The Complete Illustrated
Book of
CLOSE-UP MAGIC

The Complete Illustrated
Book of
CLOSE-UP MAGIC

*Professional Techniques Fully Revealed
by a Master Magician*

by WALTER B. GIBSON

DOUBLEDAY & COMPANY, INC., GARDEN CITY, NEW YORK
1980

The photographs in this book were taken by Milton H. Wagenfohr, Stone Ridge, New York, and Robert Haines, Kingston, New York.

Photographs are of the author's hands demonstrating the sleights.

Library of Congress Cataloging in Publication Data

Gibson, Walter Brown, 1897–
    The complete illustrated book of close-up magic.

    Includes index.
    1. Conjuring. 2. Tricks. I. Title.
GV1547.G512   793.8

A NOTE TO THE READER

This book has been illustrated with photographs wherever the author has thought they would help toward an understanding of the instruction text.

There is also a comprehensive listing of Contents. It will show how the material in the book is classified and where every division and subdivision can be found.

The glossary index at the back of the book includes special terms related to close-up magic that are not covered in the text.

INTRODUCTION

The term "close-up," as applied to magic, is of comparatively recent coinage, but its roots date back a century or more. From those roots have sprouted such aptly named categories as impromptu magic, pocket tricks, table magic, after-dinner tricks, and parlor magic. All these are somewhat interchangeable, so to avoid confusion it is preferable to classify close-up work according to the objects involved, such as coins, balls, thimbles, match boxes, matches, and a variety of other articles.

During the gradual development of modern magic, the usual learning procedure was to begin with smaller tricks and develop them into larger effects. Tricks with cards originally headed the list, particularly in the impromptu, or close-up, field. The repertoire expanded rapidly when card workers adopted techniques and artifices used by the professional gamblers. Added to that, the introduction of prepared packs and specially printed cards, as well as a host of new principles, expanded card magic to such an extent that it has become as large as all other categories of magic combined.

That fact was well emphasized in *The Complete Illustrated Book of Card Magic,* the forerunner to this companion volume, dealing with all other phases of close-up and manipulative magic, which also have experienced a remarkable growth in popularity during recent years. Headed by coins, billiard balls, and thimbles, this book includes a specialized section on table magic, covering effects limited to that restricted area, plus another on mental magic, a rapidly increasing field that frequently demands skilled close-up work at times when spectators least expect it. Lesser categories are also included to round out this volume.

To limit close-up magic to the strictest interpretation of the term would mean ruling it out entirely. This was proved some sixty years ago at a meeting of the National Conjurers' Association in New York, when a performer presented the "last word" in close-up effects, a very appropriate title, as it has never been heard of since. He showed a human hair, several inches in length, would it around his fingers, then drew it out and showed that a series of tight knots had formed along the hair. Winding it again, he finally drew it forth and showed that the knots were gone.

Here was a trick that seemingly depended on a minimum of appliances, a few strands of hair; but such was not the case. In order to convince us that the knots were real, the performer had to hand out half a dozen microscopes so that we could examine the hair before and after the knots appeared to make sure that they were real. That reduced the trick to the level of a mere puzzle.

About the same time, Houdini featured a unique effect in which he placed a pack of needles on his tongue and apparently swallowed them; then did the same with a long thread that he had rolled into a tiny ball. After drinking a glass of water and showing that his mouth was empty, he placed his fingers to his lips and drew out the thread, giving its end to a committeeman so that he could back away twenty feet or more, revealing the swallowed needles strung along the thread at regular intervals.

Houdini provided a flashlight so that members of the committee could make sure his mouth was empty during that remarkable close-up demonstration, but he wasn't performing it just for that small group. He was doing the Needle Trick for a packed house at the Hippodrome, the largest theater in New York City. To spectators in the top balcony, the needles were tiny specks that glinted in the spotlight along a thread they could not even see, but they took the word of Houdini and the volunteer committee that the nearly miraculous feat had been accomplished.

Back in that same era, Harry Bouton, an upcoming magician, amazed his fellow magi by vanishing six cards singly at his fingertips and showing his hand, back and front, before reproducing the cards at a range of only a few feet. This trick was so effective that he put it in his vaudeville act. After a few seasons, he changed his name to Blackstone and gradually expanded his act to a full-evening show that won him the title of America's Number One Magician thirty years later. All that time, he continued to present his six-card manipulation along with the latest and biggest stage illusions.

The most famous of coin manipulators, T. Nelson Downs, developed new sleights by plucking money from under the noses of his friends, who encouraged "Tommy," as they called him, to put on his act in vaudeville. He did, and as the King of Coins, he played extended engagements in England and Europe, finally retiring after his return to America. Yet, for thirty years more, he continued to baffle even magicians with his close-up work, occasionally putting on his stage act in all its glittering glory.

When Nate Leipzig, the master card manipulator, appeared in vaudeville, he staged a climax to his card work by producing eight red thimbles on his fingertips. Like Houdini's needles and Downs's coins, the thimbles caught the glare of the spotlight and brought waves of applause from all parts of the house. Through the efforts of these performers, manipulative magic became an accepted part of the theatrical scene until the decline of vaudeville reversed the trend; then such skilled performers as Cardini, Frakson, Manuel, and Rosini met the situation by adapting their work to the limited range of nightclub floors, thus bringing close-up magic back into its own.

Today, table magic serves as a testing ground for new performers, but many are turning it into a specialty involving intricate routines and mechanical devices. Working from basic methods described herein, readers can expand as they proceed, since gimmicks and other appliances are now available from magic dealers, whose ads are found in the Yellow Pages. Some table tricks can be performed on any surface, while others require a tablecloth. For specialized work, many performers use close-up pads, with a soft, pliable finish.

The matter of angles enters into all close-up work including table tricks, and demands more attention with manipulations. Many coin moves can be done in strictly close-up fashion, but billiard balls require a somewhat longer working range. Thimbles, too, are vulnerable unless closely checked. Remember, however, that practically *all* moves fall into the close-up category when presented for a single observer or only a few persons seated directly in front of the performer, which is why they have been included in this book.

With mental magic, the same rule applies when using special moves, but here the performer has an advantage because such moves are often unsuspected. Mental effects are distinctly a branch of close-up magic, but where subterfuge alone is involved, no skill whatever is required in their presentation. However, since they are particularly suited to close-up audiences—who do not know the difference—they have been purposely included in this volume.

CONTENTS

COIN MAGIC	1
Basic Manipulations	1
Single-coin Palms	1
Display Position	2
Fingertip Display	3
Finger-bend Palm	3
For a Vanish	3
For a Production	4
Standard Palm	6
For a Vanish	9
For a Production	9
Edge Palm	9
For a Vanish	9
For a Production	9
Thumb-crook Palm	11
Thumb-fork Palm	12
For a Vanish	12
For a Production	12
Alternate Thumb-fork Palm	13
Downs Palm	14
For a Vanish	16
For a Production	17
Back and Front Palm	17
For a Vanish and Production	22
Front-finger Clip	22
Back-finger Clip	23
For a Vanish	25
Back and Front Clip	25
For a Vanish	26
Back Thumb Clip	27
Coin Vanishes	28
Pull-away Vanish	29
Reverse Vanish	30
Thumb-palm Routine	33
Alternate Routine	36
Take-away Vanish	38
French Drop	39
Palm Off	40
Back Palm Off	40

False Drop	41
Fist Vanish	44
Slow-motion Vanish	46
Squeeze Vanish	49
Coin Roll	50
Coin-roll Vanish	51
One-hand Coin Roll	53
Two-hand Coin Roll	53
Coin Changes	53
Palm-to-palm Change	54
Palm-drop Change	54
Palm Drop 2	54
French Drop Change	54
Pickup Change	55
Multiple-coin Manipulation	55
Multiple Finger Bend	55
For a Production	55
Slide Vanish	57
Side-drop Vanish	57
Multiple Standard Palm	58
For a Production	59
For a Vanish	59
Pickup Vanish	60
Throw Vanish	60
Multiple-edge Palm	60
To Produce Coins Singly	60
To Vanish Coins Singly	61
Multiple Downs Palm	61
Simple Coin Productions	62
Fingertip Production	62
From the Elbow	62
Fron the Knee	62
Spread-away Production	62
Sweep Production	62
Change-overs	63
Simple Change-over	63
Sleeve Action	63
Brush-over Change	64
Change-over Placement	64
Multiple-coin Transfer	64
One-by-one Vanish	65
Coin-star Production	66
Coins and Glass	68
Throw-over	68
Four-coin Vanish and Recovery	69
Five-coin Routine	71

Coins Through Body 72
   Alternate Version 75
   Comedy Coin Routine 76
The Miser's Dream 76
      Recommended Palming Methods 79
      Follow-up to Regular Production 80
   Full-front Miser's Dream 80

BILLIARD BALLS 85
Basic Manipulations 86
   Palming a Ball 86
   Basic Display Position 87
   Finger-bend Palm 87
   Standard Palm 88
   Thumb Palm 88
   Double Palm 89
   Back Palm 90
Billiard-ball Productions 91
   Fingertip Production 91
   Alternate Fingertip Production 92
   Ball on Fist 93
   Alternate Fist Production 94
   Reverse Fingertip Production 95
   Thumb Squeeze 97
   Draw-apart Production 99
   Through the Hand 100
   Slow-motion Production 101
   Production from Elbow 102
   Production from Knee 102
   Ball from Wand 103
Billiard-ball Vanishes 104
   Simple Palm Vanish 105
   Throw Vanish 105
   Hand-to-hand 105
   Pour Vanish 105
   French Drop 106
   Swallow Vanish 108
   Pincer Vanish 108
   Push Vanish 109
   Simple Roll Vanish 111
   Fingertip Roll 112
   Thumb-roll Vanish 114
   Toss Vanish 116
   Two-hand Toss 116
   Swing-about Toss 118
   Fingertip Vanish 118

Simple Fist Vanish   119
Improved Fist Vanish   120
Hit-down Vanish   121
Ball and Silk Vanish   122
Snatch Vanish   122
Slow-motion Vanish   124
Lay-over Vanish   125
Change-overs, Transfers, and Flashes   126
Basic Change-over   127
Improved Change-over   128
Delayed Change-over   129
Notes on Change-overs   129
Transfers   131
Simple Transfer   131
Reverse Transfer   132
Thumb and Finger Steal   133
Slow-motion Steal   134
Back-palm Transfer   135
Turn-around Transfer   137
Reverse Turn-around   138
Double Turn-around   138
Flashes   140
Forearm Flash   140
Sleeve Flash   140
Combination Change-over and Flash   141
Crisscross Flash   141
Thumb Flash   143
Thumb-front Flash   145
Turnabout Flash   145
Finger Flash   147
Color Changes   149
Fist Color Change   149
Roll-over Color Change   153
Roll-over Alternate   154
Full-front Color Change   155
Throw Color Change   156
Sample Color-change Routines   157
Multiplying Billiard Balls   158
Standard "One to Four" Routine   158
Rapid "One to Four" Routine (with solid balls)   163
Ball and Shell   168
Two-way Twirl   170
"One to Four" (with shell)   171
Final-ball Vanish   178
"Four to Eight" Production   179
White and Red Transposition   181

Four-ball Twirl   184
"Four to One"   187
Fifth-ball Routine   192
Special Color Change   193

THIMBLES   197
  Basic Manipulations   197
    Display Position   197
    Thumb Palm   198
      For a Vanish   198
      For a Production   199
    Thumb-bend Palm   199
    Center Palm   200
    Finger-bend Palm   201
      For a Vanish   201
      For a Production   201
    Thumb to Finger Bend   202
      For a Vanish   202
      For a Production   203
    Tip Palm   203
    Thumb and Finger Clip   203
    Simple Finger Clip   204
    Back and Front Palm   204
      Note on Thimble Palming   207
  Thimble Vanishes   208
    Take-away Vanish   208
    Inward Take-away   209
    Poke Vanish   210
    Draw-off Vanish   212
    Twist-away Vanish   213
    Finger-switch Vanish   214
    Swallow Vanish   215
    Slow-motion Vanish   215
  Thimble Productions   216
    Standard Fingertip Production   216
    Pop Production   216
    Various Production and Recoveries   217
      From Behind the Hand   217
      From the Elbow   217
      From the Knee   217
      From Trouser Cuff   217
      From Shirt Collar   217
      From Pocket   217
      From Vest Pocket   217
  Multiplying Thimbles   218
    "One to Four" Production   218

"Four to Eight" Production   220
    Special Thimble Holders   224
"Full Front" Routine   225
Rapid "One to Eight" System   226
Change-overs and Flashes   233
    Double Change-over   233
    Fingertip Flash   236
    Full-front Flash   237
    Back-palm Flash   240
    One-hand Flash   243
Color Changes   244
    Finger-switch Change   244
    Repeat Switch   246
    Push-through Change   247
    Repeat Push-through   248
Thumb the Thimble   248
    Alternate Thumb the Thimble   251

MENTAL MAGIC   253
Message Reading   253
    Billet Switching   254
        In the Crystal   257
        From the Ashes   258
        Behind the Tablet   259
        Find the Word   260
    Center-tear Method   261
        Reading the Message   263
        Through the Crystal   263
        From the Glass   264
        Name for Name   264
        Time out of Mind   265
        Without the Watch   267
Turn-over Coins   267
    Multiple Turnover   268
Find the Coin   269
Cards and Dice   270
Triple-color Test   273
Mental Moves   274
    Double-coin Surprise   275
Six-symbol Test   277
Matched Thought   278
Number Prediction   279
    Color Cards   282
Sixth Card—Sixth Sense   284
Paired Cities   285

MATCHBOX MAGIC 287
  Drop the Box 287
  Magnetized Matches 288
    Modern Magnetic Matches 290
  Looping the Matchbox 290
  Mystic Knot Vanish 292
  Heads Away 294
  Matchbox Vanish 297
    Alternate Matchbox Vanish 298
    Appearing Matches 299
    Vanishing Matches 300
    Instant Vanishing Matches 301
    Turnabout Heads 302
    Through the Table 303
    Matchbox Do as I Do 303
    Turnabout Match 306
    Alternate Turnabout 307
  Penetrating Matches 309
    Alternate Penetration 311
    Half-match Penetration 311
    Match Through Hand 312

TABLE MAGIC 315
  Four-coin Baffler 315
  Magic Sugar Lumps 319
    Four-lump Assembly 319
    Through the Table 323
    Come-back Lump 324
  Coins Through Table 326
    Latest Variant 329
    Straight Through 330
    Hand-to-hand 333
    Throw-over 333
    Simple Passage 334
    Mutual Attraction 334
    Transposition 334
  Jump-over Dice 335
  String a Ring 336
  Magnetic Pencils 338
    Improved Method 339
  Perfect Magnetic Pencil 341
  Magnetized Knife 342
  Supermagnetism 342
  Salt Vanish 344
    Alternate Routine with Reproduction of Salt 345
    Fist to Fist 346

Vanishing Salt Shaker 347
Supersalt 348
Roll the Bills 349
Turn-up Glasses 351
Five-glass Fooler 351
Full and Empty 352

SPECIAL EFFECTS 353
Dime to Dollar 353
Quick Dime Vanish 354
Coin Through the Hand 355
Slow-motion Penetration 356
Coin Through Handkerchief 358
Alternate Penetration 360
Advanced Penetration 361
Looper Dooper 363
Link the Clips 364
Triple Links 366
Triple-knot Trick 366
Multiple-knot Trick 368
Quick-knot Vanish 368
Knot and Ring 369
Ring and Triple Knot 370
Tube and Knots 372
Color-changing Silk 373
Special Color Change 377
Silk to Egg 380
Okito Coin Box 382
Improved Okito Coin Box 386
Coin Through Card 390
Transparent Okito Coin Box 392
Coin Through Card (with transparent box) 394
Super Coin Box 395
Multiple-coin Penetration 397
Alternate Procedure 399
Repeat-cigar Production 400
Restored Paper Napkin 403
Alternate Routine 411
Glossary/Index 413

The Complete Illustrated
Book of
CLOSE-UP MAGIC

COIN MAGIC

BASIC MANIPULATIONS

There are two general classes of modern coin magic: the manipulative, in which only coins themselves are involved; and the impromptu, which utilizes additional items or appliances. Both are well suited to close-up magic, since coins are objects that everybody handles. The present section covers coin magic of the manipulative type, including most of the basic sleights; while other coin effects will be found under such heads as special magic or table magic.

The coins commonly used by skilled manipulators are either of half-dollar or silver-dollar size. This may come as a surprise to many beginners, who rather logically suppose that smaller coins should be easier to handle where concealment is concerned. However, the case is just the opposite. Larger coins are easier to palm and can be more conveniently clipped between the fingers; while, best of all, they are showy and more impressive from the audience's viewpoint.

For small hands, half dollars are best; for large hands, the dollar size is preferable. Often, however, magicians with hands of an in-between size have wished for a seventy-five-cent piece, which for them would be a perfect fit. Actually, there are various foreign coins that come close to that specification, as a check-up of coin shops will prove. Some magic dealers, in their turn, supply special "palming coins" that have been produced in both half-dollar and dollar size. Their advantage, aside from being cheaper than real money, is that they are thinner than regular coins, and enable the performer to handle more coins at a time; and they also have sharply milled edges, making it easier to palm them.

SINGLE-COIN PALMS

The palming of a single coin is the prime requisite of all coin manipulation. It serves as a form of concealment and is also used to vanish or produce a coin; hence such procedures will be detailed along with the palming action. As a preliminary to a vanish, the coin is usually shown in

1

the right hand, which palms it while apparently placing it in the left, which is later shown empty. The right hand may then reproduce the coin by apparently plucking it from nowhere.

To make these moves most effective, the coin should first be held in:

DISPLAY POSITION

Grip the coin near its lower edge between the tips of the thumb and first two fingers, keeping the coin straight upright, so that most of its surface is in full view. Have thumb in back, fingers in front, as you face the audience directly, so that you view it from the thumb side (Fig. 1) while the finger side represents the audience's view (Fig. 2).

As you turn your right side toward the audience, it is a simple matter for the thumb or fingers to draw the coin downward and inward — the first step in the palming action, as will be described under various heads. Conversely, once the coin has been drawn downward, it can be displayed anew by simply pushing it upward in reverse fashion. To show still more of the coin, you can use the —

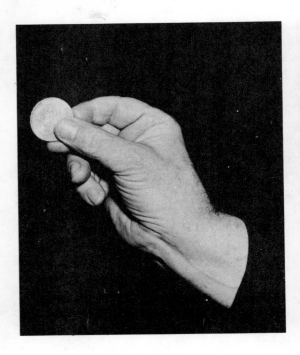

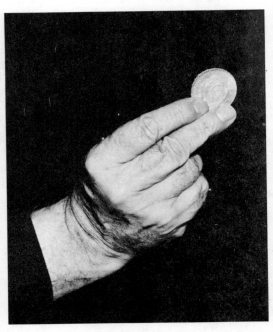

Fig. 1. Coin in display position (performer's view).

Fig. 2. Display position (as viewed by the audience).

FINGERTIP DISPLAY

Starting from display position (Fig. 1), push the coin upward with the thumb until the coin reaches the tip of the second finger, at the same time bringing the tip of the forefinger around in back of the coin, pressing it against the second finger. Both fingers are immediately extended to full length, giving the effect of the coin being produced at the very fingertips (Fig. 3). In certain methods of palming, as will be described, the coin is vanished and produced at the fingertips, bypassing the usual display position.

Methods of palming follow:

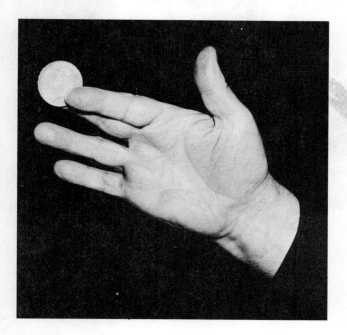

Fig. 3. Fingertip display. Hand may be turned either way.

FINGER-BEND PALM

In this simple but effective move, the term "palming" is loosely used, as the coin is not actually concealed in the palm itself. From display position, with the back of the hand toward the spectators (Fig. 2), draw the coin downward with the thumb while extending the fingers almost to full length. This brings the coin into the bend of the last three fingers, which are immediately bent inward sufficiently to retain it while the thumb is raised clear (Fig. 4).

For a Vanish: Hold the left hand cupped toward the audience, so its open palm is visible. Make a short throwing motion with the right hand as though dropping the coin into the left, which immediately closes into a fist. To add to the deception, the left hand is turned downward and forward so its back is toward the spectators; then it is raised to shoulder level, so the

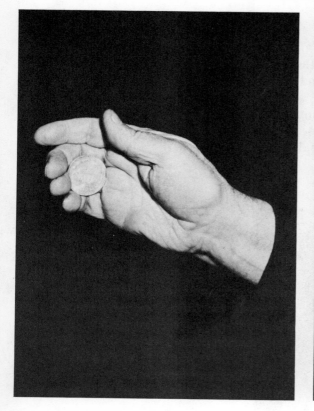

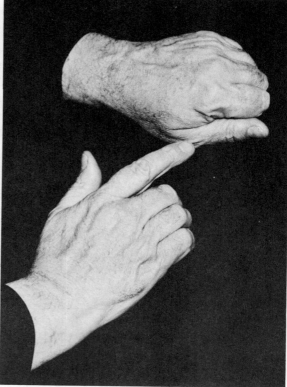

FINGER-BEND PALM
Fig. 4. Coin palmed in finger bend. Thumb being raised after drawing coin down from display position (performer's view).

Fig. 5. Spectator's view of vanish. Coin is secretly retained in right finger bend after apparently being thrown into left hand.

right forefinger can point upward toward the left hand as though reminding everyone that the coin is there (Fig. 5). The left hand is then opened and shown empty.

Once this simple sleight is acquired, it can be done almost automatically, the motion of the right hand allowing the coin to slide down into the finger-bend position. The little finger should be kept slightly inward to stop the coin at that point.

For a Production: Reach forward and upward with the right hand, at the same time bending the thumb inward. Push the coin upward with the thumb until the coin reaches display position (Fig. 1). From the audience's view, it is apparently plucked from the air by the fingers and thumb (Fig. 2). This is practically a reversal of the palming move. However: Instead of pushing the coin up, some performers prefer to insert the tip of the thumb beneath the lower edge of the coin and press the upper edge between the tips of the first two fingers. The thumb then flips the coin upward and forward to display position. This is particularly effective with a dollar-size coin.

The finger-bend palm has a special advantage in that the right hand can be shown practically palm front, if desired. To do this, face the audience directly and swing the right hand over to the right and hold it so the tips of the bent fingers are directly toward the audience (Fig. 6). Here the fingers effectively hide the coin although most of the palm is clearly shown.

This comes under the head of a "flash" move, and the hand should be shown only briefly in that position. However, for a vanish, you can stand with your left side toward the audience and apparently throw the coin from the right-hand display position into the cupped left hand, the back of the left hand coming up in front of the right hand to hide the palming action of the right.

At the same time, the body is turned frontward, with the left hand forming a fist and swinging to the left, while the right hand allows a "flash" of its interior (Fig. 6) and then points diagonally toward the left. You can then swing farther to the left and vanish the coin in the usual fashion.

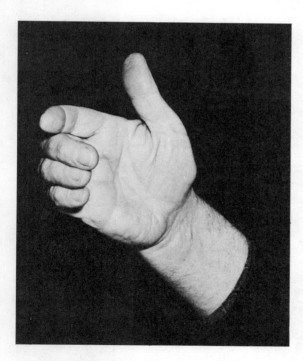

Fig. 6. Showing right hand apparently empty when turned palm frontward. Coin hidden in finger bend.

Or you can vanish the coin while you are still face front, then swing to the right, keeping the coin concealed as in Fig. 6 and bring the right thumb into the finger bend to start the push-up. As you complete the move, your left side will be toward the audience and your right hand will be palm front so that they see the reproduced coin in display position, but with the thumb in front (Fig. 2). Timed to an upward swing of the right hand, this is highly effective, apparently an open-hand production.

STANDARD PALM

This is the type of concealment from which the term "palming" was derived. Stand with your right side toward the audience and hold the coin in display position (Fig. 1) so that the audience sees the back of the hand with the coin projecting from fingers and thumb (Fig. 2). With the thumb, slide the coin to the tips of the two middle fingers, and at the same time tilt the hand straight downward, keeping the fingers well bent. Lift the thumb, leaving the coin balanced on the fingertips (Fig. 7).

STANDARD PALM
Fig. 7. Thumb withdrawing to leave coin balanced on middle fingers of right hand, ready for palming action (performer's view).

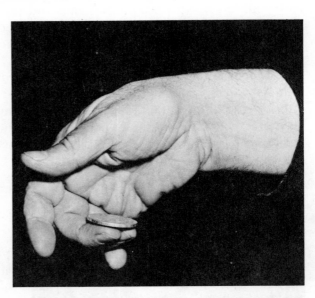

Fig. 8. Fingers pressing coin firmly into right palm, between base of thumb and other side of palm (performer's view).

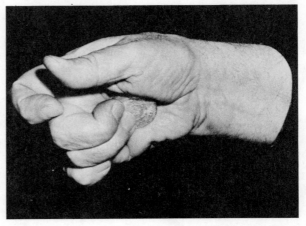

The fingers then press the coin upward into the hollow of the palm, where it is firmly gripped between the base of the thumb and the opposite side of the palm (Fig. 8). This allows the fingers to be straightened, with the coin retained in the palm, the hand now being raised vertically, with the thumb pointing upward (Fig. 9). From the audience's viewpoint, the back

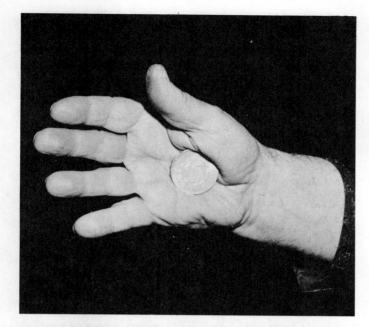

Fig. 9. Coin fully gripped
in Standard or Center
Palm (performer's view).

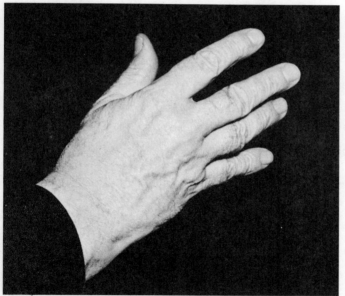

Fig. 10. Spectator's view
of performer's hand,
which is secretly retaining
coin in Standard Palm.

of the hand appears exactly as it would if empty, with thumb and fingers
spread normally (Fig. 10).

Beginners may have trouble gaining a good grip; hence the larger the
coin and the more sharply milled its edges, the easier it is to handle. With
practice, the muscles become developed and can retain the coin without
cramping the hand. But no matter how good the grip, the thumb and fingers
should never be spread wide, in "starfish" pattern. Far from proving the
hand empty, this advertises the fact that it is concealing something.

EDGE PALM

Fig. 11. Thumb moving clear after drawing coin into finger grip preliminary to Edge Palm (performer's view).

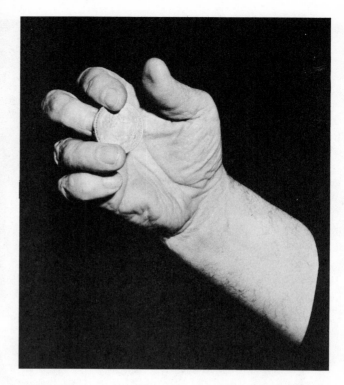

Fig. 12. Fingers planting coin edgewise in palm with base of thumb supplying needed grip (performer's view).

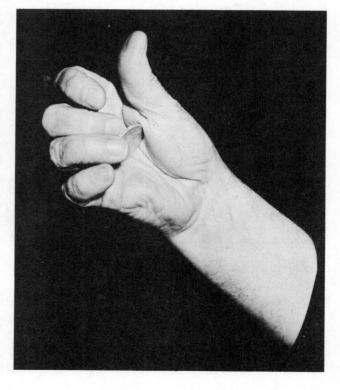

For a Vanish: The right hand apparently throws the coin into the left, actually retaining it as with the Finger-bend Palm. Since the right hand dips downward when balancing the coin on the fingertips, it is first brought. upward with a short recoil during the palming action, the sudden halt helping to plant the coin more firmly in the right palm. The pretended throw is made downward or toward the left, according to the best position for the left hand, which is held cupped to start and closes as the "throw" is made.

For a Production: Tilt the right fingers downward, then double them up into the palm, releasing the coin so it drops on the second and third fingertips. The thumb immediately presses from above, the hand is tilted upward, and the thumb pushes the coin up to display position (Fig. 1) while the right hand is raised with an upward sweep, hiding the lesser action of the thumb and fingers. The process is a reverse of the vanishing moves and is much easier.

EDGE PALM

This development of the standard palm is preferred by many advanced manipulators, so once the standard palm is acquired, it is a good plan to work on this one. Start with display position (Fig. 1) and draw the coin downward with the thumb so the tips of the first and third fingers can be extended over the edge to the lower side, or thumb side, while the tip of the second finger is doubled above the coin. The thumb is immediately withdrawn, leaving the coin gripped between the fingertips (Fig. 11).

The three fingers are then bent inward, pressing the inner edge of the coin deep into the palm (Fig. 12), which retains it while the fingers are extended. The back of the hand can then be shown as with the standard palm (Fig. 10), allowing a normal spread of the thumb and fingers.

For a Vanish: The right hand makes a short throwing action toward the left, palming the coin in process; or it can pretend to place the coin in the left hand, first palming it, then dipping the right fingertips into the cupped left hand. The right thumb and fingertips are compressed together during the final action, making it quite deceptive. The left hand is opened and the coin is gone.

For a Production: Tilt the right hand downward so that the extended thumb is exactly level. Bring the tip of the thumb against the tips of the middle fingers and turn your left side toward the audience, extending your right hand at full length. The tips of the fingers hide the coin during this sweeping action, and thumb and fingers can then be spread again, with the coin remaining concealed behind the base of the level thumb (Fig. 13).

To produce the coin, bend the second and third fingers inward and grip the coin above and below (Fig. 14). Draw it forward and outward with those two fingers only, keeping it edgewise behind the extended thumb, which amply hides it (Fig. 15). As the coin reaches the tip of the thumb,

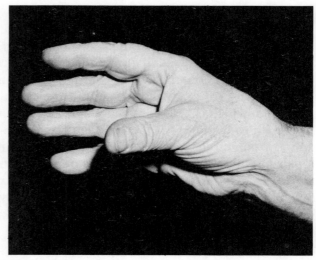

Fig. 13. Showing hand apparently empty with edge-palmed coin, concealed by base of thumb, ready for production.

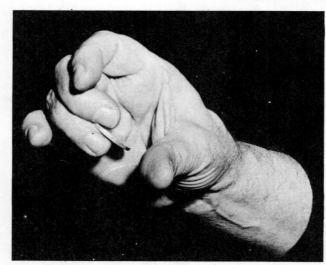

Fig. 14. Middle fingers gripping coin for edgewise production behind extended thumb (performer's view).

Fig. 15. Edge of coin just coming into sight, ready for thumb to flip it up to display position.

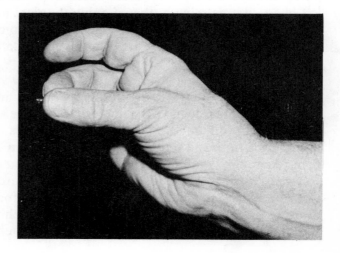

give the hand a short upward thrust, and at the same time swing the thumb beneath the coin and use it to flip the coin upward into display position (Fig. 1).

With your left side toward the audience, the right hand will be thumb frontward when the coin appears, exactly as in Fig. 1. This makes a very neat production with the coin being plucked into sight quite surprisingly. It can also be produced with your right side toward the audience, the action being precisely the same; but in this case, people will see the back of the hand, the coin emerging above the fingertips (Fig. 2), as with more conventional productions.

In contrast to the really modern manipulation just described, we have the now outmoded—

THUMB-CROOK PALM

Starting with the coin in display position, thrust the thumb straight outward and draw the fingers inward, bringing the coin with them, so that it lodges in the crook of the thumb between the upper and lower joints (Fig. 16). By lowering the thumb down into the hand or keeping the thumb pressed against the forefinger, the coin will be hidden when the fingers are extended. However, the fingers should be kept close together to make sure.

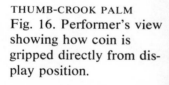

THUMB-CROOK PALM
Fig. 16. Performer's view showing how coin is gripped directly from display position.

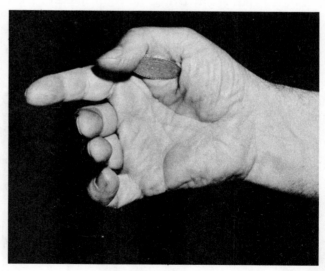

Originally, this move was used with a throwing vanish and also as a production, by simply reversing the action and pushing the coin from the thumb crook back to display position. Today, however, it serves chiefly as a utility device (see page 39), as it has been superseded by the smoother and far more effective—

THUMB-FORK PALM

Hold the coin in display position (Fig. 1) but lower the hand so the thumb is directly above the coin, which will then be resting on the tips of the first two fingers. Swing the thumb well to the left and double the first two fingers inward, pressing the coin firmly at the root of the thumb (Fig. 17).

Immediately swing the thumb to the right, pressing it against the side of the hand, with the outer edge of the coin between. Extend the fingers full length and the coin will be firmly gripped in the fork of the thumb (Fig. 18). Tilt the hand so the thumb is upward, thus bringing the back of the hand toward the audience, the coin being concealed within. Spread the fingers just a trifle, but not too much. The thumb must stay close against the hand, and this action would be noticeable if the fingers were spread wide.

For a Vanish: Make a short throwing motion with the right hand, palming the coin almost at the start. Finish by planting the first two fingers of the right hand in the left hand, which promptly closes its fingers (Fig. 19). The right fingers are then withdrawn, as though leaving the coin there. From the audience's view the fact that the first two fingers of the right hand are necessarily kept close together makes the thumb's position all the more natural, and no one will suspect that the coin is really gripped in the thumb fork. When the left hand is opened, the coin has apparently disappeared.

For a Production: Bring the right hand upward and double the first two fingers inward, one above the coin, the other below, so they can grip the far edge between them (Fig. 20). Extend the fingers full length, carrying the coin directly to fingertip display (Fig. 3). This is a very effective production.

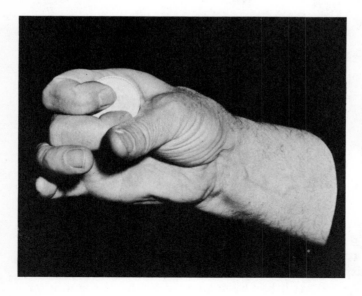

THUMB-FORK PALM
Fig. 17. First action:
Doubling fingers inward,
planting coin at root of
thumb (performer's view).

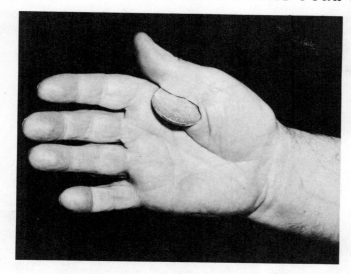

Fig. 18. Thumb thrust up-
ward and outward, grip-
ping coin in fork of thumb
(performer's view).

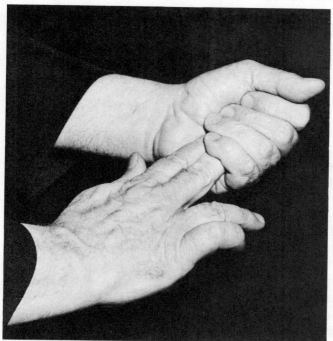

Fig. 19. Vanishing
process as spectators see
it. Coin apparently
planted in left hand by
right fingers is palmed in
fork of right thumb.

ALTERNATE THUMB-FORK PALM

As an alternate to the sleight just described, you can start with the coin already at the right fingertips in standard production position. Bend the fingers inward and run the coin edgewise along the thumb until it reaches the root (Fig. 21). Ease the thumb a trifle beneath its edge of the coin; then give it an upward, outer flip, turning the coin over and automatically clamping it in position at the fork of the thumb (Fig. 18). Some knack is

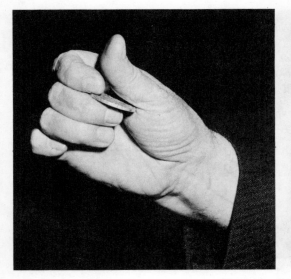

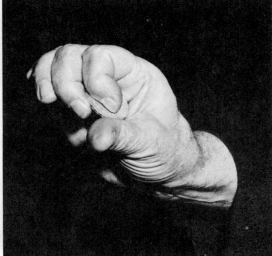

Fig. 20. Producing coin from thumb fork by gripping edge between first two fingers and extending them (performer's view).

Fig. 21. Fingers sliding coin inward along thumb, Used as alternate for Thumb-fork Palm or as initial move in Downs Palm (performer's view).

needed in gaining the exact position, but once acquired it becomes almost automatic. This is excellent for any routine in which a coin is repeatedly ·vanished and produced, as the Miser's Dream, page 76.

DOWNS PALM

This version of the thumb palm was a favorite with T. Nelson Downs, the famous "King of Koins." For many years after his retirement from the vaudeville stage, "Tommy," as we knew him, baffled magicians as well as uninformed observers with his masterful close-up coin work, which depended chiefly on the following sleight:

Start with the coin in display position (Fig. 1) and shift it to fingertip display (Fig. 3). Then bring it inward along the thumb to the root as with the alternate thumb-fork palm just described (Fig. 21). Here, however, the move is suddenly and surprisingly simplified; in a sense, there is no further move at all. The coin is simply left where it is, gripped edgewise in the root of the right thumb, while the fingers are extended (Fig. 22).

With the right side of the body toward the audience, the back of the hand is in view, with the fingers a trifle spread, giving the impression that the hand is empty (Fig. 23). It will be noted that the thumb is practically out of sight, but this is natural enough and not apt to attract attention if the hand is kept slightly in motion.

An excellent excuse for this sleight is to bring the tips of the thumb and second finger together, as though about to make a finger snap. As a follow-up to that action, face the audience directly and swing the right hand

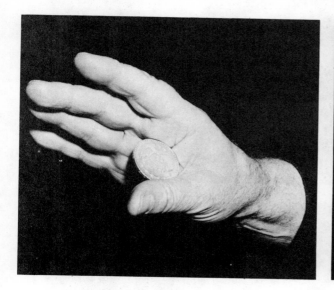

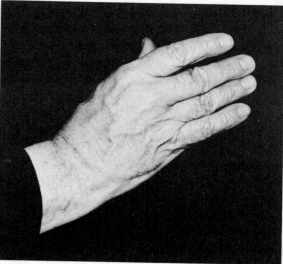

DOWNS PALM
Fig. 22. Coin is gripped edgewise at root of thumb. Hand tilted downward to show performer's view.

Fig. 23. Audience's view of back of hand while coin is secretly retained in Downs Palm.

straight forward, again pressing the tips of thumb and fingers together as though about to deliver another snap (Fig. 24). All that the spectators see during this maneuver are the backs of the fingers, which hide the coin completely.

Without pausing, turn further to the right, so the left side is toward the audience. Upon completing the snapping action, the tips of thumb and fingers are separated and the fingers spread wide while the thumb maintains its horizontal position. The hand then appears quite empty because the thumb still conceals the coin, even though the hand is being shown palm front (Fig. 25).

Here, the hand should pause only for a momentary flash; then, resuming its motions, the moves just described are immediately reversed. The body swings to the left, the tips of thumb and fingers are brought together during transit, until the right side is toward the audience, with the back of the right hand in view (Figs. 23, 24, and 25).

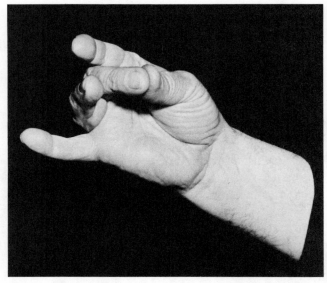

Fig. 24. Tips of thumb and second finger pressed for snap, fully concealing palmed coin as hand is turned palm front.

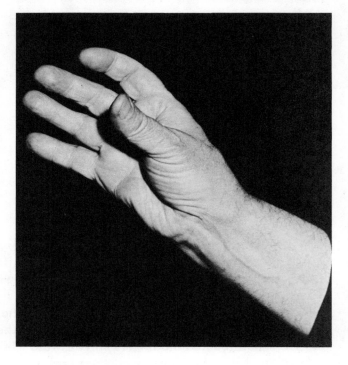

Fig. 25. After the snap. Hand shown palm front, apparently empty. Coin retained by Downs Palm.

For a Vanish: The coin may be palmed with a throwing action while the first two fingers are pretending to place it in the left hand. This is similar to the vanish used with the thumb-fork palm (Fig. 19) except that the thumb dips out of sight beneath the first two fingers, since the Downs palm is being used. Or the right hand can display the coin at the fingertips (Fig. 3). The hand comes down, then up with a long sweep, apparently tossing the coin in the air, though actually the fingers bend inward, bringing it into the

Downs palm (Fig. 22). The fingers are extended during the upward sweep, which is usually done with the back of the hand toward the audience (Fig. 23), though it may be varied with the thumb frontward (Fig. 25).

For a Production: Bend the first two fingers inward, grip the coin edgewise between them, and draw it outward behind the thumb (Fig. 26) to the very tip. The thumb goes beneath its edge of the coin, flipping it up and over to display position. The back of the hand is toward the audience (Fig. 23) so the coin appears behind the fingertips (Fig. 2). As variation, the hand can be shown thumb frontward (Fig. 25) so the coin appears behind the thumb (Fig. 1). Either way, the coin can be immediately shifted to fingertip display (Fig. 3), thereby being ready for another vanish.

Some manipulators, hearing of this sleight, may have supposed that it would be both awkward and suspicious. But all who ever saw Downs use it were quick to change their opinion. He could snap his fingers emphatically through all the stages, so he seemed to be vanishing and producing coins as a result of the snaps. He added misdirection by snapping the fingers of both hands, which is a great help for a budding manipulator as well.

Rather than risk losing his grip upon the palmed coin, the tyro can merely simulate the snapping of the right thumb and fingers, at the same time actually providing a sharp snap with the thumb and fingers of the empty left hand, letting observers think that the sound came from the right hand.

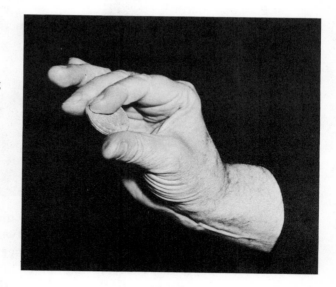

Fig. 26. Fingers producing coin from Downs Palm. Practically a reversal of palming move (Fig. 21). Hand tilted downward to give performer's view.

BACK AND FRONT PALM

This is a method originally used by Tommy Downs in his stage performances, but it is also suited to close-up presentation, with various additions or modifications. Stand with the left side toward the audience and show the coin in the right hand, holding it in display position with the thumb toward the audience (Fig. 1).

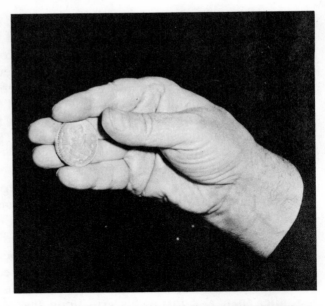

BACK AND FRONT PALM
Fig. 27. Thumb withdrawing after pressing coin in front finger grip in readiness for Back Palm.

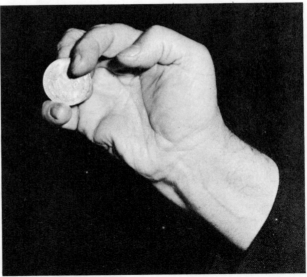

Fig. 28. First and fourth fingers gripping coin while middle fingers pivot lower edge. (Motion of hand covers move.)

The thumb then draws the coin downward until it can be gripped between the first and fourth fingers midway between the tips and the first joints (Fig. 27). This is known as the "front-finger grip" and it has special uses of its own, but in this case it is maintained only momentarily. The two middle fingers are promptly bent inward, pressing their tips against the lower edge of the coin, causing it to pivot forward or inward, between the gripping fingers (Fig. 28). As the coin does its half revolution, the middle fingers are extended in front of it, hiding the coin behind them. The hand then appears to be empty, with all fingers pressed together (Fig. 29). The coin is now held in a Back-finger Grip which is also termed a Back Palm in magical parlance (Fig. 30).

The next step is to show the back of the hand without revealing the "vanished" coin. To do this, point the fingers at a downward angle (Fig. 31). Then form the hand into a loose fist by bringing the heel of the hand down in front of the fingers, completely concealing them. The fingers can then be bent inward and up into the palm, while the thumb is extended beneath their tips (Fig. 32).

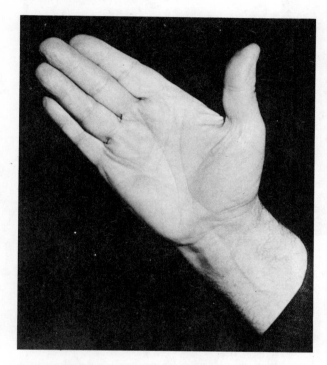

Fig. 29. Hand shown empty with vanished coin back-palmed.

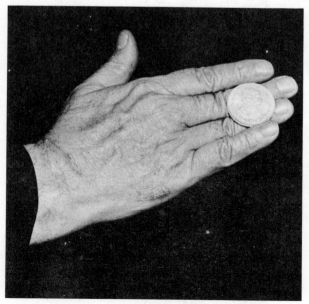

Fig. 30. Rear view of hand showing the back finger grip, which retains coin in back-palmed position.

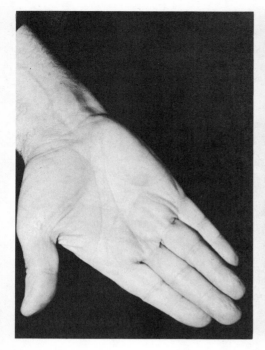

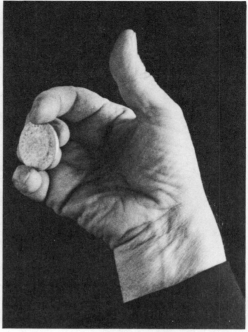

Fig. 31. Hand pointed downward, preparatory to bringing back-palmed coin to front of hand.

Fig. 32. Back palm. Swiveling coin from back of middle fingers to front. Hand turned away to hide this action (back view).

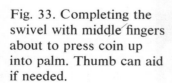

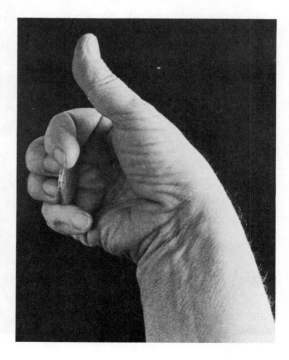

Fig. 33. Completing the swivel with middle fingers about to press coin up into palm. Thumb can aid if needed.

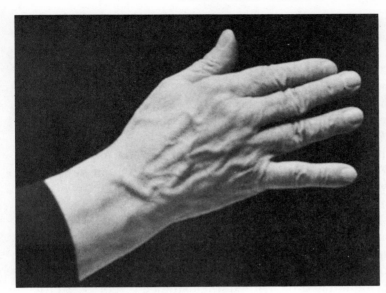

Fig. 34. Front view showing back of hand with coin now in Standard Palm (see Figs. 7–9).

The two middle fingers, thus hidden, again perform a swivel action, which is practically the opposite of the previous pivot—that is, they double past the coin and swivel it toward the fingertips. (Fig. 33). However, you do not merely return the coin to the front-finger grip, as the back of the hand would look both awkward and suspicious if shown in that fashion. The sleight, to be effective, must be progressive. Therefore:

In completing the swivel, the knuckles are turned directly downward so the coin rests on the tips of the middle fingers, which immediately press it upward into the standard palm (Figs. 7 and 8). The back of the hand may then be shown with thumb and fingers spread, the thumb pointing downward in this case (Fig. 34), since the left side of the body is toward the audience.

To show the front of the hand again, you reverse the action just described. Close the fist with its back toward the audience, dip the knuckles, and press the tips of the first and fourth fingers well into the palm so they can grip the opposite edges of the coin. The palm muscles release the coin, letting it rest on the tips of the middle fingers. Until then, the thumb is necessarily extended to allow the finger action, but now it is brought beneath the coin to control it (Figs. 32 and 33).

This is quite similar to the previous swivel, but in this case the thumb plays a more important part. It can press the edge of the coin while the fingers are being straightened back to their earlier position, where the front of the hand is shown with the fingers pressed together (Fig. 30). After allowing a brief view of the empty hand, the middle fingers swivel the coin quickly to the front grip (Fig. 28), and the thumb immediately pushes it up to display position (Fig. 1).

With practice, the transfers from front to back and back to front again, can be done without utilizing the thumb (as shown in Figs. 31 and 32). In that case, the thumb simply remains extended, letting the fingers do the work. Here the problem is drawing the coin from the standard palm (Fig. 8) with the very tips of the first and fourth fingers in order to gain the grip for the swivel (Fig. 32). To facilitate this, the hand should be lowered directly toward the floor, knuckles downward, so the coin can be dropped from the palm into the bend of the fingers. From there, it is an easy matter to gain a front-finger grip (Fig. 27) and swivel the coin to the back-palm position (Figs. 28, 29, and 30) while bringing the hand upward.

Do not bring the hand too high, as an exaggerated motion may excite suspicion. Ordinarily, the entire back-and-front manipulation can be kept just above and below shoulder level; whereas if the hand is to be lowered to the full, the manipulation can stay just above and below hip level. Either way, care must be taken to turn the hand so the coin is continually out of sight between the start and the finish. By testing it in slow motion in front of a mirror, the angles can be checked and the proper twists of fist and wrist will soon be noted.

In short, the moves should first be learned, then studied or corrected to fill individual requirements. It is quite possible to do the front and back transfers by bringing the hand inward behind the body just long enough for the necessary action, which will thus be completely hidden. In that case, the hand should start at shoulder level, come down to the hip when hidden, and up to the shoulder after the swivel. Although lacking in artistry, it provides surety.

If difficulty is experienced in reclaiming the coin from Standard-palm position, after showing the back of the hand, the Edge Palm can be used instead. You do not have to grip the outer edge of the coin between the two middle fingers; just stop the swivel halfway. The first and fourth fingers can then place the inner edge of the coin in the palm, while the second and third fingers go to the outer edge and press it home.

With the coin edge-palmed (Fig. 12), the back of the hand is shown (Fig. 34), with thumb and fingers spread. To regain the coin, tilt the fingers downward, grip the sides with the tips of the first and fourth fingers, and relax the palm muscles. Keep the middle fingers at the outer edge to steady the coin while the first and fourth fingers adjust their grip. This is almost identical with the placement move, but with no pressure at the outer edge.

For a Vanish and Production: The routine can be shortened by vanishing the coin and then reproducing it directly from the back-palm position, without showing the back of the hand at all. This is good policy in a coin-catching act where the vanish and production are frequently repeated, as showing the back of the hand too often lengthens the procedure and thereby detracts from its effectiveness.

Akin to palming methods we have the—

FRONT-FINGER CLIP

From display position (Fig. 1) draw the coin down to the second finger and press the upper edge with the forefinger, clipping it at right angles between the first two fingers (Fig. 35). With your right side toward the audience, they see the coin displayed behind the fingertips (Fig. 2), and then it is suddenly gone from view.

For a vanish, clip the coin between the right fingers while pretending to place it in the cupped left hand. This is like the thumb-fork vanish (Fig. 19), but the left fist is kept loose, since the coin is edgewise. For a production, flip the coin up to display position (Fig. 1) so spectators see it appear suddenly at the fingertips (Fig. 2).

FRONT-FINGER CLIP
Fig. 35. Thumb moving away after drawing coin down to finger-clip position (performer's view).

BACK-FINGER CLIP

Stand with the left side toward the audience and show the right hand holding the coin at basic fingertip display with the palm of the hand in open view (Fig. 3). Bend the fingers inward, pressing the edge of the coin against the tip of the thumb, which retards it while the fingers bend still farther inward until the edge of the coin is gripped at the back of the first and second finger joints (Fig. 36).

When done neatly, the coin actually revolves along the tip of the thumb, which is kept toward the audience until the coin is hidden by the flesh of the fingers, which are then extended palm up, the first two being kept together to grip the coin while the third and fourth are spread a trifle (Fig. 37). The clipped coin is perfectly hidden behind the fingers (Fig. 38).

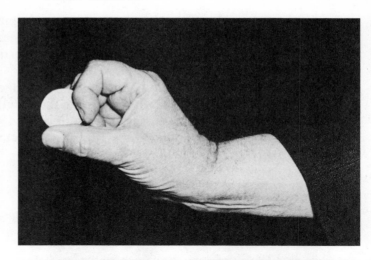

BACK-FINGER CLIP
Fig. 36. Performer's view of thumb pressing coin toward back of first two fingers. Action can be covered by keeping thumb directly toward viewers.

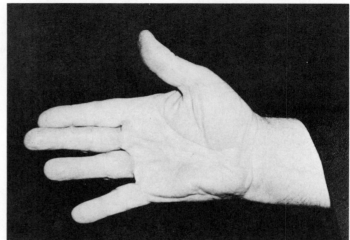

Fig. 37. Audience view of hand being shown empty with coin secretly clipped behind first two fingers.

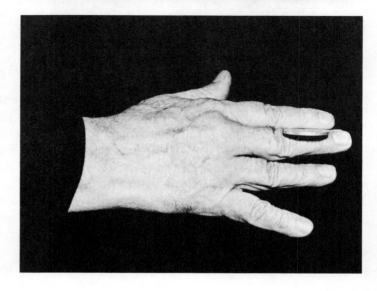

Fig. 38. Rear view showing how coin is kept from sight by back finger clip.

You can also start from display position with the thumb toward the audience (Fig. 1) and lift the forefinger, brining it over the coin and down in front, pressing the coin edgewise between the first and second fingers. The thumb, pressing the edge of the coin, revolves it forward while the fingers are doubled inward (Fig. 36). The fingers can then be straightened with the coin secretly clipped (Figs. 37 and 38).

For a Vanish: Use either sequence of moves, as just described. For a production, reverse the second procedure. From clipped position (Figs. 37 and 38) bend the fingers inward, revolving the coin toward you with the tip of the thumb (Fig. 36). Move the thumb beneath its edge of the coin and flip the coin up to display position (Fig. 1). It can then be shifted to finger display (Fig. 3) if so desired.

The back clip can also be used with the back palm. Go from the Front-finger Grip (Fig. 27) to the Back-finger Grip (Figs. 29 and 30). From the Back-grip position tilt the hand slightly so that the lower edge of the coin rests on the extended little finger. This enables the first finger to move a trifle backward and down over the upper edge of the coin, clipping it against the second finger. By drawing the forefinger upward and forward, the coin is retained in the Back-finger clip (Fig. 38). Seen from the front, the hand appears empty, with the third and fourth fingers a trifle spread (Fig. 37). A reversal of this process will put the coin again in a Back-finger Grip.

BACK AND FRONT CLIP

There are various maneuvers whereby a clipped coin can be shifted from between the first two fingers to similar positions between the other fingers, thus showing the hand back and front with a series of slow turn-overs. Downs personally described such a routine in his treatise on coin manipulations, but he seldom utilized it—if ever. Later manipulators modified these moves and thereby improved them, even using coins with special flesh-colored edges so they could not peek from between the fingers.

However, except for the Front-finger Clip and the Back-finger Clip, as just described, few of these additional moves are worth the effort and certainly none are suited to close-up presentation. So in final analysis, they are nothing more than finger exercises, and there is no need to delve into them. But out of this welter, there emerges one fairly modern and somewhat overlooked combination of sleights that simulates the Back and Front Palm but is easier of execution. This Back and Front Clip, as it has been styled, is performed thus:

With left side toward the audience, display the coin in the right hand and vanish it with the "Back-finger Clip" as described under the head (see Figs. 36, 37, and 38). Then close the fist as with the Back and Front Palm, when about to transfer the coin from back to front (Fig. 32). There is a dif-

ference in the thumb action, however. Since the coin is projecting from between the fingers, the thumb simply comes alongside it (Fig. 36) and grips
it with the old-style Thumb-crook Palm as described on page 11 (Fig. 16).

Since the fingers are gripping the upper edge of the coin, the thumb is
limited to the lower portion, but that is a help, not a hindrance. By pressing
the thumb firmly to the right, the bulk of the coin is wedged at the base of
the thumb, thus shifting from the Thumb-crook Palm to the Thumb-fork
Palm (Fig. 18). The fingers can then be extended showing the back of the
hand with the thumb downward, the coin being hidden in the thumb fork.

To show the front of the hand again, bend in the fingers and grip the coin
between the first and second fingers, as though to produce it at the fingertips (Fig. 20). But instead of producing the coin, keep the back of the hand
toward the audience and use the tip of the thumb to push the coin into the
back-finger clip. Then point the fingers straight downward, open the fist,
and bring the hand and thumb upward, showing the palm completely
empty (Fig. 37), with the coin finger-clipped in back (Fig. 38).

For a Vanish: Proceed as with the back finger clip unless you prefer to
start with the Back Palm and shift from the Back-finger Grip (Fig. 30) to
the Back-finger Clip. For a production, again proceed as with the back-
finger clip, bringing the coin to display position (Fig. 1).

Here, however, you have a very effective option that will enhance any
coin-catching routine. After showing the back of the hand with the coin in
Thumb-fork Palm position, turn your body half about so that your right
side is toward the audience. At the same time, swing the right hand down,
across in front, and up again in a long pendulum action, its back always
toward the audience, and finishing with the thumb pointing upward (Fig.
18). You are then set to produce the coin from the Thumb-fork Palm at the
very fingertips (Fig. 3).

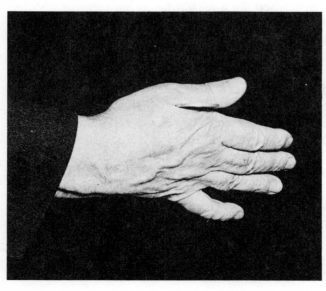

BACK THUMB CLIP
Fig. 39. Rear view of coin
retained edgewise behind
the fork of the thumb.

BACK THUMB CLIP

This was devised by Downs as a climax to the series of clipping moves, and as such it comes under the head of manipulative gymnastics. But it also serves a practical purpose, with the coin being neatly clipped behind the fleshy fork of the thumb (Fig. 39) so that the hand can be shown apparently empty in front (Fig. 40). In some cases, the coin is secretly placed there, making this strictly a utility move, which will be described under Change-overs. Still, it can figure both as a direct vanish and production with the following moves:

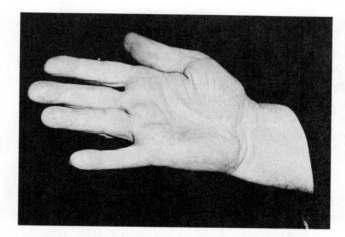

Fig. 40. Spectator's view of empty hand with coin held in back thumb clip. Note how closely the thumb is held.

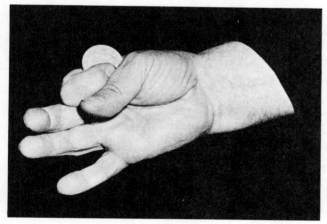

Fig. 41. Forefinger presses coin toward base of thumb, which swings upward to grip coin with back clip.

With the left side toward the audience, show the coin in display position (Fig. 1). With the thumb in front, push the coin onto the tip of the forefinger, partially balancing it there but with the edge resting against the second finger, so the thumb can be bent inward toward the palm of the hand.

Tilt the hand palm upward and bend the forefinger straight inward, carrying the coin along with it to the very base of the thumb (Fig. 41). This is similar to the Thumb-fork Palm on page 13, but since only the forefinger is used, the coin arrives at the back of the fork instead of at the front. The thumb is then pushed back to its normal position and the hand is raised with the thumb straight upward, showing the hand empty (Fig. 40) with the coin hidden in back.

Done with a down-and-up motion of the hand, this is quite illustrative, giving the impression that the coin vanished when tossed in the air. To recover the coin and produce it, the hand is tilted forward, the thumb is lifted, and the fingers are fisted all in one short, quick, circular action, in which the hand is brought forward and turned downward so its back is toward the audience. The hand may then be turned about and opened to show the coin.

This can be helped by thrusting the hand high, so that the coin actually comes down into the fist while the latter is still going upward. But quick actions are always suspicious, and there is often a chance that the audience may catch a glint of the coin. So for a safer and more deliberate recovery, the following is preferable:

After the vanish turn farther to the right so that your back is partly toward the audience. In the same action, bring your right hand straight inward so that your body hides it. At that moment, tilt the hand forward and close it as just described, letting the coin fall into the fist smoothly and easily. The upward action is provided by thrusting the hand above your head, turning the back of the fist toward the audience as you do.

Turn toward the audience, swing the right hand outward at shoulder level, with fingers frontward. Open the fist and show the vanished coin back again.

As an added bit, when raising your clenched hand above your head, you can press the coin into standard palm position (Fig. 8) and then spread your thumb and fingers. In fact, the coin does not actually have to be palmed if you tilt the back of the hand downward and forward, for the coin will then rest in the hollow of the palm. Either way, the fist is then closed and reproduced when you turn toward the audience as described.

NOTE: In all the foregoing, only the simplest and most direct vanishes and productions have been given with the various palms and clips. Other and more subtle ways of utilizing these devices will be detailed in the ensuing chapters.

COIN VANISHES

The vanishing of a coin may be rightfully classed as the basis of all close-up coin magic, as well as expert manipulation. The reason is that to be effective, it must constitute a form of delayed deception. As a basic example, the right hand shows a coin at its fingertips and places it in the left hand; or the left hand may simply take it from the right hand. Either way, the left hand closes over the coin; and when it reopens, the coin is gone.

To emphasize this, the fingers of the right hand may brush the empty left palm; then the back of the left hand may be turned toward the spectators so the right fingers can stroke it also. Finally, as part of the routine, the palm of the right hand is turned frontward to show that it, too, is empty. To the beginner, these moves may seem superfluous, but the advanced performer learns to appreciate their value, as they frequently furnish misdirection that helps to cover follow-up moves.

Unlike a production, where the sudden appearance of a coin at the fingertips can catch people by surprise, spectators may become skeptical of a coin vanish from its very start. The mere handling of a coin, its placement by one hand into the other, can remind them of something that fooled them before and this time makes them alert to solve the riddle. Even after the vanish, they will want to make sure the coin is really gone.

To counter that, the performer must practice different types of vanishes, each designed to draw the spectator's mind from the trail it has begun to follow while watching a similar routine. The vanishes that follow fulfill that requirement, so the more of them you practice, the more deceptive they will all become.

PULL-AWAY VANISH

An excellent alternate for the simple vanish used with the thumb fork palm where the first and second fingers of the right hand apparently place the coin in the left hand (Fig. 19), which closes as the right fingers withdraw. The simple vanish, used repeatedly, may excite some suspicion. That is when the pull-away will throw keen observers off the trail.

With your right side toward the audience, actually slap the coin into the open left hand with the first two fingers of the right. Tilt the left hand upward and forward; then press the tips of those same right fingers against the lower edge of the coin to keep it in place. You deliberately close the left fingers over the coin, withdrawing the right fingers a second or so later. When the coin suddenly vanishes from the left hand, the effect is surprising indeed.

It all hinges on one bold, deceptive move. As the left fingers close, push the tips of the right fingers up to the top edge of the coin. A slight raising of the hands will cover this action and the hands will appear exactly as with the simple vanish (Fig. 19). But now the right first and second fingers press hard against the coin and pull it straight along with them as they draw downward.

The pull should be almost like a snap, and the moment the right fingers are clear of the left hand, they double inward, retaining the coin in their bend (Fig. 42). The coin is then well on its way to the thumb fork palm (Fig. 18), where it can be placed by the right fingers while attention is centered on the left hand. By keeping the right thumb beneath the fingers dur-

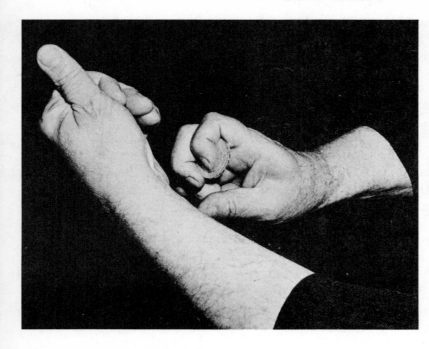

Fig. 42. Side view as seen by performer, showing right fingers doubling inward, secretly bringing coin along.

ing the pull-away, the thumb can aid with the palming action if the fingers lose their grip.

REVERSE VANISH

In this effective sequence, you stand with your right side toward the audience. The right hand then shows a coin in display position, turning it about so the thumb is toward the audience, while the left hand is extended at shoulder level, with its back toward the audience. From this position (Fig. 43) the left hand comes down over the coin and draws it away (Fig. 44). A moment later, the coin vanishes from the left hand and both hands are shown empty, front and back.

REVERSE VANISH
Fig. 43. Start of sequence. Audience view of left hand about to cover coin displayed by right hand.

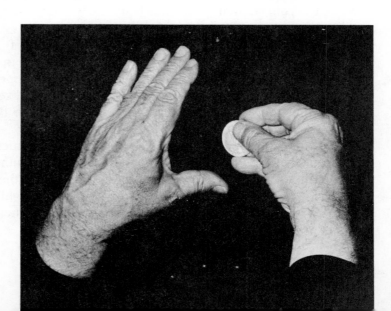

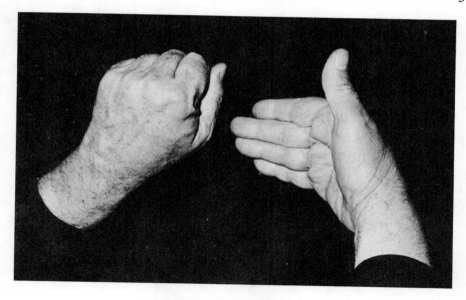

Fig. 44. Left hand has closed over coin and is now moving upward, apparently drawing coin away.

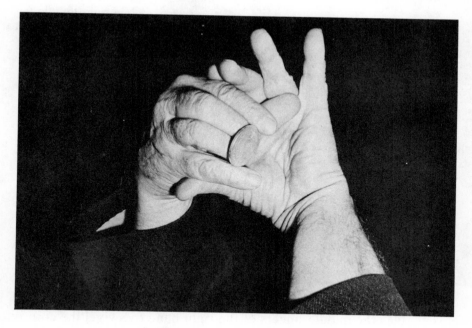

Fig. 45. Rear view of left hand covering right, with right fingers back-palming coin as left hand pretends to take it away.

This series of moves depends upon the back and front palm (see page 17), but it is well disguised throughout. From the original position (Fig. 43) the left hand covers the coin and immediately the right thumb slides it into front-finger grip position between the first and fourth fingers, so the middle fingers can swivel it to the back of the hand. This action (Fig. 45) is concealed from the audience by the left hand.

The left hand moves upward, forming a fish as though drawing the coin upward, leaving the right hand apparently empty (Fig. 44). Actually, the coin is now back-palmed by the right hand, but the fact that the fingers are pressed together excites no suspicion, as they were originally that way. The left hand is then turned so its fingers are toward the audience, and it is opened with a flourish as though tossing the coin in air, while the right hand is doubled into a fist, with its fingers away from view (Fig. 46).

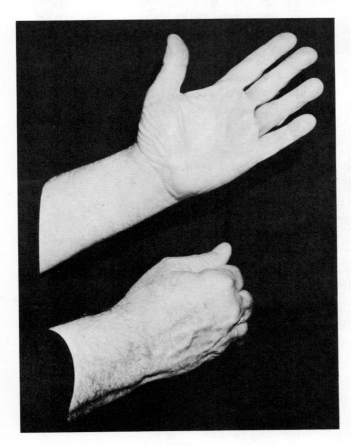

Fig. 46. Left hand vanishing coin with upward toss while right middle fingers secretly bring coin into palm.

This enables the middle fingers of the right hand to swivel the coin into the palm, continuing the deception (Fig. 33). The backs of both hands can then be shown with fingers well spread (Fig. 47), thus making the surprising vanish quite complete.

A neat touch may be added immediately after the vanish. The left hand pauses after its toss, thus holding attention while the right hand completes

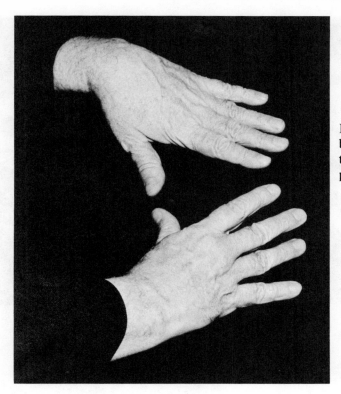

Fig. 47. Showing backs of both hands to conclude the vanish. Coin now palmed in right hand.

its palming process. The right hand then moves upward, back to the audience, and the right fingers brush the left palm to emphasize its emptiness. The back of the left hand is then turned toward the audience and the right fingers add another brush, both hands finishing back toward the audience.

As another variation, the right hand can remain palm front (as in Fig. 44) while the left hand makes its toss vanish. In this case, however, the fingers of the left hand should be held close together, like those of the right hand. After giving the audience this flash of both hands palms front, they are turned over simultaneously to show the backs. In the turnover, the left hand should form a fist exaclty like the right, making the action all the more natural.

The coin may be reproduced by any of the usual methods, but the brush production is probably the best. Turn the left palm toward the audience and sweep it from wrist to fingers and back again with the right hand, which drops the coin into the left hand on the return sweep. The left hand closes as it receives the coin and subsequently opens to reveal it.

THUMB-PALM ROUTINE

This routine combines a vanish, change-over, and reproduction of a single coin in smooth, convincing fashion. Standing with your right side toward the audience, you place a coin in the left hand, from which it

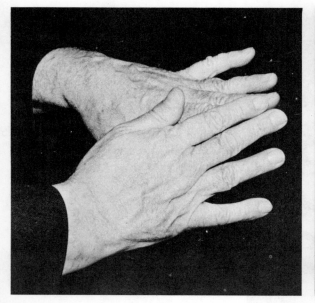

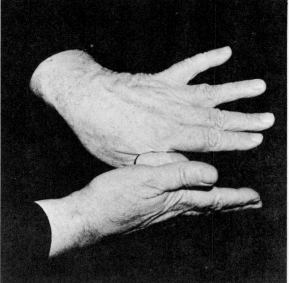

Fig. 48. Right hand brushing back of empty left
hand to show that coin
has really vanished, in
readiness for transfer.

Fig. 49. Performer's view
from above, showing
transfer of coin from
right thumb fork to back
of left thumb fork.

vanishes. The right fingers brush the left hand front and back; then both
palms are turned toward the spectators and shown completely empty.
After another brush by the right fingers, the left hand is closed and again
reopened to show that the coin has returned.

Begin by displaying the coin with the right hand (Fig. 1) and extend the
left hand, thumb upward. The right hand apparently puts the coin into the
left hand, but actually the right hand retains it by the Thumb Fork Palm
(Figs. 17 and 18). To complete the vanish, the right fingers are withdrawn
as usual from the position shown in Fig. 19, but in this case the back of the
left fist is immediately turned toward the audience, so the tips of the right
fingers can brush it lightly. That done, the left fist is turned frontward and
opened to show that the coin is gone.

To emphasize the vanish, the right fingers brush the empty left palm, this
time with a bold, sweeping stroke from the left wrist clear past the left
fingertips. The right fingers return to the left wrist, and the left hand is
turned thumb downward, so the right fingers can stroke the back of the left
hand, clear past the left fingertips. Now comes the vital move:

The right hand, having conclusively proven that the left hand is empty,
front and back, returns slowly toward the left wrist. This brings the fork of
the right thumb, with its palmed coin, directly in front of the left thumb
(Fig. 48). That enables the fork of the left thumb to grip the far edge of the

coin (Fig. 49), thus taking it from the fork of the right thumb, which obligingly releases it. Here, the left hand uses the Back Thumb Clip (as described on page 27), so by turning the left hand thumb upward and palm front, the coin can be kept from sight behind the left hand.

There is just one danger: Observers may catch a flash of the coin during the transfer. That is easily covered by the following device: As the left hand turns palm front, the right hand swivels to the left (Fig. 50). This affords perfect coverage for the reversal of the left hand, preventing anyone from gaining a glimpse of the "vanished" coin (Fig. 51).

The rear view shows how beautifully the transfer works, but during it the hands should be lifted to shoulder level or above and tilted backward at a sufficient angle for the coin to reach a horizontal position. That gained, the right hand continues to the left wrist; then the right hand sweeps the left palm with new gusto well past the tips of the left fingers.

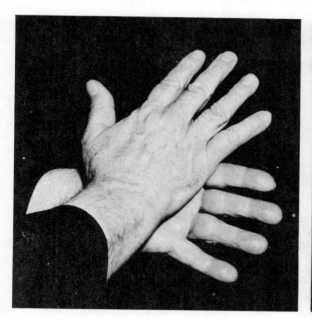

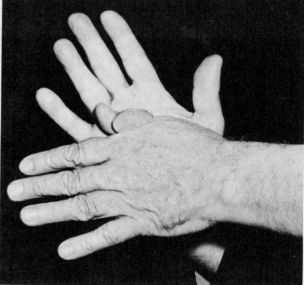

Fig. 50. Right hand swiveling upward to the left, covering left hand as the latter is turned palm front.

Fig. 51. Rear view. Left hand is being turned palm frontward, showing how coin is hidden during action.

Without pause, the right hand is brought inward directly below the left hand and the right hand is turned palm front, with its fingers pointing up to the extended left hand (Fig. 52). This shows the right hand as completely empty as the left, something that keen observers may have doubted up to that point. The natural backward tilt of the left hand keeps the coin perfectly concealed by the back thumb clip.

Don't linger too long at this point; a matter of two seconds should be about the limit. Then go into a reversal of the moves already described. Turn the back of the right hand toward the audience, and bring the right hand up in front of the left hand, toward the left wrist (Figs. 50 and 51). There, the back of the left hand is turned toward the audience so the fork of the right thumb can secretly regain the coin from the back of the left fork (Figs. 49 and 50). This is done during the turnover, and as the transfer is completed, the right hand moves to the left wrist, then gives the back of the left hand a sweeping brush clear past the left fingertips.

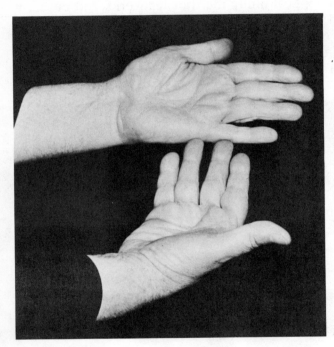

Fig. 52. Audience view of hands being shown full front. Coin concealed at back of left thumb fork.

The left hand is then turned palm toward the audience, with thumb upward, so the right hand can return to the left wrist and give the palm of the left hand another finger brush. Following that, the right hand reproduces the missing coin from the thumb fork palm (Fig. 18), bringing it from behind the left hand or from the left elbow, or by reaching out and "catching" the coin at the tips of the right fingers (Fig. 3).

ALTERNATE ROUTINE

Here is an alternate for the Thumb-palm Routine with a surprise finish. It starts as usual, with the coin vanishing from the left hand, which is shown absolutely empty. Then the right hand is shown independently to be quite as empty, the coin having actually gone from both hands. Then, as an

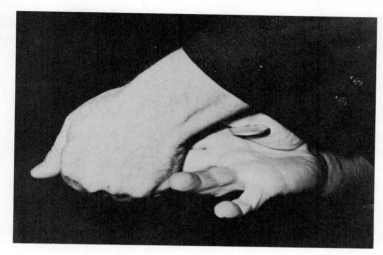

Fig. 53. Alternate Thumb-palm routine. Rear view of coin being dropped from right thumb fork into left sleeve.

added twist, the coin is reproduced by the left hand instead of the right hand.

The only flaw in this routine is that it involves sleeve work, which is frowned upon by most skilled sleight-of-hand performers, due to its uncertainty and lack of artistry. In recent years, however, "sleeving" has been coming to the fore, deserving due consideration; and in this particular instance, good misdirection is involved, both in disposing of the coin and in reclaiming it.

Start by apparently placing the coin in the left hand, actually thumb-palming it with the right (Fig. 18) so that the first two fingers of the right hand are gripped within the closed left hand (Fig. 19). At this point, raise both hands so the left forearm is at a 45-degree angle and you will note that the fork of the right thumb comes just above the cuff of the left coat sleeve (Fig. 53).

Maintaining that position momentarily, the right thumb releases the coin, letting it fall into the sleeve. As the coin drops, the right fingers are withdrawn from the left fist and go through the brushing motions—as with the Thumb-palm Routine—to "vanish" the coin from the left hand and prove the latter empty, front and back. Following that, turn the body to the right and show the right hand empty, back and front, much in the manner of the Back and Front Palm, as described on page 17, lowering the right hand to knee level as you do.

In this case, the right hand is really empty, as is proven when you finally spread its fingers. While attention is thus centered on the right hand, the left hand is simply dropped from shoulder level straight down beside the body, with the back of the left hand toward the spectators and the fingers loosely cupped. The coin drops from the left sleeve into the bend of the left fingers, which retain it in the Finger-bend Palm (Fig. 4).

The right hand is raised with palm front; the left hand follows, back toward audience, pointing to the empty right hand. The left hand continues to the right elbow and produces the coin from there, a very effective climax, as the left hand was shown so thoroughly empty earlier.

TAKE-AWAY VANISH

One of the neatest, yet simplest of coin vanishes. Stand with the right side toward the audience and extend the left arm at shoulder level, keeping it slightly bent with the back of the left hand toward the spectators, left thumb pointing downward. Hold the coin at the tips of the right first and second fingers, in fingertip-display position (Fig. 3).

Swing the right hand toward the left and carry the coin over and in back of the left hand, placing the coin therein. Having completed this dipping action, the right hand is brought upward and forward, then lowered. The left hand, having formed a fist to retain the coin, is turned with its thumb toward the audience and is opened to show the coin exactly where you placed it.

The right fingers take the coin again and the whole maneuver is repeated. This time the left hand is opened with a slight tossing motion, and the coin has mysteriously vanished!

It is all done during the repeated dip. The right fingers, instead of placing the coin in the left hand, simply keep it clipped between them. The left fingers close into a loose fist, as though retaining the coin as before, while the right hand comes back upward, outward, and downward, its fingers still bent inward.

The back of the right hand is kept directly toward the audience with knuckles upward, which completely hides the coin (Fig. 54). While the left hand is being turned thumb front for the vanish, the right hand continues downward, thumb-palming the coin in progress so it can be shown with fingers spread when it points to the empty left hand.

Fig. 54. Right hand drawn upward from left hand, retaining coin between fingers (rear view).

FRENCH DROP

A truly fundamental vanish, this is still as deceptive as it was in its heyday more than a century ago. The coin is held by the left hand with the tip of the thumb at one edge, the tips of the first two fingers at the other edge, and with one side tilted toward the spectators. The right thumb is then inserted in the space beneath the coin, so that the right fingers can close over it (Fig. 55).

FRENCH DROP
Fig. 55. Start of sequence. Right thumb is inserted beneath coin, right fingers are closing over it.

With the closing, the right fist apparently takes away the coin, thanks to the lifting action of the right thumb. But when the hand swings to the right and provides a rubbing action, it is immediately opened and the coin has disappeared.

The move itself is both simple and subtle. As the right fingers cover the coin, the left thumb is lifted just as the right thumb starts its upward move. As a result, the coin drops into the bend of the left fingers (Fig. 56). The back of the left hand is raised toward the audience, retaining the coin in the Finger Bend (Fig. 4). The left forefinger is then pointed toward the right hand when the latter is shown empty.

Fig. 56. Side view of French Drop, showing coin dropping into left finger bend as right fingers close down from above.

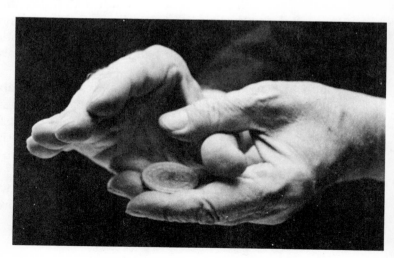

The bolder the original display of the coin (Fig. 55), the stronger the subsequent effect. Unfortunately, however, the very ease with which the French Drop may be acquired has led to its own undoing. Beginners fail to show the coin openly and also make the move too quickly, which is fatal, as the beauty of the Tourniquet—as the French Drop was originally termed—depends upon its deliberation.

Far from weakening the effect of the French Drop, such problems have led to the creation of still more subtle moves, specially designed for the sharp onlooker, as follows.

PALM OFF

Here the right hand deliberately takes the coin from the left hand, without performing the French Drop. You then extend your right hand toward the sharp spectator and say, "Here, take the coin." If he looks toward your left hand in a knowing way, as though thinking the coin is still there, you spread your right hand, palm downward, above his open hand, retaining the coin with the Standard Palm (Fig. 9).

That the back of the right hand is shown freely (Fig. 10) and the right forefinger can point to the left hand are added convincers that the coin is still there, until you open the left hand and show the acute observer that it is just as empty as he supposed the right hand to be. By then he is so sure that the right hand was really empty that he is totally baffled.

However, when working with a group of spectators, the majority will assume that the right hand really took away the coin, so you must fool them legitimately along with the few sharpies who are sure you let the coin drop in your left hand. This dual feat may be accomplished in two ways. First by:

BACK PALM OFF

Face obliquely toward the left, exhibiting the coin between the tips of left thumb and fingers, in readiness for the French Drop (Fig. 55). Actually take the coin with the right hand and immediately pivot toward the right, lowering the empty left hand with its back toward the audience and fingers bent inward.

Meanwhile, the right fist is extended at about waist level, with its knuckles downward, and fingers bent inward beneath the coin. The tips of the first and fourth fingers immediately press the opposite edges of the coin, applying the front-finger grip (Fig. 27) in readiness for the Back Palm, which is executed as you complete the body pivot to the right (Figs. 28 through 30).

This move can be deliberate at first, ending with a quick upward sweep or toss as the hand is shown empty. Then, before observers fully note that the right fingers are still pressed together, the right hand is again lowered to waist level, with fingers pointing downward, and the hand is fisted, so the fingers can swivel the coin to the front of the hand (Figs. 31 and 32).

This is simply a continuation of the regular Back and Front Palm (pages 17 and 18), but this time, in completing it, pivot the body fully to the left while pressing the coin upward into the Standard Palm (Figs. 8 and 9). During this action, swing the right hand upward and forward, keeping its back toward the audience. At the same time extend the left hand to the left at shoulder level so the right hand, coming upward like a pendulum, finishes its swing by pointing to the left hand, which is casually shown empty, front and back.

The vanish itself will baffle the average onlooker, and the aftermath of showing the left hand empty will nonplus the know-it-alls, making this brief routine highly effective. As a follow-up, the coin may be reproduced by brushing the left hand with the right, as with the brush production (page 33). However, the vanish itself is so complete that it is also good for a final getaway in which the coin is either pocketed or laid aside, as convenient.

FALSE DROP

Here an outright effort is made to fool anyone familiar with the French Drop. Start with the backs of the left fingers directly toward the onlookers and tilt the left thumb toward you so that the coin is actually hidden before you begin the familiar move shown in Fig. 55. In making the move, bring the right fingers down in front of the left fingers, covering the latter from view. This enables the left thumb and second finger to plant the edge of the coin behind the fork of the right thumb (Fig. 57).

FALSE DROP
Fig. 57. Performer's view of right hand covering coin at start. Left thumb and fingers are holding coin.

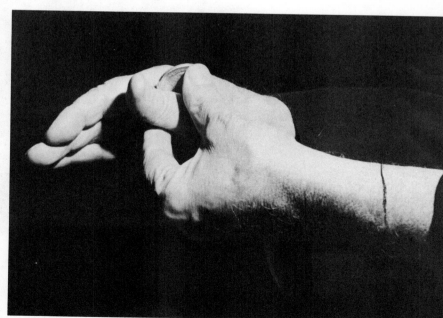

This move is done secretly, and the more deliberately the better, since any hesitation gives the impression that the regular drop is underway. The right hand is immediately fisted and brought upward and backward to the right, keeping the coin continually from view. A good way to insure this is to aim the back edge of the coin straight toward the right shoulder, keeping it on target until the hand is almost there. The left hand, meanwhile, is lowered suspiciously in cupped fashion, as though retaining the coin (Fig. 58).

By the time the right hand nears the right shoulder, the right knuckles should be pointing directly upward. You then pivot the body slowly to the right, tilting the right hand downward and backward, still keeping the clipped coin completely from view. This brings the bent fingers toward the audience, with the thumb resting level upon them. In the same action, the right hand is extended to half-arm's length, and the fingers are opened and spread slightly, showing the hand apparently empty (Fig. 40). Actually, the coin is retained from sight by the Back Thumb Clip (Fig. 39).

Audience attention promptly shifts to the left hand (where you want it). You extend the left hand toward the spectators, open it, and spread the fingers wide, palm upward, then downward, showing it empty, too. Then, to certify the surprise, point the left fingers up below the right hand, showing both palms front—the left hand vertically, the right hand horizontally.

The vanish is then all but complete, the final touch being to show the backs of the hands as well. To do this, slide the fingers of the left hand up in back of the right hand until the left thumb nears the center of the right palm (Fig. 59). At the same time, elevate both hands higher than your shoulder, tilting them backward and downward so the right hand is at a 45-degree angle and the left hand is almost level, its fingers pressed together and extending straight backward (Fig. 60).

Fig. 58. Audience view of right fist (with coin concealed in back thumb clip) while left hand draws attention.

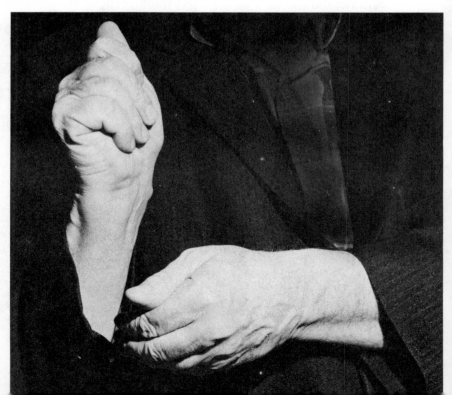

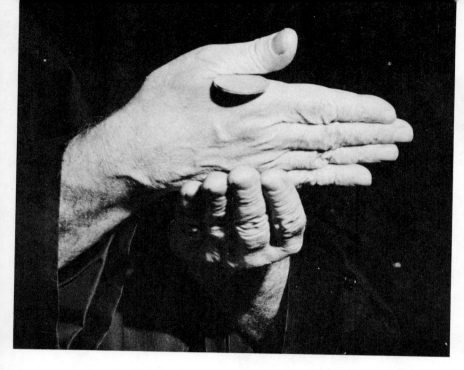

Fig. 59. Rear view of left fingers coming up behind right hand while left thumb presses against right palm.

During that motion, raise the right thumb slightly, letting the coin drop unseen from the back clip into the bend of the left fingers (Fig. 61), which grip it in the Finger Bend Palm (Fig. 4). The hands are then lowered toward waist level while the left hand is being turned palm downward under cover of the right hand, the tip of the left thumb still pressing the right palm and serving as a pivot.

Fig. 60. Audience view of right hand tilting backward to hide dropping of coin into left finger bend.

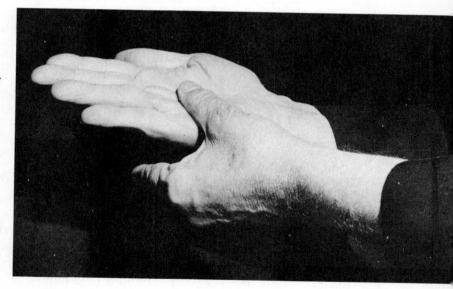

As the back of the left hand comes directly toward the audience, raise the right hand alone to shoulder level, turning its back toward the audience, with thumb straight downward. The left hand follows upward, its forefinger pointing to the back of the right hand, which is then turned

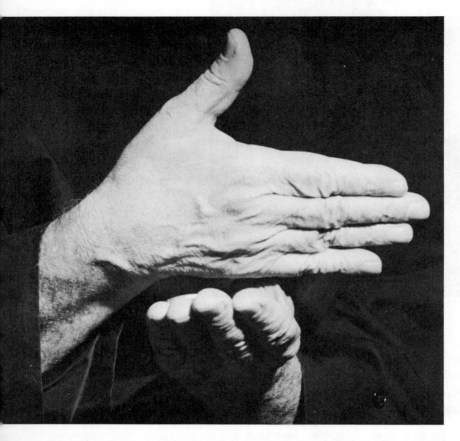

Fig. 61. Rear view show-
ing completion of the
move. Coin in finger bend
of left hand while right
hand rises to vertical with
thumb spread wide.

thumb upward to show the front as well. This eliminates any lurking suspicion of the right hand and the routine is now complete, the coin being
safely palmed in the bend of the left fingers.

FIST VANISH

This sleight, though simple, may be classed as advanced because it
demands exact timing and a sure grip. The right hand openly tosses a large
coin into the left, which closes its fingers over the coin, forming a loose fist,
which is turned so its back is toward the audience. The right hand casually
strokes the left fist, which is turned about and opened. The coin is gone!

Stand with the right side toward the audience. Hold the coin with the
right hand in display position and toss it so that it lands close to the base of
the left middle fingers. The left hand is held palm upward; now, as it forms
a loose fist, it is turned forward and downward, so that the coin falls into
the bend of the left fingers. Simultaneously, the left thumb is doubled inside the left fist, where it guides one edge of the coin between the lower
knuckles of the left middle fingers, which hold it there (Fig. 62).

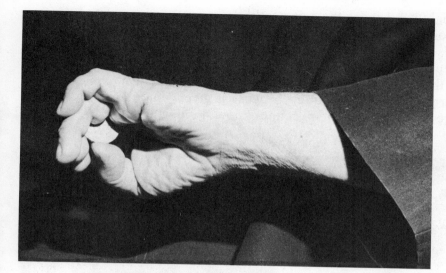

Fig. 62. Rear view of left hand, showing how thumb edges the coin between middle fingers. Back of hand is actually toward audience, with fingers pressed closely together, hiding the coin.

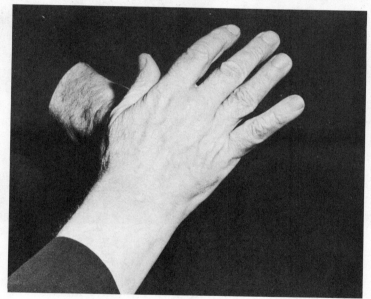

Fig. 63. Audience view of right hand momentarily covering left as hands are raised to shoulder level.

As you raise the left hand to shoulder level, with its back toward the audience, bring the tip of the left thumb to the inner edge of the coin. Bring the right hand upward so it covers the left fist (Fig. 63), and with the left thumb thrust the coin forward between the middle fingers so the right hand can grip it with the familiar Edge Palm (Fig. 64). To facilitate this vital move, the hands should be practically at right angles to each other.

Once the right hand gains its grip, lower it slightly and brush the back of the left hand with the right fingers, increasing the sweep as the right hand is lowered still farther, and finally pointing upward to the left hand, which is tightened into a firmer fist with the thumb slipping to the outside. The left hand is opened with a self-rubbing motion and is spread wide to complete the vanish. The right hand keeps the coin neatly and secretly edge-palmed (Fig. 12) while pointing to the empty left hand.

The crux of this deceptive routine is the well-timed transfer of the coin. Later, you can reproduce it as preferred. But the steal, if done neatly, can be made before the onlookers suspect that anything is due to happen. Moreover, the larger the coin the better, because it gives you a stronger grip with the edge palm, which the spectators know nothing about.

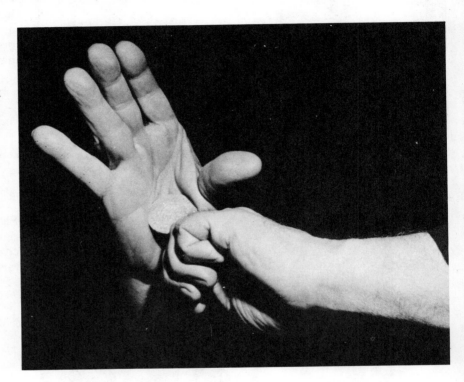

Fig. 64. Rear view of left hand thrusting coin between fingers, with right hand gripping coin in Edge Palm. Left fist continues upward so right fingertips can brush it.

SLOW-MOTION VANISH

To go from one gem to another, consider the Slow-motion Vanish. As its name implies, it consists of an open placement of a coin in the left hand, a deliberate showing of the empty right hand, and an absolute vanish of the coin from the left.

Stand with your right side toward the audience, display the coin with the right hand, and drop the coin into the center of the left palm, which is held upward to receive it. Close the left fingers over the coin and turn the left hand forward and downward, letting the coin rest on the tips of the middle fingers, as though about to produce it from Standard Palm position. Instead, the fingers push the coin to the heel of the hand, so that it protrudes there.

To cover this, the left hand is turned with its back directly toward the audience, and the left hand promptly tightens its fist, pressing the tips of the middle fingers against the edge of the coin so that it comes to a vertical position between the fingernails and the heel of the hand, putting it outside the fist. The right hand approaches and strokes the back of the left hand, finally tapping it with the right forefinger, as though to emphasize that the coin is really in the left hand. Then:

The right hand, its forefinger still pointing to the left hand, is turned palm front, showing the right hand empty, as absolute proof that the coin is

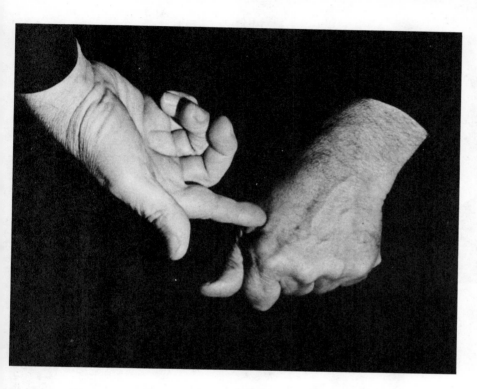

SLOW-MOTION VANISH
Fig. 65. Right hand, palm turned openly toward audience, points to left fist containing coin.

really in the left hand (Fig. 65). The right hand is now turned around, rotating leftward, with the forefinger still pointing, but with the remaining fingers bending inward so that their knuckles come directly below the left thumb (Fig. 66). All is then ready for the vital move:

As the hands are raised toward shoulder level, the left hand is turned downward, bringing the outer edge of the coin down between the middle fingers of the right hand, which spread slightly and then close tightly, clipping the coin between them. This transfer (Fig. 67) is completely hidden by the right hand, which is still held knuckles upward.

The left hand continues its turning motion until its fingers are directly toward the audience. At the same time it rises higher while the right hand is lowered, still pointing at the left. The left hand is then spread wide and shown empty, while the right thumb, bending inward, comes beneath the coin and secretly brings it into the fork of the thumb, where it is promptly palmed (Fig. 18).

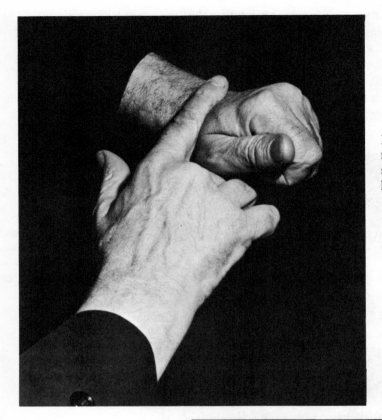

Fig. 66. Audience view of right hand completing turn so knuckles come below left thumb.

Fig. 67. Rear view of same vital position, showing how right middle fingers secretly clip coin between their knuckles.

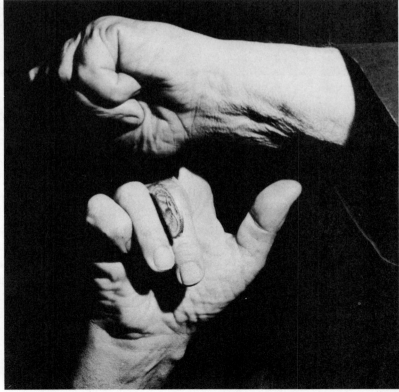

SQUEEZE VANISH

The closer you view this vanish, the more it is likely to deceive you. The performer holds a large coin edgewise between the tips of his right thumb and forefinger, keeping it slanted very slightly downward. He brings his left hand over the coin, hiding it from above. The left fist closes slowly over the coin with a tight, squeezing action; then the left hand turns upward and spreads its thumb and fingers to show that the coin has vanished.

Meanwhile, the right hand has remained stationary, the tips of its thumb and forefinger pressed together as mute testimony that the left hand forced them together when it removed the coin in its tight fist. But if you think that the coin is in the right hand, you are wrong. Like the left hand, the right is opened palm upward with no trace of the missing coin.

This is another of those instances where sleeve work is justifiable, as it is very artfully applied in this case. As the left hand covers the coin, the right thumb and forefinger provide a sharp squeeze of their own to the opposite edges of the coin (Fig. 68). As they do, they point the coin directly toward the left sleeve. The pincer action propels the coin straight into the sleeve, often as far as the elbow (Fig. 69). From there on, it is simply a case of opening the hands to show the coin gone. The left hand should be tilted up to match the downslant of the right. Later, the left hand is dropped to the side, where the coin is allowed to slide from the sleeve into the bend of the left fingers, which can later reproduce it.

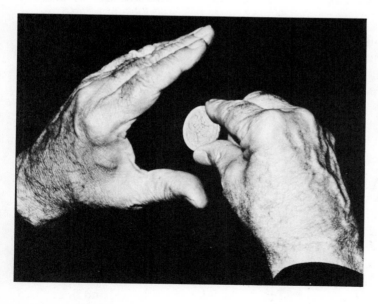

SQUEEZE VANISH
Fig. 68. Start viewed from directly above. Note pincer grip of right thumb and forefinger.

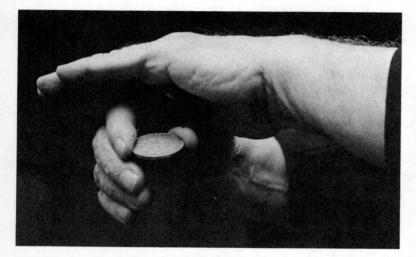

Fig. 69. Side view from below, unseen by spectators. Left hand has covered coin from above. Right thumb and forefinger are beginning their squeeze.

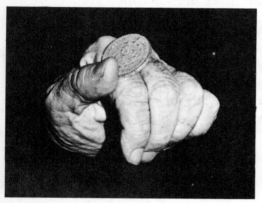

COIN ROLL AND VANISH
Fig. 70. Start of sequence with left thumb pushing coin up over forefinger.

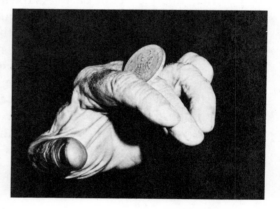

Fig. 71. Forefinger tilting coin over second finger, with third finger raised to bring down far edge of coin.

COIN ROLL

This is primarily a flourish used between tricks to emphasize the performer's digital dexterity without revealing any of his deceptions. The right hand places a large coin between the thumb and forefinger of the left hand, which is held with knuckles upward (Fig. 70). With a slight upward push, the left thumb rolls the coin across the forefinger, so the far edge of the coin tilts downward and is trapped between the forefinger and the second finger (Fig. 71), which raises slightly to receive it and then moves downward, piston fashion, so that the coin rides over the second finger and is trapped by the third finger, which also comes up to control it.

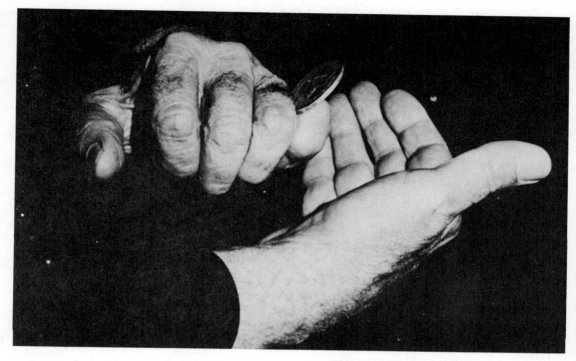

Fig. 72. Roll has carried over left third finger, with little finger about to topple coin into cupped right hand.

With the same piston action, the third finger propels the coin onward to the space between the third and fourth fingers, where the fourth finger, in its turn, continues the rolling action, sending the coin over the fourth finger (Fig. 72) so that it rolls completely clear of the left hand and drops into the right hand, which meanwhile has been cupped palm upward in order to receive it. The right hand then replaces the coin between the thumb and lower portion of the left forefinger and the roll can be repeated time and again.

Once the rolling has been practiced to the point where it becomes both smooth and steady, it can be used as forerunner to the following deception:

COIN-ROLL VANISH

Here the performer finishes the repeated coin roll by apparently carrying the coin away in the right hand instead of replacing it between the thumb and forefinger of the left. The right hand is fisted, raised, and opened with a rubbing motion of thumb and fingers, whereupon the spectators are surprised to see that the coin has vanished. To cap that puzzling result, the performer points his right forefinger toward his left hand, and they are even more amazed to find that the coin has returned there and that the left fingers are again rolling it from knuckle to knuckle as before.

In short, the coin vanishes from *within* the right hand and reappears upon the *back* of the downturned left hand, almost as if the coin roll had not been interrupted!

Actually, the roll is not really interrupted; it is merely shortened. To work the vanish, you must face directly toward the spectators so that the back of your cupped right hand is toward them as well. You start the roll as usual, letting the coin flip openly into the waiting right hand, but after a few repeats, you speed the action by bringing your right hand up more rapidly, so that the onlookers barely see the coin tumble over the left little finger and into the right hand because the back of the right hand intervenes.

All is then ready for the crucial move, which takes place during the next roll. As the coin crosses the third finger of the left hand, both hands are tilted upward and inward toward the body. This hides the coin as it comes between the third and fourth fingers and enables the fourth finger to lift high enough to halt the coin's progress without being observed. Simultaneously, the left thumb is thrust beneath the left fingers, clear to the base of the little finger, where it engages the lower edge of the coin. The third and fourth fingers immediately relax and the coin slides downward, so that it is practically balanced on the tip of the left thumb, which can easily retain it by pressing it up into the bend of the other fingers (Fig. 73).

All this is completely covered by the right hand, which now closes into a fist and moves upward and to the right as the body is turned in that direction. Spectators see the left hand partly closed with knuckles upward, as if waiting for the right hand to replace the coin so the roll can be continued.

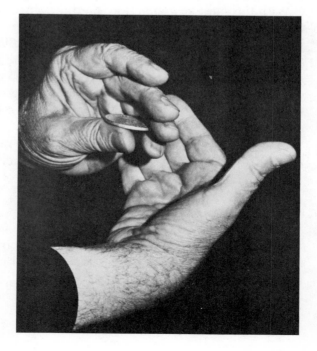

Fig. 73. Rear view of vital move in Coin Roll and Vanish, showing left thumb secretly receiving coin while right hand covers.

If the move is neatly done, they never suspect that the coin is still in the left hand. While their eyes follow the right hand and its "vanishing" motions, the left thumb brings the partly balanced coin out from beneath the fingers and presses it up against the forefinger. Just as the right hand opens, showing itself empty, the left thumb thrusts farther upward, starting another coin roll (Fig. 70), and as the spectators follow the point of the right finger, they see the roll actually in progress.

Done nonchalantly, this has a highly baffling effect, which is concluded by simply completing the standard coin roll, this time letting the coin drop legitimately into the right hand.

ONE-HAND COIN ROLL

The coin roll can be presented as a one-hand flourish by simply following the moves just described under the Coin-roll Vanish, but with no attempt at deception. The left thumb starts the coin rolling over the forefinger (Fig. 70), which relays it on across the third finger, but as it comes between the third and fourth fingers, they spread so that the coin slides down to the tip of the thumb, which by then has been extended to receive it. The thumb brings the coin back to the starting point, and the flourish is repeated as often as desired. For a finish, the thumb simply retains the coin within the hand, which is turned palm upward to show the coin.

TWO-HAND COIN ROLL

By practicing the roll with both hands, the following flourish can be used effectively. Start with the usual roll—say with the left hand—but keep the right hand turned knuckles upward just like the left. When the left third finger is ready to flip the coin over the fourth finger, extend the right hand just beyond and just below the left, so that the coin drops edge downward between the first and second fingers of the right hand, which retain it momentarily there. In fact, by tilting the left hand forward, the left hand can practically place the coin there instead of dropping it. The right hand then continues the roll on past its little finger, where by then the left hand can be waiting to receive and continue the roll. This double action may be repeated as long as desired.

COIN CHANGES

The secret exchange of one coin for another serves two special purposes: (1) the apparent transformation of one type of coin to another, such as a half dollar magically becoming a silver dollar; or a silver coin turning into one of copper—an excellent climax to a series of vanishes and reproductions, or as an intervening surprise; (2) the substitution of a special coin for an ordinary coin, or a coin belonging to the performer for one he has borrowed from the audience.

Since these involve sleights already described, they will be given in brief, with appropriate references:

Palm-to-palm Change: Very easy and very good. Have the substitute coin palmed in the left hand, which is back toward the audience, as you face the audience and display the original coin with the right hand. Turn to the left and bring the left hand palm upward, keeping its fingers cupped to hide the coin. Simultaneously, the right hand apparently places the original coin in the left hand, actually palming it, with the Standard Palm, just as with a vanish. The left hand closes, then opens, exhibiting the substituted coin.

With a transformation, this is highly effective, as the right hand can apparently throw the coin into the left, with the observers believing that they really "saw it go" over a gap of several inches. To play that to the full, the left hand should transfer the transformed coin back to the right hand, which then displays it between thumb and fingertips, boldly covering the fact that the original coin is neatly and secretly nestled away down in the right palm.

Palm-drop Change: Here the substitute coin is palmed in the right hand, while the original is displayed at tips of thumb and fingers, as you face directly toward the audience. Show the left hand empty and swing toward the left, as though to throw the visible coin into the left hand.

Instead, the right thumb draws the original coin downward behind the fingers, at the same time releasing the palmed substitute so that it falls into the left hand, which closes over it. All in the same move, the right fingers press the original coin into the right palm, retaining it there with the Standard Palm (Fig. 9).

This is a wonderfully deceptive move, with this proviso: The substitute coin must be released a split second before the original coin is palmed; otherwise they will click as they pass and thus ruin things completely. That is why some very capable performers have shunned this move, thinking that they must be quick in palming the original before releasing the substitute. Let the substitute drop first and you will have no trouble palming the original in the right hand, which naturally recoils to the right while the left hand carries the substitute leftward, drawing all attention in that direction.

Palm Drop 2: An excellent variation to the method just described. Have the substitute coin palmed in the right hand. Display the original (as in Fig. 1) and pretend to throw it from the right hand into the left, actually palming it in the right hand with the Thumb Fork Palm (Figs. 17 and 18), releasing the palmed substitute instead. Here the original may be palmed first and the substitute released immediately afterward, with no chance of a click.

French Drop Change: With the substitute coin palmed in the right hand, show the original coin in the left, holding the original coin in position for the French Drop (Fig. 56). The right hand apparently takes the coin from the left, but actually executes the French Drop so that the original coin drops into the bend of the left fingers, while the right fingers close over the palmed substitute. Later, the right thumb pushes the substitute coin to the tips of the right fingers, as with a production, but in this case the coin is exhibited in more casual style.

Pickup Change: A neat reversal of the Palm-to-palm method. Have the substitute coin palmed in the right hand. Show the original coin between the tips of the right thumb and fingers, then toss it into the palm of the left hand, which is upturned to receive it. Point the tips of the right thumb and fingers downward around the original coin, as though to pick it up; but instead, press it firmly into the left palm, which retains it as the left hand is immediately turned downward. Simultaneously, the right hand moves upward and away, letting the substitute coin drop to the tips of the right fingers, which are bent inward to receive it. The right thumb then pushes it into sight as though it were the original coin.

NOTE: In all the changes so far described, the substitute coin is normally retained by the Standard Palm (Fig. 9) at the outset. However, in most instances, the Finger-bend Palm (Fig. 4) may be utilized instead, depending on the choice of the individual performer. In the next change, the Finger-bend Palm is utilized both at the start and the finish. It is called:

MULTIPLE-COIN MANIPULATION

This phase of coin manipulation follows the general pattern applicable to single coins, but with certain limitations and extensions that will become obvious when tested. As with a single coin, palming is the primary requisite when multiple manipulation is involved, so for convenience, each palming device will be followed by descriptions of productions and vanishes appropriate or adaptable to that particular method.

The basic difference between single and multiple manipulation is this: A single coin, if acquired secretly, or brought unnoticed from the pocket, can be automatically palmed during that action, whereas a group of coins, usually handled as a stack, must be placed in the desired palming position. This will be covered by the Change-over Placement (page 64), involving a single coin, and its follow-up, the Multiple-coin Transfer (page 64), which serves as starting point for the next sleights.

MULTIPLE FINGER BEND

Here placement is automatic. In picking up a stack of as many as six coins, they are worked into the finger bend and treated exactly like a single coin (page 3).

For a Production: Push the coins upward, one by one, with the right thumb to the tip of the right forefinger, as with the single-coin production (page 4). The left thumb and fingers take the coins as they appear, exhibiting them in fanwise fashion, as in Fig. 74, which shows the production in progress. Usually, the back of the right hand should be kept toward the audience; but if the angles are not too bad, the palm can be turned frontward for the production of the last few coins, provided the finger bend is sufficient to hide them until they are pushed up.

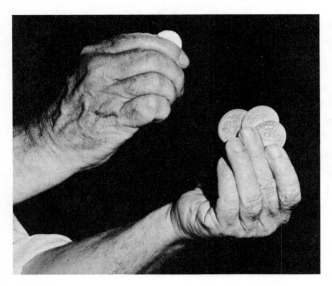

MULTIPLE FINGER BEND
Fig. 74. Performer's view of coins being produced singly from finger bend of right hand with upward thrust of thumb. Those already produced are transferred to left hand.

To produce the coins uniformly, keeping the remainder of the stack intact, relax pressure of the middle fingers and push up lightly with the thumb. The stack will stay in position because of its own weight, so that each successive coin can be thrust upward without dragging others along. However, as an added safeguard against that contingency, the right forefinger may be bent inward above the stack (Fig. 75) so each coin must be pressed against the finger and worked past it in the course of production. This automatically keeps the remaining coins in place.

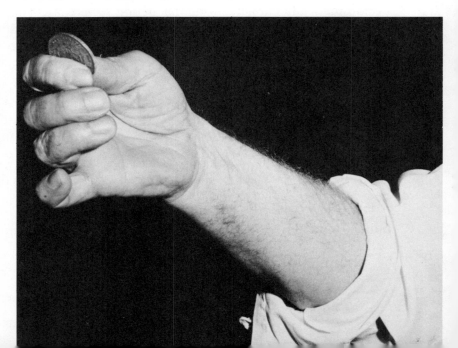

Fig. 75. Production from finger bend with hand turned palm toward audience. Bend of fingers provides needed concealment.

Slide Vanish: Lay three or more coins in overlapping fashion on the out-stretched right palm. Turn the right side toward the audience, and during that action, point the right fingers downward and apparently let the coins slide down into the open left hand, which is held palm upward to receive them (Fig. 76). The left hand is promptly closed and raised; later, the coins vanish from it.

The action is quite simple. The right hand turns its back toward the on-lookers as it begins the slide, and simultaneously bends its fingers inward so that the coins land in the bend of the right fingers instead of the left hand (Fig. 77). By cupping the left fingers slightly upward, the bend of the right fingers is unnoticeable and the left hand closes as though carrying away the coins while the right hand retains them in the Finger-bend Palm (Fig. 78).

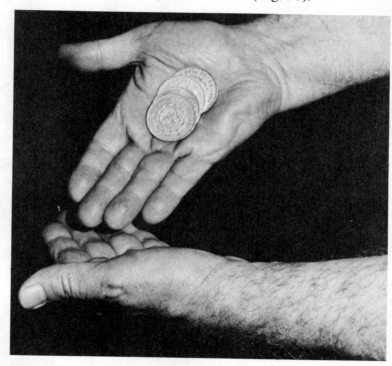

Fig. 76. Start of Slide Vanish with right hand displaying overlapped coins, ready to slide them down into the left.

Side-drop Vanish: Here the coins are overlapped on the first two fingers of the right hand (Fig. 79), which turns sideward and inward as though let-ting the coins drop into the cupped left hand, which is promptly closed as if containing them. Actually, the coins are halted by the right third finger, which is bent inward to retain them, acting like a temporary ledge (Fig. 80), with the little finger bent farther inward for added insurance. From that position they can be worked into the Finger-bend Palm with the aid of the right thumb, while audience attention is on the left hand.

This move was frequently used by T. Nelson Downs, in whose hands it was extremely deceptive. While easy to perform, it requires considerable practice to create a perfect illusion of the coins being practically thrown from the right hand into the left.

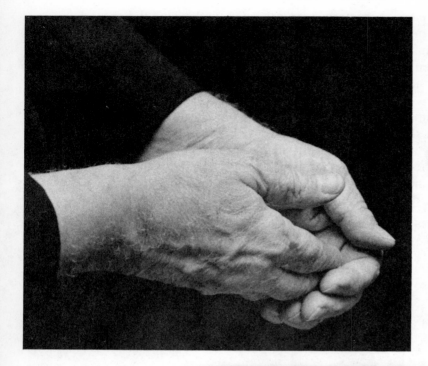

Fig. 77. With right side turned toward audience, right fingers point directly downward. The left hand is cupped to receive coins.

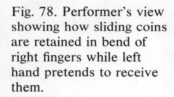

Fig. 78. Performer's view showing how sliding coins are retained in bend of right fingers while left hand pretends to receive them.

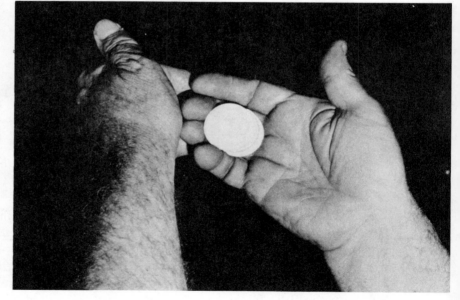

MULTIPLE STANDARD PALM

Here a stack of coins is retained in the Standard Palm position as described on page 6. One way is to start with the coins in the Finger-bend Palm, tilting the fingers downward so the coins can be worked toward

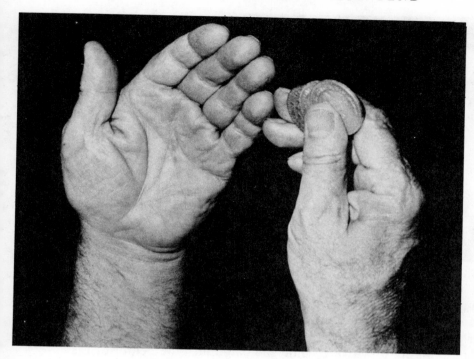

Fig. 79. Right hand holding coins in readiness for Side-drop Vanish with left hand ready to receive them.

Fig. 80. Performer's view of Side Drop. Right third finger acts as a ledge to retain the coins.

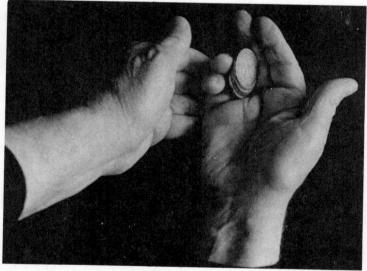

the fingertips with the aid of the right thumb. There they rest on the middle fingers, which press the coins upward into the palm, as with the single coin.

For a Production: The simplest method is to shift the coins to the Multiple-finger Palm and produce them as described under that head. One notable exception is with the Coins and Glass routine (page 68).

For a Vanish: Stack the coins on the tips of the right middle fingers, pressing down with the right thumb to steady the coins. Then palm the stack exactly like a single coin, while the right hand is apparently transfer-

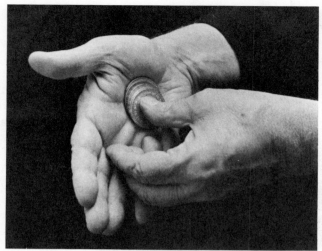

Fig. 81. For Pickup Vanish, coins are pressed into stack.

ring the stack to the left hand. Here a side grip on the coins can be applied by the right forefinger and little finger to momentarily steady the stack when the thumb is lifted.

Pickup Vanish: A reverse of the Slide Vanish (page 57). Lay the coins so they overlap on the outstretched right palm. The left hand approaches and its fingers, pointing downward, slide the coins into the center of the right palm, with the left thumb in readiness to help pick up the stack. Instead, the left thumb presses the stack firmly into the right palm (Fig. 81), and as the performer faces to the left, the back of the right hand is tilted upward, while the left hand closes with its back toward the audience as though carrying the coins away. Later they are vanished from the left hand.

Throw Vanish: Set the stack squarely in the center of the right palm and compress the right hand to grip them while making a throwing motion toward the left hand, which closes as though receiving the coins. Another excellent vanish is the One-by-one, described on page 65.

MULTIPLE-EDGE PALM

The performer faces to the right with the coins palmed in the bend of the left fingers and plants the stack edgewise in the right palm as he turns his body and faces to the left. The left thumb grips the stack from above, thus aiding the planting process (Fig. 82).

To Produce Coins Singly: Slide the third finger beneath the stack and draw the bottom coin forward until it can be gripped by the forefinger or the second finger from above and produced exactly like a single coin (Fig. 83). This is repeated with the remaining coins; and any time the stack tends to loosen, it can be tightened by bending the fingers inward and pressing the coins in place. As the coins are produced, they are either taken by the left hand or dropped in a receptacle.

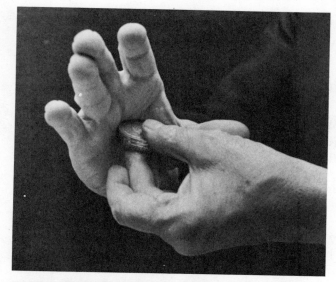

MULTIPLE-EDGE PALM
Fig. 82. Left hand plants stack in right palm while right fingers provide cover.

Fig. 83. Concealed move. Second and third fingers gripping bottom coin to produce that coin.

To Vanish Coins Singly: Hold the coins fanwise in the left hand. After single palming of the first coin, grip each succeeding coin between the second and third fingers of the right hand and slide it into position beneath the previous coin, ending with the entire stack edge-palmed.

MULTIPLE DOWNS PALM

This is a specialty in itself, and as such it is covered under the headings of Four-coin Vanish and Recovery (page 69) and Five-coin Routine (page 72).

Other types of single palms do not lend themselves to multiple manipulation, with the exception of the Back and Front Palm, which some of the most famous coin manipulators have handled in highly skilled fashion.

Though effective at long range, these are not adaptable to close-up presentation; hence the methods already covered are preferable.

SIMPLE COIN PRODUCTIONS

These are particularly effective following a vanish, as observers who are wondering where the coin went will be all the more surprised by its sudden reappearance. These run as follows:

Fingertip Production: This has been described with the following palming methods. To bring the coin back, you simply produce it at the tips of the fingers, by thrusting it there. Always effective, but needs variation, such as:

From the Elbow: Here, with the right side toward the audience and the coin palmed in the right hand, bring the right hand up behind the extended left forearm, working the coin toward the right fingertips. Turn the right hand palm frontward, pressing the coin against the back of the right sleeve. Raise the left hand at an upward angle while the right fingers slide the coin downward to the left elbow, where it is drawn into sight between the very tips of the right thumb and the second finger.

From the Knee: Again, with the right side toward the audience and the coin palmed in the right hand, lower the right hand to the outside of the right knee and press it there as you face frontward. This makes it easy to drop the coin to the bend of the right fingers, hiding it behind the trouser leg while gripping the cloth between the tips of the right thumb and fingers. The hand is turned palm frontward and the right fingers work the coin into sight as though drawing it edgewise through the cloth itself.

Spread-away Production: With the coin palmed in either hand, and that same side toward the audience, keep the fingers of both hands close together and press the tips of each hand against the other. The fingers are cupped so the thumbs may be extended side by side, with the tips of the thumbs pressing the tips of the forefingers. All this is done in one continued action and the hands are pointed downward, letting the coin drop to the tips of the cupped fingers.

Swing frontward, raising the hands to shoulder level, and in the same motion lower the tips of the thumbs behind the fingers, so they can press the coin and retain it in position. The fingertips are then drawn apart to reveal the coin between thumbs and fingers, as though it were making a mysterious reappearance. This effect can be enhanced by turning the hands outward and bringing the tips of thumbs and fingers from the horizontal to a vertical position so they seem to peel the coin into sight. The thumbs provide an upward thrust as the climax.

Sweep Production: With the coin palmed in the right hand, using the Standard Palm, and the right side toward the audience, the right forefinger points to the empty left hand, which is held palm frontward. The left hand is turned over and the right fingers brush the back of the left hand from the wrist past the fingertips, immediately returning to the left wrist. The left hand is then turned frontward and the right hand again brushes it in the same manner, but during the return to the left wrist, the right palm comes directly over the left palm and drops the coin therein. The left fingers close over the coin during that brief coverage, and when the left fist is opened, the coin has mysteriously appeared there.

CHANGE-OVERS

The secret transfer of a coin from one hand to the other is termed a change-over and gives the impression that both hands are empty while placing the coin — or coins — in position for some further manipulation, usually a production. Since the various change-overs depend on palming methods already described, they can be explained in brief form as follows:

Simple Change-over: With a coin palmed in the right hand, face at an angle toward the left, casually showing the left hand empty, the back of the right hand being toward the audience. Bring the hands together, palm to palm, the right diagonally across the left, raising them to a horizontal position, as you swing frontward.

During that action, the right hand releases the coin so that it drops into the left palm, which grips it. Then, as you swing more to the right, separate the hands just enough to swivel them in opposite directions as you turn them completely over, bringing the left hand uppermost. Now, faced at an angle toward the right, you carry the right hand farther in that direction, drawing attention to the fact that it is empty; while the left hand, now palming the coin, remains where it is, its back toward the spectators.

This simple change-over works well with the Standard Palm once you have acquired the proper grip (Fig. 9). It is still better with the Edge Palm (Fig. 12), as the grip is easier, but the hands must be cupped during the transfer. It is very easy with the Finger-bend Palm (Fig. 4), as in that case the bent right fingers simply drop the hidden coin into the bend of the left fingers, and the palms of both hands are completely viewed during the entire turnover. But even that can excite suspicion rather than allay it, unless the transfer is reduced to a point where it becomes insignificant. That aim can be attained by utilizing:

Sleeve Action: Here, as preliminary to the Simple Change-over, you face well to the left. You use your right hand, with its secretly palmed coin, to draw up your left sleeve, while the left hand is shown conspicuously empty. Then, swinging frontward and continuing well to the right, you make the change-over and finish with the left hand, now palming the coin, drawing up the right sleeve, while the right hand is shown just as obviously empty, with its palm toward the audience.

This emphasizes the finest element in misdirection: that of a greater motion covering a lesser. Eyes that would look the wrong way in response to a swift or abrupt move will automatically follow a long move and literally overlook whatever occurs during its progress. Keep that in mind with the following:

Brush-over Change: Start with a coin Standard Palmed in the right hand. Turn obliquely to the left and extend the left hand downward at a forty-five-degree angle, palm frontward, completely empty. With the right hand —back toward the spectators—brush the left hand from heel to fingertips and beyond. Turn frontward, bringing the right palm directly over the left fingertips and drop the coin thereon, bringing the left hand up to level.

The right hand, still tilted forward, now screens the left fingers as they come upward and inward, pressing the coin into the left palm in Standard Palm position, with the left hand turning downward to receive it. Keep swinging to the right during this continuous action, finally turning the right hand palm upward to prove it empty. By then, the left hand, back upward, has reached the right wrist; from there, it brushes the right hand past the fingertips at the same forty-five-degree angle used at the start.

This change-over can be worked from right to left by simply reversing the process. Either way, it can begin and end with the sleeve action as previously described.

Change-over Placement: Here the purpose is to transfer a coin from the bend of the left fingers to some other type of palm in the right hand. Start with your left side toward the audience, so that the left hand can pull up the right sleeve. Then extend the left hand, keeping the thumb within it, and lay the empty right hand directly across it, so the right palm is cupped above the left fingers (Fig. 84).

Swing your body leftward so your right side comes toward the audience. During that action, the left thumb pushes the coin to the tips of the left fingers, enabling them to do one of the following:

    a. Press the coin firmly into the right palm, which retains it with the Standard Palm (Fig. 9).
    b. Thrust the coin edgewise into the right palm, which grips and retains it with the Edge Palm (Fig. 12).
    c. Raise the coin to the gap between the right thumb and the base of the right forefinger, which is kept wide so the coin can be gripped horizontally at the root of the right thumb with the Downs palm (Fig. 22).

Whichever method is used, the misdirection is carried farther. To complete the change-over, the left hand is raised back upward, swivel fashion, with the tip of the left thumb linked lightly to the tip of the right forefinger. This holds attention on the left hand as it continues upward and turns palm frontward to display itself completely empty, as the right forefinger still points toward it.

Multiple-coin Transfer: This is the Change-over Placement with two or more coins. The only difference is the action of the left thumb, which presses down upon the coins, keeping them clamped against the left fingers until they are placed in whichever palm position the right hand intends to

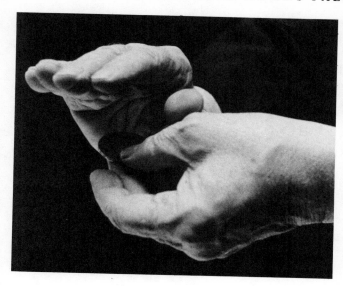

Fig. 84. Here's how left hand should place coin for Change-over Placement. This is the transfer.

use. Follow with the same swivel action to show the left hand back and front, the left thumb being guided by the right forefinger, tip to tip, as the left hand is raised back upward.

This multiple change-over is very useful and sometimes essential after obtaining a load of four or more coins from the trouser pocket or elsewhere. It works well prior to an open-hand coin production. Both the Change-over Placement and the Multiple Coin Transfer can work from right hand to left, as well as from left hand to right.

ONE-BY-ONE VANISH

The performer shows three or more large coins of the same size and places them on the table. With his right side toward the audience, he picks up the coins one by one with his right hand and drops each into his left hand, where people hear them clink against any that are already there. Finally, the left hand is opened with a rubbing motion to show that all the coins have vanished.

Actually, the coins are palmed singly in the right hand, which utilizes the Standard Palm. Each coin is exhibited in display position between the tips of the right thumb and fingers, which approach the closed left hand to drop it there. The left hand opens only when it is partly covered by the right so that no one can see that it is empty. The right hand immediately palms the coin and purposely clinks it against the previous coin. This simulates the sound of a coin dropping on those supposedly in the left hand and is a very effective auditory illusion.

The left hand closes as the right moves away to pick up the next coin; this action continues until all the coins are apparently in the left hand, which goes through the vanishing action and shows itself empty. For a prompt reproduction of the vanished coins, the right hand shifts them to finger-bend position (see page 13) and pushes them upward with the right thumb, as though plucking them one by one from midair (see page 4).

With five coins, this vanish can be followed by the Coin-star Production, a very effective climax.

COIN-STAR PRODUCTION

This simultaneous production of five coins ranks high among manipulations and is particularly effective after vanishing the coins, as their reappearance furnishes a real surprise. In effect, the performer moves his hands up and down in rhythmic fashion, palm to palm; then, with an upward thrust, he extends his thumbs and fingers, tip to tip, spreading them to resemble a star, with a coin appearing between each pair of tips (Fig. 85).

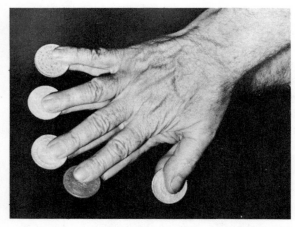

COIN-STAR PRODUCTION
Fig. 85. Position of coins at finish.

Practice is the keynote of this sleight, but it is well worth the effort, for the moves are not difficult, but merely painstaking—somewhat like the touch system used in typing. In the simplest form, which should be practiced first, the coins are palmed in the bend of the right fingers and the performer stands with his right side toward the audience. The left hand is shown empty, usually following a vanish, and is then brought palm to palm with the right hand, while doubling its fingers inward, like those of the right hand.

Both thumbs are brought inward as well, and under cover of the right hand, the left thumb and fingers grip the coins in a stack that is slanted a trifle to the left and lifted upward as the right thumb is inserted beneath (Fig. 86). This enables the right thumb to slide the top coin upward, so the left thumb can follow upward and press the coin against the right thumb (Fig. 87) while the tip of the right forefinger is free to press the next coin and start it upward, aided by the tip of the left forefinger.

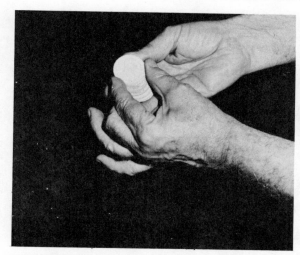

Fig. 86. Coin stack
slanted left and up by left
thumb and fingers.
Note right thumb at top
edge of stack.

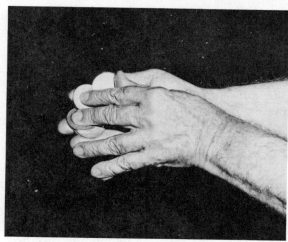

Fig. 87. Spreading begins.
Motion of arms helps con-
ceal action.

So it continues, finger by finger, until the coins are all in place. This production is partly covered by the up-and-down motion of the hands. Even if the coins are glimpsed during the action, the effect is still good, as the coins seem to be budding at the fingertips, and this is somewhat magical in itself. Added coverage can be gained by turning farther to the left, so that the tips of thumbs and fingers are pointed away from view. As the fingers finally spread to form the star, the body is swung back to its original position, displaying the coins to full advantage.

The ultimate aim is to spread the coins in one smooth action so that their appearance is almost simultaneous. This knack can be acquired through long and continuous practice, along the pattern just described. Another way is to place the coins in the bend of the right fingers as the left hand makes its approach. The right thumb first presses the entire stack well into the lower bend of the right forefinger, then spreads the coins toward the tip of the left little finger (Fig. 88). This arranges the coins evenly across the hand, and the palm is tilted a trifle upward to retain the coins in position.

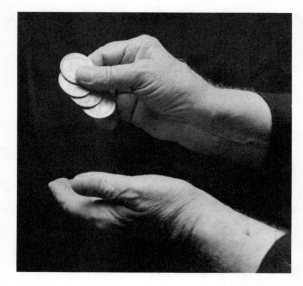

Fig. 88. Alternate spread starts separation of coins well before left hand joins action.

The left thumb and fingers can then be pressed directly against their respective coins, holding them there while the right thumb goes beneath its coin and presses upward. This enables the right fingers to find their proper coins from below, beginning the spreading process as they do. Once acquired, this flourish adds to the "simultaneous" appearance.

COINS AND GLASS

An excellent addition to any coin routine, especially as a follow-up to the Miser's Dream (page 76). Several coins are shown in the right hand and transferred to the left, while the right hand picks up a drinking glass and holds it at the tips of the thumb and fingers, which are pointed downward. The left hand makes a downward stroke, opening as it reaches the back of the right hand; and the coins are apparently driven through the right hand, landing in the glass with an emphatic clank.

In apparently placing the coins in the left hand, they are palmed in the right by the Multiple Standard Palm, (page 58) using any "vanishing" move described there. Thus in picking up the glass, the coins are actually retained above it — still concealed in the right palm, which simply releases them when the left hand makes its downstroke, so the coins arrive in the glass automatically as well as magically, as though actually driven down through the right hand.

Throw-over: Originally the coins were dispatched from the left hand into the glass by a sideward throwing motion, giving the effect that they traveled invisibly through the air and penetrated the glass itself. Though the effect is good, it is not well adapted to close-up presentation unless done very quickly, as observers may note that the coins drop from above, instead of arriving from the side. The downward penetration through the hand makes the drop more natural. Bringing the hands together is also effective, as the left hand can begin its downstroke almost while the right hand is picking up the glass.

In throwing the coins, experts made a series of left-hand gestures as if sending the coins one by one, while the right palm released them singly to conform to the illusion. This required such careful timing and precision that it demanded more practice than the effect was worth. Moreover, the surprise lessened with the passage of each succeeding coin, so no matter how artistic the procedure, it lost its real effect if done deliberately enough for the single releases.

However, if done rapidly, with one quick gesture after another, the coins can be dropped in clumps by relaxing the right palm with each left-hand throw, with practically the same effect as if the coins dropped singly. This can be applied to the modern penetration where the left hand drives the coins down through the right hand. A series of quick slaps accounts for each penetration, and any time coins fail to drop, the left hand slaps harder on the next try.

With comparatively little practice, it will be found that the slaps help jar the coins from the right palm; hence there is little need for the right hand to relax its grip, making the action all the easier. Another point that seems to have been overlooked with this striking effect is the size of the glass used. By experimenting with narrow and wide-mouthed tumblers or goblets, as well as those of in-between sizes, a performer can find the type best suited to his hand, thereby enabling him to release the palmed coins more effectively.

FOUR-COIN VANISH AND RECOVERY

This highly effective routine was a specialty with Welsh Miller, an eccentric but skillful coin manipulator who was probably the only performer who might have fairly challenged T. Nelson Downs for the title "King of Koins" when both were in their prime. Oddly, although the presentation was Miller's, the Downs Palm is utilized exclusively throughout the routine.

The performer begins by displaying four coins between the tips of the thumb and fingers of his left hand, which are spread-eagled to accommodate them. Keeping the left hand nearly full front, the performer stands with his right side toward the audience and clips the nearest coin between the first two fingers of his right hand (Fig. 89) in order to display it separately. He apparently tosses the coin in air, only to have it disappear; then, clipping the next coin, he vanishes it the same way. He continues the procedure with third and fourth coins, until all have completely vanished.

Showing the right hand empty, back and front, snapping his fingers in the meantime, the performer reproduces the coins, one by one, between the tips of his right fingers, and replaces them between the tips of his out-

FOUR-COIN VANISH AND RECOVERY
Fig. 89. Coins are arranged between each finger in left hand at start. Right hand clips nearest coin between first and second fingers.

stretched left fingers, exactly as they were at the start. He drops them singly into his outstretched right palm and the routine is completed.

As already stated, the Downs Palm is the only sleight required; hence the vanish of the first coin is simply a case of bending the fingers inward, palming the coin, and extending the fingers during an upward sweep, as described on page 14. The subsequent coins, however, demand more subtle handling, and this is where the real artistry enters. The first coin is palmed as in Fig. 22; then:

With the second coin, the right fingers bend inward during the toss, bringing the coin beneath the one that is already there (Fig. 90). When the second coin is almost in place, the right forefinger is extended beyond the outer edge of the coin and presses it firmly home, while the right second finger presses upward, bringing the faces of the coins firmly together (Fig. 91). The same process is applied with the third coin and finally the fourth, and it forms the real crux of the vanish, as the coins must be practically clamped together to prevent them from wobbling and coming loose.

Still more care is needed in the one-by-one reproduction of the coins. Here, the right second finger is brought beneath the coins and the palming grip is relaxed, so that the second finger bears most of the weight. This enables it to move forward, bringing the bottom coin along with it (Fig. 92), and simultaneously, the tip of the right forefinger is pressed firmly against the edges of the upper three coins, so the palming grip can be fully regained. The loose bottom coin is then clipped between the tips of the first two fingers, which are extended to produce the coin in display position between the thumb and fingertips. It is then replaced between the spread fingers of the left hand.

This move is repeated with the bottom coin of the remaining three; then the bottom coin of two; and finally, the one remaining coin is reproduced in simple fashion and added to the left-hand group.

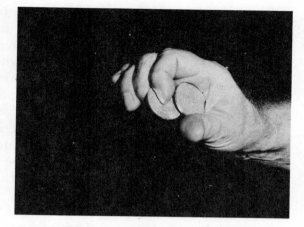

Fig. 90. Concealed placement of second coin. Forefinger and second finger clip coin and ease it beneath first coin.

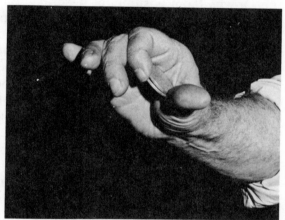

Fig. 91. First and second finger action firmly plants bottom coin. Note how second finger presses upward against forefinger and, thus, the bottom coin.

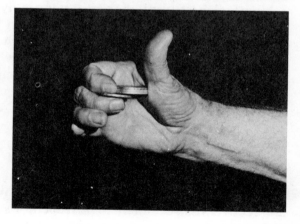

Fig. 92. Production begins when palm grip is eased and right second finger can move bottommost coin forward.

FIVE-COIN ROUTINE

Here is a neat adaptation of the Four-coin Vanish and Recovery with a decidedly different effect, although the moves are essentially the same. The performer starts by showing his hands empty; he then plucks coins from the air with his right hand, placing them between the outstretched fingers of his left hand, until all four spaces are filled. Then the right hand produces a fifth coin, but having no place to put it, the right hand vanishes the coin with a toss, then does the same with the left-hand coins, one by one. For a climax, the hands are brought palm to palm and the thumbs and fingers are spread in star fashion, reproducing the five vanished coins between their tips (Fig. 85).

Start with the five coins palmed in the bend of the left fingers while facing toward the right. The left forefinger points toward the empty right hand and the hands are brought together, with the right hand covering the left in front of the body, which makes a full turn toward the left. During the swing, the hands execute a change-over, with the left thumb and fingers simply planting the five coins at the base of the right thumb and fingers in the Downs Palm position, as described on page 14.

The right hand then produces the coins one by one, as in the Four-coin Recovery, placing them between the fingers of the outspread left hand (Fig. 89). The fifth coin is produced and vanished; and the other four coins follow, exactly as with the Four-coin Vanish, except that the right hand in this case palms five coins instead of only four. After the vanish of the fifth coin, the body can turn frontward, with the thumb and fingers of each hand pointing at an angle toward the audience, and providing a snapping action.

This move is very effective, as the left thumb and fingers supply the sound that the right thumb and fingers merely simulate, while keeping the stack of coins well hidden. Then, in turning toward the left, the left hand is shown empty with a brief flash, giving the impression that the right hand is equally clear, particularly as the right hand relaxes at that moment and tilts far enough forward to let the stacked coins ease into the finger bend.

Now facing leftward, the performer simply brings his hands together and reproduces the vanished coins by the Coin Star Production, bringing the routine to a very effective climax. Although five coins are used, this is no more difficult than the four-coin routine previously described, since in this case, the coins are planted prior to producing them; and after they have been vanished, they do not have to be reproduced singly, thanks to the Star Production.

COINS THROUGH BODY

One of the most spectacular of manipulative effects, this five-coin vanish and recovery is seemingly impossible in its original form as presented by T. Nelson Downs. However, with a slight touch of unsuspected fakery, its operation can be greatly simplified, bringing it well within the range of the average manipulator, who will thereby find it an outstanding close-up effect.

Facing the audience directly, the performer asks a spectator to stand on his right, also facing frontward. Holding five coins in his left hand, the performer extends his right hand palm upward and spreads its thumb and fingers, star fashion. Then, carefully, the left hand balances coins one by one upon the tips of the right thumb and fingers. Slowly raising his right hand almost to the spectator's eye level, the performer suddenly sweeps his right hand at a downward angle, clamping the thumb and fingers close together, so the coins come between them.

To prevent the coins from scattering, the right hand plants them squarely in the upturned left hand, which immediately forms a fist around them. The left arm is thrust forward and the performer wheels to the right, bringing his left fist squarely in front of the spectator's chest. With a count of "one — two — three — " the performer makes appropriate gestures toward the spectator, opening his left hand on the final count as he slaps the helper's chest.

Facing frontward, the performer raises his left hand and shows it empty, much to the surprise of the audience. But the big surprise is yet to come. While the left fist has been tapping the spectator's chest, the right hand has casually and quite naturally edged itself behind the spectator's back. Now, as the performer takes a step to the left, the right hand emerges again, bringing the five vanished coins balanced precariously on the tips of its thumb and fingers, exactly as they were at the outset. As carefully as he placed them, the performer removes them one by one with his left hand, thus concluding a masterpiece of close-up manipulative magic.

For sheer effect, this trick is unbeatable. The opening position is so precarious that observers are sure the right hand dumped the coins into the left, so they suppose that the performer is about to begin all over. Instead, the coins have suddenly vanished and their reproduction, in the same precarious state, is truly magical. Hence the performer depends upon surprise and misdirection to cover the moves, which are comparatively simple.

In placing the coins on the right fingertips, they are set at a slightly forward angle (Fig. 93), so that when the fingers are closed, the coins come between them, step fashion, with the thumb bringing its coin down upon the forefinger's coin (Fig. 94). Thus instead of being planted loosely in the left fist they are actually retained by the right thumb and fingers. By then,

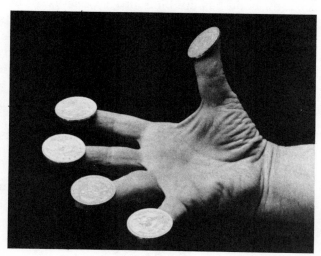

COINS THROUGH BODY
Fig. 93. Showing coins
balanced on tips of right
fingers and thumb at start.

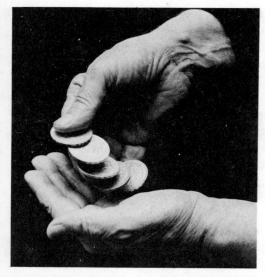

Fig. 94. Secretly retaining coins between right thumb and fingers while apparently placing them in left hand.

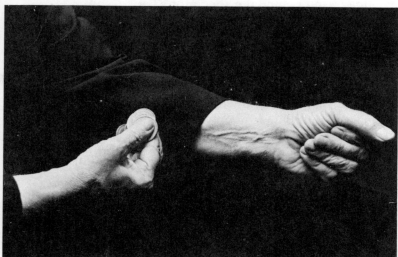

Fig. 95. Rear view of left forearm covering right hand and coins retained therein.

the right hand has doubled into a loose fist of its own, and in retaining this position, it keeps the gripped coins perfectly concealed. In thrusting the left arm forward and wheeling to the right, the left forearm completely covers the fisted right hand (Fig. 95) so that the right hand can move away unseen and go in back of the spectator. There, while the left hand is driving the coins through the victim's body, the right hand reverses its original move, bringing the coins back to their original position on the outspread thumb and fingers.

This recovery presents a double problem. First, returning four coins to their balanced positions on the fingers is difficult indeed, as they must be handled simultaneously without the aid of the left hand. Second, getting the fifth coin back onto the ball of the thumb is impossible by a mere reversal of the original move, because in the vanish, the coin was clamped downward by its own inertia, while when the thumb is lifted, the coin will slide off at an angle. Hence, some added move or device is necessary for the thumb to retain it.

It is generally assumed that Downs solved this problem with the aid of a special coin that had a dab of adhesive wax imbedded in the center of one side, which was kept downward when the left hand placed the coin upon the thumb. Though Downs depended upon sheer skill in most of his manipulations, he knew the value of a "gimmick" under special circumstances. Granting that he may have used one, modern manipulators can adapt the idea to great advantage by applying a square of "double stick" Scotch tape to an ordinary coin. Adhesive on both surfaces, it is completely transparent; therefore this trick will elude detection even if both sides of the coin are shown.

What goes for one coin will therefore go for all five. By giving each a square of "double-stick" tape, they can be balanced on the thumb and fingers with impunity, and the hand can be tilted at an angle without losing them. This converts a highly difficult manipulation into one of the easiest. Since the coins "stay put" during the entire process (Fig. 93), the vanish does not have to be hurried, hence, and is much more effective. The recovery, hidden behind the spectator's back, can be as deliberate as desired. The mere act of spreading the right thumb and fingers makes the recovery automatic.

Here, another factor should be noted. In doing the routine the hard way with unprepared coins, the dollar-size coins are best. They are the heaviest available and are the easiest to balance, particularly during the recovery. But being large, they are harder to hide when the right hand is fisted. Today, however, coins of half-dollar size are preferable. The tape retains them more securely and they are more effectively concealed when the right hand is fisted because they are lighter and smaller.

That leaves just one problem: how to proceed with other manipulations involving unprepared coins, particularly those in which the coins may be handled by the spectators.

The solution is quite simple. Have five duplicate, unprepared coins in the change compartment of your right coat pocket. Gather the taped coins with the left hand, and stack them on the outstretched right hand, in position for the Slide Vanish or the Side-drop Vanish (page 57). Execute the preferred vanish from right to left and after showing the left hand empty, dip the right hand into the pocket, leaving the taped coins there and bringing out the ordinary batch that you have in readiness.

ALTERNATE VERSION

As an alternative, Downs occasionally performed the Coins Through Body alone, when working before a very small group, or under conditions where introducing an assistant caused complications. The operation is similar, but in this case the performer swings well to the left when apparently placing the coins in the left hand. Then, as the closed left fist is extended farther to the left, his doubled right hand is brought across the body to the right hip, carrying its concealed coins.

Then, facing straight forward, the performer slaps his left hand against his chest, while the right hand goes behind his back and recovers the coins with the usual spread. Here an effective climax is for the performer to turn his back completely toward the audience, letting them see the coins resting on his thumb and fingers before he carefully brings his hand forward with a slow twist of the wrist that enables him to transfer them to the left hand.

COMEDY COIN ROUTINE

This was used by Downs as a follow-up to the more artistic Coins Through Body, but chiefly for the benefit of fellow magicians or with intimate groups. Under such circumstances, it is highly effective, since the astonishment of the spectator who serves as volunteer assistant is humorous indeed.

The performer stands facing the audience with the helper slightly to his right. Showing five coins in his right hand, the performer raises them under the spectator's nose, then apparently throws them into his left hand, using either the Slide Vanish or the Side-drop Vanish. He turns leftward as he does this, stepping back so that the spectator can see his left fist as he extends it; then, with a comment such as "Here—step closer, so you can hold my left sleeve—" he places his right hand on the volunteer's left shoulder and draws him toward the left.

The spectator thinks the coins are in the performer's left hand, but actually they are palmed in the right. This enables the performer to set them in a stack on the spectator's shoulder. He then strokes his left fist with his right hand, which he shows empty; then he opens his left hand to show it empty, too, while the spectator stares dumbfounded, to the delight of the remaining onlookers who see the coins resting on the volunteer's shoulder.

Meanwhile, the performer says, "Come a little closer—" and again rests his right hand on the volunteer's shoulder, this time regaining the coins. Bringing his right hand down to his left, he cups them together and reproduces the coins with a rubbing motion, leaving the victim still more puzzled.

THE MISER'S DREAM

This is a classic of coin conjuring that has retained its popularity for a century or more because the magician demonstrates an ability that everyone would like to possess: that of plucking coins from the air in seemingly unlimited quantity. From the magician's standpoint, it is easy to perform and highly deceptive in effect, which are further reasons for its long survival.

The accepted procedure is to produce coins singly at the tips of the right fingers and drop them into a receptacle held in the left hand. In the early days, a borrowed top hat was the usual receptacle, as the coins landed there with an emphatic plunk, with added clanks as they increased in number. When high hats went out of style, a performer would ask for a derby hat instead, or even supply one of his own, as those became scarce. Soft hats were not so good, but would sometimes do if a plate or ashtray was placed inside the hat to serve as a sounding board for the dropping coins.

Today, a fairly large canister is perhaps the best receptacle, with metal the preferred material, as it gives off the loudest sound. Special coin buckets have been designed for this purpose; but a bowl or a child's sand-pail can also be pressed into service. In any case, the performer either borrows the receptacle or passes it out for examination and meanwhile gets set for a stupendous production, which nobody even begins to suspect:

In his left trouser pocket, or left coat pocket, if need be, the performer has a stack of coins, ranging from a dozen upward. "Upward" simply means as many as can be conveniently gripped in an extended finger bend, running from the bend of the fingers into the palm itself. The tendency is either to take too few, thinking in terms of the simple finger bend; or to take too many, since the stack can be extended almost to the heel of the hand. However, experience will prove that there is a happy medium, which may be best described as the maximum that can be handled efficiently.

While picking up the receptacle with his right hand, or simply showing it with his right hand, the performer turns his right side toward the audience, enabling his left hand to go to the pocket and pick up the stack of coins as described. As the left hand emerges, the performer turns frontward and here the performer introduces a subtle touch that is finely suited to close-up work, particularly with spectators seated at side angles. The left hand glides upward, close to the body, keeping the coins fully concealed in the bend of the fingers, until it reaches the lapel of the coat, which is gripped by the thumb and tips of the fingers, a very natural move.

With a final showing of the receptacle, the magician continues his swing to the right, bringing the receptacle toward the left hand and at the same time tilting its mouth toward the audience. This enables the left hand to grip the rim, with its fingers carrying the stack of coins inside the receptacle, which it raises mouth upward, as the right hand leaves the receptacle and the left hand and moves away. By now, the left side is toward the audience, with the right hand gesturing upward, palm wide open, to carry attention in that direction. All is now ready for the production.

The magician makes a few futile grabs, as though trying to snatch something from the air; then swings to the left and makes a quick grab in that direction, adding a nod of satisfaction, as though having actually caught a coin. All in the same action, he pretends to throw the coin into the receptacle, at the same time releasing the innermost coin from the left-hand stack, so that it lands in the receptacle. To emphasize his success, he reaches in and brings out the coin, displaying it at the tips of his right thumb and fingers.

Now he apparently drops the coin openly into the receptacle, but actually palms it in the right hand, simultaneously feeding the next coin from the left-hand stack, so that it falls instead. Reaching in the air with his right hand, he produces the palmed coin at his fingertips and pretends to drop it in the receptacle, again palming it as he releases another coin from the left hand. The whole procedure is so natural that the performer can continue on and on, catching coins and dropping them, until the hidden supply is exhausted.

The whole routine is quite easy, for it requires only the repeated palming and reproduction of a single coin by the right hand. The feeding action of the left fingers is completely concealed within the receptacle, enabling the fingers to work each coin into exact position prior to its release. However, the Miser's Dream requires continued practice to acquire the precision that assures the deception. By slanting the stack of coins inward (Fig. 96), working the first coin to the fingertips, and retaining the rest in place (Fig. 97), perfect timing can be attained.

MISER'S DREAM
Fig. 96. Producing a coin in the Miser's Dream. Left hand is purposely tilted at side angle to show its hidden stack of coins.

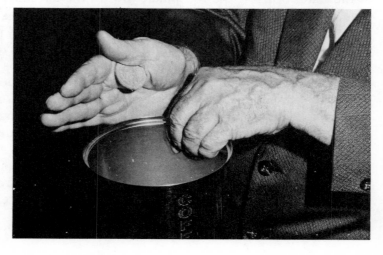

Fig. 97. Performer's view of dropping coin in container, actually palming it (in fork of right thumb) while left hand releases a hidden coin.

From long experience dating from derby hats onward, these points must be considered:

If the left hand is slow on the feed, throw it from the right hand anyway. The lack of a plunk will pass unnoticed.

If the left hand pushes two (or more) coins into position instead of only one, don't worry. Let them all go and the plunk will merely be more emphatic.

However, if the left hand is fast on the feed, either restrain it or hurry the right hand's action to conform with it. Nothing is more disconcerting to a performer, or more enlightening to skeptical onlookers, than a sudden clank of a coin arriving in the receptacle before the right hand has dropped it there. If you can't avoid it, at least try to cover it by stepping up the tempo of the right hand's productions.

If you hurry it too much, you can always pause just after palming the coin, keeping the right hand closed above the receptacle, as though you intended to show the coin again. Then, as a hidden coin finally falls from the left hand, you can open the right hand, timing the pretended drop to the sound of the arriving coin.

To avoid the hazards just described, devices may be introduced to the performer's advantage. One very effective procedure is to toss a coin in the air and actually palm it in the right hand. The performer keeps looking upward, expecting it to return, which it does by plunking into the receptacle, which is extended to catch it. Any delay in the arrival of the invisible coin is accounted for by an appropriate thrust of the left hand; and if it fails to "land" on schedule, another thrust is made, as though its whereabouts were still unknown. This simply adds to the comedy.

Another comedy bit is to take a man's necktie, a lady's handkerchief, or some other item with the right hand and shake it above the receptacle, letting one or more coins drop from the left hand during the process. This creates the illusion that the coin—or coins—actually came from the borrowed object.

Recommended Palming Methods: Although the Finger-bend Palm (page 3) may be used for the Miser's Dream, by palming a coin when pretending to throw it in the hat and then producing what appears to be another coin at the fingertips, the Standard Palm (page 6) is preferable, as it gives a more open-handed impression. The same applies to the Edge Palm (page 9), with the added advantage that the body can be swung to the right and a coin produced by reaching in that direction. Ordinarily, the performer should swing back toward the left before pretending to drop the coin into the receptacle, but a partial turn toward the front will prove sufficient, if the performer's timing is exact.

For fast, smooth productions, some performers prefer the Alternate Thumb Fork Palm (page 13), producing each new coin between the tips of the first two fingers; then immediately forking it with a pretended throw into the hat and producing more in the same rapid fashion. Each time the coin is shown in Fingertip Display (Fig. 3), bypassing the conventional display position (as recommended on page 3).

The Downs Palm (page 14) is best of all, provided it has been practiced to the point where it becomes almost automatic. The performer can face left or right as desired, apparently dropping each coin straight downward into the receptacle, with a vertical motion that covers the palming action, whether the back of the hand is toward the audience, or the thumb is kept frontward. This was the way Downs did it, not only on the stage, but also in the very midst of a group of people who were viewing his hands from all angles.

By utilizing the thumb and finger snap (as described on page 17), the presence of the palmed coin can be covered under the very noses of the onlookers, provided that the hand is kept at proper level, particularly when thumb front, with the tips of thumb and second finger pressed together. That makes it perfect where close-up magic is concerned, yet it does not detract from the palming methods previously recommended. They, too, are suited to close-up work, and are easier to execute, but require more attention to the angles.

Follow-up to Regular Production: After the hidden supply of coins in the left hand has been exhausted, the performer dips his right hand into the receptacle and brings up as many as a dozen coins, letting them trickle from his hand in true miserly fashion. He repeats this a few times to prove that he has produced a surprisingly large quantity of coins; and the final time, he secretly retains most of the coins in the finger bend, so that only a few fall back into the receptacle.

The right hand is then raised and goes into a continuous production, with the thumb pushing coins upward one by one as described under Multiple Finger Bend (page 56) and shown in Figs. 74 and 75. In this case, instead of transferring the produced coins to the left hand, they are allowed to drop into the receptacle, as a continuation of the Miser's Dream.

FULL-FRONT MISER'S DREAM

This is without doubt the neatest and most deceptive version of the Miser's Dream ever devised, but it lay latent for many years, simply because it was necessary for the magician to use a receptacle of his own, instead of a borrowed hat. Hence it lacked the impromptu touch that was regarded as a "must" in bygone days. Now that high hats and derbies have become "old hat" in their own right, audiences expect to see a magician drop coins into a bowl instead of a bowler, so this improved version has come into its own.

There is no fakery in the receptacle used in this production, but it must be a type with an upright handle, such as a child's sandpail, or better still, an ice bucket. This can be made of metal, but a glass bucket of the type depicted here is ideal, as each dropping coin can be seen through its entire course.

In effect, the performer stands with his left side toward the audience, holding the handle of the bucket with his left hand, while he shows his empty right hand full front. Reaching in the air, he plucks a coin from the void and lowers his hand toward the bucket. Dipping his fingers forward, he lets the coin slide from their tips directly into the bucket. Again reaching into the air, he produces another coin and drops it into the bucket in the same fashion; then another and another, until he has produced a dozen or more coins so openly that the result appears phenomenal.

The basic sleight used in the production is the Back and Front Palm (pages 17–19), requiring only a single coin, which is manipulated entirely by the right hand. This coin is palmed in the right hand at the outset, either with the Finger-bend Palm (page 3) or the Standard Palm (page 6). (The performer faces toward the left.) It is naturally concealed there while the right hand picks up the bucket by the handle and displays it from various angles. During that procedure, the left hand picks up a stack of a dozen or more coins from the left trouser pocket, as with the regular Miser's Dream. These are palmed in the bend of the left fingers.

Keeping the left hand close to the body, the performer swings to the right, thus enabling the left hand to grip the handle of the bucket in the bend, above the stack of coins. As the performer faces directly to the right, the concealment is perfect, as the back of the left hand is toward the audience and the bend of the fingers is natural. Meanwhile, the right hand drops to the right side and swivels the coin to back-palm position. Looking upward, the performer raises his right hand, showing its empty palm, while the left hand is thrust forward with the bucket (Fig. 98).

FULL-FRONT MISER'S
DREAM
Fig. 98. Audience view at start of Full-front Miser's Dream production. Right hand, apparently empty, about to produce its back-palmed coin.

Fig. 99. Right hand pro-
ducing coin and dipping
toward bucket to drop the
coin therein.

Fig. 100. Coin dropping
from right fingertips into
bucket. Note how natu-
rally right hand comes
down behind left.

The first coin is "caught" by simply swiveling it to the front grip and
then to display position (Fig. 99). The right hand begins a deliberate
forward dip to drop the coin into the bucket because the slower the move,
the easier the subtle switch that follows. In order to dip into the bucket, the
right fingers naturally come down behind the left hand, and the moment
they go from sight, they swivel the coin to the back-palm position, while the
left thumb thrusts the top coin of its stack toward the descending right
hand (Fig. 100).

Note that the stack is kept upright, not slanted in the bend of the left fingers. This facilitates the action of the left thumb, so that as the right-hand
coin regains its back-palm position, the left thumb releases its coin, letting
it drop on the fingers of the right hand (Fig. 101). This is also hidden from
the audience, so when the right fingers emerge below the left hand a
moment later, the onlookers suppose that the coin they see there (Fig. 102)
is the one the right hand plucked from the air.

After letting the visible coin drop into the bucket, the right hand reaches

Fig. 101. Side view of right hand descending toward bucket and backpalming coin under cover of left hand, which pushes off first coin of its hidden stack.

Fig. 102. Side view of right hand, with its own coin back-palmed, receiving coin fed by left hand; now set to drop it into bucket.

up and repeats the production sequence with the back-palmed coin (Figs. 98 through 100), while the left hand "feeds" another coin from its stack (Figs. 101, 102) so the right hand can again back-palm its coin and proceed with another production. This continues until the left hand has fed its entire store to the right hand. Even magicians can be baffled by this subtle sequence, thinking at first that the performer has three or four coins backpalmed; then realizing as the production continues that it would be impossible with so many; while the action of the left hand is too well hidden to excite suspicion.

The follow-up recommended with the regular production (page 4) can be used with this version of the Miser's Dream as well, but since the back of the right hand is toward the audience, the performer should face forward while dropping the coins singly into the bucket, somewhat deliberately and at much the same angle as in the original production, to maintain the impression already created.

BILLIARD BALLS

Magic with billiard balls was introduced nearly a century ago, utilizing ivory balls of 2-inch diameters in contrast to the 4¼-inch type used on the billiard table. Even the 2-inch size was too large for most hands and too heavy for easy manipulation, so special wooden balls were manufactured, ranging in diameters from 1¼ to 2 inches, with other sizes in between. When highly polished, these closely resembled actual billiard balls and, to further that impression, they were usually painted red or white, the colors used in the standard game of billiards.

As ball manipulation increased in popularity, other colors and textures were included. Some attractive sets were made of silver-plated hollow metal. Others were composed of celluloid, which later gave way to heavier plastic used in a type of ball very popular today. In magical terminology, all were classed as "billiard balls," with one notable exception: As the game of golf gained in importance, magicians began using golf balls instead of billiard balls in some of their routines.

Here, the size was right for many hands—1¾ inches—but their weight was not. Substitutes soon cropped up in the form of plastic golf balls and others made of a fairly soft rubber, which can be squeezed during manipulation—a very helpful factor in some ball routines. Such balls are also easy to grip when palming or rolling them between the fingers, which is often difficult when working with polished wooden balls. However, coating wooden balls with a sparkling crusted surface gives them a good grip and causes them to glitter in the light when they appear at the magician's fingertips.

All these balls can be purchased from reliable magic dealers, who also furnish a "shell ball" with their sets. This is a half of a hollow ball, just large enough to receive and hide a solid ball, which can be rolled from there to the tips of the fingers, and thus gives the effect of one ball multiplying into two.

While these balls and shells are often important in advanced manipulations, it is quite easy to find balls suitable for immediate practice. These include:

Colored rubber balls of 1¾-inch diameter, used by children for bouncing, and sold at many variety stores;

Decorative balls of foam plastic, which though lightweight are easily gripped and can therefore be handled effectively;

Hollow balls with crusted surfaces also used for decorative purposes and easily gripped;

Imitation golf balls used for practice strokes; and

Ping-Pong balls of the heavier, more durable type used in table-tennis matches.

To make a shell ball, a plastic ball can be cut in half; in fact, there are many that break apart quite easily. The best of this type are plastic "Easter Eggs" the size of real eggs that come in various colors and are made to open so that they can be filled with candy. The lower portions are so well rounded that they form an ideal shell. The only problem—as with other improvised shells—is to find balls that fit into them snugly.

If you have trouble on this score, the answer is to fashion a ball of the required size. You can do that by using a small hard rubber ball for a core and wrapping it in a square of soft tissue paper, which is then dampened so that you can roll it between your hands until it forms an outer layer around the ball. Continue this process with more squares of tissue paper, dampening each layer as you go along, until you finally have a ball that fits the shell. Squeeze out the surplus water, round the ball as exactly as you can, press down any slight protuberances, and let the ball harden overnight, or for a few days.

Such a ball will be the right size and it will have the right weight and proper surface for capable manipulation. If colored tissue paper is used, you may be able to match the shell as closely as is needed; if not, you can paint the ball, shell, or both until they correspond. Additional balls and shells can be fashioned to complete an entire set to go with any of the routines described in this chapter. As for shells, some magicians have even made them from rattles that babies have outgrown, so improvising your own equipment can be fun in itself.

BASIC MANIPULATIONS

PALMING A BALL

Modes of palming billiard balls are few but simple and therefore are subject to constant repetition, but this passes unnoticed because a great variety of moves are involved, making them all the more difficult to follow. In competent hands, they are seldom exactly alike. Though a ball is bulky and therefore requires special care in its concealment, it is also spherical and therefore easily rolled in and out of a palming position. It may be placed in different positions prior to a vanishing procedure, which thereby becomes all the more deceptive. Hence the display position about to be described may be regarded as a mere preliminary to others that are more effective and will be detailed in due course.

BASIC DISPLAY POSITION

Hold the ball at the tips of the thumb and all four fingers, turning it directly toward the spectators, or holding it with fingers pointing directly upward, so that a slight squeeze will push it to the very tips. A slight relaxation will let it sink down to the original position, where the principal grip is supplied by the first and fourth fingers at opposite sides of the ball, with the second and third fingers pressing lightly against it. The thumb merely rests against the ball, ready to move away when required.

Methods of palming follow:

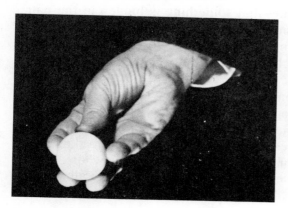

Fig. 103. Display position preliminary to palming action in which the back of hand is turned toward audience.

FINGER-BEND PALM

Simply let the ball ease downward to the base of the fingers, which are bent inward to retain it with a natural grip, the back of the hand being turned toward the audience. Since the ball is round, the little finger can be bent in more than the others, while the forefinger can be extended slightly, even being used as a pointer if desired (Fig. 104). This is very effective with a simple vanish, where the right hand palms a ball while pretending to place it in the left, which closes its fingers loosely about the imaginary ball and apparently rubs it into nothingness.

Fig. 104. Finger-bend Palm shown from performer's viewpoint.

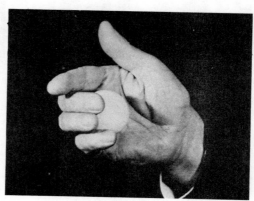

STANDARD PALM

Here the two middle fingers press the ball into the very center of the palm, where it is gripped between the base of the thumb and the side of the hand (Fig. 105). The fingers and thumb are then extended, with the back of the hand toward the audience, the ball being fully concealed in the palm.

Both these terms—"extended" and "concealed"—have special significance in billiard-ball manipulation. To begin with, the muscles of the hand must be considerably contracted to gain a proper grip on the rotund ball. Hence any spreading of the thumb and fingers may make the hand look awkward from in back, suggesting that something is hidden in the palm. Again, the spaces between the fingers may allow a glimpse of the ball from certain angles. So it is better to keep the fingers close together; and the same applies to the thumb, which should be almost parallel to the side of the hand (Fig. 106).

Practice this by closing the hand into a fist, then opening it gradually, even gingerly, increasing it by degrees to attain the maximum suited to the hand. Stretching it too far can thus be avoided. If the hand is slightly moist, light pressure will create an adhesive effect, causing the ball to cling to the palm of its own accord. Ease of palming becomes a habit where billiard balls are concerned. For a simple vanish, using the Standard Palm, follow the procedure described under the Finger-bend Palm.

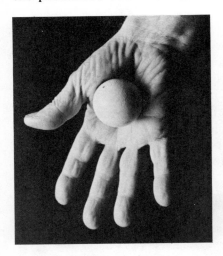

Fig. 105. Standard Palm showing full extent to which the hand can be spread. Performer's view.

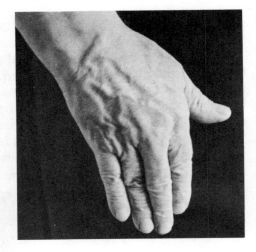

Fig. 106. Audience view of right hand with ball concealed in Standard Palm. Fingers are kept close together.

THUMB PALM

This can be used as an alternate for the Standard Palm. From display position, the fingers are bent inward, bringing the ball beneath the thumb, which is extended over it, gripping the ball in its curve (Fig. 107). The grip is not only firm, but also sure; and any objection that it is technically awkward is offset by the fact that if the hand is kept in motion and the palming is of brief duration, nobody will notice that the thumb is absent.

In fact, if the hand is tipped slightly downward when using the Standard Palm, the thumb will go from sight automatically, which often happens. The danger there is that the ball will show from below, so the position must be avoided. But with the thumb palm (as just described) there is no downward tilt, so the ball cannot show below. Yet the absence of the thumb is no problem, any more than with the Standard Palm. So for purposes of practice, the thumb palm will do while working on the standard palm; and after progressing further in the field of billiard-ball manipulation, it may not really matter which type of palm is used. Either, if properly executed, can prove sufficiently deceptive.

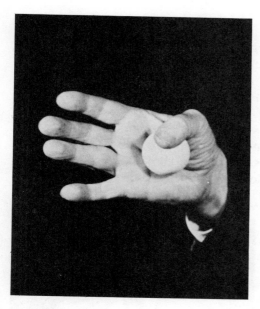

Fig. 107. Performer's view of Thumb Palm, used as substitute for Standard Palm.

DOUBLE PALM

A valuable device with various sleights and routines, this is simply a combination of the Standard Palm and the Finger Palm. One ball is first gripped in the Standard Palm; then another ball is picked up and finger-palmed (Fig. 108). By pressing them lightly together, they are retained more effectively, and each ball may be produced singly. Instead of the Standard Palm, the Thumb Palm may be used to grip the first ball.

With smaller balls, a "triple palm" is feasible, a third ball being wedged between the other two and retained by a modified thumb palm, the others being held by the Finger Palm and Standard Palm respectively. This, however, is not apt to be often used.

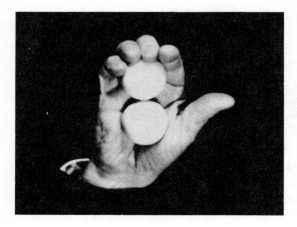

Fig. 108. Double Palm,
combining finger bend
with Standard Palm. Per-
former's view.

BACK PALM

From display position, the ball is gripped between the first and fourth
fingers, allowing the two middle fingers to double inward and come beneath the ball (Fig. 109). By straightening the two middle fingers in front of
the ball and turning the palm toward the audience, the ball, still clipped by
the first and fourth fingers, is hidden behind the middle fingers, in what is
termed a "back palm" position (Fig. 110).

For a simple vanish with a fairly small ball, this move can be executed
with an upward toss; then, after momentarily showing the hand empty, the
ball may be reclaimed with a downsweep and a short upward lift, during
which the middle fingers double under and in back, so the ball is shown in
original display position (Fig. 103).

Fig. 109. Right fingers
swiveling ball into
Back-palm position.

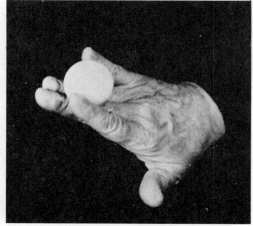

Fig. 110. Back-palm posi-
tion. Rear view, showing
how ball is retained and
concealed.

BILLIARD-BALL PRODUCTIONS

Since many billiard-ball routines open with the production of a ball, and many vanishes are necessarily followed by reproductions, the greater the variety, the more effective such manipulations should be. Surprisingly, however, most manipulators are limited to very few such sleights, making ball productions a really neglected field. Fancy vanishes and moves to show the hands empty will wind up cold if followed by the repeated process of drawing the missing billiard ball from the elbow or the knee. Yet those two devices have long been the stock-in-trade of many capable manipulators, simply because they were not acquainted with other methods.

Fortunately, the scarcity of production sleights is not as serious as generally supposed. There are actually enough to vary the procedure, as often as required, but some are little known and others have been little used. Yet oddly, both of these categories include some of the best. This statement is backed by long years of observation and experience; so to clinch it, productions will be treated first among the sleights, not only because of their novelty, but also because they represent truly basic manipulations.

In each production, the performer begins with a ball secretly palmed in one hand. Whenever "right" or "left" is mentioned, the reader should understand that the situation is reversible or interchangeable; that it is given one way simply for brevity or convenience. When a ball is palmed in the right hand, the performer usually stands with his right side toward the audience; and vice versa with his left. Any exceptions to this rule will be noted.

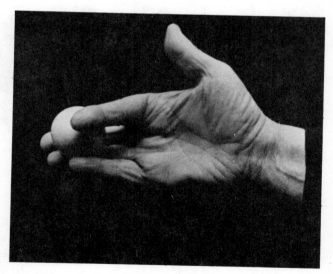

PRODUCTIONS
Fig. 111. Right forefinger beginning roll-up for Fingertip Production (rear view).

FINGERTIP PRODUCTION

A ball is palmed in the right hand, by the Standard Palm (Fig. 105).

Stand with the right side toward the audience and point the fingers of the right hand at a forty-five-degree angle toward the floor, letting the ball drop to the Finger-bend Palm (Fig. 104). At the same time, ease the little finger a trifle wide of the rest and bring it inward, forming a step on which the ball rests. In the same move, bend the forefinger completely inward so that its knuckles press against the ball (Fig. 111).

Now swing the right hand from forty-five degrees downward to forty-five degrees upward, and as you do, straighten the forefinger, rolling the ball up between it and the second finger (Fig. 112). After the two swings will the fingers are fully extended, and from the audience's viewpoint, the ball will appear suddenly and mysteriously between the tips of the first two fingers (Fig. 113).

A rotary motion of the right hand, first outward and downward, then upward and inward, will not only facilitate the manipulation, but also will enable the moves to blend smoothly and effectively, while a forward thrust at the finish covers the final stage of the roll-up.

Fig. 112. Completion of roll-up, with ball at finger-tips (rear view).

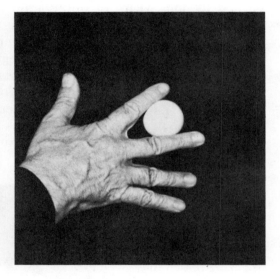

Fig. 113. Fingertip Production as viewed by audience.

ALTERNATE FINGERTIP PRODUCTION

This is similar in effect to the regular production, but the action of the hand varies. Double the thumb inward and bring the ball from Standard Palm position to the Thumb Palm, at the same time tilting the hand slightly inward to keep the ball hidden. In practically the same move, bend the second finger inward below the ball, where it presses upward (Fig. 114) and rolls the ball forward to the tip of the thumb, enabling the forefinger to press the ball downward from above (Fig. 115).

Fig. 114. Alternate Fingertip Production: Ball raised to Thumb-palm position, so second finger can come beneath (rear view).

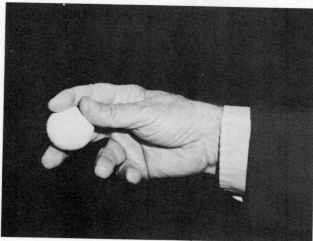

Fig. 115. Thumb and second finger extended, putting ball between fingertips. (see Figs. 112 and 113).

The forefinger relieves the thumb, and the fingers are extended, with the thumb following long enough to make sure the ball is properly placed, should that be necessary. The ball then makes its appearance at the fingertips (Fig. 113). Though not as smooth and rapid as the usual fingertip production, some performers may find this method easier, particularly with a large ball.

BALL ON FIST

From Standard Palm position (Fig. 105), dip the hand forward and outward, letting the ball fall into Finger-bend Palm position (Fig. 104), but in this case as far toward the forefinger as possible, regardless of whether the ball is momentarily visible to the spectators, because:

In that very same moment, the thumb is bent inward and is stretched across the hand, to the base of the little finger (Fig. 116). Coming below the ball, the thumb is ready to lift it, so in a continuation of the move, the hand comes upright, closing loosely to form a fist, with the thumb automatically bringing the ball on top, where from the audience's view (Fig. 117) it seemingly arrives magically. Here again, the moves can be blended with a rotary motion of the hand, preferably ending in a short upward thrust.

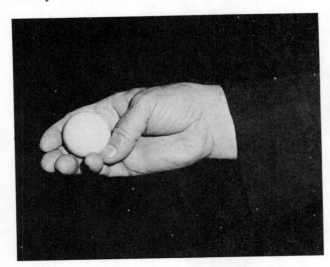

Fig. 116. Start of Ball on Fist. Inserting thumb beneath ball to raise it from Finger-bend position (rear view).

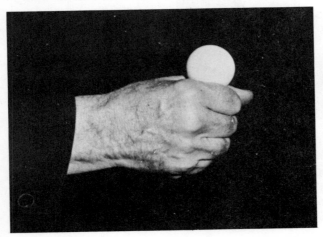

Fig. 117. Finish of Ball on Fist.

ALTERNATE FIST PRODUCTION

The same production can be accomplished by bringing the ball to Thumb Palm position (Fig. 107), then simply closing the fist beneath it (Fig. 118), so that the thumb can be swung away from the audience, over the ball and down in back where it joins the fist, and the ball is seen resting upon it, as in Fig. 115. A rotary motion, in which the hand is tilted toward the spectators in the first stage of the move, speeds the production and gives it an illusory effect.

REVERSE FINGERTIP PRODUCTION

A very surprising sleight as it comes at an unexpected moment and forms an excellent variation to the usual fingertip production. In this case, the left side is toward the audience and the right hand is extended toward the right, but with its thumb downward, so that only the back of the hand is seen, the fingers pointing directly to the right. The hand moves downward, then upward, and the ball suddenly appears between the tips of the third and fourth fingers (Fig. 119).

Fig. 118. Alternate Fist Production: Ball being brought to Thumb Palm so fist can be closed beneath it (rear view).

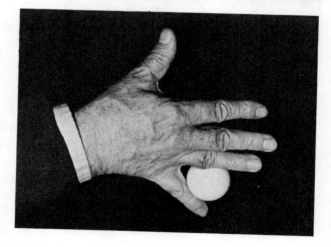

Fig. 119. Ball appearing between last two fingers, climaxing Reverse Fingertip Production as seen by audience.

The ball is in Standard Palm position (Fig. 105) to start. During the wavy motion, the third finger bends inward and draws the ball forward, enabling the thumb to bend inward and press the ball from in back (Fig. 120). Together, they roll the ball farther forward and upward, so the little

Fig. 120. Rear view of
third finger working ball
toward thumb, so latter
can aid in coming roll-up.

Fig. 121. Thumb and third
finger completing roll-up,
producing ball as pre-
viously shown (see Fig.
119).

finger can swing down over the ball to the tip of the thumb (Fig. 121). The
fingers are extended and spread, with the little finger rolling the ball
upward into the production position shown in Fig. 119, which represents
the audience's view.

This sleight can be worked with the right side toward the audience, the
thumb of the right hand upward. It is easier in that fashion, as the ball rolls
downward to appear between the tips of the third and fourth fingers. However, the reverse production, with the thumb downward, is much more
surprising. It can be done while standing with the right side toward the audience, thumb upward, by giving the right arm a pendulum swing downward past the body and straight out in back, the ball being produced at the
finish of the long sweep, which not only makes the move easier, but also
helps to hide the action of the thumb and fingers.

THUMB SQUEEZE

This production is both easy and effective, as timing is more a factor than deftness. The ball is palmed in the right hand, in standard palm position, with the right side toward the audience. The left hand is turned palm front and the left forefinger points to the tip of the right thumb, which is pointed upward (Fig. 122), indicating that the ball is to be produced from there.

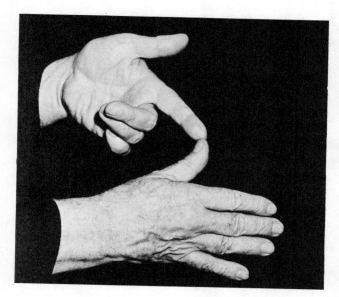

Fig. 122. Start of Thumb Squeeze Production as viewed by audience. Ball secretly palmed in right hand.

The left hand then swings downward below the right and comes upward, palm to palm, fingers pointing diagonally upward (Fig. 123), which like the previous position represents the audience's view. This enables the left hand to grip the ball secretly between the base of the left thumb and forefinger, in order to thrust the ball upward along the right thumb (Fig. 124). Timed to that smooth and rather rapid action, the hands are turned so their fingers are toward the spectators, with the right thumb tilting downward to the horizontal.

Fig. 123. Left hand brought palm to palm with right hand, but pointed upward as shown (audience view).

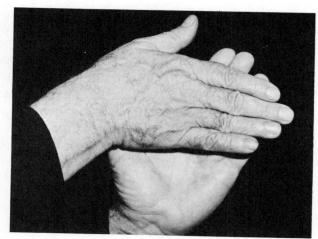

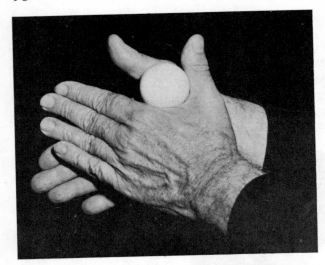

Fig. 124. Left hand moving upward, gripping ball between base of thumb and fingers (rear view).

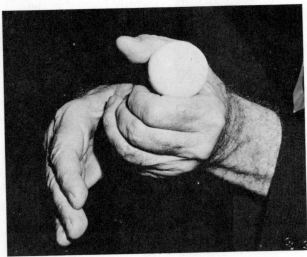

Fig. 125. Left hand forming fist and turning toward viewers as ball apparently emerges from tip of right thumb.

Thus the ball comes into sight, as though squeezed from the tip of the right thumb (Fig. 125), the very thing that the performer indicated by his earlier gesture. Since the right thumb partly hides the slide-up and the hands are meanwhile in motion, the arrival of the ball is quite deceptive. In keeping with the "squeeze," the left thumb forms a loose fist, with the left thumb and forefinger lightly encircling the ball, so that its bulk projects in full view, but the ball is still safely gripped.

By tilting the left hand upward and slightly tightening the fist, the ball can be balanced on it, as with the climax of the fist production (Fig. 117). Or the left thumb and fingers can simply relax and work the ball to display position (Fig. 103).

DRAW-APART PRODUCTION

A very easy production, in which a ball appears by degrees, creating an excellent illusory effect. Start with the right side toward the audience, with the ball palmed in the right hand, in Standard Palm position (Fig. 105). Bring the hands palm to palm, keeping them horizontal, and press the tips of the thumb and fingers closely together. Now turn the body full front, swinging the hands so the fingertips point directly toward the audience (Fig. 126).

Almost in the same move, spread the palms a trifle and tilt the hands forward so the ball rolls down toward the fingertips, being concealed by the thumbs, which are still pressed together side by side. Then tilt the hands upward, so the hands can spread wider, as though hinged at the fingertips, which still conceal the ball from in front. This enables the thumbs to separate and press their tips against the opposite sides of the ball, retaining it between them.

Fig. 126. Tips of fingers brought together full front for Draw-apart Production.

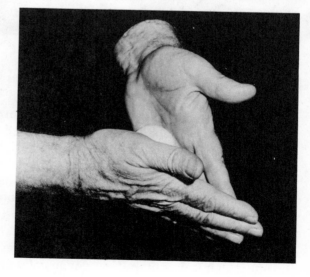

Fig. 127. View from downward angle, showing thumbs drawn apart as preliminary to next action, with ball secretly between palms.

This is clearly shown in Fig. 127, which is pictured at a downward angle to give the exact details. The thumbs then press the ball against the fingertips, which draw away in opposite directions with a peeling action (Fig. 128). The effect is that the ball grows between them, finally coming into full view, as though emerging from the fingertips themselves (Fig. 129). A neat twist is to finish the "peeling" with a downward action, so that the fingertips point at an upward angle. From there, either hand may then take the ball and exhibit it in display position.

Fig. 128. Downward view showing thumbs pressing ball so fingers can be drawn apart.

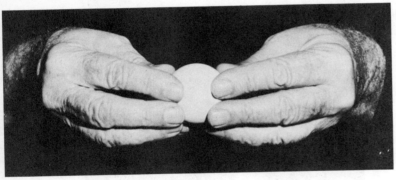

Fig. 129. Audience view of fingers "peeling" ball into sight.

THROUGH THE HAND

This is a neat production, or rather a reproduction, as it is partially a vanish, in which the ball is apparently placed in the left hand, but is actually palmed in the right. Standing with the right side toward the audience, extend the left fist at shoulder level with its back toward the audience as though it held the ball. The right hand, with ball in Finger-bend Palm (Fig. 104), points to the left; then approaches it and plants the ball against the back of the left hand.

The right thumb presses against the ball, which is brought into sight between right thumb and fingertips by a rotary motion to the right, giving the effect that it was literally and magically drawn through the back of the hand. By finishing with a downward twist, the ball is brought to display position in the right hand with thumb and fingers pointing upward. The left hand is then turned palm toward audience and opened to show that it is empty, to the surprise of skeptics who suppose that a second ball was used.

NOTE: This move can start with ball palmed in Standard Palm position (Fig. 105) or Thumb Palm position (Fig. 107). In either case, the right hand, in approaching the left, sets the ball against left knuckles. The right hand is then drawn inward, automatically rolling the ball to the required Finger-bend Palm position at the back of the left hand.

SLOW-MOTION PRODUCTION

This is an excellent opener for a billiard-ball routine. A ball is palmed in the right hand; and with right side toward the audience, the right hand points to the open left hand, which is shown empty, palm frontward.

The tips of the right fingers now come upward at an angle and deliberately fold the left fingers inward, pressing against the left fingernails (Fig. 130), forming the left hand into a loose fist, which is turned with its back toward the audience. The left hand is then slowly turned frontward and opened to show itself still empty.

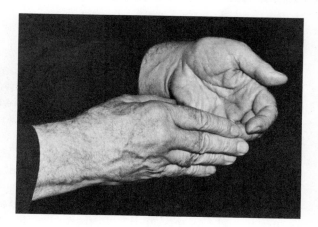

Fig. 130. Start of Slow-motion Production with right fingers folding left fist inward. (Ball palmed in right hand.)

The same move is repeated, but this time the right fingers go higher and at less of an angle, giving the left fingers more coverage as it closes them. Again, the left hand is fisted, turned backward and then frontward, to be shown empty. Then:

For the third time, the right fingers perform the closing action, but this time they are practically level with the left fingers; and the tips of the right fingers go well past the first knuckles of the left. This enables the right palm to release the ball, automatically transferring it to the bend of the left fingers (Fig. 131), which retain it. In closing the left hand, the right completely covers it until the left hand has been turned back toward the audience.

Then the left hand is raised, turned frontward, and opened to show that a ball has appeared there, at the same time rolling it upward with the thumb until it reaches display position with the right forefinger innocently pointing toward the left hand all the while.

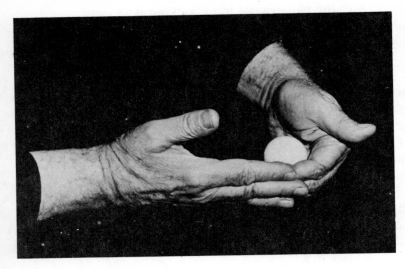

Fig. 131. Repeat of folding process. View from above showing transfer of ball from right palm to bend of left fingers.

PRODUCTION FROM ELBOW

As stated earlier, this is a routine production that is quite effective if not overdone, being specially suited to the recovery of a ball that has been vanished earlier. Standing with right side toward the audience, raise the left arm and extend the left hand at an upward angle, showing it empty. The right hand, with a ball palmed, comes up to the left elbow and dips the fingers just beneath it, pointing them away from view. The ball drops to Finger-palm position, if not already there, enabling the right fingers to push it up behind the left elbow (Fig. 132). The right hand then moves slowly downward, palm front, as the left arm is raised a trifle higher, so that the ball comes in sight as though drawn from the elbow by the tips of the right fingers (Fig. 133).

PRODUCTION FROM KNEE

Standing with the right side toward the audience, the right hand, with the ball palmed, swings downward to the outside of the right knee. In the same action turn frontward, so the right hand can go behind the knee and also turn frontward, rolling the ball into sight at the fingertips, as though drawing it from behind the knee, ending with the ball in display position between right thumb and fingers.

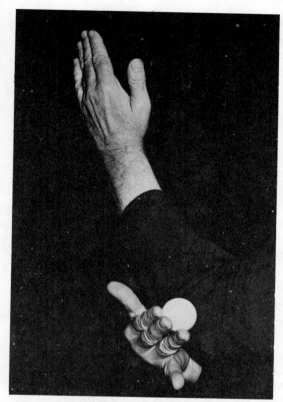

Fig. 132. Elbow Production. Rear view of right hand planting ball behind left elbow.

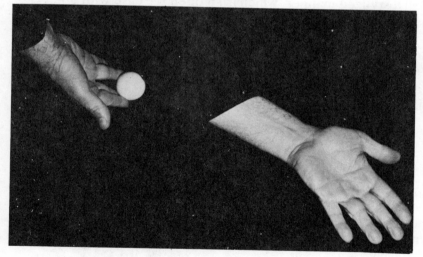

Fig. 133. Audience view of right hand drawing ball into sight with rolling action, from behind left elbow.

BALL FROM WAND

An old but effective opening production. With the right side toward the audience and the ball palmed in the right hand, hold a wand upright in the left hand, which is palm front. Simply run the right hand up the wand and rest the ball on the tip, so that the right thumb and fingers can ease downward around the ball, revealing it in display position. An upward push of the wand at the final moment helps create the illusion of the ball being drawn from the wand-tip.

BILLIARD-BALL VANISHES

While most billiard-ball vanishes follow a basic pattern, they also offer a greater variety than those involving other objects, such as coins and thimbles. This is because billiard balls are specially adapted to sleight-of-hand, due to the ease with which they can be rolled into positions that allow for deceptive moves, usually in the form of a continuous action.

Generally, a vanish consists of one hand apparently placing an object in the other, from which it later vanishes; or, in contrast, one hand supposedly takes it away from the other and then vanishes it. Switching from "placement" to "take-away" or vice versa is always good policy, as it throws keen observers off the trail; and with billiard balls, that rule can be carried still farther, since the principles can be combined as well as alternated.

The mere rolling of a ball between the hands, or a toss back and forth, can create an optical illusion, leaving an onlooker totally baffled as to when a vanish actually begins. This means that vital moves can be varied instead of being treated in a stylized manner, which is so often the case with other objects. The only admonition is to avoid fancy moves or unusual positions unless they have a definite purpose or logical reason.

Still, the occasional introduction of such showy sleights is always effective during the course of an extensive routine, particularly when working before a larger audience than the average close-up group. So all this adds to the zest of billiard-ball magic for the performer as well as his audiences.

POUR VANISH
Fig. 134. Beginning of pouring action with right hand openly letting ball roll into left hand.

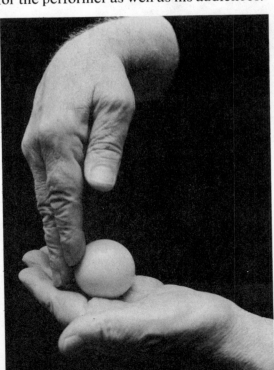

SIMPLE PALM VANISH

Stand with the right side toward the audience and show the ball in display position in the right hand. Swing the right hand toward the left, palming the ball in the right, which is turned back toward the audience as its fingers pretend to plant the ball in the left hand, which apparently closes over it. The left hand is then raised, turning its back toward the spectators, while the right forefinger points to the left hand to indicate where the ball went. The left hand is then turned frontward and opened with a rubbing motion of the fingers to show that the ball has vanished. Finger Palm, Thumb Palm, or Standard Palm may be used.

THROW VANISH

Similar to the Simple Palm Vanish, but the right hand instead of planting the ball in the left, makes a throwing motion in that direction, palming the ball as it does. The left hand closes loosely as though receiving the ball and in the same action moves upward, turning its back toward the audience and then comes frontward, completing the vanish with a rub-away motion. Choice of palming method is optional.

HAND-TO-HAND

This is the Throw Vanish, but as preliminary, the performer stands face toward the audience and throws the ball from right hand to left, then back and forth, turning leftward as he does, and finishing with the pretended throw, which is followed by the usual vanish.

POUR VANISH

Easy but deceptive. The right hand is outstretched, palm upward, with the ball lying on it. The right fingers are then pointed downward, letting the ball roll into the left hand, which is brought palm upward to receive it (Fig. 134). The left hand replaces the ball on the right palm and the pouring ac-

Fig. 135. Repeat of pouring action with back of right hand toward audience and left hand apparently closing over ball.

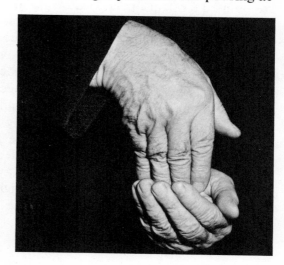

tion is repeated, but the body is turned more to the left, so the back of the right hand is toward the audience (Fig. 135). The right hand retains the ball by either the Standard Palm or the Thumb Palm, while the left fingers close in cup fashion, pretending to receive it (Fig. 136). The left hand is then raised and proceeds with the usual vanish. With a small ball, the right hand can let it roll down into the finger bend, palming it there.

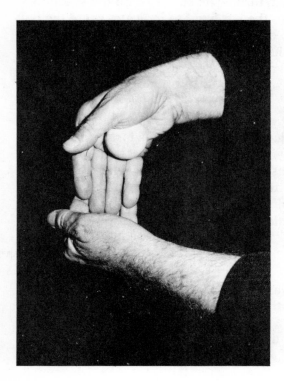

Fig. 136. Rear view of repeat action with right hand secretly retaining ball by Standard Palm.

FRENCH DROP

Standing with the right side toward the audience, the ball is held in the right hand between the tips of the thumb and the first two fingers, which are pointed straight upward, allowing people to look directly through the space beneath, a mere modification of the usual display position. The left thumb is thrust directly through that space from in back (Fig. 137), the left fingers close down over the ball from above (Fig. 138), and the right hand is simultaneously tilted upward, so its back is toward the audience.

At the moment of complete coverage, the right thumb and fingers release the ball, dropping it into the bend of the right fingers (Fig. 139), which either retain it there, or preferably press it into the Standard Palm position (Fig. 105) or even grip it with the Thumb Palm position (Fig. 107). In any case, a slight swing to the left, with a lift of the hands, completes the illusion that the ball has been taken away in the left fist and insures the concealment of the palmed ball in the right hand.

Fig. 137. Beginning of French Drop. Left thumb is thrust openly beneath ball held by right thumb and fingers.

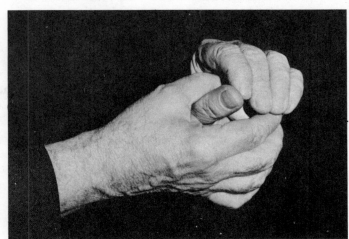

Fig. 138. Left fingers closing down over ball as though to remove it.

Fig. 139. Right thumb and second finger holding ball in pincer grip against left palm (rear view).

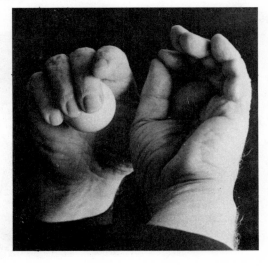

This automatically enables the left hand to turn back toward the audience with the right finger pointing to the left hand as though it still held the ball, the familiar position that precedes the frontward turn and "rub-away" action, which presumably accounts for the vanish of the ball.

SWALLOW VANISH

A whimsical follow-up to the French Drop. Instead of "vanishing" the ball immediately, the left hand is raised to the performer's mouth and he pretends to place the ball there. The left hand is then lowered and casually shown empty, while the performer thrusts his tongue deep into the right cheek to represent the ball. The right hand, which actually has the ball palmed, comes up and presses the imaginary ball with its forefinger. The tongue is drawn back and the performer gives a gulping motion, as though swallowing the ball, which can later be produced elsewhere by the right hand. This forms a very useful bit of byplay in connection with various billiard-ball routines.

PINCER VANISH

A very deceptive sleight in which the ball is held between the tips of right thumb and the second finger, similar to the French Drop, but is then set squarely against the palm of the left hand, which is turned toward the audience and held in vertical position with thumb above (Fig. 140). The left hand then turns completely over in a forward direction, bringing its back toward the audience and completely covering the ball (Fig. 141).

Timed to that action, the right hand makes a quarter turn downward, to the rear. It retains the ball in a pincer grip between the tips of the thumb

Fig. 140. Ball placed against left palm at start of Pincer Vanish. Palm faces audience.

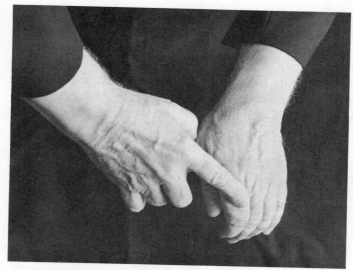

Fig. 141. Left hand turning its back toward audience, covering ball while right hand tilts downward.

Fig. 142. Rear view of left hand pretending to take ball that right hand secretly retains in pincer grip.

and second finger, which are doubled close against the palm, and the ball hidden there, as in Fig. 142, which represents a rear view. The left hand closes as though taking the ball and moves upward, with the right forefinger pointing toward it. Moments later, the left hand is turned frontward and shown empty, the right hand meanwhile palming the ball with the aid of thumb and fingers.

PUSH VANISH

With the right side toward the audience, the right hand places a ball in the curve of the left thumb and fingers, which practically encircle it. The right thumb pushes the ball into the left fist (Fig. 143) until it is completely out of sight (Fig. 144) when the left hand is raised, turned frontward and opened to show that the ball is gone.

The vital move comes at the climax of the push. There the left fingers relax, so the right thumb actually rides over the ball instead of pushing it farther. This allows the ball to drop into the bend of the right fingers, which are extended beneath the left hand (Fig. 145). From there the ball is easily palmed in the right hand while the left fist is being raised.

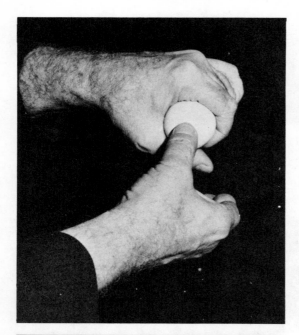

Fig. 143. Beginning of Push Vanish with right thumb openly thrusting ball into left fist.

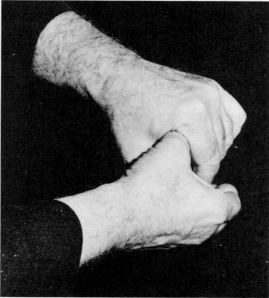

Fig. 144. Audience view of completion of push vanish with right fingers coming up beneath left hand.

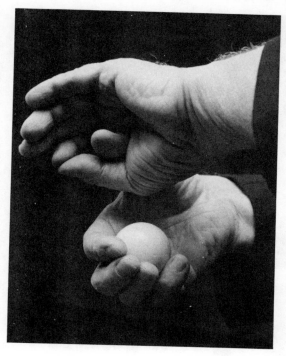

Fig. 145. Rear view of left hand secretly dropping ball into bend of right fingers.

SIMPLE ROLL VANISH

Facing the audience, the performer keeps rolling a ball in a circular fashion between the palms of his hands, which are held horizontally, right hand above, left hand below (Fig. 146). Turning to his right, he brings his left hand to a vertical position, thumb upward and with the back of the hand toward the audience. As though continuing the roll, the right hand points its fingers downward and apparently draws the ball to the tips of the left fingers, while it closes as though carrying the ball away (Fig. 147).

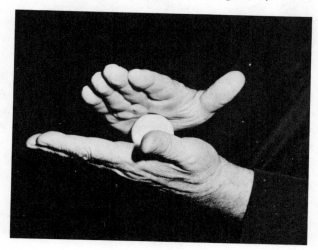

Fig. 146. Start of Simple Roll Vanish. Hands are held horizontally while ball is rolled between them.

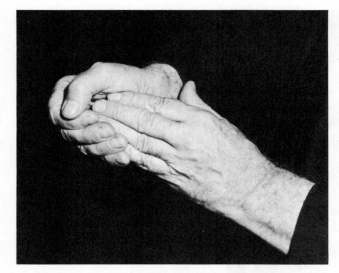

Fig. 147. Left hand brought to vertical position as ball is supposedly rolled into right hand.

Fig. 148. Rear view. Ball is actually palmed in left hand, which points upward as right hand pretends to carry ball away.

The right hand then turns its back toward the spectators, and the left forefinger points to the right hand as it opens and shows that the ball has vanished. Actually, the ball is palmed in the left hand at the conclusion of the roll, being pressed there firmly by the right, which merely goes through the pretense of drawing it away (Fig. 148).

FINGERTIP ROLL

Here both hands are pointed directly toward the audience, with the ball displayed between the tips of the fingers, which are pressed together (Fig.

149). The right fingers draw the ball inward, pressing it against the left hand, then curling around it (Fig. 150), continuing to roll it into the right fist. Simultaneously, the performer turns to the right, raises his right fist, and turns its back toward the audience, as the left forefinger points up to the right fist.

Fig. 149. Start of Fingertip Roll with ball at tips of fingers, viewed from above.

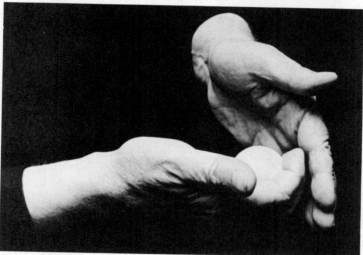

Fig. 150. Right fingers openly curling around ball and taking it away as prelude to vanish. Viewed from above.

This is done openly, with the fingers tilting downward (as in Fig. 150) as prelude to the artifice that follows. The right hand opens, brings the ball to display position (Fig. 103). From there it is replaced at the fingertips (Fig. 149) and the move is apparently repeated, but with this vital difference: The performer turns to the right as he begins the roll, so the left hand hides the action of the right. This time, instead of curling around the ball, the right fingers are doubled, so they ride over it (Fig. 151), and by continuing the roll, the right knuckles press the ball into the left palm, which retains it

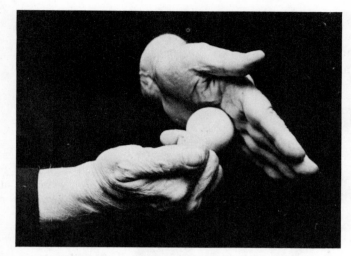

Fig 151. The actual vanish. Right fingers doubling so knuckles press ball into left palm. Back of left hand hides this action (rear view).

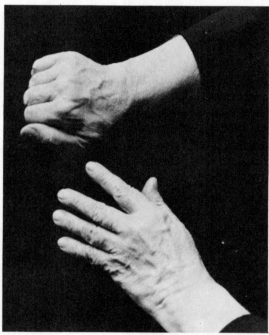

Fig. 152. Left hand palms ball and points to right hand, which is raised fisted, as though containing ball (audience view).

while the right hand is fisted and raised back toward the audience (Fig. 152). The right hand is then turned frontward and opened with the usual rubbing motion or given a toss to complete the vanish.

THUMB-ROLL VANISH

Stand with the right side of the body toward the audience. The left hand is extended with the palm toward the audience, and the right thumb presses the ball against the heel of the left hand, down toward the outside edge (Fig. 153). The right thumb then rolls the ball at an upward angle to the center of the left palm so that the left hand can close around the ball, turn its back toward the audience, and carry the ball upward in its closed fist. The ball is then shown, replaced in the right hand, and the move is repeated; but this time the ball vanishes from the left hand.

The move is practically automatic and utterly deceptive. For the vanish, the right thumb simply continues its upward roll after the ball reaches the center of the left palm (Fig. 154) so that the ball rides over the lowest knuckle of the left forefinger, the left hand being turned forward and downward to facilitate the action (Fig. 155). This enables the left knuckle to press the ball into the palm of the right hand, which adds a rotary motion, pointing its fingers upward. This facilitates the palming process, and the left hand, closing under cover of the right, is raised empty, with its back toward the audience. The usual vanish follows.

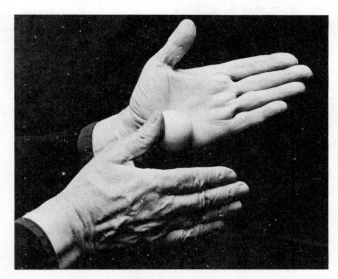

Fig. 153. Start of Thumb-roll Vanish. Right hand rolls ball upward, from heel of right hand toward center of left palm.

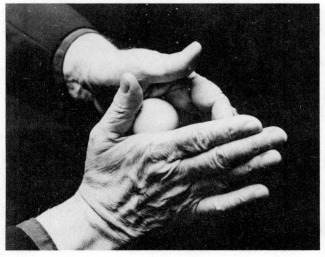

Fig. 154. Ball reaches center of left hand, which is closing loosely around it as if to carry it away (view from above).

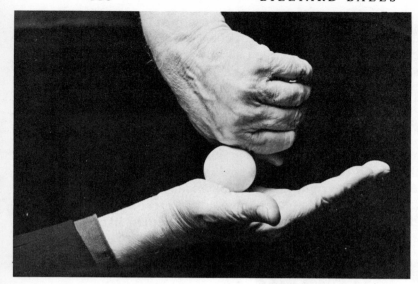

Fig. 155. Performer's view of right hand continuing roll over back of left hand. Left knuckles secretly press ball into right palm.

TOSS VANISH

Simple but effective. The performer keeps tossing a ball upward and catching it with his right hand, while gradually turning his right side toward the audience. On the fourth or fifth toss, he simply retains the ball, palming it while the back of his hand is toward the audience. Convincingly done, this produces an optical illusion of the ball vanishing in midair. Each toss should be at least two feet, preferably increasing by degrees, and if the performer follows the ball with his own eyes, he will carry the audience's gaze along, enhancing the effect.

TWO-HAND TOSS

A highly advanced form of the simple toss, this is one of the best of vanishes, thanks to a subtly delayed action. With the right side toward the audience, the right hand is extended at about waist level and gives the ball an upward toss to the left hand, which is held with its back toward the audience and catches the ball at about shoulder level (Fig. 156).

Closing about the ball, the left fist is turned frontward and gives the ball a short toss, letting it drop to the waiting right hand (Fig. 157). The double move is repeated a few times, the left hand making its toss quite deliberately, until suddenly the ball vanishes by apparently dissolving in midair, for the left hand is shown entirely empty.

Here both optics and imagination are involved. After the right hand has made a few tosses, it repeats the action but palms the ball as it comes upward, while the left hand simultaneously imitates its usual backhand catch. (Fig. 158 shows a rear view.) The illusion is perfect. Having seen the ball traverse the space before, people will imagine they saw it again, and will be positive the ball is in the left hand.

Hence the vanish from the left hand comes as a complete surprise, and some highly imaginative observers may think they saw the ball disappear in midair when tossed by the left hand, although it wasn't there to start with. This makes the vanish absolute. An onlooker has to retrace two steps and not merely one, as in the simple toss.

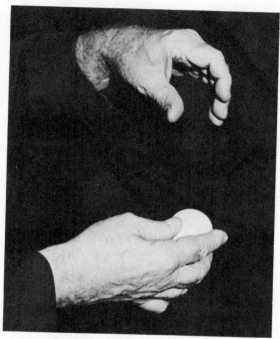

Fig. 156. Right hand about to toss ball openly to left hand.

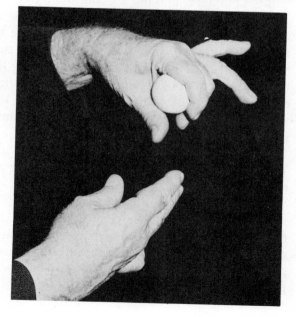

Fig. 157. Completion of preliminary toss. Left hand has caught ball and is about to drop it back into right hand.

Fig. 158. Rear view of
right hand palming ball as
it repeats the toss with
left hand pretending to
catch ball.

SWING-ABOUT TOSS

This is a follow-up to the Two-hand Toss whereby the disposal of the
ball is complete, making a good finale to a series of manipulations. After
pretending to catch the ball with the left fist (Fig. 158), swing the body to
the right so that the left side is toward the audience. The left hand then
makes its upward toss, but with its back toward the audience as in the
simple Toss Vanish. The right hand, being out of sight, simply drops the
ball in the coat pocket, while the left hand draws attention upward. Immediately swing back to the left, showing the left hand empty, and bring the
right hand up to the left, brushing the palms together and showing both
hands empty as you face full front.

FINGERTIP VANISH

Standing full front, the right hand holds the ball between the tips of its
first two fingers, with thumb straight upward, the remaining fingers bent
slightly inward. The left hand comes in front of the ball (Fig. 159) and apparently removes it, turning back toward the audience with the right hand
pointing toward it. A rubbing motion of the right hand and the ball
vanishes.

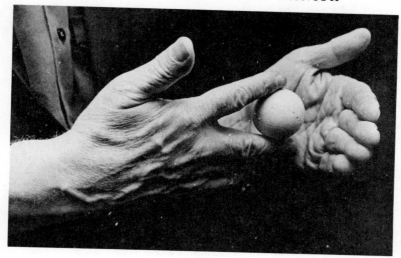

FINGERTIP VANISH
Fig. 159. Left hand about to cover ball held at tips of right first and second fingers.

In apparently removing the ball, the left hand completely screens it and at the same time gives it a slight jolt, sending it into the right palm, where the third and fourth fingers of the right hand are bent inward to press the ball in place in a Standard Palm. The fingers are then fully extended and the left hand closes as though removing the ball. The body is immediately turned to the left, with the right hand palming the ball (Fig. 160) and pointing to the left as it pretends to carry the ball away. This is a very effective routine after producing a ball at the right fingertips (see page 91), as it is already in position for the vanish.

SIMPLE FIST VANISH

Facing slightly to the right, the performer places a ball on his left fist and encircles it with his right hand (Fig. 161), which is held thumb upward. Next, the right hand apparently carries the ball away to the right, turning

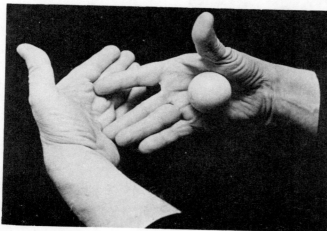

Fig. 160. Rear view showing ball palmed in right hand where it has been pressed by third and fourth fingers.

its back toward the audience, as if keeping the ball loosely gripped. The left hand points at the right, which is then opened and the ball is gone.

Simplicity is the keynote here. During the right hand's circling action, the left fist relaxes, allowing the ball to drop down into the left hand, which promptly palms it, as shown in Fig. 162, while the body turns farther to the right, completing the move as described in the Fingertip Vanish, and reverse the hands as necessary.

IMPROVED FIST VANISH

Here the left side is directly toward the audience at the start, with the left hand extended almost at arm's length. The ball is resting on the left fist and the right hand, thumb turned down, comes in front of it as a screen

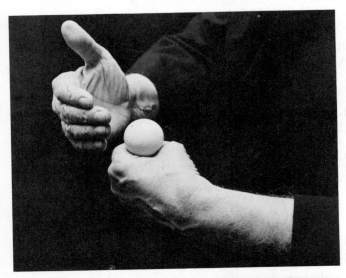

SIMPLE FIST VANISH
Fig. 161. Side view showing right hand closing around ball on left fist.

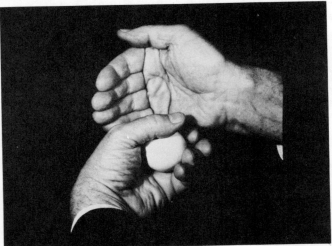

Fig. 162. Rear view of ball secretly dropping into left palm as right hand apparently takes it.

(Fig. 163), as if to sweep it away in a loose fist of its own, from which it vanishes after the right hand is turned back toward the audience.

The ball actually drops into the left fist under cover of the right hand. The left hand does not begin its palming action until the right hand has been lifted up and away, as though carrying the ball with it. This is an excellent vanish to follow the Fist Production (page 94), as the ball is in position to start.

Fig. 163. Improved Fist Vanish with right hand, thumb downward, about to sweep ball from left fist (side view).

HIT-DOWN VANISH

A very effective alternate for the Simple Fist Vanish, which begins with the performer facing directly front. The ball is shown on the left fist, but instead of encircling it, the right hand is brought palm downward, in cupped fashion, as though driving the ball down into the left fist. In fact, it can be done that way to start, then shown in the left hand and replaced on the fist ·for a repetition of the move.

In the repeat, however, the cupped right fingers actually grip the ball and bring it upward in Finger Palm position following the downward hit. Simultaneously, the body is turned to the left, so the left fist can turn thumb downward with its back toward the audience, while the right forefinger points upward with the other fingers concealing the ball in Finger Palm fashion. The left hand is then opened to show the ball gone.

BALL AND SILK VANISH

A special adaptation of the Simple Fist Vanish starting with the ball on the left fist, with the right hand holding a silk handkerchief, which it lays over the ball and apparently takes it away in the folds of the silk. When the silk is shaken by the right hand, the ball has vanished.

What happens is this: The right fingers pretend to grip the ball through the folds of the silk, but actually let it drop into the left fist, which opens to receive it. The right hand presses its fingers deep into the doubled center of the cloth and turns palm frontward, as though it still gripped the ball through the silk. The left hand grips the "neck" of the cloth, so that the center retains the exact shape of the ball. Actually, the ball is palmed in the left hand, as shown in the rear view, with the hollow bulge of the silk giving the impression that the ball is still there.

So the right hand has only to take a corner of the handkerchief, give it a vehement shake, and show that the ball has vanished from it, while the left hand — which retains the palmed ball — points innocently and helpfully to the right. Both hands then spread the silk to show that the ball is really gone, and bundle it up with the ball inside it, so either hand can pocket it, ball and all.

SNATCH VANISH

A rapid move that reverses the usual trend, but is highly effective when properly done. While facing directly toward the left, a ball is openly placed in the left hand, which is closed, turned back toward the audience, and extended at arm's length. The right hand makes a few quick passes in front of the left, and when the left hand is turned frontward and opened, the ball has vanished.

As the title implies, the ball is literally snatched away by the right hand. When the left hand is turned back toward the audience, its fingers secretly roll the ball as far toward the wrist as possible (Fig. 164, rear view). In making one of its quick passes (Fig. 165), the right hand comes directly below the knuckle of the left thumb. At that moment, the left fingers release the ball so that the right hand snatches it as it drops and carries it away (Fig. 166).

In practicing this, cup the right hand slightly upward to make the snatch in scoop fashion, allowing no space between it and the left hand; otherwise people may glimpse the ball, no matter how rapidly or adeptly the move is executed. It is best to snatch the ball on the first or second sweep; then repeat the action a few times, but with the right hand well below the level of the left, so that the vital move is accomplished before observers can even suspect it. The right hand can add a few circling motions, going farther and farther away from the left hand before the latter is finally opened.

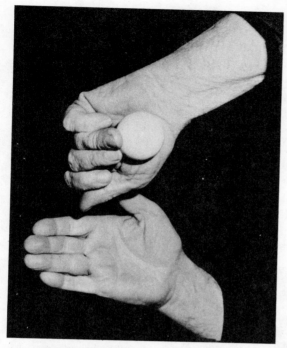

SNATCH VANISH
Fig. 164. Rear view of left fingertips secretly pressing ball toward wrist. Right hand is poised for snatch from below.

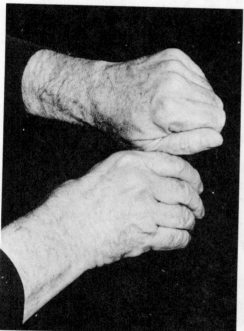

Fig. 165. Right makes snatching action while left hand secretly releases ball (audience view).

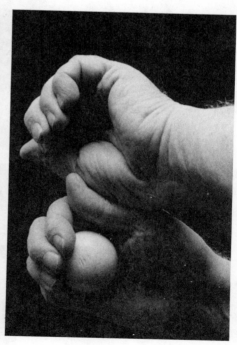

Fig. 166. Completion of snatching action. Right hand palms ball from finger-bend position (rear view).

SLOW-MOTION VANISH

This is in direct contrast to the Snatch Vanish, yet it involves a similar procedure; hence one makes a good alternate for the other. A ball is placed openly in the left hand, which is turned back toward the audience. Facing to the left, the right hand points toward the left fist, then, as an afterthought, the right hand is turned palm frontward and shown empty, just to assure onlookers that the ball is really in the left hand (Fig. 167).

Note that the backs of the right fingers rest naturally against the back of the left hand. Meanwhile, the left fingers have worked the ball to their tips as with the Snatch Vanish (see Fig. 164). Now the right hand is turned back toward the audience, again pressing its fingers against the back of the left hand and immediately the left fist is turned toward the audience, one move blending into the other. This brings the ball directly into the right palm, where it is pressed home by the tips of the left fingers (Fig. 168).

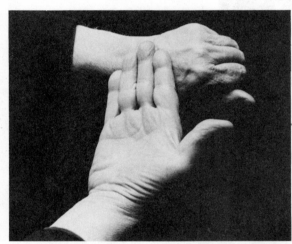

Fig. 167. Start of Slow-motion Vanish. Right hand shown empty after placing ball in left fist.

Fig. 168. Rear view of hands revolving. Left hand secretly presses ball into right palm.

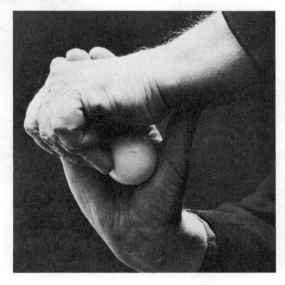

Without pause, the left hand is raised slowly upward and the right hand is brought inward and downward, so it can point to the left fist, which is now frontward (Fig. 169). Since the left fist must be kept loose as if it still held the ball, it is a good plan to bend the left hand inward toward the body to help the illusion, particularly if a fairly large ball is used. The left hand is then turned back toward the audience and the ball is deliberately "vanished" with the usual rubbing action.

This is an excellent alternate for either form of the Roll Vanish (page 111), in which the ball is apparently placed in the left hand but really retained in the right. The same quick passes can be used with a Roll Vanish, but no snatch is necessary, as the ball is already gone. By working one method, then repeating with the other, the spectators will be doubly misdirected. As a finish, the ball can be reproduced either from the left elbow, at the right fingertips, or on the right fist. (See pages 117, 132.)

LAY-OVER VANISH

Very easy, deliberate, and effective. Facing to the left, the left hand is extended, back toward the audience, thumb downward, forming a loose fist. The right hand holds the ball in display position and reaches over the left hand, apparently laying the ball therein. The right hand is withdrawn, the left is opened, and the ball is gone.

Actually, the right hand simply retains the ball, finger-palming it while pretending to leave it in the left but bringing it upward and out again. Moving downward, the right hand keeps pointing up toward the left hand, which is raised, turned frontward, and shown empty, while the right hand, still moving downward, eases the ball from Finger Palm position to Standard Palm position.

This move can be facilitated by pressing the ball against the upper edge of the left hand, practically rolling it from display position into the Finger Palm.

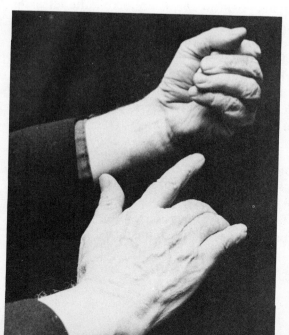

Fig. 169. Left hand turned toward audience and about to vanish ball. Ball is palmed in right hand.

CHANGE-OVERS, TRANSFERS, AND FLASHES

The beauty of billiard-ball manipulation lies in the variety of its moves, which include not only productions and vanishes but also multiplication and color changes, all providing elements of surprise. The final touch, however, depends upon the introduction of subtle supplementary sleights whereby the hands are shown apparently empty before productions, after vanishes, or in between. Here variety is more essential than ever, for if the action were confined to one process, its repetition might arouse suspicion. But the moves that follow offer a wide range of choices, some being suited to specific purposes, adding that much more to their novelty.

These sleights were originally termed "change-overs," a short form of "change-over palm," signifying that the ball is secretly transferred from the palm of one hand to the other, so that each hand may be shown empty in turn. But there is a distinction between a change-over and a direct transfer; and from those have developed moves in which both hands are shown apparently empty simultaneously. Now, the important difference from the manipulator's standpoint is the matter of timing, which has generally been overlooked. Productions and vanishes can be executed according to the performer's natural or preferred tempo, fairly deliberately or reasonably rapid. But the in-between moves must be sped or slowed to suit the immediate conditions.

On that basis, these sleights have been placed in three classes, each with its own process:

1. *Change-overs*, in which the performer starts with his right side toward the audience, shows his left hand empty, and swings about so that his left side is toward the audience, enabling him to show his right hand empty. This can be done slowly, because the swing from left to right, or vice versa, is a time-taker in itself; and therefore it cannot be hurried, or it will not be appreciated.

2. *Transfers*, where the performer keeps his right side toward the audience throughout, never changing his position. Or, if preferred, the left side is toward the audience, but the moves are exactly the same. Either way, the action must be smooth and continuous, with brief pauses emphasizing the emptiness of the hands, making it a step-by-step procedure.

3. *Flashes*, which really are the best of all, with the audience given only a momentary view of the empty hands — so brief, in fact, that almost before the most skeptical observers are convinced that there is nothing there, the hands are doing something else.

Summarized: The tendency is to make the *change-overs* too rapidly. Keep them slow and emphatic, as if they were mere gestures. With *transfers*, too much speed looks too manipulative; too much delay lets observers analyze the moves, so try to keep a medium tempo. With *flashes*, just don't waste time. The approach and even the departure can be slow or studied, but the vital move — the crux, so to speak — must be momentary. Keep these points in mind as you put the following moves to the test:

BASIC CHANGE-OVER

The performer stands with right side toward the audience, a ball palmed in his right hand. The right forefinger points to the empty left hand (Fig. 170). The palms are brought together with the ball directly between them while the performer swings to the right. Now the fingers, kept close together, point toward the audience (Fig. 171). At this point, the right palm

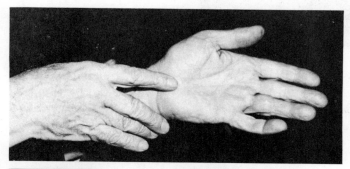

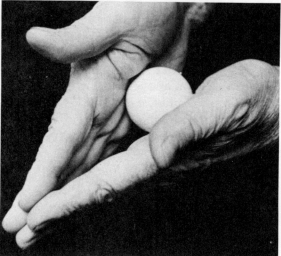

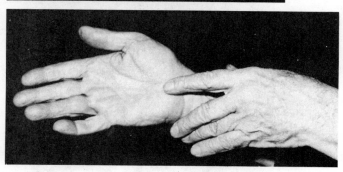

BASIC CHANGE-OVER
Fig. 170. Spectator's view at start of change-over. Right hand secretly retains ball in Standard Palm position while pointing to empty left hand.

Fig. 171. Change-over at halfway mark, showing hands brought together, palm to palm. Fingers point toward audience (performer's view).

Fig. 172. Body now turned to right. Left hand has ball in Standard Palm position and is pointing to empty right hand (spectator's view).

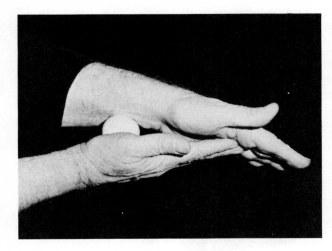

IMPROVED CHANGE-OVER
Fig. 173. View from above. Right hand presses ball against left wrist, rolling it forward as palms are brought together.

relaxes pressure, and the left palm grips the ball instead. The swing is continued until the left side is toward the audience. By now the ball has been transferred from the right palm to the left palm, so the right hand can be shown empty with the left forefinger indicating that fact (Fig. 172).

IMPROVED CHANGE-OVER

Here a rolling process is introduced, making the change-over more natural and more deceptive. The right hand, pointing toward the left, rests its fingers against the left palm and presses the palmed ball against the left wrist, as in Fig. 173, which represents a view from above. During the body turn to the right, the right hand is thrust forward and the left hand is drawn backward simultaneously. Thanks to this lateral action, the heel of the right hand rolls over the ball. The ball, in turn, rolls over the heel of the left hand as the swing continues (Fig. 174). The ball is brought into the left palm, and the left fingers rest against the right palm. At midpassage, tips of thumbs and fingers are pressed together, as with the Basic Change-over (Fig. 171), the difference being that the ball is between the heels of the hands.

Fig. 174. View from above. With fingers now pointing toward audience (as shown in Fig. 171), ball is being rolled into left palm.

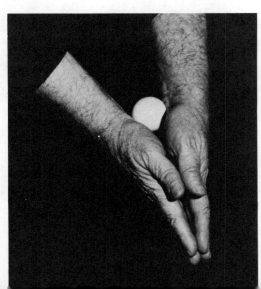

DELAYED CHANGE-OVER

Starting with sleeves well rolled up and with right side toward the audience, the right hand, with ball palmed, points to the left hand and plants the ball against the left forearm, fairly close to the elbow. The body swings to the right, and the right hand is thrust forward, while the left hand is drawn back, much as with the Improved Change-over, but with this difference:

At the midpoint of the change-over, when the hands are palm to palm, pointing directly toward the spectators, the ball is still between the wrists. Keeping the hands heel to heel, they are opened fanwise, giving observers a view of two empty palms (Fig. 175). This delay should be timed to give the audience a brief "flash," no more, the opening and closing of the hands being at about the same tempo as the change-over action.

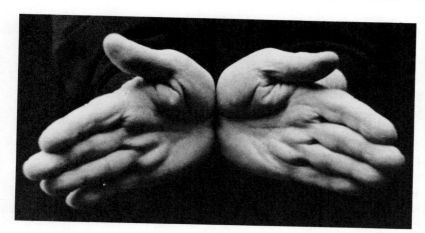

DELAYED CHANGE-OVER
Fig. 175. Spreading hands to show empty palms at midpoint of change-over. "Flash" as viewed by audience.

This can be prolonged by continuing the swivel during the flash — that is, start the flash just before the midpoint, while the fingers are still pointing at a slight angle to the left; and end it just after the midpoint, so that they will be pointing at a slight angle to the right. Either way, the ball will be temporarily stalled between the wrists, as shown in Fig. 176, which gives a view from above. Following the flash, the swing to the right is continued, bringing the ball into the left palm as the latter nears the right elbow.

This move is particularly effective when using a rubber ball of a somewhat compressible type, as the closer the wrists are pressed together, the wider the hands can be spread, automatically prolonging the flash, while giving a fuller view of the empty plams. However, constant motion is essential, as the hands are in an awkward position at the crux of the sleight; but that will pass unnoticed if no one is given time to analyze it.

Notes on Change-overs: Change-overs are particularly useful as adjuncts or preliminaries to other moves, as they suggest that the hands are empty, without deliberately asserting so. A good reason for shifting from one side to the other is to draw up each sleeve in turn, With the Basic Change-over, the performer would simply use his right hand to tug his left sleeve slightly,

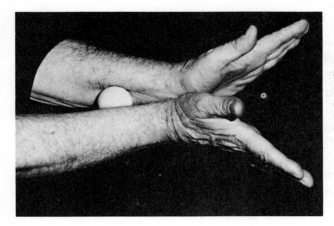

Fig. 176. View from above, showing exact position of hidden ball while empty hands are momentarily spread.

then make the change-over and use his left hand to tug his right sleeve, as verification of the initial act.

With the Improved Change-over, it is better to be more emphatic. The right hand draws the left sleeve emphatically upward, the hands go into the change-over, and the left hand draws the right sleeve upward in the same emphatic style. Observers will later avow that you couldn't have done that so emphatically unless your hands had been completely empty before and after.

With the Delayed Change-over, preliminary action can really take over. If you start with your sleeves rolled up – and high up! – you can follow the routine as described. But with the sleeves down, there is a chance for dramatic presentation, since you have to roll them up to start. That must be specially handled, as follows:

Standing right side toward the audience, the performer extends his right arm and rolls up his right sleeve with his left hand. Nobody knows that he has a ball palmed in his right hand. He then extends his left arm, showing his left hand empty, and rolls up his left sleeve with his right hand, which everyone by then is sure must be empty. This puts him in prime position

SIMPLE TRANSFER
Fig. 177. Right hand, ready to sweep across opened left, holds palmed ball.

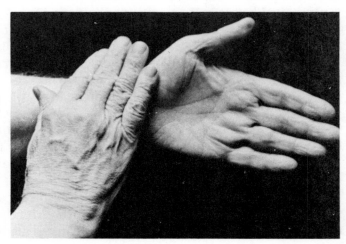

for the "delayed" procedure, which requires arms bared to the elbows, though only the performer knows it.

Change-overs furnish the further function of enabling the performer to turn from one side to the other in the course of his manipulations. Experience will show how valuable this is. As an example: With his left side toward the audience, the performer executes the Improved Fist Vanish (page 120), where the ball is apparently taken away by the left hand, from which it vanishes, but is actually palmed in the right hand. By following with a change-over, the performer can bring his left side toward the audience and appropriately reproduce the ball on his left fist, using the Ball on Fist production (described on page 93).

TRANSFERS

In contrast to the cross-body sweep of the hands that renders the actual change-over almost unnoticeable, transfers involve a one-sided action within a limited area. Thus, instead of casually indicating that the hands are empty, the performer must emphasize the supposed fact. Where misdirection can automatically cover a change-over, a transfer must provide its own, since attention is focused on the hands throughout. That is done through a continuous, rhythmic motion, inserting pauses only when needed or indicated. If the motion is too rapid, the effect is lost; if too slow, onlookers can follow the moves too closely. So the proper procedure is to blend the moves into a series of transfers, which may be regarded and treated as a unit, subject only to specified variations.

SIMPLE TRANSFER

Stand with your right side toward the audience. The ball is palmed in the right hand, which has its back toward the audience, with fingers closed and pointing upward in front of the left wrist. The left hand is extended horizontally, palm front (Fig. 177). The right fingers sweep the left hand from heel to fingers, to emphasize that the left hand is entirely empty. The right hand then returns to its original position at the left wrist, and the left hand is turned over so its back is toward the audience. The right hand then sweeps the back of the left hand clear past the fingertips to emphasize its emptiness further.

Again, the left hand is turned palm front and the sweep is repeated; but this time the right hand pauses in front of the left palm and plants the ball there (Fig. 178). Under cover of the right hand, the left turns its back toward the audience and the right completes its sweep. Again returning to its original position, the right hand is turned front and shown empty as the ball is now palmed in the left hand, which still has its back turned toward

Fig. 178. Right hand passes during slow sweep and secretly transfers ball from right palm into left.

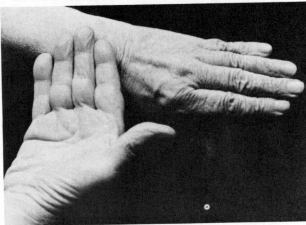

Fig. 179. Right hand completes sweep, returns to original position (at left wrist), and is now shown empty.

the audience (Fig. 179). The right hand now turns its back toward the audience and sweeps the back of the left as before.

Apparently, the series of sweeps has merely been repeated. Actually, a secret transfer has been made so that the right hand is shown all clear at the very time when spectators are most apt to suspect that it is palming the ball.

NOTE: The procedure can be shortened by eliminating the two preliminary sweeps, particularly during an extensive manipulative routine; but always, when ready for the transfer, the right hand should sweep the palm of the left, return and make the transfer, then sweep the back of the left hand, before the right returns and shows itself empty, as that leaves the spectators one step back.

REVERSE TRANSFER

By a reversal of the moves just described, the ball can be effectively transferred back from the left palm to the right. With the right hand shown empty and the ball palmed in the left hand (Fig. 179), follow a brief pause by turning the back of the right hand toward the audience and sweeping the back of the left. Then return the right hand to the left wrist and turn the left hand frontward under cover of the right (Fig. 178), switching the ball from the left palm to the right, and continue by sweeping the right hand past the left fingers, all in the same move. An added touch here is again to turn the back of the left hand toward the audience and give it a fleeting sweep with the tips of the right fingers, before producing the ball with the right hand.

However, the reverse moves may be entirely eliminated by means of the following move, which also brings the ball back into the right palm, but in much swifter fashion:

THUMB AND FINGER STEAL

With ball palmed in the left hand, the right fingers sweep the back of the left, halting slightly beyond and below it, showing the backs of both hands. The right hand, in returning toward the left wrist, moves at an upward angle, the thumb and little finger of the right hand bent slightly inward so they can be extended up behind the left hand, one on each side of the thumb (Fig. 180).

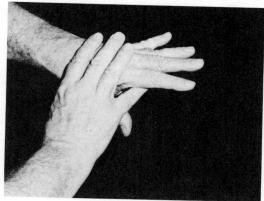

THUMB AND FINGER STEAL
Fig. 180. Right hand, returning toward left wrist, halts short to extend thumb and little finger up into left palm.

There, the right thumb and little finger grip the ball between their tips (Fig. 181) and carry it down to the right with another sweep (Fig. 182), palming it during the action by pressing inward with the middle fingers. The left hand is turned palm front and the right hand, pointing upward, returns to brush the left from wrist to fingertips, thus certifying the left hand's emptiness.

During the vital downsweep (Fig. 182), the right thumb and little finger should be doubled inward to prevent spectators from gaining a glimpse of the ball from a side angle. This momentary cramping goes unnoticed as the hand is in motion and it is all part of the palming action. In fact, the hand can practically be fisted on the downsweep, finishing with the ball in Finger Palm position or Standard Palm position, as preferred.

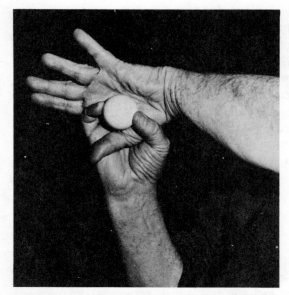

Fig. 181. Right thumb and little finger take pincer grip on ball to draw it downward from left palm (rear view).

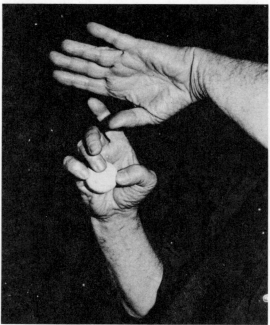

Fig. 182. Right hand continues downward while third finger presses pincer-gripped ball to start palming action (rear view).

SLOW-MOTION STEAL

As an alternative transfer, starting with the ball palmed in the left hand, the right begins its usual sweep, but very slowly, pausing at the left fingertips before continuing down to the right. The sweep is repeated, still more slowly; and under cover of the right hand's pause, the left fingers are bent inward, gripping the ball and immediately bringing it forward to Finger Palm position. Timed to that action, the right thumb is extended up beneath the left fingers, and the right second finger comes down from above, enabling them to grip the ball between their tips, as shown in the rear view, Fig. 183.

The right hand immediately continues its slow motion to the right, carrying the ball away as the left fingers are automatically extended (Fig. 184). The right hand, increasing speed, palms the ball on its downward sweep, and the left hand is turned palm toward the audience, so that the right forefinger can point up to avow the left hand's emptiness.

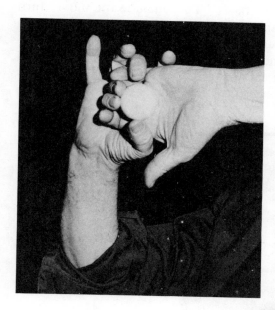

SLOW-MOTION STEAL
Fig. 183. Rear view of follow-through. Right hand carries ball entirely clear and left fingers are extended.

Fig. 184. Audience view of right hand secretly palming ball while right forefinger begins upward point.

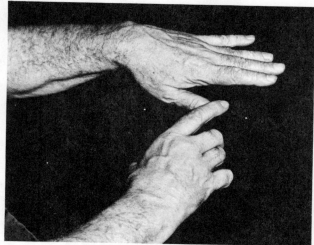

BACK-PALM TRANSFER

Another move to follow the Simple Transfer, when the ball is palmed in the left hand which is back toward the audience while the right hand is palm front with fingers pointing up toward left hand. The left hand is then turned palm front, and presses the ball against the back of the right fingers which conceal it. (Fig. 185). The first and fourth fingers of the right hand immediately grip the ball between them and the right hand is drawn straight downward until its middle fingers can be inched back against the edge of the left hand (Fig. 186). Both hands then appear empty, but the ball is actually back palmed by the right.

The left hand aids in the concealment, but it is by no means angleproof. So unless the spectators are few and directly in front, their view of the empty palms should be limited to a "flash." To conclude the move, turn the left hand forward and downward, covering the right fingers; then turn the right hand full about under cover of the left so its back is toward the audience. This enables the right hand to bring the ball into Standard Palm position, by doubling its middle fingers inward and bringing them up over the ball, thereby pressing it into the palm. The backs of both hands are then shown.

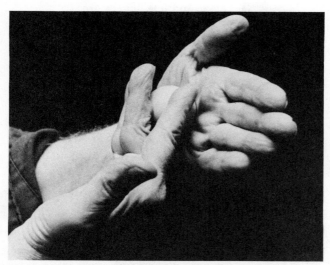

BACK-PALM TRANSFER
Fig. 185. Left hand turns frontward to press palmed ball against back of right fingers. Left hand should be cupped to hide ball from angles (side view).

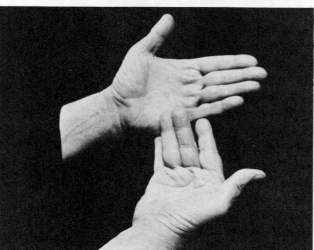

Fig. 186. Right hand drawn downward, bringing ball gripped between first and fourth fingers. Middle fingers provide cover.

TURN-AROUND TRANSFER

A ball is palmed in the right hand, which sweeps the back of the left hand, then the front, from wrist to fingertips, as with the preliminary to the Simple Transfer. Returning, the right hand presses the ball against the palm of the left hand while its own fingers are doubled inward (Fig. 187). The ball is then rolled inward over the knuckles of the right fingers until it nears the left wrist, as shown in Fig. 188, which represents a view from above.

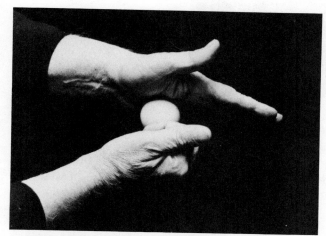

TURN-AROUND TRANSFER
Fig. 187. Start of sequence. Right hand presses palmed ball against left palm as right fingers double inward (view from above).

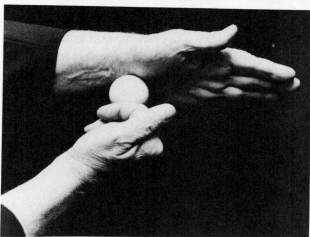

Fig 188. Right hand rolls ball inward over knuckles. Fist conceals ball from front (view from above).

At that point, the right fist conceals the ball from the front, and the roll is continued to the left wrist by extending the right fingers toward the left wrist, so that both palms are shown openly, in horizontal fashion. This, incidentally, is one of the neatest poses of manipulative magic. Viewed from above, the actual position of the ball is plain, as the performer sees it. But to stop there would make it obvious that the hands were concealing something.

So the best thing to do is to prove otherwise with an equally neat swivel

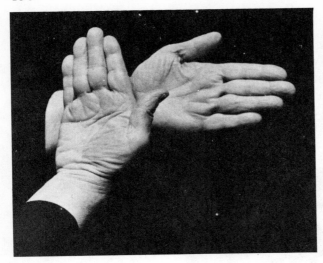

Fig. 189. Right hand swivels upward to the right and gives audience a full view of open hands. Position of ball remains unchanged.

move. Simply twisting the right hand from the horizontal to the vertical, without disturbing the ball at all (Fig. 189), thus showing both hands "empty," is as natural and emphatic a position as anyone could wish.

Now, having attained the peak of perfection, the problem is how to descend from it, or get back to where you were. The simplest way is by a—

REVERSE TURN-AROUND

The right hand swivels back to where it was, fists itself, and knuckles the ball into the left palm (as in Fig. 187). There the right fingers can straighten out, enabling the right hand to roll the ball forward and palm it, regaining the original position. Or, instead:

The left palm can retain the ball when the right knuckles press it there (Fig. 187). The right hand then extends its fingers, while the left hand turns upward and backward, taking the palmed ball with it, so the backs of both hands are shown. The right hand can then be turned palm front and shown against the left, ready to reclaim the ball by any of the moves already described.

DOUBLE TURN-AROUND

Done in easy, slow-motion style, this represents the ultimate in manipulative magic. Starting with the Turn-around Transfer, bring the hands to the position where both are shown empty, the right hand pointing upward, the left hand outward, both palms front (Fig. 189). The ball, of course, is between the wrists, putting it in readiness for the following moves:

Slowly turn the left hand palm downward, while automatically rolling the ball downward behind the right hand. The right hand remains palm

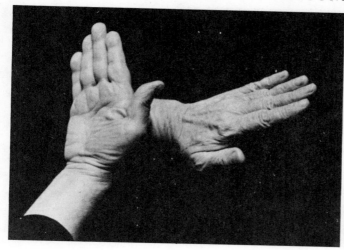

DOUBLE TURN-AROUND
Fig. 190. Left hand turns forward and downward to secretly roll ball between back of left wrist and back of right hand.

front, while the back of the left hand is now displayed (Fig. 190). Swivel the right hand to the horizontal position where its fingers point inward (Fig. 191) and knuckle the ball outward behind the right fist and along the back of the left hand (Fig. 192) until the right hand naturally palms the ball (Fig. 193) and the backs of the hands can be shown separately. For a neat finish, the left hand can sweep the back of the right from wrist to fingertips; the left hand is then turned palm front, and the right forefinger points to it, thus carrying attention in its direction.

Fig. 191. Right hand reverses swivel so that fingers point inward horizontally. Ball is still hidden between right hand and left wrist.

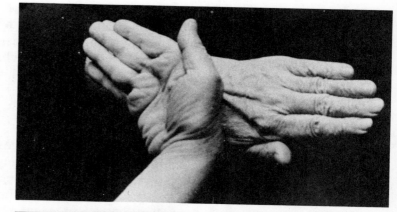

Fig. 192. View from above shows right fist rolling ball over knuckles toward palm of right hand.

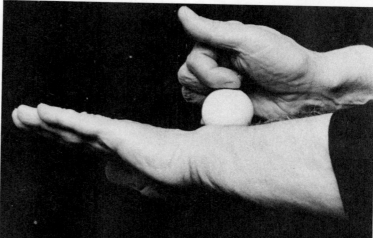

Fig. 193. Ball is now palmed in right hand, and both hands can be shown separately.

Done smoothly, deliberately, and even in slow motion, this series of manipulations is very effective. The ball should be fairly small and preferably have a rough or frosted surface. A ball of the compressible rubber type is also well adapted to such moves.

FLASHES

Elements of the "flash," in which both hands are simultaneously shown empty, but only briefly, are found in the Delayed Change-over, the Back-palm Transfer, and the Turn-around Transfer, when followed by the Return Turn-around, all described under their respective heads. In those, however, the emphasis is on palming action, whereas with most flashes, other modes of concealment are generally used.

FOREARM FLASH

This is simply the Turn-around Transfer (page 137) with the right hand planting the ball against the left wrist and pointing toward the left hand as though beginning the Improved Change-over (Fig. 173). Instead, the right hand doubles into a fist, is drawn inward along the left arm, and swivels its fingers upward, so the ball is hidden between the back of the right hand and the left forearm, showing both hands empty and wide apart. A prompt reversal of the move brings the ball back to its original position in the right palm.

SLEEVE FLASH

Similar to the Forearm Flash, but instead of rolling up the sleeve, it is used as a background for the right hand, which begins the move from well above the left wrist, finishing close to the left elbow. Again, a reversal of the process brings the ball back into the right palm.

COMBINATION CHANGE-OVER AND FLASH

Starting with the left side toward the audience, with ball palmed in the left hand, which points to the right, the performer executes the Improved Change-over (page 128) as he turns to the left. This automatically brings the ball into his right palm in readiness for the Forearm Flash, which is executed as an immediate continuation of the change-over.

There should be no hesitation whatever; in fact, the right fingers can start to double inward before the right side is fully toward the audience, thus blending one sleight into the other so that the change-over, which suggests that both hands are empty, is concluded with a flash that certifies the fact. This is followed by the usual return, as already described.

CRISSCROSS FLASH

Facing a trifle toward the left, with the ball palmed in the right hand, the right hand is placed against the back of the left hand (Fig. 194). The left hand is then swiveled to the right, so that the fingers of both hands are pointed toward opposite elbows (Fig. 195). Swing the body to the front, and turn the arms inward. The right hand is cupped, particularly at the outer edge, and keeps the ball hidden as the hands are brought palm front (Fig. 196).

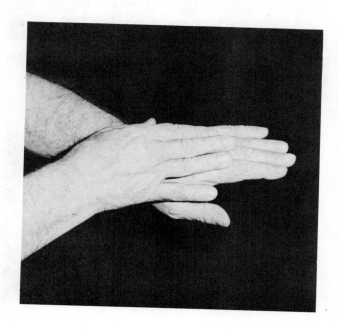

CRISSCROSS FLASH
Fig. 194. Preliminary position for Crisscross Flash. Right hand presses palmed ball on back of left hand.

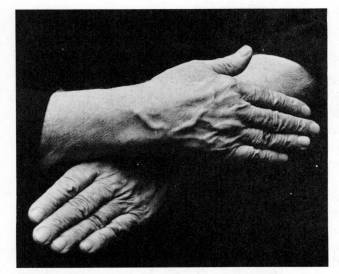

Fig. 195. Left hand swivels downward to the right as body is turned forward. Note cupped position of right hand.

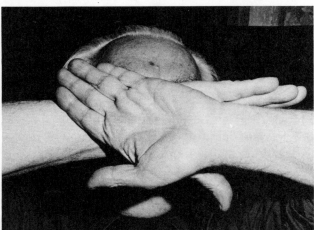

Fig. 196. Hands raised and turned palms frontward at eye level. Right hand conceals palmed ball by pressing it against back of left hand.

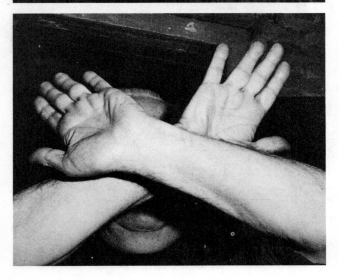

Fig. 197. Hands now thrust toward opposite elbows, showing both palms empty. Ball rolls between wrists and is concealed there.

The right hand is then pushed toward the left elbow and the left hand toward the right elbow. Maintain the horizontal position of the forearms while rolling the ball between them to the wrists. The arms are then raised above eye level, and in the same action, the hands are swiveled toward each other to form an X. The ball serves as a pivot. This brings the right palm into view along with the left, and both hands are shown empty (Fig. 197). An immediate reversal of the process brings the ball back to the right palm.

NOTE: This flash was a favorite with Okito, who worked in oriental costume and crossed his arms when showing his hands actually empty, both as a preliminary gesture and following a series of manipulations. The same policy can be applied to other moves, the more they are adapted to the performer's natural style, or the more he conforms his style to the moves, the more effective and deceptive they become.

THUMB FLASH

This starts like the Cross-over Flash, but is kept within a limited area, which speeds the action and makes it effective at very close range. Facing at an angle to the left, the right hand, with ball palmed, is cupped against the back of the left (Fig. 194), with fingers of both hands toward the left. That position is maintained as the body is turned straight front, the palms being raised toward the audience, the ball being hidden behind the left hand (Fig. 198). Simultaneously, the right hand shifts the ball to Thumb Palm position, so the tip of the right thumb can be doubled against the ball (Fig. 199).

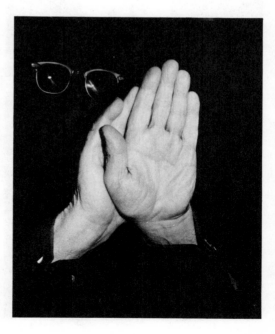

THUMB FLASH
Fig. 198. Performer now turns front and points hands upward. Ball has been shifted to Thumb-palm position behind left hand.

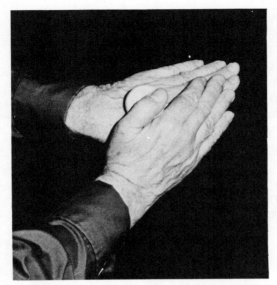

Fig. 199. Rear view shows shift in progress. Right thumb presses ball to new position.

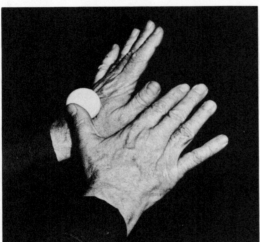

Fig. 200. Hands spread as right thumb presses ball behind left hand (rear view).

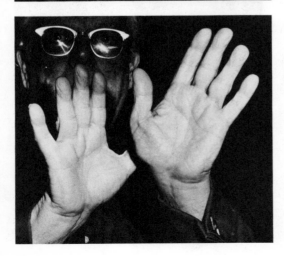

Fig. 201. Audience view of the flash at its final moment, before moves are reversed. Both hands appear empty.

From there the hands simply swivel outward, and the ball serves as a pivot for the right thumb, which keeps the ball in position behind the left hand (Fig. 200). From the audience's view, the hands are perfectly empty (Fig. 201), and the move is so natural that the missing tip of the right thumb seems of no consequence, if it is noticed at all. Rather than allow time for people to think about it, however, the moves should be immediately reversed, to bring the ball back into the right palm so that the right forefinger can point to the empty left hand as the body is turned farther to the left.

THUMB-FRONT FLASH

In this variant of the Thumb Flash, the performer faces the audience directly throughout, thus eliminating body swings. The hands are raised with backs toward the spectators; then turned and shown palms front. Finally, the backs are again shown, all in one continuous action, which is both deliberate and deceptive.

To start, the ball is palmed in the right hand. Both hands are raised to show the backs, with the tips of the little fingers touching so the hands form an inverted V. The left hand is turned palm front, partly screening the fingers of the right hand. The right hand immediately bends inward, planting the ball against the back of the left hand. The right thumb presses the ball there, so that the right hand can be spread to the right, with the tip of the thumb holding the ball hidden so that both hands can be shown apparently empty, exactly as with the Thumb Flash (see Figs. 200 and 201).

A reversal of these moves brings the hands back to the original position, and with practice the moves can be blended so that the turning of the hands seems almost simultaneous, although the right hand actually gyrates under cover of the left. Although body swings are unnecessary, they are not taboo. The performer can start while facing toward the left, swing front, then left again; but the actual moves all take place while facing frontward.

If preferred, the ball can be palmed in the left hand to start; in that case, the left thumb keeps the ball out of sight behind the right hand.

TURNABOUT FLASH

With the right side turned to the audience and the ball palmed in the right hand, this begins like the preliminary to the Simple Transfer (page 132) in which the right hand points to the empty palm of the left (Fig. 177) and sweeps the left hand from heel to fingertips. As the right hand is about to return, it pauses, and this makes all the difference.

With the left hand held horizontally and the right hand held vertically, the right fingers rest lightly on the left fingertips (Fig. 202). The left little

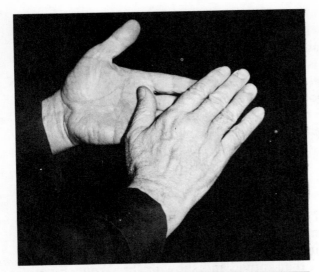

TURNABOUT FLASH
Fig. 202. Right hand, with ball secretly palmed, pausing in front of extended left fingers in preparation for transfer.

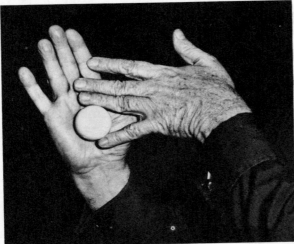

Fig. 203. Rear view shows left third and fourth fingers spread to take away palmed ball under cover of the right hand.

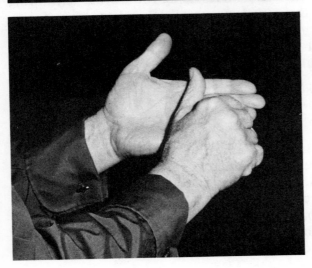

Fig. 204. Right hand forms fist in front of ball while still concealing it. Right fist begins its turnabout.

finger, however, is lowered as the right hand approaches, so that the right hand secretly inserts the palmed ball between the tips of the left third and fourth fingers, which grip it as shown in Fig. 203, a rear view.

The right fingers are then doubled down into a fist that hides the gripped ball (Fig. 204). Pressing its knuckles against the ball, the right hand revolves to the right, opening its fist as it does, so that the right fingers are pointed upward, and the right palm is wide open, and facing the audience (Fig. 205). The ball is still hidden behind the right knuckles. The right fingers are pressed together closely during the entire move.

Even the spread of the little finger is hidden along with the ball, but as with other "flashes," it would be unwise to linger. The moves are immediately reversed, and the hands are returned to their original positions (Figs. 202 and 203). The right hand again palms the ball while the left hand is raised and shows itself unmistakably empty. Its back is then turned toward the audience, and the right forefinger points toward it.

Since the right hand is plainly shown to be completely empty, the direction of attention to the left hand tends to allay whatever suspicion may lurk in skeptical minds.

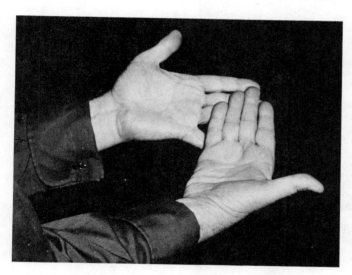

Fig. 205. Right fingers point upward, hiding ball, as palm turns frontward. Both hands are apparently empty.

FINGER FLASH

With the right side toward the audience and a ball palmed in the right hand, the right forefinger points upward toward the left hand, which is shown empty, back and front. While attention is thus directed toward the left hand, the right thumb and second finger bend inward and gain the ball in a pincer grip between their tips. The left hand, now palm front, comes down in back of the right forefinger and rests against the inbent thumb and second finger of the right hand, thus forming perfect coverage for the ball (Figs. 206 and 207).

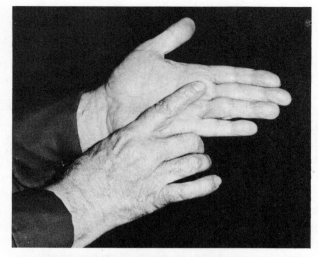

FINGER FLASH
Fig. 206. Right hand laying forefinger on left palm to prove its emptiness. Note how lower edge of left hand rests against right second finger.

Fig. 207. Rear view showing right thumb and second finger using pincer grip to tilt ball up behind left hand.

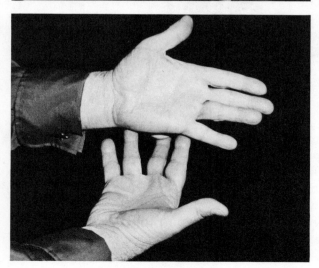

Fig. 208. Right fingers spread, with hand twisted palm-front. Ball is hidden by left hand, held by right second finger (angle exaggerated here to show placement).

This enables the right thumb and second finger to press the ball up in back of the left hand, where it is retained by the tip of the right second finger, thus enabling the right hand to twist palm front, showing itself empty, with fingers pointing upward (Fig. 208). Only the very tips of the right fingers (with the exception of the little finger) are completely out of sight behind the left hand, with the second finger supporting the ball. Again, a brief flash is followed by a reversal of the moves, bringing the ball back to the right-hand pincer grip (Fig. 206), from which it is palmed in the right hand, while the left is being shown front and back.

This flash is a good follow-up to the Pincer Vanish (page 108), as the ball is retained in the pincer grip during the vanish, putting it in position for the flash.

COLOR CHANGES

These represent a highly effective phase of ball manipulation, wherein a ball apparently changes color, usually from red to white, or vice versa, though other colors may be involved. From the audience's view, this appears truly magical; but from the performer's standpoint it consists in a secret exchange of one ball for another, combining various sleights, such as vanishes and change-overs toward that purpose.

FIST COLOR CHANGE

Facing at an angle toward the left, the performer shows a white ball in display position (Fig. 103) and places it openly on his left fist (Fig. 209). He circles his right hand around the white ball and swings his body toward the right. Drawing his right hand away and turning it palm front, he shows that the ball mysteriously changed its color from white to red.

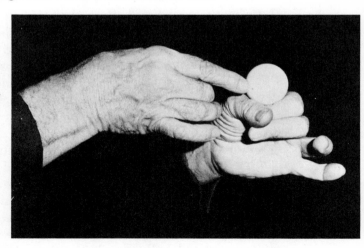

FIST COLOR CHANGE
Fig. 209. Start of Fist Color Change. Right forefinger points to white ball resting on left fist.

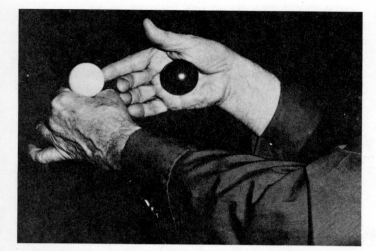

Fig. 210. Rear view of starting position, showing red ball palmed in right hand.

Fig. 211. Right hand screens white ball, so it can sink into left fist during frontward turn (rear view).

The red ball is palmed in the right hand at the start (Fig. 210). Thus, after placing the white ball on the left fist, the right hand is supposedly empty when it screens the white ball with an encircling action. The performer is turning to the right at the time, and when the hands are about full front, the left fist relaxes, letting the white ball sink into it (Fig. 211). This, of course, is still screened by the right hand; and once the white ball is deep in the left fist, the left thumb is brought above it, so the right right hand can set the red ball on the left fist with no danger of one ball clicking against the other (Fig. 212).

Continuing his swing to the right, the performer automatically brings his right hand palm frontward, revealing the red ball on his left fist, thus completing an apparent color change of the original ball.

As a follow-up, the empty right hand takes the red ball between the thumb and first two fingers. This enables the left hand to open its fingers, retaining the white ball in Standard Palm position, while the left forefinger points to the red ball (Fig. 213). In so doing, the left hand presses the

Fig. 212. White ball is now fully settled in left palm, and right hand secretly places red ball on left fist (rear view).

Fig. 213. Audience view of the left forefinger pointing to red ball in right hand. Left hand has palmed white ball in readiness for change-over.

palmed white ball against the right wrist (Fig. 214). This puts the hands in position for the Improved Change-over (page 128).

The Improved Change-over is promptly executed by pushing the left hand forward and drawing the right hand backward, at the same time swinging the hands from right to left, so that the palms slide across each other in the usual manner. This brings the white ball almost into the right palm (Fig. 215) as the right thumb and fingers reach the position where they can openly transfer the red ball to the left thumb and fingers (Fig. 216). Leaving the ball there, the right hand is drawn farther back along the left wrist, completing the palming of the white ball by pressing it firmly as it rolls into the right palm.

Thus the right hand finishes by resting against the left wrist and pointing its forefinger to the red ball now held by the left thumb and fingers. Thus by the natural act of transferring the red ball from the right hand to the left,

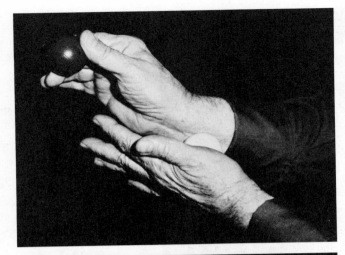

Fig. 214. View from above, showing start of change-over of white ball from left palm to right. Red ball is openly displayed throughout.

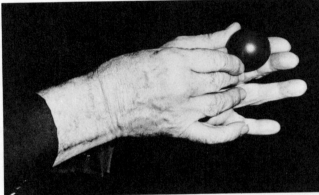

Fig. 215. Left thumb and fingers taking red ball from right hand during course of the change-over.

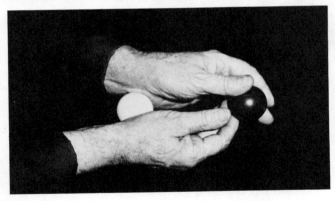

Fig. 216. View from above, showing position of white ball during transfer of red ball. By keeping fingers close together and pointed toward audience, white ball is fully hidden.

both hands have been shown apparently empty while secretly transferring the palmed white ball from the left hand to the right.

The right thumb and fingers then take the red ball again, keeping the back of the hand toward the audience. This enables the left hand to close itself into a fist as before, so that the right hand can place the red ball upon it. The color change is then repeated (as shown in Figs. 209-212), the only difference being that a red ball turns to white. Another change-over will show both hands empty. All is then set for a repetition of the original change from white to red; and so on. Or the performer may follow with:

ROLL-OVER COLOR CHANGE

This is a simple but effective change, whether worked in combination or on its own. The left hand shows a white ball in display position, then grips it in the curl of the left thumb and forefinger, tilting the hand forward so that the ball is directly toward the audience, with the right forefinger pointing toward the ball. Keeping his right side toward the audience, the performer extends his right hand beyond his left (Fig. 217) and draws his right hand toward him, brushing the white ball with his right fingers. As a result, the ball changes color from white to red.

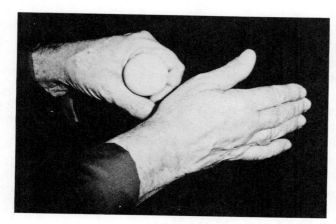

ROLL-OVER COLOR CHANGE
Fig. 217. Start of Roll-over Color Change. Right hand extended beyond left hand, ready to be drawn across white ball.

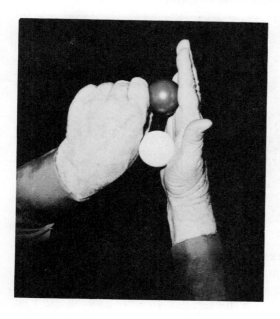

Fig. 218. Rolling action nearing completion with red ball supplanting white ball in left hand (view from above).

The move may be immediately repeated, changing the red ball back to white. In the course of repeated changes, the left hand may at any time be tilted upward, turning its palm full front, showing it to be empty, with the right forefinger indicating that fact.

The method is clear indeed, when viewed from above. The red ball is originally palmed in the right hand, which goes far enough beyond the left to press the red ball against the knuckle of the left forefinger. This action brings the heel of the right hand against the white ball. While pressing firmly, the right hand is drawn inward as it rolls the white ball over the left thumb, so that it automatically comes into the right palm. Simultaneously, the right fingers roll the red ball inward, bringing it into the position vacated by the white ball (Fig. 218).

ROLL-OVER ALTERNATE

In repeating the Roll-over Color Change, the emphasis on the emptiness of the left hand is apt to raise a question in an astute observer's mind: "What about the right hand?" The answer is to turn frontward and show the right hand empty.

The move is very simple. No roll is needed. Instead, bring the white ball directly against the red ball (Fig. 219) and push the red ball into the left fist, leaving the white ball in view when the right hand is drawn away (Fig. 220). With wooden balls, do this carefully to avoid any telltale "click." Then show the right hand empty as just described. The left hand can't be shown empty at that moment, but it doesn't matter, since all attention is focused on the right hand. However, this can be followed by the same change-over used with the Fist Color Change, thus:

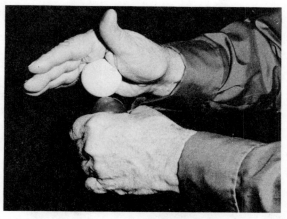

Fig. 219. View from above. Right hand uses palmed white ball to push red ball into left fist.

Swing the body to the right, stressing the empty right hand, at the same time turning the back of the left hand toward the audience and bringing the left fist upright. All the while the white ball is in open view, and a slight squeeze of the left hand will perch it on the left fist, exactly as with the Fist

Fig. 220. View from rear showing completion of change. White ball now hides red ball in left fist.

Color Change (Fig. 209, page 149). The right hand takes the white ball, enabling the left hand to assume the change-over position (Figs. 213 and 214) so the palmed red ball is secretly transferred from the left hand to the right hand as the body swings to the left.

Here, however, the right hand, instead of setting the white ball on the left fist, can place it in the curl of the left thumb and forefinger (Fig. 217) in readiness for a repetition of the Roll-over Color Change or the Roll-over Alternate. In short, the performer can switch from the Roll-over to the Fist Color Change or vice versa at any time he pleases. As a further choice he can introduce the—

FULL-FRONT COLOR CHANGE

With the right side toward the audience, the right hand places a white ball between the tips of the left thumb and the first two fingers (as in display position), and the right forefinger points to the otherwise empty left hand. The right hand is then extended upward and beyond the left hand. From there, the right hand is brought downward at a forty-five degree angle toward the body, sweeping across the white ball, which changes to a red ball during the process.

The move is simply a modification of the Roll-over. The heel of the right hand presses against the white ball, rolling it downward until the tips of the left fingers can press the red ball. Continuation of the slanting roll brings the white ball into the right palm, which retains it, while the left thumb is extended to grip the now-visible red ball along with the left fingers. After the color change, the move may be repeated, changing the red ball back to a white; then the white to a red; and so on.

To show both hands empty following a color change, the fingers of the right hand are doubled inward against the palmed ball, and the rolling action is continued past the left wrist. This enables the right hand to execute the Forearm Flash (see page 140), showing both hands palm front. In this case the Forearm Flash may be prolonged a few moments, since attention can be diverted to the red ball by twirling it slightly with the left thumb and fingers. This is in contrast to the usual Forearm Flash, where spectators are viewing the empty hands alone, making it unwise to linger longer.

The white ball, of course, is safely hidden between the back of the right hand and the front of the left wrist. As with the usual Forearm Flash, the right hand reverses its action, bringing the white ball back into the right palm, as at the conclusion of the color change. Here there is chance for further misdirection. Since the right fingers, in straightening, are approaching the red ball, they simply continue that approach, and the right thumb and the first two fingers pluck the red ball from the left hand.

As a follow-up to that natural action, the left hand is shown back and front, drawing attention in that direction. The right hand, already shown convincingly empty, now has the white ball safely and secretly palmed, while showing the red ball in display position. From there the performer can continue with further color changes of any type; but the sleight can also serve as climax to a routine, with the performer calmly pocketing the visible ball and dropping the palmed ball along with it.

THROW COLOR CHANGE

As a quick color change, this is also an effective prelude to the disposal of the extra ball. Apparently, a ball changes color when thrown from the right hand to the left. This may be repeated, then followed by a surprise vanish and reproduction to complete the routine. Since the whole procedure is fast but simple, it can best be described from the performer's viewpoint as follows:

Start with the red ball in display position in the right hand, which has the white ball palmed. With right side toward the audience, the left hand is shown back and front. The right hand pretends to throw the red ball into the left hand, but actually retains it in the bend of the fingers (see Finger Bend Palm, page 87) and releases the white ball instead. The left hand immediately closes and is raised with its back toward the audience, with the right forefinger pointing in that direction.

The left hand is then turned frontward and opened to show that the ball has changed from red to white. While attention is thus drawn to the left hand, the right fingers press the red ball into Standard Palm position. This enables the right thumb and fingers to take the white ball from the left and repeat the color change. The "throw" should be nothing more than a "drop" of a few inches, but by swinging both hands toward the left and carrying the left hand well away from the right hand, the exchange of balls is easily masked, while the action is exaggerated to the proportions of a throw.

For the sequel—as the vanish and reproduction of a red ball, with the disposal of the white—pretend to "throw" the red ball as usual, retaining it in the bend of the right fingers, but retain the white ball as well, in the Standard Palm position. Thus the left hand is actually empty when raised back toward the audience, both balls being concealed in the right hand. The right forefinger keeps pointing toward the left hand, which is turned frontward and opened with a rubbing motion to show that the red ball has vanished. The right hand immediately dips into the right coat or trouser pocket, releasing the white ball from the Standard Palm position and bringing out the red ball between the tips of the right thumb and fingers, leaving the white ball pocketed.

At first trial, the final throw and getaway may seem overbold, and the right hand somewhat cramped, but brief practice and neat timing will offset that. Since observers anticipate another "color change," the element of surprise is sufficient to hold attention on the left hand, while the right is dipping into the pocket. As an alternate, the left hand can perform the "vanish" with a tossing action, carrying eyes upward, while the right hand makes a leisurely dip.

SAMPLE COLOR-CHANGE ROUTINES

Here, in brief, are some suggested routines involving the various "color changes" just described. They have been "engineered" with misdirection fully in mind, introducing enough repetition to hold continued interest without overdoing it. The individual performer can choose whichever he likes best, or combine routines in whatever way seems best suited to his style.

Routine One: With right side toward audience and white ball palmed in right hand, place visible red ball on left fist. Swing front, executing Fist Color Change and continue to right, showing right hand empty. Transfer visible white ball to right hand and swing left, making "change-over." Put white ball on left fist and swing to the right, using Fist Color Change to turn white ball back to red. Swing left, making "change-over," and visibly thrown red ball into left hand, Repeat action, using "Throw Color Change to turn red into white. Repeat action, "vanishing" red ball from left hand, dipping right hand into pocket to bring out red ball and leave white ball.

Routine Two: With right side toward audience and white ball palmed, place visible red ball in curl of left thumb and forefinger. Execute Roll-over twice, changing red to white and back to red; then the Roll-over Alternate, leaving red ball in left fist. Swing to right, showing right hand empty, and take visible white ball in right hand. Swing to left, executing "change-over" to show left hand empty. Place white ball in curl of left thumb and forefinger; change it to red, with Roll-over Color Change. Show left hand empty, rolling red ball to tips of left thumb and fingers; then do the Full Front, changing red ball to white. Repeat, changing white back to red, but this time finish with the Forearm Flash, showing both hands apparently empty. Reclaim red ball with right thumb and fingers; drop it in pocket, along with the palmed white ball.

Routine Three: Start with right side toward audience, with white ball palmed in right hand. Place red ball in left hand, in curl of thumb and forefinger. Work Roll-over three times, so ball changes to white, red, white. Then use Roll-over Alternate, bringing white ball in view. Swing to right, so left side is toward audience, and put white ball in curl of right thumb and forefinger, with red ball still in left hand.

Now work the "Roll-over" from the left instead of the right side, a very neat variation, turning white to red; then red to white. Stop there; display white ball at right thumb and fingertips; swing to the left, doing a "change-over", placing white ball at tips of left thumb and fingers, with red ball palmed in right hand. Follow with the Full-front Color Change, turning white to red; repeat, turning red to white, finishing with the Forearm Flash.

Reclaim white ball and drop both in pocket, or follow with the Throw routine, changing white to red, vanishing red and bringing it from pocket, leaving the white ball there.

MULTIPLYING BILLIARD BALLS

STANDARD "ONE TO FOUR" ROUTINE

This is a basic "one to four" production incorporating standard sleights with billiard balls and allowing individual variations. It can be presented under exacting conditions, making it specially suitable to impromptu work, especially with balls of comparatively small diameter.

Four balls of the same size and color are used, one in each trouser pocket, with the third placed well up under the left arm and retained there, while the final ball is palmed in the right hand. Thus in readiness, the procedure is as follows:

Stand with the right side toward audience, keeping the left elbow close to the body. Extend the right arm, so the left hand can pull up the right sleeve; then bring the right hand inward and pull up the left sleeve at the elbow, both actions being merely preliminary gestures. The right forefinger points to the empty left hand, then proceeds with the Slow-motion Production, page 101, the first ball appearing in the left hand.

The right side of the body is kept toward the audience, and the right hand takes the ball between the thumb and the first two fingers, so the left hand can execute the French Drop (page 106). As the left hand opens to show that the ball has vanished, the right hand goes to the left elbow and reproduces it from there (see page 113).

Again, the ball is vanished from the left hand, either by the French Drop or the Thumb Roll (page 115). As the right hand again goes toward the left elbow, the left arm is extended and the right hand reclaims the ball from beneath the left arm. Actually, the right hand retains the palmed ball and brings out the ball that was already concealed beneath the arm, showing it in display position.

To multiply the ball from one to two, place it between the tips of the thumb and forefinger of the left hand, which is held palm toward the audience (Fig. 221). During this action, point the right fingers directly upward and tilt the left fingers a trifle downward. This puts the left first and second fingers in perfect position to grip the ball concealed in the right palm (Fig. 222). Almost in the same move, the left hand is raised, turning its back toward the audience, while the right forefinger points upward. When done with a flourish, this gives the effect of a second ball suddenly appearing above the first (Fig. 223).

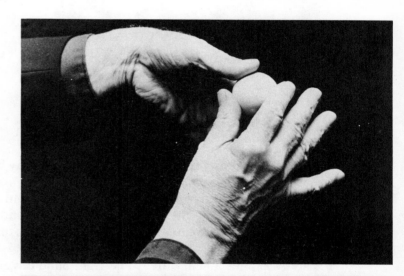

STANDARD "ONE TO FOUR" ROUTINE
Fig. 221. Right hand places visible ball between left thumb and forefinger, thus enabling left first and second fingers to gain ball from right palm.

Fig. 222. Back view of left fingers secretly taking ball from right palm, so left hand can be brought upward.

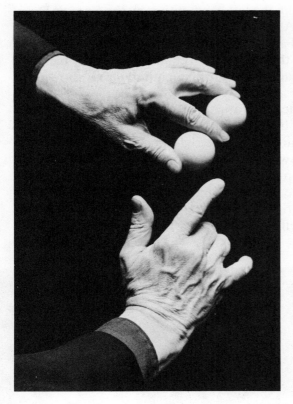

Fig. 223. Completion of
move. Right hand points
to left-hand production of
both balls.

For a close-up production, another touch may be introduced: As the left
hand is raised and turned frontward, the right hand follows it, hiding the
action of the left hand with a rapid, wavy action, as though making mystic
passes. When the right hand slows its motion and gradually draws away —
behold! — the multiplication has been accomplished by seemingly magical
means.

Now comes a neat move. The right hand covers the lower ball and pretends to pluck it from between the left thumb and forefinger, but the ball is
actually retained. While the right fist is slowly closing, the left hand is tilted
forward and downward so that the back of the left second finger is directly
toward the spectators when the right fist moves away (Fig. 224). Due to
the tilt of the left hand, the upper ball held between the left forefinger and
second finger partly hides the lower ball, which is still gripped between the
left thumb and forefinger.

To complete the effect, the left third finger is moved inward between the
balls until it presses the side of the left forefinger, and the fourth finger
moves along with it (Fig. 225). Even the left thumb can aid in the concealment by moving a trifle below the ball but toward the forefinger while the
left third and fourth fingers press down upon the hidden ball, thus helping
to retain its position.

This move is extremely easy, because the hand is simply tilted to hide
one ball behind the other. Compressing the fingers in the manner described

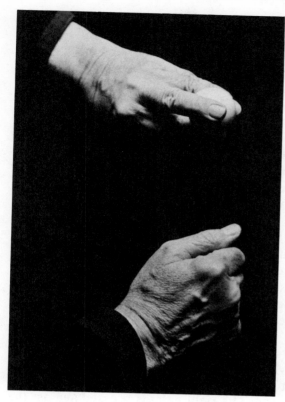

Fig. 224. Left hand tilts
so back of second finger is
toward spectators. Upper
ball hides lower ball,
which right hand pretends
to take away.

serves as a cover-up if the audience is not directly opposite the front ball. Keeping the left hand in motion also helps to hide the ball, so lower the left hand toward the left side, while the right hand draws attention its way by moving downward and then upward with a quick tossing action. These moves give the effect of the ball disappearing in air from the right hand.

Fig. 225. Rear view
shows how left fingers
help to conceal lower ball.

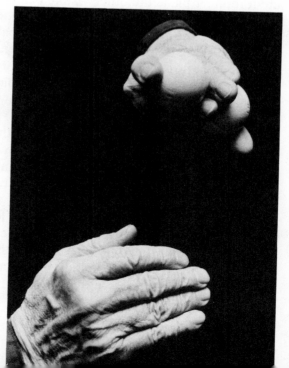

The right arm should be immediately to the right so that the palm of the right hand can be turned toward the spectators and shown empty, with its fingers pointing upward.

Looking upward, the performer exclaims: "Gone! Up there? No—" and turning toward the left, he brings his left hand upward with a rapid sweep and halts it at shoulder level as he adds, "It's back up here!" With that the left hand is displayed back and front, showing that the vanished ball has returned. Done briskly, this is deceptive. Even if sharp spectators catch on, it serves as a preliminary gag to soften them for the neat move that follows.

Again, the right hand covers the upper ball, but this time actually plucks it from the left, which immediately tilts forward and downward as before. The right hand, with its back toward the audience, then makes a tossing motion, exactly as before. This time the ball is retained in the right palm (see Toss Vanish, page 116), but the back of the right hand is kept toward the audience, as the right hand points upward and the performer comments: "Up there? No!" Naturally, the "wise" spectators look toward the left hand and the others also expect it to reappear there, but they are all fooled when the performer raises his left hand and shows the single ball, back and front, saying, "Up here? No!"—and adds, "It's down here, in my pocket."

Dipping his right hand in his trouser pocket, he retains the palmed ball and brings out the extra ball, which is in readiness there. The right hand places the ball between the first and second fingers of the left hand, which is turned palm toward the audience. The right palm is pressed against the left and the body is turned to the right, bringing the left side toward the audience, enabling the hands to execute a "Change-over Palm" (see page 127), leaving the hidden ball in the left palm.

The right thumb and forefinger take one ball from between the first two fingers of the left hand. The right hand turns palm front and the left thumb and forefinger place the other visible ball between the tips of the right first and second fingers. This enables the second and third fingers of the right hand to take the third ball from the left palm, and the right hand swings upward, turning its back toward the audience with a brisk rotary motion, now showing three balls instead of only two.

The left hand plucks the topmost ball from between the right second and third fingers, while the right hand drops downward and backward, to carry attention momentarily in that direction. The left hand repeats the Toss Vanish, retaining the ball in its palm; and the right hand swings upward as the performer comments, "Up here? No—down here—in the pocket." Only two balls are showing in the right hand, and to reclaim the third, the left hand dips into the trouser pocket and brings out the fourth ball, keeping the third palmed.

With left side toward the audience, the left hand places the visible ball between the second and third fingers of the right hand, which is held palm front. This enables the right third and fourth fingers to grip the final ball between their tips (Fig. 226), taking it secretly from the left palm. With an

Fig. 226. Rear view of left hand placing third ball between second and third fingers of right hand enabling right third and fourth fingers to take final ball from left palm.

upward swing, the right hand turns its back toward the audience, and there is the fourth ball, mysteriously produced, to complete a "full hand" of four balls between all the fingertips.

The left hand takes the balls singly and knocks them against the others to prove their solidity, then lays them one by one on the table, as a finale to the "one to four" production. Or they can be dropped in the coat pocket, if preferred. By having an odd ball of a different color in the upper section of the right coat pocket, the performer can retain one ball in his left hand and put the other three in his right coat pocket, picking up the odd ball on the way out and palming it in his right hand. He is then set for a series of color changes with the ball he kept in his left hand. See Color Changes, pages 149 to 157.

RAPID "ONE TO FOUR" ROUTINE (WITH SOLID BALLS)

For a quick, somewhat impromptu multiplication from one ball to four, the following is quite effective, especially as the four balls can be handed around immediately following their appearance, proving that all are quite solid. You must be "set" for this effect so that you can present it without delay, but that is not really a drawback, as the preparation itself can be done rapidly, while you have turned away on some trifling pretext.

Set up the four balls as follows: Ball 1, which is shown openly, between the tip of the right thumb and the joints of the forefinger, so the fingers can be extended in a direct line with the hand. Put Ball 2 in Back Palm position between the first and the fourth fingers of the right hand. Balls 3 and 4 are double palmed in the left hand by the Finger Bend and Standard Palm positions, respectively.

Stand with your left side toward the audience, right hand well extended at shoulder level, palm front, but tilted a trifle forward. Keep the left hand

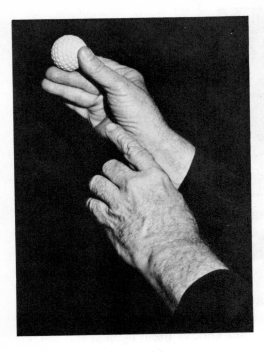

Fig. 227. Start of sequence. Left forefinger indicating ball displayed in right hand.

loose at the left side, its back toward the audience but ready to make a pointing gesture up toward the right. By gauging the proper angle, Ball 1 helps to conceal Ball 2 by filling the slight gap between the first two fingers, with the right thumb providing added coverage, while the forward tilt prevents people from glimpsing the hidden ball through the gap between the third and the fourth fingers.

Here the natural manner in which Ball 1 is exhibited, even to the spread of the first two fingers, offsets the ordinarily cramped position of the "back palm." Ostensibly, the second finger is extended forward to support Ball 1, though the thumb and forefinger provide the actual grip. The result is a perfect preliminary display (Fig. 227).

This hides the real situation (Fig. 228), and to cover it further, the right hand should begin a rather rapid rotary action, finishing with a forward, downward sweep that brings the knuckles upward. With the sweep, draw your two middle fingers inward (Fig. 229), so their tips can move upward and around the hidden Ball 2, which is safely clipped between the first and the fourth fingers. This brings the middle fingers on top of the second ball, enabling them to roll the ball a trifle forward, with the little finger providing a helpful shove to complete the action. This brings the ball directly above the forefinger, where it can be retained by the second finger alone, making a very effective production of the second ball (Fig. 230).

These moves, though exacting, are not difficult, as they can be done gradually, with some comment, as: "Here you see a solitary billiard ball, which doubles itself into two —" With that, the left hand moves upward, takes Ball 2 between thumb and forefinger, placing it between the right

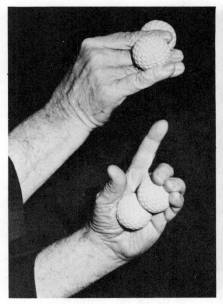

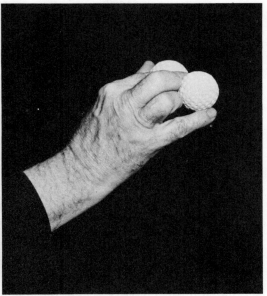

Fig. 228. Rear view of setup. Second ball is back-palmed in right hand and two more are double-palmed in left.

Fig. 229. Middle fingers are drawn inward so they can be carried up and over the back-palmed ball, still clipped between other fingers (rear view).

Fig. 230. Right middle fingers roll ball to top forefinger, completing production of second ball.

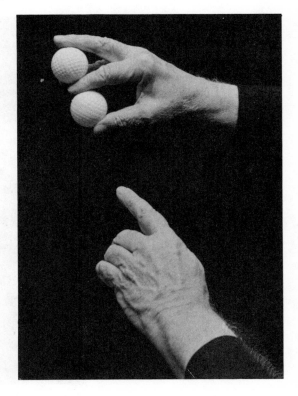

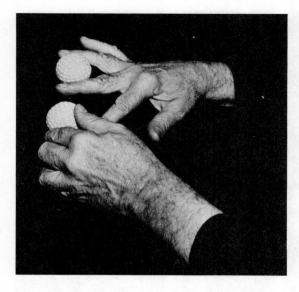

Fig. 231. Left hand moves Ball 2 up to space between right middle fingers and is now moving Ball 1 to space between right thumb and forefinger.

second and third fingers. Then, moving downward, the left hand takes Ball 1 between thumb and forefinger and places it between the right first and second fingers (Fig. 231).

Completion of that action brings the hands in perfect position to pluck Ball 3 from the bend of the left fingers, which it does immediately (Fig. 232). Then, practically as a continuation of that hidden action, the right hand gives a quick twist, bringing its thumb upward and its palm frontward, displaying three balls instead of only two (Fig. 233).

Fig. 232. Rear view shows right thumb and forefinger secretly plucking Ball 3 from bend of left fingers.

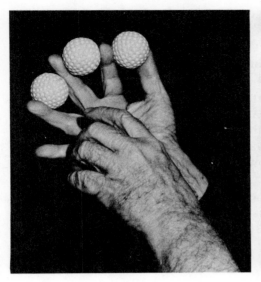

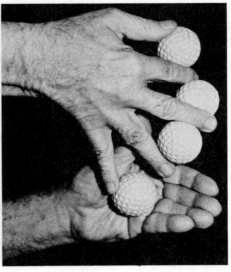

Fig. 233. Finish of right hand's upward twist brings palm frontward to show third ball.

Fig. 234. Rear view of right third and fourth fingers plucking Ball 4 from left palm.

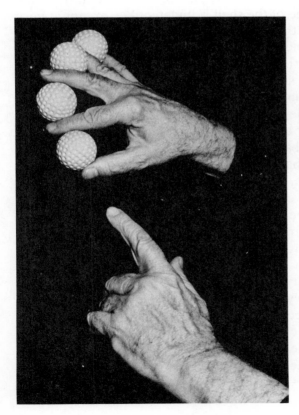

Fig. 235. Right hand sweeps upward and turns back toward audience as it "produces" fourth and final ball.

A good procedure during the action just described is to count the balls while placing them: "One—two—," then make the twist, adding emphatically: "And three!" But the action does not stop there. The left forefinger verifies the count by tapping the three balls in order, beginning with the ball between the right thumb and forefinger, continuing outward from there. As you count, "One, two, three—" your left palm comes directly in front of the space still remaining between the right third and fourth fingers, enabling them to pluck Ball 4 from the left palm (Fig. 234). All in the same action, the right hand makes an upward sweep, turning its back toward the audience. The left hand points upward as you announce: "And one is four!" (Fig. 235).

Be sure to turn the right hand far enough forward so that the fourth ball can be plainly seen between the last two fingers; the effect will be truly magical as the ball is hidden all during the turn and therefore appears to pop from nowhere.

BALL AND SHELL

As an adjunct for multiple billiard ball manipulation, the half "shell" is both useful and unique. It consists of one half of a hollow ball, which fits snugly over a solid ball, so that from the front, the two appear to be a single, solid ball. If both are the same color, the "ball" can be shown back as well as front, as the thin edge of the shell is undetectible, except at very close range; and even then, if the hand is kept in motion, as by turning it back and forth, the edge will not be noticed.

When a ball of another color is inside the shell, the ball cannot be seen if the shell is kept full front; and similarly, the shell itself will appear to be a solid ball if held alone in the same manner. In that case, care must be taken in regard to angles, though the shell itself can be shown as close up as desired to a single spectator or a clustered group. Hence angles should be "covered" by moving farther back.

The ball and shell may be handled as a single ball, as long as care is taken to keep the shell in place. For manipulative purposes, they are usually shown as a single ball between the tips of the thumb and the forefinger (Fig. 236), with the back of the hand toward the audience. Both sides of the "ball" can be shown by turning the hand palm front, then back again, provided—as already specified—that ball and shell are both of the same color. The thumb and forefinger, pressing both the edge of the shell and the ball itself, provide the necessary clamp to keep the two in place.

To cause one ball to "multiply" to two, which is the primary purpose of the Ball and Shell, bring the second finger down behind the thumb, press the finger against the ball, and continue with an upward motion that automatically rolls the ball out of the shell (Fig. 237). This action is covered by a wavy or circular motion of the hand, or by a long swing of the arm. This

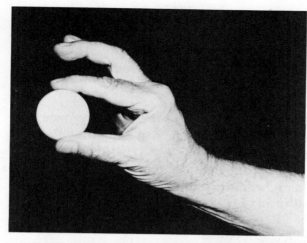

BALL AND SHELL
Fig. 236. Ball and shell
shown as a single ball.
Shell is toward audience.

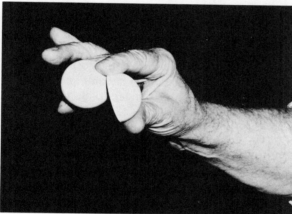

Fig. 237. Side view of
second finger rolling ball
backward and upward
from shell.

is continued until the ball is over and above the forefinger, where it is retained by downward pressure of the third finger (Fig. 238). To spectators, it seems that a second ball has instantly appeared above the first. A reversal of the moves causes one ball to vanish, leaving only a single, as at the start.

Fig. 238. Second ball appearing between first two fingers. Shell passes for original ball.

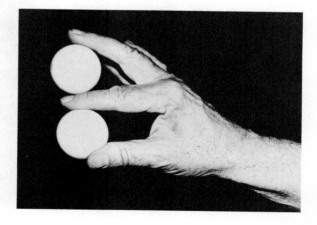

TWO-WAY TWIRL

The single ball can be shown front and back if the hand is kept in motion to hide the edge of the shell. When the shell and ball are shown as two, the shell must naturally be kept full front—that is, with its rounded or convex side toward the audience, but by use of a clever two-way twirl, both balls can apparently be shown back and front.

As soon as the solid ball has been rolled above the forefinger (see Fig. 238), bring the third finger immediately below the ball and swing the second finger backward, carrying the ball from the forefinger to the third finger (Fig. 239). The second and third fingers are then swung downward, bringing the ball below the thumb, which places the shell on the second finger, still keeping the shell full front (Fig. 240).

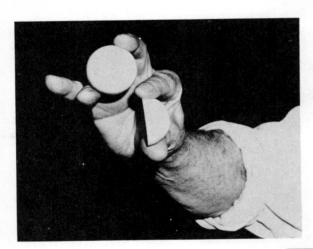

TWO-WAY TWIRL
Fig. 239. Start of twirl.
Ball is shifted to position
between second and
third fingers (side view).

Fig. 240. Second and
third fingers swing down-
ward and thumb places
shell on second finger
(side view).

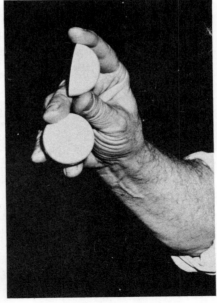

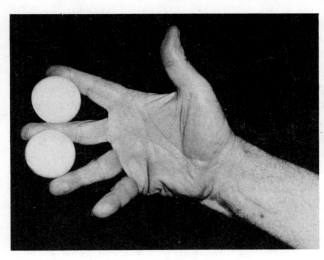

Fig. 241. Audience view of completed twirl. Shell (between first two fingers) and ball (between second and third fingers) still appear as two solid balls.

Once the shell is firmly pressed between the second and third fingers, the thumb can be freely raised and the whole hand spread wide, with the open palm toward the audience, showing the shell between the forefinger and the second finger and the ball between the second and third fingers, each appearing to be a solid ball (Fig. 241).

After a momentary pause, the moves are reversed. Bring the thumb beneath the shell, so it can be taken between the thumb and forefinger (Fig. 240) and then brought down in front of the solid ball and below it (Fig. 239). This enables the second finger to roll the ball from the third finger onto the forefinger so the shell and ball again are displayed as they were originally (Fig. 238).

In effect, two solid balls have been given a double twirl, showing them back and front from all angles; but in actuality, the shell has not moved at all. It serves practically as a pivot, with the hand being swung forward, then backward around it, as a test will show. Some practice is required to do the move smoothly, but once acquired it is highly deceptive and worth the time spent in perfecting it. You can always pause to let the left hand approach and adjust the ball or shell in order to avoid a slip.

This move is used with the One to Four and other multiplication effects that follow, along with other twirls that will be described in due course.

"ONE TO FOUR" (WITH SHELL)

This original routine is worked with the regulation set of three balls and a shell—all one color—as sold by most magic shops. Ramifications involving extra balls, some of different colors, will be described later. Beforehand, place the ball and shell in your right trouser pocket, a single ball in the left trouser pocket, and another ball in the right coat pocket, along with an ordinary handkerchief to be used with the routine.

When ready to perform, turn away long enough to get the ball from the right coat pocket and palm it in readiness for a production. If you have to do this rather openly, bring the handkerchief from your pocket and lay it on the table, or hand it to someone, saying that you will need it later. This gives you an excuse for going to your pocket, and in so doing, you secretly palm the first ball while bringing out the handkerchief. You are then ready to go.

Either produce the first ball immediately, a good method being the Fingertip Production (page 91), as the subsequent productions will all be at the fingertips. Or begin by showing both hands empty, with a suitable change-over, transfer, or flash, singly or in combination; then produce the first ball. Here one or two vanishes and reproductions may be injected, according to your skill in or liking for single-ball work. Then proceed with:

Ball to Ball and Shell: Using either the French Drop (page 106) or the Roll Vanish (page 111), apparently take the ball in your right hand, actually retaining it in the left hand, with your left side toward the audience. Pretend to place the ball in your mouth with your right hand, press your tongue into your left cheek so as to resemble the ball, and give the bulge a push with your left forefinger, following with a gulp as though swallowing the ball. Show your right hand empty, dip thumb and fingers into your trouser pocket, and bring out the ball and the shell together, showing them as a single ball, which spectators think is the original ball, which you now have palmed in your left hand.

One Ball to Two: With the left side still toward the audience, use the roll-up to bring the ball from the shell, thus making one into two. This can be followed by the Two-way Twirl, which naturally adds to the effect. Either way, you will have the shell between your right thumb and forefinger, with the solid ball between forefinger and second finger (Fig. 238). This puts you in position to "load" the palmed ball from the left hand, a simple but highly vital procedure with the "multiplying" routine.

You bring up your left hand in order to take the upper ball from between the right forefinger and second finger. In raising the left hand, keep its fingers downward, so that the palmed ball eases into the finger bend, where it remains concealed in the Finger-bend Palm (page 87). The left thumb and forefinger start to take the shell, but merely adjust it slightly (Fig. 242). That brings the other left fingers behind the shell, enabling them to introduce the palmed ball from the finger bend into the shell, a very neat and well-concealed maneuver (Fig. 243).

The left thumb pauses only long enough to guide that action, then continues upward, along with the forefinger, so they can take the upper ball instead of the lower ball and shell. Don't go for the upper ball too rapidly, or you may have to load the shell in downward fashion, which spoils the rhythm, because the moment the left thumb and forefinger grip the single solid ball, the hands should be drawn apart, leaving the united ball and shell between the right thumb and forefinger.

Here the left hand swings down below the right, so that if wooden or

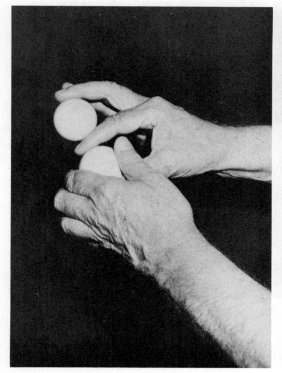 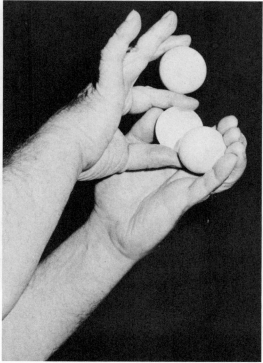

"ONE TO FOUR"
Fig. 242. Left hand ad-
justs shell, which sup-
posedly is the original
ball. Left hand holds
palmed ball.

Fig. 243. Left hand in-
troduces hidden ball into
shell from Finger-palm
position.

thick plastic balls are used, they can be rapped together to emphasize their
solidity (Fig. 244). In that case, you can keep your left side toward the audience, though a momentary frontward turn will impress the rapping
process upon viewers at your left. But when using lighter or compressible
balls, it is better to face full front, so that the hands can be spread apart at
shoulder level, as though comparing one ball with the other.

Third-ball Production: Swing to the right again, keeping shell and ball
between right thumb and forefinger, while the left hand places its solid ball
between the right second and third fingers, leaving a gap (Fig. 245). Here
some skilled manipulators prefer to replace the upper ball between the
right forefinger and the second finger, as shown earlier (Fig. 238). The
right third finger can then be lowered below the ball to roll it up between
the second and third fingers.

Either way, the production of a third "ball" is now a simple matter.
From the position shown, the left second finger is lowered beneath the ball
and shell, so it can bring the ball from the shell with a backward and

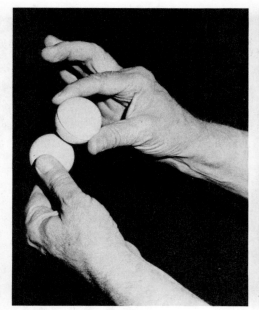 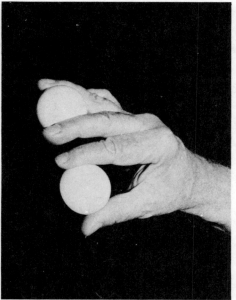

Fig. 244. Left thumb and forefinger bring down single ball so right thumb and forefinger can tap it with ball and shell.

Fig. 245. Audience view of shell and ball combination between right thumb and forefinger, and solid ball between second and third fingers.

upward roll (Fig. 246). This produces a third ball between the fingertips (Fig. 247), which, reading upward, actually consist of shell, ball, ball.

However, instead of the conventional roll-up, a very deceptive reverse move may be used that gives the effect of a twirl. With ball and shell between right thumb and forefinger (Fig. 245), tilt the hand backward, bring it palm front, and then transfer ball and shell from between thumb and forefinger to the gap between right forefinger and second finger. If you want, you can spread the hand wide, keeping it tilted slightly backward, so the shell will stay on the ball, with its rim resting against the first two fingers. Then bring the thumb to its previous position (Fig. 248).

Now swing the hand forward and downward, pressing the thumb against the bottom edge of the shell. The shell stays full front between the tips of thumb and forefinger, while the ball is retained between forefinger and second finger. The ball is then rolled up automatically from the shell, and comes into sight when the back of the hand is toward the audience in the customary three-ball position (Fig. 249).

Getting Final Ball: Grip the top ball between left thumb and fingers, carrying it downward behind the lower ball and the shell (Fig. 250). As you do this, nestle the ball in the bend of left fingers and ease it into the shell (Fig. 251). Close the left fist with its back toward spectators. Pretend to

Fig. 246. Side view of right second finger rolling ball from shell to fill gap between shell and other solid ball.

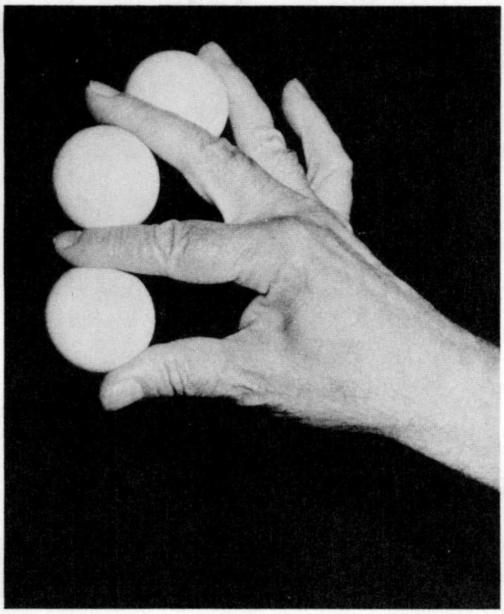

Fig. 247. Solid ball fills gap after conventional roll-up, thus giving the appearance of three balls.

Fig. 248. Start of alternative reverse move. Right thumb places ball and shell appearing to be a single solid ball, in gap.

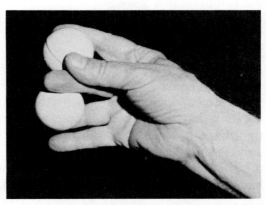

Fig. 249. Side view of right hand completing forward downswing. Ball remains in gap and shell is carried downward.

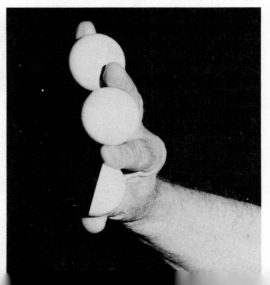

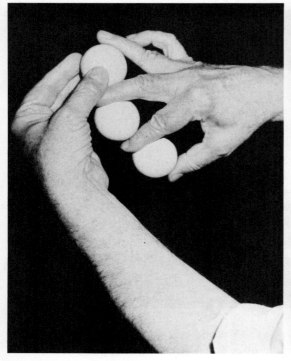

Fig. 250. Left hand takes
top ball to bring it down
behind lower ball and
shell. Note left thumb in
front, ready to press ball
into bend of left fingers.

Fig. 251. Rear view show-
ing left hand secretly introducing ball from finger
bend into waiting shell.

place the ball in your mouth with the left hand and go through the swallowing imitation, or pretend to squeeze it away with your left fingers. Turn the
right hand palm front so that spectators see only two balls there. The left
hand is shown empty. Dip left hand into your trouser pocket and bring out
the solid ball. Place it between the second and third fingers of your right
hand, as though you had simply reproduced the vanished third ball (Fig.
252).

Fig. 252. Replacing third
ball between right fingers
after bringing it from
pocket with left hand.

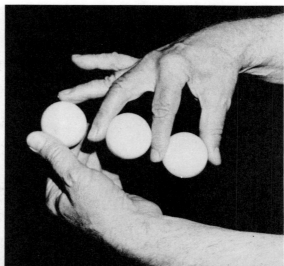

Fourth-ball Production: The left hand, in adjusting the balls at the tips of the right fingers, can palm off the shell and then take the top ball between the left thumb and forefinger, so that the right hand can rap the other two against it, demonstrating their solidity, or simply to compare them for size. The left side is kept constantly toward the audience, so the left hand can secretly add the shell to the ball by simply squeezing the ball in the hand. The right hand lays the other two beside it, then picks up ball and shell between the right thumb and forefinger.

The left hand then places one ball between the right second and third fingers and another between the right third and fourth fingers. Now there is a gap between the right forefinger and second finger, so the right hand can be raised and waved slightly as it produces a fourth ball exactly as it did the third. This can be done with a roll-up by the second finger, or by the reverse action, where the hand is turned frontward (Fig. 253). However, with either of these, some performers are apt to have difficulty retaining all four balls in place, particularly if large balls are used.

Fig. 253. Fourth-ball production using conventional roll-up or reverse twist (side view).

Here is a good answer to that situation. After bringing the third ball from the left trouser pocket, place it between the second and third fingers of the right hand (Fig. 250) so that the only empty space is between the third and fourth fingers. The left hand then moves downward, adjusting the middle ball, and finally does the same with the bottom ball, which actually consists of a ball and shell.

During that action, the right hand is tilted downward, so that the bottom ball drops into the bend of the left fingers, under cover of the left hand (Fig. 254). As the left hand is lowered with the ball, spectators still see the shell and take it for a solid ball. As the right hand is raised, still exhibiting three balls, the left presses its stolen ball into the conventional palm. The left forefinger then points to the shell and balls displayed by the right hand while you count, "One—two—three."

Then, with your left side constantly toward the audience, you thrust the left hand forward, counting "Four!" With that, you produce the palmed

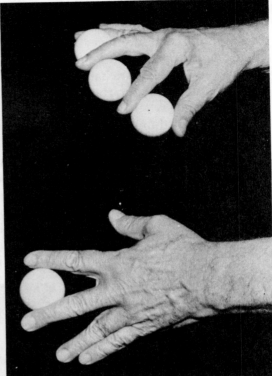

Fig. 254. Rear view showing fingers of left hand stealing ball from shell so ball can be palmed in readiness for production.

Fig. 255. Left hand produces ball at fingertips (see page 91), while right hand displays shell and two balls to resemble three balls.

ball by the Fingertip Production (page 91). Thus you have produced a fourth ball in the same magical fashion as the previous three, at your fingertips (Fig. 255), but with your left hand instead of your right, which serves as a neat variation. The left hand then places its ball between the uppermost fingers of the right hand, thus filling all spaces.

FINAL-BALL VANISH

This is an excellent device for the close-up worker, for it enables him to climax a billiard-ball routine by getting rid of the final ball entirely. This is done with the aid of an extra ball, identical to the others in the set, which is previously prepared as follows:

Take a yard of cord elastic and pin one end to the ball with a thumbtack while pressing the thumbtack firmly in place. Run the free end of the elastic through the belt strap of your trousers just in back of your left hip and draw it through the belt straps in back, around your right side, and clear to the front, until the ball reaches the left hip strap. Then tie the free end of the cord to the nearest belt strap, allowing a slight slack, so the ball will dangle a few inches in front of the left hip strap, where it is hidden by your coat.

At the finish of a ball routine, when you are down to a single ball, face the audience and vanish the ball from your right hand by the French Drop, so your left hand, which secretly palms the ball, can reproduce it from the right elbow. Repeat the vanish from the right hand, but this time turn your right side toward the audience, remarking that the ball has gone to your left hip pocket. Reach beneath your coat with your left hand, keeping your left side out of sight, and actually put the ball in your left hip pocket, leaving it there.

Bring your left hand forward and pick up the duplicate ball that is dangling from your hip strap. Hold it at the tips of thumb and fingers so that the thumbtack and the attached elastic are completely concealed between the left thumb and fingertips and then swing boldly to the right, bringing your left hand fully into view with the reproduced ball at the very tips of your left thumb and fingers.

There, you really have hooked them, as the saying goes. They think that it is the same ball that you vanished, but they would like to see you do it again, so that they could really catch it. And that's when you really do it. With your left side toward your audience, the ball at your left thumb and fingertips, and the stretched elastic concealed behind your left forearm and underneath your coat, you simply bring your right hand forward and downward, cup it over the ball, as if to take it away—and let go with your left hand!

The ball will be gone before anybody knows it, you included, except you don't tell them where it went. Just wring your hands together as though hoping it would be gone, then turn front as you spread your hands to show that it has gone. The ball will be right back where it started, dangling from the belt strap that's just behind your left hip.

That's magic!

"FOUR TO EIGHT" PRODUCTION

When performing the "one to four" production before a sizeable audience, a surprise climax can be introduced by displaying the four balls with a wide sweep of the right hand and then coming up with an instantaneous production of another set of four in the left hand, thus concluding the routine.

This is accomplished with the aid of a special gimmick consisting of four balls, preferably of rubber, which are strung together on a double length of wire. The upper end is turned downward to form a hook, while the lower

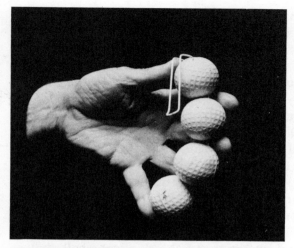

"FOUR TO EIGHT"
PRODUCTION
Fig. 256. Back view of
four-ball gimmick used in
"Four to Eight" Produc-
tion. Double length of
wire supports balls and
ends in hook at top.

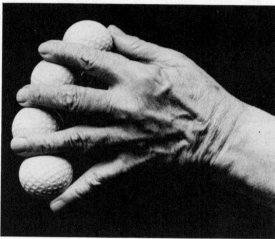

Fig. 257. Gimmick as
seen by audience. Per-
former appears to produce
four additional balls in-
stantaneously with left
hand after completing
"One to Four" Produc-
tion with right hand.

ends are simply bent back into the fourth or lowermost ball of the set. The
wire is curved so that the tips of the thumb and fingers can gain a grip on
the balls from in front, with the hook extended downward in back, as
shown in Fig. 256.

The appliance shown here is hung in the right inside pocket of the coat,
with the hook over the upper edge. Standing with the left side toward the
audience, the right hand completes the "one to four" routine, being extended nearly at arm's length. The right hand then makes a long, downward sweep to knee level as the body pivots forward, and continuing the
sweep, the right side is turned toward the audience, so that the right hand
can be extended an arm's length to the left.

Just as the body reaches the frontal position, the left hand is thrust beneath the coat and the left thumb and forefinger grip the uppermost ball of
the wired set, drawing it upward from the inside pocket and upward
toward the shoulder, so that by the time the right side is toward the audi-

ence, the gimmick is entirely clear of the pocket, allowing the left hand to lower it beneath the coat.

The right hand then makes a reverse sweep back to its original starting point, pivoting the body so the left side is again toward the audience. During that action, the left hand is drawn from beneath the coat and follows along behind the right forearm. This automatically brings the back of the left hand toward the audience, so that the hooked end of the gimmick is hidden behind the uppermost ball and the four balls appear to be an ordinary set of singles, as shown in Fig. 257. As the right hand is extended to arm's length, the left hand is brought up beside it and the doubling from four to eight is complete.

Either a box or a bag should be handy so the two sets of balls can be dropped out of sight; or a few loose items should be lying on a table so that the wired set can be laid behind them. If doing the "one to four" left-handed, the gimmick should be the reverse of the one shown here, so it can be hung in the left inside pocket of the coat.

WHITE AND RED TRANSPOSITION

This excellent routine with two white balls and a red can be performed at close range with baffling results. You display the three balls in conventional fashion at the fingertips of your right hand; then drop the red ball in an empty box, measuring about five inches in each dimension. Stating that you will magically transpose a white ball with the red, you vanish a white ball from your right hand, while your left hand plucks the red ball from your right elbow and replaces it between the right fingers. Then, dipping into the box, the left hand brings out the missing white ball.

To prove that miracles can happen twice, you repeat it in reverse. You drop the white ball back into the box, showing a white and a red in the right hand. Instantly, the lone red vanishes and is found in the box, while the white ball that was in the box appears at your right elbow. Then, for a climax, you leave the red ball in the box, vanish one of the two whites, and find it with the red ball. All three balls may then be given for examination.

All this is accomplished with the aid of a "ball and shell," which are utilized purely for a "vanish" and not for "multiplication." The requirements are a white shell and ball, a single white ball, and a red ball. To start, you place the white ball and shell between the right thumb and forefinger; the single white ball between the tips of the right forefinger and second finger; the red ball between the tips of the right second and third fingers. This gives you two whites and a red, which can be shown as three solid balls, back and front.

With your left hand, you pick up the cubical box and show it to be entirely empty. Setting it upright on the table, your left hand takes the red ball and either knocks it against the white to prove "all solid," or simply shows it and replaces it between the fingers. Either way, this gives you sufficient reason to adjust the three balls, and in doing that, your left hand secretly steals the lower white ball from the shell in the bend of the left fingers, which shift it to the standard palm. The left thumb and fingers then take the red ball and dip into the box, as you state that you will drop the red ball there. Actually, your left hand drops the palmed white ball and palms the red ball instead.

As matters now stand, the right hand apparently shows the two white balls at the tips of the right thumb and fingers, but the lower white ball is actually the shell. The left hand has the red ball secretly palmed, and there is a solid white ball in the box where the red ball is supposed to be.

Stating that you will cause a visible white ball to change places with the red ball in the box, you begin a wavy motion with your right hand, enabling the right second finger to roll the solid white ball down into the shell. The left hand goes to the right elbow and produces the palmed red ball, promptly placing it in the space between the right forefinger and second finger from which the white ball just vanished. The left hand is turned palm frontward, showing itself entirely empty, and dips into the box, bringing out the missing white ball.

Here, the left hand can temporarily place the white ball between the tips of the right second and third fingers, so that the left hand can pick up the box, tip it forward, and show that it is definitely empty. The left thumb and fingers then take the upper white ball and drop it back in the box, without dipping the left hand from sight.

Tipping the box to show it empty is not absolutely necessary, so if you prefer, you can simply drop the white ball back into the box after bringing it out. Either way, you now are showing a solid white ball—actually ball and shell—between the right thumb and forefinger, with a solid red ball above it, between the right forefinger and second finger, while there is a white ball in the box. So you state that you will repeat the transposition, but this time in reverse, bringing the the white ball from the box by sending the red ball there.

Adjust the right-hand balls with your left hand, and in the process steal the white ball from the shell, retaining it in the bend of the left fingers. Follow with an up-and-down motion of the right hand, rolling the red ball down into the white shell. Be careful to keep the shell straight front, as a bad angle might give some spectators a glimpse of the red ball, which you have temporarily "vanished." With your left hand, immediately produce the white ball from the right elbow and insert it between the forefinger and second finger of the right hand, replacing the vanished red ball. All in the same action, steal the red ball from the shell in the bend of the left fingers, shifting it to the Standard Palm position as you dip your left hand into the box and bring out the red ball at the tips of your left thumb and fingers, casually turning the left palm frontward to show the hand otherwise empty.

Done briskly and smoothly, this is perhaps the neatest and most deceptive of "ball and shell" manipulations ever devised. The red ball is vanished in a twinkling, the white ball produced an instant later, and the red ball found in the box immediately after replacing the white ball in the right hand. By keeping a jump or two ahead of your audience, you not only have them baffled by what has occurred so far, you also have set the scene for further deception. To all appearances, you are back about where you started, with two white balls at the tips of the right thumb and fingers, plus a red ball in the left hand, ready to go in an empty box.

But actually, people are viewing a white shell below a white ball, each representing a solid ball. The red ball, of course, is solid; but the box, instead of being empty, contains a solid white ball, with its presence unknown to anybody except yourself. Taking advantage of that situation, you drop the red ball back into the box, stating that this time you will cause a white ball to pass invisibly from your right hand and join the red ball in the box as a result of magical attraction.

With the usual up-and-down motion, the right second finger rolls the solid ball down into the shell and you show it back and front, proving conclusively that one of the white balls has vanished. Turning your left hand palm frontward, you let everyone see that it is completely empty; then you dip your left hand into the box and bring out the red ball and the white ball, between the tips of your left thumb and first two fingers. By facing full front, you can then point your left thumb and fingers toward the audience, which enables the right hand to place its white ball and shell between the tips of the left second and third fingers, with the shell full front. This wedges the ball and shell firmly in place between the fingers.

The left hand, with thumb upward, can then be shown from all angles, if kept sufficiently in motion to hide the join of the ball and the shell. The right hand removes the ball and the shell as one, placing them together in the right coat pocket; then does the same with the solid white and solid red ball, giving each a slight toss before pocketing it.

Another way, especially suited to exacting close-up conditions, is for the right hand to work the shell and the ball into the bend of the fingers, with the fingers cupped around the shell. The right hand then places the ball between the second and third fingers of the left hand, retaining the shell in the bend of the right fingers. The left hand can then show the three balls under the very eyes of the spectators, even giving them for examination, while the right hand picks up the box by the rear edge, with fingers inside and thumb outside. This enables the right hand to tilt the box forward, showing it empty, while keeping the shell concealed in Finger Palm position within the bend of the fingers.

The right hand can then lay down the box and pocket the balls one by one, adding the shell to the first ball that it takes from the right fingers. Or, if the balls have been given for examination, the left hand can take them back singly, transferring each ball to the right hand, which pockets a ball while the left hand is reaching for another. The shell simply goes along with the first ball. Another way is for the right hand to set the box upright and simply let the shell slide down into it, adding the three balls singly and putting the box away.

Instead of a box, a bowl can be used, or even a round cardboard container, provided it is deep enough to prevent anyone from looking in at a downward angle and seeing a ball that has been temporarily left there. If the box or container has a lid, you can carry the balls inside, opening it to take out the balls and start the routine, then putting them away and closing the box at the finish. Balls—and shell—of any contrasting colors may be used, as two greens and one yellow; but two whites and a red are best, as they make up the set of three commonly used in the game of billiards, and therefore are appropriate for the trick.

The great feature of this effect is that although a shell is used, no multiplication is involved. People therefore suppose that only three balls figure in the routine; and the fact that you have an extra white at your disposal, thanks to the shell, goes totally unsuspected. Instead of producing balls from the elbow, as already described, the left hand can pluck them from the air with a grasping motion, or between the tips of the first two fingers, by the Fingertip Production. Timed to the "vanish" of a ball from the right hand, this is very good.

A particularly effective close-up procedure is worked as follows: Instead of "vanishing" a ball from one hand and "producing" one from the other, bring the left hand with its palmed red ball in front of the right hand, covering the white ball that the right hand is showing in the space above the shell, which passes as a white ball. The right second finger rolls the white ball down into the shell, and the left hand leaves the red ball in its place, moving away to reveal the transformation. This same move can be used to change a red ball to a white and to take away an upper white ball, which the left hand can then pretend to throw into the box.

FOUR-BALL TWIRL

Following the production of the fourth ball, you can introduce a real "convincer" in the form of a simple "twirl," which apparently shows all four balls front and back, to prove their solidity. With the shell appearing as a ball between the right thumb and forefinger, along with the three solid balls between the other fingertips, you begin a slow, emphatic count of "one—two—three—four" starting with the shell, which you tap lightly with your left forefinger.

Keeping your left forefinger against the far edge of the shell, you turn your right hand downward, so its palm comes toward the audience. Simultaneously, the pressure of your left forefinger keeps the convex side toward the audience, so that it continually appears to be a solid ball. Actually, the shell remains stationary. It is the hand that rotates from back to front. (Fig. 258).

The twirl takes place on the count of "one," while the left forefinger presses the edge of the shell as the right hand comes palm front (Fig. 259). From there, the left forefinger moves to the other balls, continuing the count. You then repeat the count in reverse, starting upward from the ball

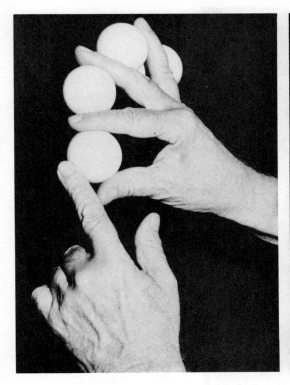

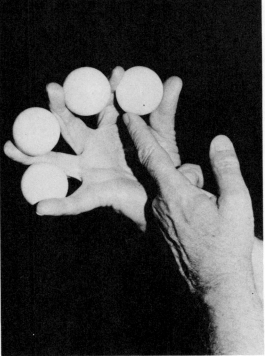

FOUR-BALL TWIRL
Fig. 258. Left hand completes downward count of four balls. Note forefinger's position in readiness for twirl.

Fig. 259. Audience view of completed twirl. Pressure of left forefinger has kept convex side of shell continually toward spectators.

between the right third and fourth fingers, which is now the lowermost ball. As you reach the shell on the count of "four," raise the right hand a trifle, so the left hand can turn its palm directly toward the spectators. This casual showing of the empty left hand enables the tip of the left forefinger to hook the lower edge of the shell (Fig. 260). The right hand is then swung upward, so its back comes toward the spectators; and the shell, retained by the left fingertip, does a reverse pivot between the right thumb and forefinger, again keeping its convex side continually toward the audience (Fig. 261).

Thus, all during the maneuver, the shell appears as a solid ball, but the difference between the forward twirl and the reversal is both subtle and essential. In the forward twirl, the shell, in a sense, is *pushed* by the left forefinger (Figs. 257 to 259). So the move should be deliberate to keep it constant, which is natural enough, as you are just finishing your count. To push it back would be impossible without changing the position of the left forefinger. Hooking the shell is therefore the only course, as the shell is

Fig. 260. Left forefinger neatly hooking edge of shell at finish of upward count in preparation for reverse twirl.

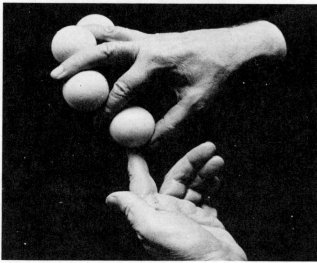

Fig. 261. Right hand finishing upward turn, bringing its back toward audience and automatically completing twirl.

pulled back into its original position (see Figs. 260 and 261). The reversal, incidentally, can be done more rapidly, which is helpful toward the next series of moves.

It is also possible to dispense with the reversal and use the following procedure: Keeping the right hand palm front (see Fig. 259), the left thumb and fingers take each ball in turn, beginning with the lowermost, and draw each ball entirely clear of the right hand, immediately replacing it, as you count upward: "One—two—three." With the count of "four," you take the shell just as if it were a solid ball, removing it entirely with the left hand, retaining it while your right hand swings upward and turns forward to reclaim it between thumb and forefinger. This puts the four "balls" exactly as they were.

Whichever procedure is used, things are now set for the next stage of the routine, which runs as follows:

"FOUR TO ONE"

Having produced a ball from nowhere and magically made it into four, you now go "down the ladder" from four to one, but with a few neat and rather necessary embellishments in between. The left hand starts proceedings by plucking the uppermost ball between thumb and fingers, to bring it down behind the other three held in the right hand (Fig. 262). The left thumb, in front, presses the ball into the bend of the left fingers, so when they reach the shell, they can secretly insert it there, with the left hand covering the action (see Fig. 251).

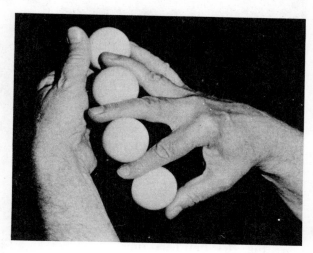

"FOUR TO ONE"
Fig. 262. Start of sequence. Right hand is about to bring top ball down behind the others.

The left hand closes into a loose fist, as though it held the ball, and by raising the left hand and blowing on it, you can apparently rub the ball away with your left thumb and fingers. At the same time, the right hand should be turned palm forward, showing only three balls there (Fig. 263). Here, by keeping the right hand slightly in motion, the shell and ball will appear as a solid ball, even though the edge of the shell is toward the audience.

Turn the back of the right hand toward the audience, adjusting the three balls with the left hand, thumb in front, fingers in back. This enables the left fingers to steal away the ball from the shell, keeping the ball concealed in the bend of the left fingers (Fig. 264).

The right second finger now rolls the "middle" ball downward into the shell, reducing its "three" to two—a single ball between the second and third fingers; and the shell and ball between thumb and forefinger. Simultaneously, the left hand presses its finger-palmed ball against the right elbow and draws it into sight (Fig. 265). Well timed, this is a very deceptive procedure, giving the effect of a ball traveling down the left sleeve and out through it. The right first and second fingers are immediately spread so that the left hand can replace its ball there, again giving the right hand three solid balls, one being a ball and shell (between thumb and forefinger).

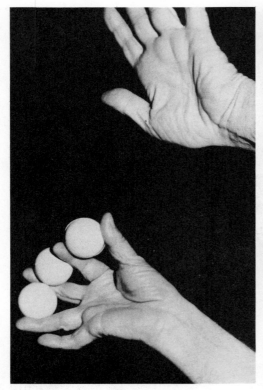

Fig. 263. Left hand rubs ball away, while right hand turns palm frontward to show only three balls left (side view).

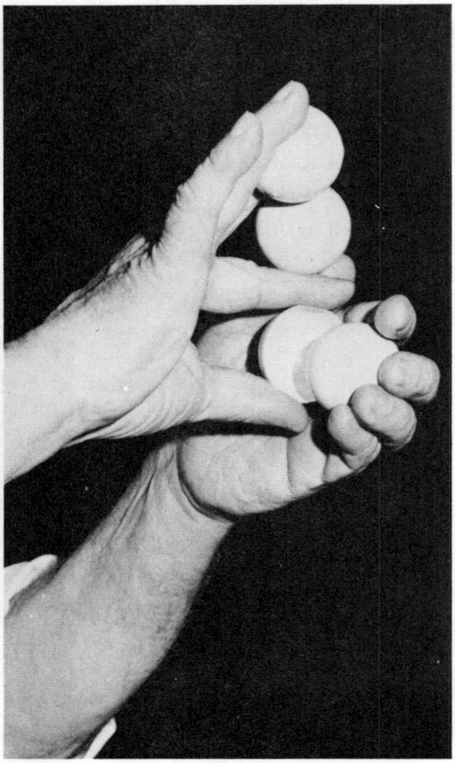

Fig. 264. Left hand steals vanished ball from shell while readjusting the "three" balls (rear view).

Fig. 265. Side view of right hand vanishing middle ball by rolling it into shell. Left hand immediately brings solid ball from right elbow.

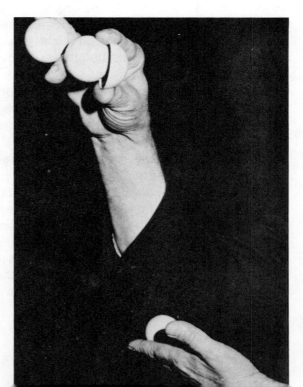

In making this replacement, you automatically steal the ball from the shell in the bend of the left fingers. The right hand again rolls the "middle" ball down into the shell, leaving the right hand with two balls instead of three. The "third ball"—which you just stole!—is already in your left hand, but instead of going to your right elbow, you reach into your left coat pocket and bring it from there. Placing it back between the right first and second fingers, you repeat the "steal" and again send a ball to your left coat pocket.

This could be done indefinitely; and actually, you should repeat it two or three times, to condition your audience for the surprise that is to follow. Your real objective is to get rid of that *extra ball* without anyone knowing it; and here is the perfect way:

Bring your left hand from the pocket, leaving the ball there, but keep your hand loosely closed as if it contained the ball. Bring your left hand up to your right, and move as if placing the imaginary ball between your right first and second fingers, which are spread to receive it (Fig. 266). Actually, under cover of your left hand, your right second finger rolls the ball up from the shell into the waiting space (Fig. 267). When your left hand moves away, people see the three balls back where they belonged, between the right thumb and first finger, first and second fingers, second and third fingers. But now they are seeing only a shell and two solid balls. The real third ball is safely stowed in your left coat pocket; and no one knows it except you!

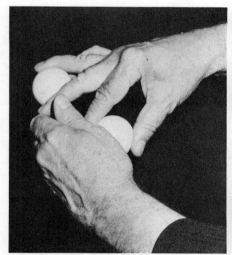

Fig. 266. Grant's move. Performer pretends to bring vanished ball from pocket and replace between other two. This is an exact copy of actual replacement.

Fig. 267. Rear view. Right second finger secretly rolling ball up from shell so left hand can move away to show it as the ball that was replaced.

This neat disposal of the third ball was devised by Gen Grant, and is utterly deceptive. The fact that the third ball already went to your pocket two or three times is enough to make even the keenest observers think that you are doing the same thing once more. This catches them on the "off-beat," ready to be baffled further.

There is, however, another very effective way of getting rid of that extra ball, which may be used as a variation. After bringing the third ball from your pocket a few times, you finally send it there again and bring out your left hand empty, simply leaving the ball in the pocket. Staring at your empty left hand in surprise, you suddenly look toward your right hand; and at that moment, roll the ball from the shell up between your first and second fingers. That puts three balls back where they belonged; and nobody will realize that you disposed of an odd ball during the process, because most people don't even know that an "extra" ball is involved.

You now proceed to get rid of another ball entirely. Simply take the top ball of the three with your left hand, bring it down behind the middle ball, and leave it in the shell, which represents the bottom ball. Keep your left hand closed, as if it contained the top ball; then simply rub the ball away, with your left thumb and fingers. That leaves you with only two, both in the right hand: one a ball and shell; the other a single ball. In adjusting them with the left hand, you "steal" the ball from the shell; then, with the right hand, you roll the other ball down into the shell, vanishing one ball, and immediately reproduce it with your left hand from your right elbow (Fig. 268).

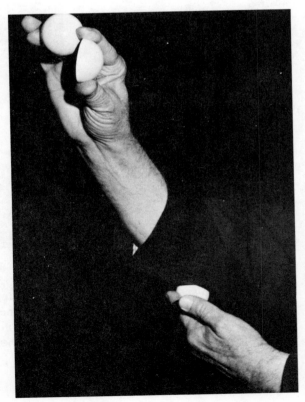

Fig. 268. Side view shows right hand vanishing upper ball by rolling it into shell, with left hand "finding" ball at right elbow.

This move is worth a repeat, as the left thumb and forefinger can replace the ball between the right first and second fingers, while the remaining fingers of the left hand steal the lower ball from the shell, palming it in the bend of the left fingers. Both actions can be blended into one, making this one of the neatest moves in ball and shell manipulation. This can be followed by another vanish of the upper ball by rolling it into the shell, while the left hand again reclaims it from the right elbow.

Good though this move is, it should not be overdone. One procedure here is to lower both hands to knee level, keeping their backs toward the audience. Each hand contains a single ball, between the tips of its thumb and forefinger; but the left hand holds a solid ball, the right hand a shell and ball showing as a single ball. Facing directly front, the left hand pretends to push the ball through the knees, actually palming it behind the left knee, then emerging with the back of the left hand still toward the audience. Simultaneously, the right hand goes behind its knee and rolls the ball from the shell, so it emerges, showing two. By a reversal of these moves, the right hand apparently sends a ball back through the knees to the left hand, which reclaims it from in back of the left knee. A bit of comedy, but still good magic, if not overdone.

Your best step here is to send the ball through the knees from right to left; then turn to the right and place the left-hand ball between the right forefinger and second finger, while the left hand steals the ball from the shell, just as you did after "finding" the ball at your elbow. In fact, you can omit the knee comedy if you want, and simply use this as a follow-up to the elbow routine. But now, when you vanish one of the balls from your right hand, your left hand dips into your coat pocket, leaves the palmed ball there, but pretends to bring it out and replace it between the forefinger and second finger of the right hand. This is simply a repeat of the Gen Grant move described earlier with the right second finger rolling the ball up from the shell under cover of the left hand's pretended replacement.

Now, with a wavy motion of the right hand, you roll the ball into the shell and turn directly frontward, showing shell and ball as a single ball. In doing this, point both hands upward, showing both palms empty. If working at very close range, keep both hands in motion, so that no one can note the edge of the shell while you are turning it with your right fingers, and so that it faces toward the onlookers. From then on it will be unnoticeable.

Your next step is to vanish the final ball. To do that, you must first dispose of the shell. One good way is to turn to the left, casually cup your right hand, so that the ball and shell sink down into the bend of the right fingers, where by rolling the ball with your thumb and fingers, you can easily bring the shell beneath. Turning farther left, you now throw the ball from the right hand into the left hand, retaining the shell in the bend of your right fingers, with the familiar "finger palm." If you still have the handkerchief in your right coat pocket, you can throw the ball openly, so that everyone sees it go into the left hand; and remarking that you now need a handkerchief, you reach into your pocket with your right hand, secretly leaving the shell there and bringing out the handkerchief.

If, however, the handkerchief is lying on the table, as suggested earlier, make a quick, short throw, hiding the ball as you transfer it from your right hand to your left hand. Then thrust your right hand into your pocket, leaving the shell there, and as eyes turn suspiciously in that direction, bring your right hand into view, showing it empty, as you remark, "You thought I tried to fool you, didn't you? Not at all. I really put the ball into my left hand." Pointing your right hand toward the left, you open your left hand and show the ball there, with no one suspecting that during this bit of byplay you got rid of the shell that nobody knew was there. You then pick up the handkerchief with your right hand.

Either way you work it, you now have the ball in your left hand and the handkerchief in your right. With your right hand, place the ball on your left fist and cover it with the handkerchief, using it to vanish the ball by the Ball and Silk Vanish, described on page 122. You finish that by rolling the "vanished" ball inside the handkerchief, which you simply thrust into your pocket.

FIFTH-BALL ROUTINE

Here is an original elaboration of the Multiplying Billiard Balls that adds greatly to the effect, as it involves the production of a fifth white ball, plus a color change from white to red under seemingly difficult conditions. For this extended routine, you need an extra white ball, which is placed beforehand in the left trouser pocket, along with the ball already there; and also a red ball, which is placed in the left coat pocket, along with a small red silk handkerchief.

Proceed with the "one to four" routine until you have produced the third ball and you are showing three balls—actually shell, ball, ball—at the tips of the right thumb and fingers. As usual, you then "vanish" the uppermost ball by sliding it down into the shell and pretending to blow it away. Your left hand then brings the missing ball from your trouser pocket, but in this case, you secretly palm the extra ball and bring it along with the invisible ball that you place between the second and third fingers of your right hand. You then turn the palm of your right hand toward the audience to show three solid balls, and you can keep it that way while you reach forward with your left hand and produce a fourth ball by the finger-tip production. The left hand places this ball between the tips of the right third and fourth fingers, giving you four solid balls, and you emphasize this by turning your right hand downward and forward, with the left hand pointing to each ball as you count them downward, "one—two—three—four."

In finishing the count, the left hand adjusts the ball and shell between the right thumb and forefinger, treating them as a solid ball. In so doing, the left hand takes away the ball in the bend of its fingers, which press it into the palm of the left hand. As part of that same move, the tip of the left fore-finger presses the edge of the shell and gives it an automatic half twirl so the right hand can turn palm front again (Fig. 269).

Now comes the neat production of the fifth ball, a real surprise! The right thumb and fingers are pointed upward, displaying the "four" balls, palm front. The left hand glides upward and is placed palm to palm with the right hand, secretly pressing the hidden "fifth" ball into the right palm. The left hand is then swung across the right wrist, revealing the fifth ball as the center of a cluster held by the right hand (Fig. 270). The right hand simultaneously tilts downward so that its fingers point outward to the right.

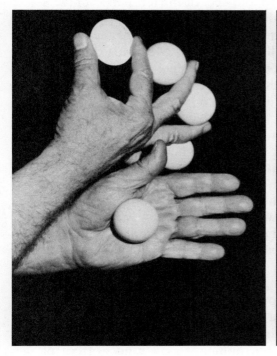

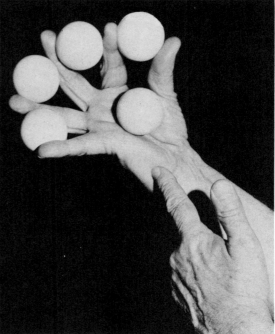

THE FIFTH-BALL ROUTINE
Fig. 269. After completing twirl, left hand (with palmed ball) goes below right hand, which has turned palm front (rear view).

Fig. 270. Left hand has moved away and points to fifth ball, which has appeared in right hand.

SPECIAL COLOR CHANGE

Here the left hand goes into the coat pocket and brings out the red silk, at the same time palming the red ball. You brush the center ball with the red silk and state that this sometimes adds color to a white ball. You then lay the red silk over your right arm and draw your left hand across your right palm, starting from near the tips of the right fingers and come directly toward the right wrist, covering the center ball in the process.

Note that during this move, the left fingers are pointing directly toward your right and are kept close together so that they hide the white ball to the last moment. When they come clear, the spectators are amazed to see that the ball has changed from white to red and you promptly repeat the process, changing it from red back to white; then from white to red again. This is an adaptation of the Roll-over Color Change, but done more deliberately and under somewhat different conditions. You extend the left hand far enough, so that as it is drawn inward, the heel of the left hand contacts the white ball held in the right palm and rolls it toward the left wrist, so that as the hands come exactly palm to palm, the left hand can leave the red ball in its place. Continuing the inward roll, the left hand overtakes the white ball and automatically palms it, so you are then nicely set to repeat the change, this time from red to white; then white to red; and so on.

Finish the changes with the red ball in view. You can then take it openly with the left hand, pick up the red silk along with it, and put them in your left coat pocket, remarking that you always keep the red ball as a souvenir. Drop the palmed white ball in your pocket along with them; and that will leave "four" balls still in your right hand that you count. Actually, they consist of a shell and three solids, so in counting them, hook the shell with the tip of your left forefinger and do the reverse twirl, turning the back of your right hand toward the audience, while keeping the convex side of the shell toward the audience. You are then all set to reduce the balls from four to one and finally vanish the last ball, as already described in the "one to four" routine.

Note on Color Change: After making the final change to the red ball, instead of pocketing it immediately, you can inject the following moves: Take the red ball openly between your left thumb and forefinger, keeping the extra white ball concealed in your left palm. Compare the red ball with the four on display in the right hand by running it slowly up in front of them, even tapping the white balls if you want. Since the palm of your right hand is toward the audience, this brings you to the shell, which represents the uppermost ball, between your right forefinger and thumb.

Keeping the back of your left hand toward the audience, you neatly hook the edge of the shell with your left second finger and turn over the right hand, so its back is toward the audience, making the twirl as you do. Now repeat the comparison, moving the red ball up the line in front of the whites, until you reach the right little finger; then bring the red ball down behind them. During the down trip, let the palmed white ball ease into the bend of your left fingers (except the left forefinger) and you can leave it in the shell when you arrive there. Now you can show both hands back and front, with four solid white balls and one solid red and nothing to hide. Finally turn the back of the right hand toward the audience, run the red ball down the line again, and steal the extra white from the shell, so you can secretly pocket it along with the red ball and the red silk. You are then ready to continue the usual routine.

Though these extra moves may seem somewhat superfluous, particularly in a fairly fast routine, they have been included because they represent a high point in manipulation. The change of a white ball to a red ball, with immediate disposal of the white ball by sliding it into the white shell, is very neat, for it is accomplished with no false moves at a time when the hands have five balls on display. It becomes a mere matter of course to pocket the red ball later, and the fact that an extra white ball goes along with it should pass completely unsuspected.

THIMBLES

Of all the items used in close-up magic, thimbles are perhaps the handiest. They can be carried in pockets and brought out at any time to be vanished, multiplied, and even changed in color. Thimbles are adaptable to all sorts of sleights and moves that are deceptive at the closest range, yet they can be effective for platform and even stage performance.

Simple metal thimbles are excellent for manipulative work, but must be painted if used in color changes. This problem can be solved by using modern plastic thimbles, however, which come in various colors and sizes and are readily obtainable. Many magicians use specially manufactured wooden thimbles, which are larger and are available in different colors. These can be seen at a distance and are also easy to manipulate, though naturally they are not suited to close-up work, as are smaller thimbles.

The same applies to some very fine thimbles set with rhinestones that dazzle audiences with their scintillating effect when shown in the right light. Although designed to render a thimble act suitable for large audiences, there is no reason why they should not be used for close-up work as well, provided care is taken to avoid bad angles and placement too close to the audience. Some performers carry two sets of thimbles: small ones for strictly close-up work, and larger ones that can be used whenever conditions allow.

Whatever the choice of thimbles, the mode of manipulation is the same, so all the methods that follow can be used for all types of thimble work, small or large.

BASIC MANIPULATIONS

Palming a thimble is swift, easy, and effective at the closest range. Several methods are available, and these are used chiefly in vanishes and productions, as will be specified in each case, but with elaborations that will follow under separate heads. However, since a thimble is designed to be worn on the tip of a finger, that is how it should be shown in:

DISPLAY POSITION

Place the thimble on the tip of the forefinger in preparation for the moves to follow. For convenience, we will assume that it is displayed on

197

the right forefinger rather than the left, though these positions are interchangeable according to individual preference. Also, if preferred, the
thimble can be shown on the tip of the second finger at the start, yet still be
handled as effectively as if displayed on the forefinger. For special purposes, it can be shown on the tip of the third finger, little finger, or even the
thumb, as will be detailed later. But starting with the conventional forefinger display, we have the:

THUMB PALM

This is the most important move in all thimble manipulation. Starting
with the thimble on the forefinger in display position (Fig. 271), the finger
is bent inward and presses the thimble into the fork of the thumb (Fig.
272). It is gripped there (Fig. 273) and the forefinger is promptly extended
along with the other fingers, the back of the hand being shown (Fig. 274)
with the thumb pressed closely enough to the hand to hide the palmed
thimble completely.

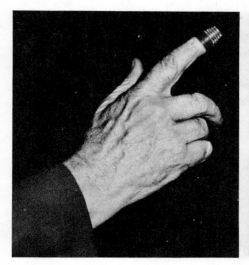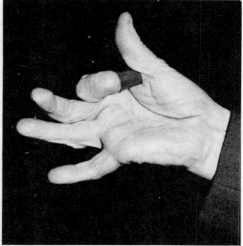

THUMB PALM
Fig. 271. Thimble in dis-
play position.

Fig. 272. Thimble being
palmed in fork of thumb
by bending forefinger in-
ward (performer's view).

For a Vanish: Stand with the right side toward the audience. Display the
thimble on the right forefinger and spread the left hand full front toward the
spectators. Swing the right hand toward the left, as if placing the thimble in
the left hand, but actually thumb-palming the thimble on the way. As the
tip of the forefinger reaches the left hand, the left fingers close around it,
forming a loose fist, which lifts upward and away, as though taking the

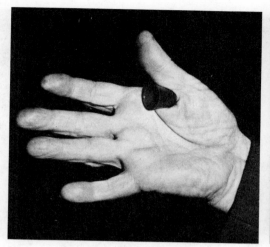

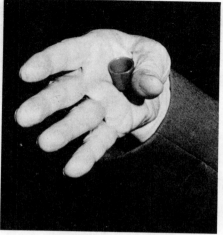

Fig. 273. Completion of
Thumb Palm. Thimble is
retained in thumb fork
while forefinger is ex-
tended (performer's view).

Fig. 274. Thimble palmed
by bending thumb inward.

thimble with it. The left hand is then opened and shown empty to complete
the supposed vanish.

This move is covered partly by the sweep of the right hand and by the
back of the hand itself, which obscures the audience's view during the pretended placement of the thimble in the left hand.

For a Production: Point upward with the right forefinger, and as the eyes
of the observers follow that motion, bring the right hand downward, press
the tip of the forefinger into the palmed thimble, and sweep the right hand
upward, at the same time extending the fingers so that the thimble appears
upon the tip of the forefinger. Here the upward sweep of the hand serves as
the coverage.

This works equally well with the forefinger and the second finger; hence
the "move" is interchangeable, so it should be utilized almost exclusively
with those fingers. It can be worked, when needed, by the third finger,
though this demands considerable flexibility. Hence, as an alternative, you
can use the:

THUMB-BEND PALM

Here the thumb is simply bent inward to press and retain one or more
thimbles against the palm of the hand (see Fig. 274). The exact position of
the thimble can range from the base of the thumb almost to its tip, according to whichever finger is involved in the procedure. Keep the hand in motion while showing its back, or lower the hand naturally to your side, and

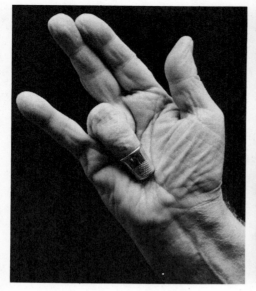

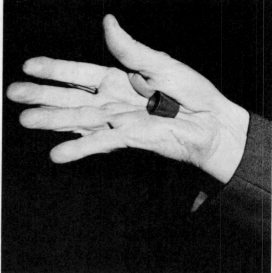

CENTER PALM
Fig. 275. Third finger
being inward to place
thimble in Center-palm
position.

Fig. 276. Fingers ex-
tended with thimble neatly
center-palmed.

the absence of the thumb will not be noticed. The vanish and the production are the same as with the Thumb Palm.

CENTER PALM

Ideal when starting with a thimble on the third finger, this consists of
bending the finger fully inward and pressing the thimble into the very
center of the palm (Fig. 275), where it is gripped and retained between the
base of the thumb and the opposite side of the hand, the finger being immediately extended (Fig. 276).

This can be worked from the tips of the second and little fingers, though
the hand may be somewhat cramped. From the forefinger, it is more difficult, but can be managed by bringing the thimble into the Thumb-bend
Palm and then rolling it to Center Palm position with the tip of the third
finger.

The vanish and the production are the same as with the Thumb Palm,
but here there are some interesting possibilities, such as vanishing a thimble from the forefinger with the Thumb Palm, reproducing it on the second
finger and vanishing it with the Center Palm, then reproducing it on the
third finger.

Or the thimble can be thumb-palmed from the second finger, produced from there by the third finger; center-palmed by the third finger and reproduced on the tip of the little finger. All such exercises give the fingers a flexibility that renders the various moves more natural and therefore more deceptive.

FINGER-BEND PALM

Start with the thimble on the tip of the right forefinger, the standard display position. As you turn the hand downward, grip the thimble between the tips of thumb and second finger so the forefinger can be drawn clear (Fig. 277). The thumb then rolls the thimble into the bend of the fingers, which encircle it loosely and retain it concealed there (Fig. 278).

For a Vanish: Perform this action with a sweep of the right hand toward the left, extending the right forefinger so that the left hand can come over it and apparently draw away the already missing thimble. The left fist is then turned frontward and opened to show that the thimble has vanished, while the right forefinger points at the left hand to emphasize that fact.

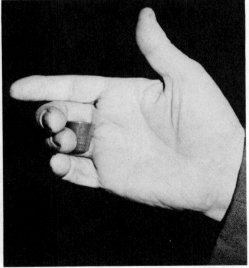

FINGER-BEND PALM·
Fig. 277. Thumb and second finger drawing thimble from tip of forefinger. Thumb then rolls thimble into finger bend.

Fig. 278. Thimble palmed in finger bend, and thumb is fully extended.

For a Production: Point upward with the right forefinger; swing the hand downward, then upward, reversing the palming moves so that the thimble appears upon the tip of the right forefinger.

THUMB TO FINGER BEND

A fairly large thimble can occasionally be exhibited on the tip of the right thumb instead of the usual display position on the tip of the forefinger. From there it can be "palmed" quickly and effectively by simply dipping the tip of the thumb into the bend of the fingers, which take away the thimble.

For a Vanish: Extend the left hand, thumb downward, back toward the audience. Show the thimble on the right thumb and thrust it up into the left hand (Fig. 279), which slowly cups as if to take the thimble (Fig. 280). Under cover of that action, the right fingers palm the thimble in their bend and the left hand moves upward, tightening into a fist, which is later opened to show that the thimble has vanished. Immediately after the thimble is palmed, the right thumb is raised to its original position, adding to the impression that the left hand carried the thimble away.

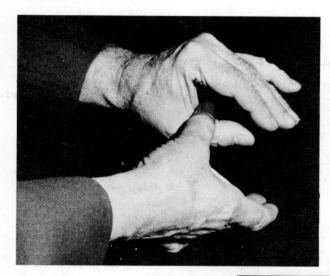

THUMB TO FINGER BEND
Fig. 279. Thimble, on tip of right thumb, is inserted into the cupped left hand (audience view).

Fig. 280. Left hand screens transfer of thimble from right thumb to bend of right fingers (rear view).

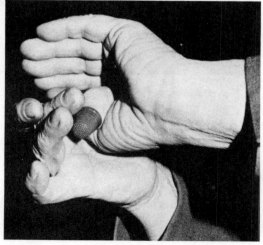

For a Production: Simply lower the right hand, keeping its back toward the audience, dip the thumb into the finger bend, and bring up the thimble on the tip of the thumb as the right hand makes an upward sweep. Or, if preferred, the thimble can be recovered on the tip of the right forefinger as described under the previous head.

TIP PALM

Though not strictly a palming method, this is so styled because it fulfills the same purpose—at least to a degree. To hide a thimble that is on a fingertip, simply bend the finger inward, keeping the back of the hand toward the audience. Thus as many as four thimbles may be simultaneously "palmed" on tips of the fingers. Generally, however, this subterfuge is used to conceal a single thimble, and to make the hand appear natural, the other fingers should also be bent inward. The one exception is the forefinger, which—if free—should point to the other hand or elsewhere to divert attention in that direction.

The Tip Palm can also be used with the thumb, provided the thimble is a fairly large one. Simply dip the thumb down into the hand so it is hidden by the fingers, which are kept close together as if in readiness for the Finger-bend Palm, which in this case is not completed. Again, the forefinger may divert attention as a "pointer."

THUMB AND FINGER CLIP

This is another device that serves as the equivalent of a palm. Starting from the display position (see Fig. 271), the thimble is taken away between the thumb and second finger, as though starting the Finger-bend Palm, but in this case, the grip is simply retained (Fig. 281) as the hand is turned

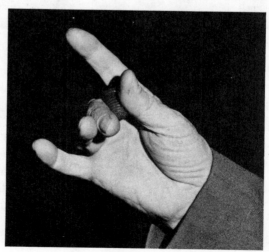

Fig. 281. Thumb and second finger take thimble from tip of forefinger, which is then extended as shown (rear view).

downward, keeping the thimble temporarily concealed. If used as a vanish, the thimble can be immediately reproduced from the Thumb and Finger Clip, or it can be fully palmed later by one of the accepted methods.

SIMPLE FINGER CLIP

Here the thimble is displayed on the tip of the second finger, which is bent slightly inward so that the first and third fingers may grip the opposite sides of the thimble and remove it (Fig. 282). The second finger is then straightened while the other fingers continue to bend inward, carrying the thimble clipped between them, thus concealing it within the hand.

A reversal of this move will bring the thimble back to the tip of the second finger; or, if preferred, it can be thumb-palmed or center-palmed by bending the second finger inward and using its tip to place the thimble in the required position.

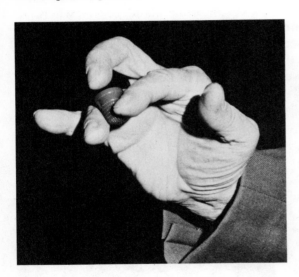

Fig. 282. First and third fingers clip thimble from tip of second finger (rear view).

BACK AND FRONT PALM

This is perhaps the neatest of all thimble sleights. Start with a thimble on the tip of the second finger, with the hand turned palm frontward (Fig. 283). Bend the fingers inward so that the first and third fingers can grip the thimble as with the finger clip (Fig. 284). Now thrust the tip of the thumb in front of the thimble to hide it momentarily. Then straighten, and in the same move bring the second finger inward and between them (Fig. 285), immediately straightening it along with the rest. This swivels the thimble to the back of the hand (Fig. 286), and the thumb is outstretched to show the hand completely empty. The fingers, of course, must be kept close together to hide the fact that the thimble is concealed in back (Fig. 287).

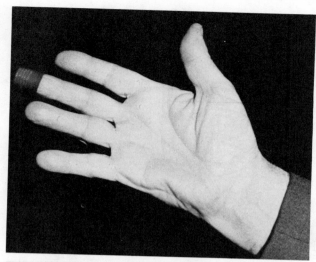

Fig. 283. Thimble shown on tip of second finger, in readiness for Back and Front Palm (audience view).

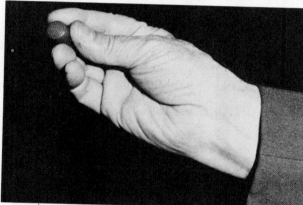

Fig. 284. Thimble clipped between first and third fingers. Thumb hides tip of second finger from audience.

Fig. 285. Second finger bends inward to swivel thimble to Back-palm position (rear view)

This completes the Back Palm, and when performed with an up-and-down motion of the hand, the vanish can be done in full view. To produce the thimble, simply reverse the moves as given, bringing it back to the tip of the second finger.

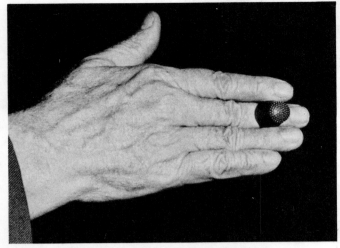

Fig. 286. Thimble clipped in Back-palm position (rear view).

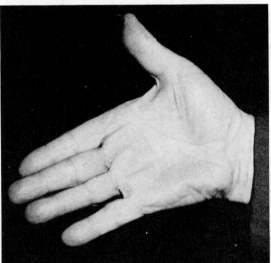

Fig. 287. Hand shown empty with thimble back-palmed. Note slight spread of little finger.

Fig. 288. Fingers doubled to hide action from audi-ence.

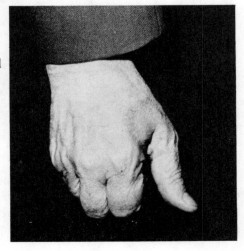

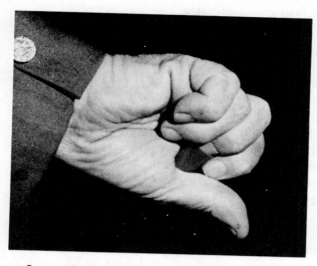

Fig. 289. Hidden action, showing tip of second finger regaining thimble and pressing it into Thumb-palm position (rear view).

Instead of producing the thimble, you can show both sides of the hand, which adds greatly to the effect. Tilt the hand so the fingers point straight downward, then double the fist by lowering the heel of hand in front of the fingers, in order to prevent the thimble from showing (Fig. 288), thus bringing the knuckles upward. Thus hidden, the second finger can double in between the first and third, inserting the fingertip in the thimble, with the thumb aiding from beneath (Fig. 289). From there it is promptly "thumb-palmed" so the hand can be straightened and its back shown.

When using the right hand, this is all done with the left side of the body toward the spectators. To bring back the thimble, you can reverse the moves as described, so that the hand comes palm front and the thimble is reproduced on the tip of the second finger. But there is another procedure that is not only effective, but also simpler; namely:

Keeping the back of the right hand toward the onlookers, turn your body well to the left, so your right side is toward the audience. At the same time bring the right hand downward and then upward with a long pendulum swing, its back staying constantly toward the spectators. As you finish the upward sweep, produce the thimble on the tip of the second finger by simply bringing it from Thumb Palm position (Fig. 273). It can be reproduced by the forefinger, but since it started from the second finger, it is more consistent for it to arrive back there.

Note on Thimble Palming: In many moves, the thumb can play a helpful but hidden part. With the Thumb Palm (page 198), the thimble can be guided into the palming position by running it down along the thumb. Whenever a thimble is produced on a fingertip, the tip of the thumb can move up and tap it firmly in place, just before its appearance. Conversely, the thumb can help loosen a thimble that is fixed too tightly on a finger.

THIMBLE VANISHES

Three basic "vanishes" have been covered under palming methods. It is best to review them briefly here, as a prelude to the more specialized routines that follow. The three basics can be classed as the "placement," where the right hand apparently places a thimble in the left, but actually retains it; next, the "draw-off," where the left hand turns back toward the spectators and apparently draws the thimble away from the right hand; and finally the "toss," in which the up-and-down motion of the right hand, ending in a quick toss, covers the actual palming action.

The difference, as by now you should know, is that the "placement" is the artistic procedure, whereas the "draw-off" is a cover-up, and the "toss" is designed to confuse the eye. But do not let those differences deceive you, for your purpose is to deceive other people. Often a placement, neat though it may be, is not too impressive to the onlookers. A draw-off, though inspired by necessity, may carry attention so effectively that the result is really uncanny; while a toss may leave the spectators so bewildered that they will accept the resultant vanish as real magic.

Keep all those points in mind when practicing the "vanishes" that follow. Vary them as needed to make the most of the audience's reactions, for that, in the final analysis, is what counts most.

TAKE-AWAY VANISH

This vanish is so simple, so clean, so effective that it has to be tried to be appreciated. When your right side toward the audience, show a thimble in display position (Fig. 271) and place it squarely in the center of the outstretched left hand. You close the left fingers and bring away the right forefinger, apparently leaving the thimble there. But when the left hand is opened, the thimble has vanished.

What you do is simply take it away on the tip of the right forefinger, by snapping the thimble straight downward and bending it inward, all in the same action (Fig. 290). Incredible though it sounds, the eye cannot follow it, even though the thimble is in actual sight during the first few inches of its descent. The move can be easy and deliberate, but not hesitant. A few tests in front of a mirror will help you time the action to perfection.

Starting with the hands at about shoulder level gives the right hand the benefit of a long downward sweep. The right forefinger should start bending inward as it leaves the left fist, and the right hand thumb-palms the thimble at the finish of the sweep. Meanwhile, the left fist is elevated slightly and turned back toward the audience, carrying attention upward. It is then turned frontward and opened with a rubbing action, with the right forefinger pointing upward to emphasize the vanish.

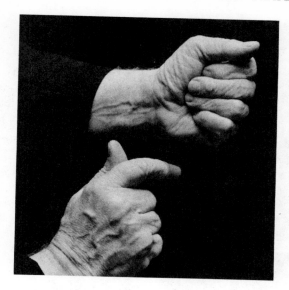

Fig 290. Left fingers close as if to snatch thimble. Right forefinger is secretly withdrawn from left palm (performer's view).

INWARD TAKE-AWAY

Similar to the Take-away Vanish but worked at a different angle, so it can be done under the very noses of the onlookers. It is also well suited to performing at a table, as you begin by extending the left hand palm upward, the fingers pointing straight away from the body. Show the thimble in display position on the right forefinger and plant it squarely in the center of the left palm, pointing straight toward the left fingers (Fig. 291), which are promptly closed to cover the thimble.

Now bring the right hand quickly toward the body, doubling the right forefinger as you do (Fig. 292). This enables you to thumb-palm the thimble in the right hand (Fig. 293), as the left hand is extended, its fist tightening, and turning downward to draw attention in that direction. The right hand makes a pass above the left, which is turned upward and opened to complete the vanish.

Fig. 291. Thimble placed in left palm at start of Inward Take-away.

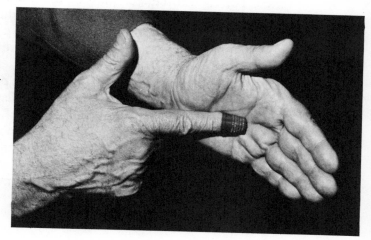

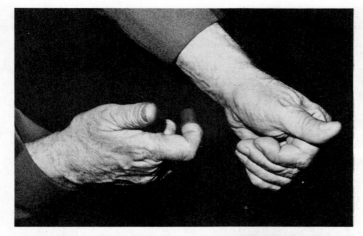

Fig. 292. Right forefinger bending inward to take away thimble as left fingers close (side view).

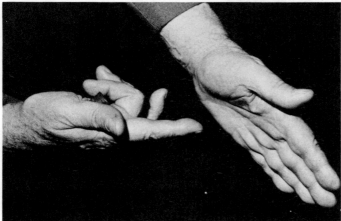

Fig. 293. Right hand thumb-palms thimble as left hand opens and is shown empty (side view).

POKE VANISH

In this deliberate vanish, the left hand is closed into a loose fist and turned at a slightly downward angle, so its back is partly toward the audience. The right forefinger shows a thimble in display position and pokes it into the left fist, apparently leaving the thimble there. The left hand is raised, turned frontward, and opened with a rubbing motion, showing that the thimble has vanished, with the right forefinger still pointing toward the left hand to emphasize the result.

The getaway is neat, indeed. During the poking action, the right forefinger is thrust almost full length into the left fist (Fig. 294), which enables the right forefinger to curl downward in back of the left thumb, where the right thumb and second finger remove the thimble under cover of the left fist (Fig. 295). As this puts the thimble in Thumb and Finger Clip position (see Fig. 281), the right forefinger can be immediately withdrawn from the left fist, pointing toward the left hand as it completes the vanish.

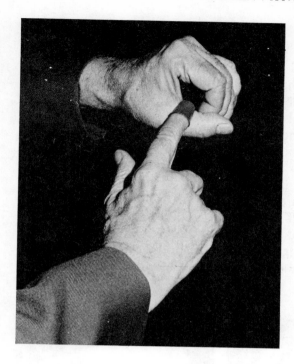

Fig. 294. Start of Poke
Vanish. Right forefinger
inserts thimble in left fist.

Or, if preferred, the left hand can finish with a tossing action, carrying attention upward, while the right, lowering a trifle, transfers the thimble to the Finger-bend Palm (see Fig. 278). Or the right forefinger can dip into the thimble and follow with the standard Thumb Palm (see Figs. 272 and 273).

Fig. 295. Right thumb and
second finger clip thimble
during poking action (rear
view).

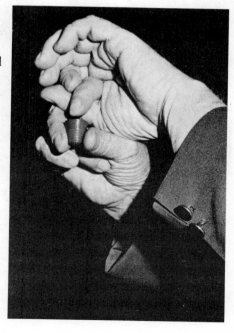

DRAW-OFF VANISH

Though similar to the Poke Vanish, this begins with the thimble in display position on the second finger of the right hand, which points straight upward so that the left hand (with back toward the audience) can deliberately encircle it in order to draw away the thimble (Fig. 296). Moments later, the thimble vanishes from the left hand.

Actually, the left hand does not remove the thimble. Instead, the right second finger is bent downward around the left thumb, so that the first and third fingers of the right hand can clip the thimble between them, thus secretly drawing it away (Fig. 297). Note that at this point, the hands should be tilted slightly downward and away from the audience, so that the left fist can pretend to draw off the thimble without revealing its actual position. The thimble is retained in the Simple Finger Clip (Fig. 281), and while the left hand is proceeding with the vanish, the right second finger bends inward, dips into the thimble, and transfers it to the standard Thumb Palm position.

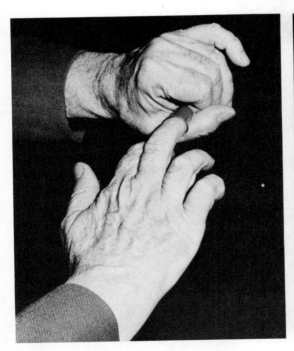 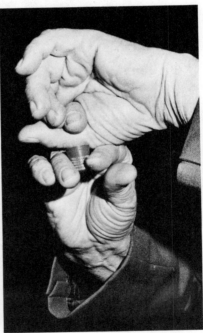

Fig. 296. Right second finger inserts thimble in left fist as start of draw-off (audience view).

Fig. 297. First and third fingers clip thimble and secretly draw it downward (rear view).

TWIST-AWAY VANISH

This move also starts with a thimble on the right second finger, with right side toward the audience: The left hand is shown palm frontward and the right hand is brought up in back of it, also with its palm toward the audience. This enables the right second finger to bend down into the left palm (Fig. 298) so that the left fingers can close around the thimble in truly open-handed fashion. The left hand apparently takes away the thimble by twisting upward so its back is toward the audience, while the right hand naturally twists inward toward the body, also bringing its back in view (Fig. 299). The left hand lifts, turns frontward, and rubs the thimble into nothingness while the right points its forefinger upward to certify the process.

The move is as easy as it is deceptive. The thimble never leaves the tip of the right second finger, which is kept bent inward while the left hand closes loosely and makes its upward twist (Fig. 300). This should be timed so the right hand furnishes full coverage as the left hand twists away. At

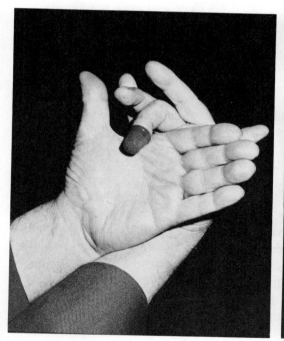

Fig. 298. Start of Twist-away Vanish showing placement of the thimble.

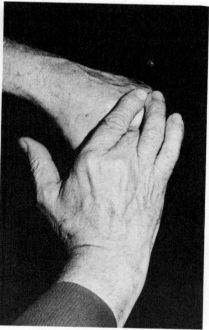

Fig. 299. Completion of the twist. Both hands rotate to bring their backs toward audience.

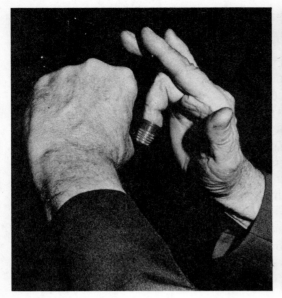 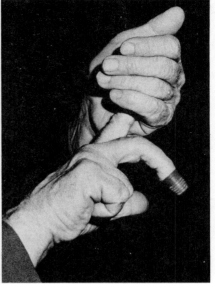

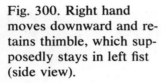

Fig. 300. Right hand moves downward and re- tains thimble, which sup- posedly stays in left fist (side view).

Fig. 301. The switch in action. Second finger dou- bles while forefinger is ex- tended (view from per- former's right).

the finish, the right forefinger points upward while the third and fourth fin- gers are bent inward along with the second finger, which retains the thim- ble by the Tip Palm (page 203).

FINGER-SWITCH VANISH

This sequence is very effective as an alternative to the basic vanishes described earlier. A thimble is shown on the right forefinger and is placed in the left hand, which exhibits it briefly and replaces it on the right finger- tip. Again, it is placed in the left hand, from which it immediately vanishes.

It all depends on a swift, easy move, plus a neat subterfuge. Face the au- dience directly, so the right hand can be held with forefinger straight upward, displaying the thimble, the other fingers being loosely fisted, with the thumb toward the body. In placing the finger in the left hand, the body should turn toward the left, so the thimble can be planted with a long, sweeping gesture. To replace the thimble on the right finger, the body is again turned full front, and that is when the subterfuge is introduced.

During the forward turn, the right forefinger is bent inward and the sec- ond finger is extended instead. This passes unnoticed, because the forefin- ger is behind the second finger, from the audience's view. The left hand places the thimble on the tip of the right second finger and continues its extension toward the left. The right hand repeats the sweeping movement toward the right, apparently planting the thimble in the left hand, which promptly closes. During the sweep, however, the right second finger is bent inward, the thimble with it, while the forefinger is placed in the left hand, which closes so promptly that no one realizes that the thimble is no longer there (Fig. 301).

With the thimble still concealed on the tip of the second finger, the right hand is slowly drawn downward, showing the tip of the forefinger bare, and the left hand is opened to complete the vanish. During that action, the right second finger can transfer the hidden thimble to Thumb Palm position if so desired.

SWALLOW VANISH

As a bit of byplay, the performer can apparently place a thimble in his mouth and pretend to swallow it; then have it appear elsewhere. This is done by showing the thimble on the tip of the forefinger and palming it while the hand makes an upward sweep to the mouth. The lips close over the tip of the forefinger, which is slowly withdrawn from the mouth as though leaving the thimble there.

If preferred, the Finger Switch can be used instead, with the right forefinger first placing the thimble in the left hand, which replaces it on the tip of the right second finger. The fingers are switched as the land swings up to the mouth, the second finger bending inward while the lips pretend to draw the thimble from the forefinger. With either procedure, the performer finishes with a gulp, as if swallowing the thimble.

SLOW-MOTION VANISH

This varies from the usual thimble vanish in that the thimble is dropped in the left hand instead of being placed there. The left hand is closed into a fist and extended with its back toward the audience. Facing to the left, the performer strokes the back of the left hand with the fingers of his right hand and the left hand is raised, turned frontward, and opened with a rubbing motion to show that the thimble has vanished.

To start, the thimble is dropped in the bend of the left fingers with its mouth toward the thumb. In closing the left fist, the tip of the thumb is pressed into the thimble with the action being covered as the back of the left hand is turned frontward. By loosening the left fingers, the thumb, carrying the thimble, is extended beyond them; the fist is then tightened, with the thumb and the thimble on the outside. This, of course is hidden from the audience and the right hand is raised toward the left at the same time.

As the right fingers stroke the back of the left hand, the left thumb is extended downward into the right palm, which grips the thimble. The left thumb returns up to the fist, which is turned frontward and opened to show that the thimble is gone, with the right forefinger pointing upward to stress that fact.

THIMBLE PRODUCTIONS

These are limited chiefly to the appearance or reappearance of a thimble on the forefinger or the second finger of either hand. Sometimes they may be produced on the tip of another finger or the thumb, with the usual procedure being to bring the thimble from one of the palm positions to the fingertip, as already described.

STANDARD FINGERTIP PRODUCTION

For really close-up work, cover the action by a quick rotary motion of the hand, during which the fingers are doubled inward in order for one to gain the thimble. That done, finish with a short inward motion followed by a sharp stab either forward or upward, during which the fingers and thumb are extended, giving the effect that the thimble has materialized from midair. This can be used either for an opening production or for the recovery of a "vanished" thimble.

When working at longer range, it is best to turn the right side of the body toward the audience and swing the hand in a larger circle, but more slowly. Bend the finger inward during the downsweep, so it picks up the thimble when the hand is at its lowest point, and extend the finger, with the thimble on its tip, during the upswing, finishing with a short stab. In this production, it is wise to run the thimble along the thumb, so that the tip of the thumb can press it home just prior to the stab. This prevents the thimble from flying loose.

POP PRODUCTION

This is the standard production with an added and highly surprising feature. As a thimble appears on the tip of the forefinger, it arrives with a popping sound, giving quite a magical effect. This was a great specialty with the famous thimble manipulator John Ramsay, adding a touch of perfection to his close-up work.

To produce a pop along with the thimble, keep the forefinger slightly bent as the hand begins its thrust, so the thimble will not be seen until the final moment. In the meantime, bring the tips of the thumb and third finger together and give them a sharp snap, just as the forefinger is fully extended. This requires both practice and precision to gain the right result, but it is well worthwhile for anyone who has the aptitude, as the illusion of the thimble delivering the pop is just about perfect.

This effect can only be used when producing a thimble on the tip of the forefinger or second finger, since the third finger must be free to provide the snap. It is just as effective at longer range, provided the pop is loud enough to carry. If not, a clucking sound with the tongue can be timed with the appearance of the thimble to produce a similar illusion.

VARIOUS PRODUCTIONS AND RECOVERIES

Instead of seemingly producing thimbles from mid air, their appearance or reappearance on the fingertips may be handled in various ways, thus adding novelty to the presentation.

From Behind the Hand: With the thimble palmed in the right hand, stand with the right side toward audience and point to the left hand, which is shown front and back. Finally turning the left hand frontward, raise the right hand up behind it and bring the thimble to the tip of right forefinger under cover of the left hand. Draw the right hand downward, so the thimble comes in sight.

From the Elbow: Again with the right side toward the audience, extend the left arm, so the right forefinger can point to the left elbow. The right hand then comes up behind the left elbow and brings a palmed thimble to the fingertip, apparently drawing it dowm from the elbow.

From the Knee: Facing frontward, with thimble palmed in the right hand, swing the right hand downward with its back toward the audience and move it inward behind the right knee just far enough to hide the action of bringing the thimble to the fingertip. The right hand then draws the thimble slowly into sight, gathering loose cloth between thumb and fingers to give the effect of pulling the thimble through.

From Trouser Cuff: For a similar production, lean forward and move the right hand below the left trouser cuff, so the thimble can be brought to the fingertip, under the fold of the cuff itself. The thimble is then slowly drawn into sight.

From Shirt Collar: This is done by simply doubling the fingers and getting the palmed thimble to the tip of the *second finger,* so the first three fingers can poke down beneath the collar, hiding the thimble between the fabric. Another device is to have a duplicate thimble already under the collar, where it can be produced by deliberately inserting the forefinger and bringing out the thimble as if it were the one just vanished.

From Pocket: Reproducing a "vanished" thimble from the trouser pocket or the coat pocket is both simple and effective, as there is ample space within the pocket to bring the thimble from Thumb Palm position to fingertip. Here again, a duplicate may be placed beforehand and brought out to represent the original. This is particularly good with a pocket that has an "inner pocket" for keys or change, as the thimble will be instantly available if placed therein.

From Vest Pocket: This lacks sufficient coverage for the reproduction of a "vanished" thimble by getting it to the fingertip, but it is ideal for bringing out a duplicate already placed there, as simple insertion of the forefinger into the pocket does the trick. For a performer who does not wear a vest, the thimble can be tucked down under the belt with its mouth upward and can be picked up with a dip of the finger and an upward twist.

Such productions and reproductions are used extensively in the following routine:

MULTIPLYING THIMBLES

"ONE TO FOUR" PRODUCTION

In standard form, this consists of producing a thimble on the tip of the right forefinger, then vanishing it and having it reappear. After a few such "passes," a second thimble appears, than a third and finally a fourth, so that all the fingers of the right hand are capped with thimbles. This is known as the "one to four" routine, and it is accomplished as follows:

Beforehand, place a thimble in the right coat pocket, this being No. 1, the original thimble. A duplicate, No. 2, is placed down inside the shirt collar at the left, mouth upward. No. 3 is similarly placed down inside the collar at the right. No. 4. goes in the trouser pocket or under the belt, mouth upward. All is then ready for the act.

Start by turning your left side toward your audience and casually reaching into your right coat pocket to obtain the thimble (No. 1), which is promptly thumb-palmed. If people are very close, you may find it expedient to drop some article into your pocket or bring out something like a handkerchief, not only as an excuse for going there, but also to help cover the palming action. For our basic routine, we will assume that you have sufficient leeway to turn left and right, as with most forms of manipulative magic; then later we can consider situations where the scope is more limited.

Turn to the left, bringing the back of the right hand toward the audience, bring the hand upward, and produce the thimble on the tip of the forefinger. Vanish the thimble by apparently placing it in your left hand, then reclaiming it from your left elbow, again on the right fingertip. Another vanish from the left hand; this time the right hand is thrust beneath the coat to reclaim the thimble, as though it had traveled clear up the left sleeve.

This is a really subtle move, since thrusting your hand entirely from sight may cause people to suspect that you are going after more than just the vanished thimble. But in bringing out the thimble on your right forefinger, you turn frontward and swing your right hand far enough to the right, showing the palm to be entirely empty. That lets wise observers realize that they guessed wrong, without actually telling them so. It in turn allays their suspicion of similar moves that follow.

Turn toward the left and again vanish the thimble from the left hand, actually palming it in the right hand. This time use the left hand to bring the duplicate thimble (No. 2) from the left side of the collar. Turn your body toward the right, extending the right arm to full length but keeping the back of the right hand toward the audience. Now the left forefinger pushes its thimble up behind the right elbow, thumb-palming the thimble as soon as it is out of sight. The left forefinger is then drawn downward, showing that its thimble has gone; and simultaneously, the right-hand thimble (No. 1) is produced on the tip of the right forefinger.

To help cover that action, the right hand is fisted so the forefinger can gain its thimble; then the right hand is turned palm front and its fingers spread wide, all in the same quick action. This gives the effect of the thimble passing from the left forefinger, along the arm, and arriving on the tip of the right forefinger, a highly magical effect. As a follow-up, turn the body to the left, keeping the back of the left hand toward the audience, and repeat the maneuver, this time sending the right-hand thimble (No. 1) from the left elbow to the tip of the left forefinger (No. 2), while turning the left hand palm front.

Now comes a rapid procedure. Face directly toward the spectators, keeping the backs of the hands toward them. Swing the left hand upward, counting "one," then down; then upward, counting "two." Come downward, thumb-palming the thimble as you do, and up again on the count of "three," showing that the thimble has gone from the tip of the left forefinger. Simultaneously, bend the right forefinger inward and obtain its thumb-palmed thimble; then thrust it upward, extending the finger so the thimble reappears on its tip.

Then reverse the process, vanishing the right-hand thimble with a tossing action (see page 208) and a count of "three," and "catching" it on the left forefinger by simply bringing back the left-hand thimble. This can be repeated a few times and then sped up with just a single toss and catch — left to right, right to left — and so on. The action can be sped still more rapidly by bending and extending the forefingers alternately without even pausing to palm the thimbles. Finally, both hands are thrust suddenly upward, stopping with both forefingers extended and a thimble on each.

Here you comment: "If you make one thimble jump fast enough, it becomes two. So we'll send one away, making it vanish in slow motion."

Turning your right side toward the audience, extend the left hand, with its thimble still on the left forefinger. Plant the right forefinger, with its thimble squarely in the left palm; then, keeping the left forefinger extended, close the other three fingers over the right forefinger. Draw the right forefinger downward, using the Take-away move (page 208) to bring its thimble with it. Then open the left fingers successively — second, third, and fourth — showing that the thimble has vanished from within the left hand.

This is a very neat and deceptive move, and while people are staring at the lone thimble still on the left forefinger, the right hand has time to thumb-palm its thimble and then go to the shirt collar, where the right forefinger draws out the thimble (No. 3) already placed there. Bring the right hand over toward the left, with the comment: "So again, we have two thimbles, one for each forefinger; and if I want a third, I just reach up and get it!"

With that, the right second finger bends inward and picks up the thumb-palmed thimble, which comes in sight as the finger is extended during an upward thrust of the right hand. The left thumb and second finger remove the thimble from the left forefinger and place it on the right third finger, so the right hand can display all three. You then remark: "Now, to vanish one of these three thimbles—"

Here you have three choices:

Perhaps the neatest is the Draw-off Vanish (page 212), in which the left hand apparently draws off the thimble from the right second finger and rubs it into nothingness, while the right hand is actually clipping the thimble and thumb-palming it. In this case, the first three fingers of the right hand are shown after the "vanish" with the thimble missing from the middle finger only, which has a very convincing effect. The fingers of the right hand are then thrust into the trouser pocket and the middle finger brings out the thimble previously placed there (No. 4). The "vanished" thimble (No. 3) is still thumb-palmed in the right hand. If the thimble is drawn from the belt instead, only the second finger needs to dip from view.

Another way is simply to vanish the thimble from the right forefinger by placing it in the left hand and using the Take-away move, thumb-palming the thimble in the right hand. With this method, it is the right forefinger that picks up the spare thimble from the pocket. Simplest of all is the Swallow Vanish (page 215), where you thumb-palm the thimble from the forefinger while apparently placing it in your mouth. Again, it is the forefinger that brings the extra thimble from the pocket.

Whichever method is used, there will be three thimbles showing on the first three fingers of the right hand, after coming from the pocket. With the left hand, you move a thimble from the right forefinger to the fourth, or little finger; then thrust the right hand in the air and produce the thumb-palmed thimble on the right forefinger, to show four thimbles in all.

"FOUR TO EIGHT" PRODUCTION

This forms a great climax to the "one to four" production of thimbles. Following the production of the fourth thimble on the right hand, the performer turns his body to the right, showing the right hand palm frontward. With his left forefinger, he tallies the thimbles, "one, two, three, four," counting from the right little finger upward (Fig. 302).

Now the right hand is turned forward and downward, covering the left forefinger (Fig. 303) and allowing the other fingers of the left hand to be extended upward along with it. When the right hand is raised and again turned frontward, spectators are amazed to see another quota of four thimbles perched on the fingers of the left hand, which is still back toward the audience. Magically, the performer has caused the thimbles to double from four to eight (Fig. 304)! Such is the effect on the spectators. Now to explain the method:

Beforehand, the four additional thimbles are placed in a row beneath the performer's belt, on the left side of his body. They are set in a row, each thimble mouth downward, so the fingers of the left hand can be brought upward beneath the belt and secretly inserted in the thimbles. If the belt is wide enough to hide the thimbles, they can be placed forward—that is, in front of the left hip; otherwise, they should be placed in back of the left hip, although some performers may prefer them that way.

Reverting to the "one to four" routine, when the performer turns to the left to produce the fourth thimble on the right forefinger, his left hand goes to his belt and thrusts its fingers up into the thimble (Fig. 305). If the fingers have trouble gripping the thimbles, the heel of the hand can aid them by bending inward and pressing downward from above. The left thumb may also aid the final action by running along the row and pressing each thimble downward.

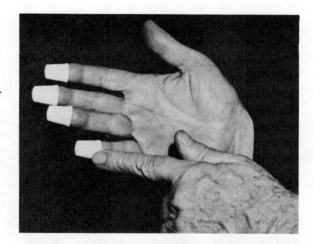

"FOUR TO EIGHT"
PRODUCTION
Fig. 302. Left forefinger little finger upward.

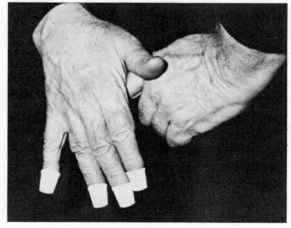

Fig. 303. Right hand lowered to cover fingers of left hand.

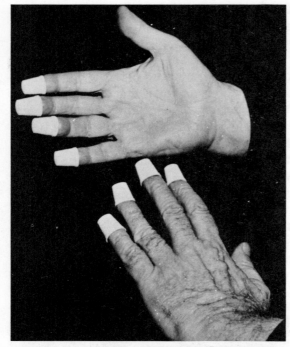

Fig. 304. Right hand raised and turned front-ward to reveal thimbles on left fingers.

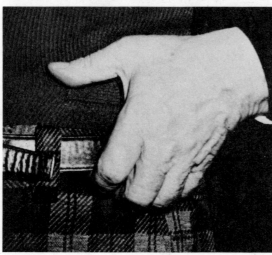

Fig. 305. Left hand thrusting fingers upward to grip thimbles and draw them from beneath belt.

This steal should be deliberate, not hurried, with the right hand provid-ing misdirection while the left is gaining its load. One way is for the right hand to make a few futile stabs high in the air before finally "catching" its fourth thimble. Another device is to pretend to produce the thimble from the left trouser cuff (as already suggested), which makes it natural for the left hand to press against the left hip while the body is bending forward.

Combining these two devices is also a neat idea. After a few high stabs with the right forefinger, the performer suddenly exclaims, "I lost it!" and

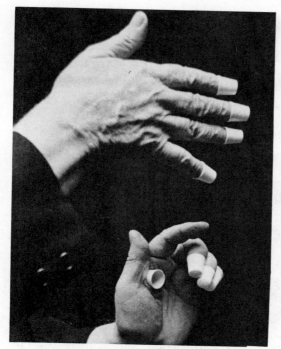

Fig. 306. Left hand has thumb-palmed the thimble from forefinger, leaving forefinger free to point to right-hand thimbles.

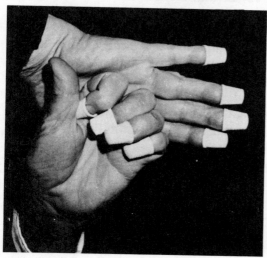

Fig. 307. Left forefinger regaining thimble from thumb palm under cover of right hand (rear view).

looks downward toward the floor, adding: "There it is, right beside my foot." That gives an excuse for stopping to catch the imaginary thimble on the right forefinger, which is finally produced from the trouser cuff or heel of the left shoe. All the while, the body is turned so that the left hand is out of sight, secretly getting its four thimbles.

That done, the left hand doubles into a fist, which is held close to the body with its back toward the audience. When the body is turned toward the right, the left hand thumb-palms the thimble from its forefinger (Fig.

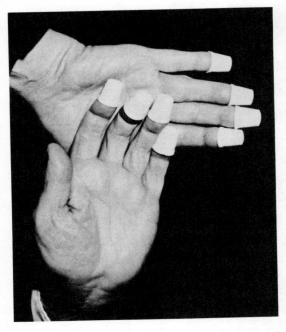

Fig. 308. Left fingers
bring thimbles upward
under cover of right hand
(rear view).

306), while the right hand is being raised and turned palm frontward. The
left hand then comes upward, with only its bare forefinger extended, and
counts the right-hand thimbles, as already described.

When the right hand turns downward and forward, covering the left fingers, the left forefinger bends inward and regains its thimble from the fork
of the thumb (Fig. 307). All four fingers of the left hand are then extended
upward under cover of the right hand, bringing the left-hand thimbles in
position for production (Fig. 308). That takes place when the right hand is
raised upward, clear of the left, so that all eight thimbles are on final
display.

If there is any problem in thumb-palming the thimble from the left forefinger while the hand is fisted, or if there is any delay in getting the thimbles
from the left, it is a good plan to keep the left hand fully fisted and leave out
the counting process. Since the right hand is holding attention by displaying its four thimbles, it is an easy matter to turn it forward and downward,
so it meets the knuckles of the left fist coming upward and no one will realize that the left fingers are completely out of sight. In this case, however,
be sure to keep the left thumb pressed close alongside the doubled forefinger, hiding the forefinger's thimble from that angle.

Special Thimble Holders: If difficulty is experienced in producing the
four extra thimbles from beneath the belt, a special holder can be used to
make the result more rapid. One type of holder can be made from a strip of
heavy cardboard or even thin metal, measuring about five inches long and
two inches wide. Eight holes are punched in the strip, in pairs forming a
row, with each pair the width of a thimble. A length of cord elastic is knotted at one end, and the other end is drawn through the first hole from the

back, then run across to the second hole and drawn through from the front. This is repeated with the remaining pairs, with the free end of the elastic being knotted at the back.

The corners of the holder are also punched with holes to receive four small safety pins. The holder can then be pinned to the trousers near the left hip, or at the lower edge of the left side of the coat. If the performer is wearing a vest, the holder can be pinned beneath it, under the left vest pocket. In all cases, these are arranged so that the thimbles can be pushed up into the wide spaces at the front of the holder, where they are retained by the elastic cord.

Another type of holder can be prepared by laying four paper clips on a similar strip of cardboard, bending their short ends outward so that a length of plastic tape can be edged beneath and pressed down to hold the long ends firmly in place. This holder also has pins at the corners, so it can be fixed in place with the short ends of the clips pointing upward. The thimbles are inserted mouth downward on the short ends, so that the fingers, pushing upward, can obtain them almost automatically.

Specially made holders are obtainable from magic dealers and are naturally more satisfactory than the types just described, so they are well worth the investment for any magician who intends to feature the full thimble act.

"FULL FRONT" ROUTINE

Since close-up manipulation may mean cramped positions, with bad angles of vision, it is sometimes necessary to do a thimble routine "full front," keeping the backs of both hands toward the audience whenever possible and producing thimbles on the fingertips by dipping the hands close to the body and bringing the fingers point upward with a sidewise swing, rather than a reaching action.

For a vanish, the Inward Take-away (page 209) is usually best, as it is designed for close-up work, but it can be varied by keeping the hands close to the body while turning to the left or the right. In palming a thimble the fingers can curve inward just enough to hide the thimble from all angles, as experiment will prove, and such curvature is natural when working in this manner.

Another device is to keep the hands fairly low and tilted a trifle downward, which will cover any observation from above. When working in a seated position, a forward lean is good for the production of the fourth thimble, as it enables the left hand to go to the belt or holder almost automatically, which naturally avoids suspicion. However, when working full front, it is preferable to have a holder pinned slantwise under the right side of the coat or to the inside pocket, or even inside the pocket itself, with the mouths of the thimbles upward.

The right hand then produces its fourth thimble with an upward swing, moving outward from the body, while the left hand slides in between the right elbow and dips its fingers directly into the holder. The left hand thumb-palms one thimble and emerges as the right hand swings downward, so the left forefinger can tap the right fingers, counting the thimbles, "one — two — three — four." The right hand then moves directly in front of the left hand, which picks up its palmed thimble with the forefinger; and the hands are simply separated, swinging the fingers upward, showing all eight thimbles.

RAPID "ONE TO EIGHT" SYSTEM

Though ideal when seated at a table, this routine can also be worked while standing, and if practiced to the point of smoothness, it will have the spectators too baffled to suspect the surprise finish. In effect, the performer starts with a single thimble on his right forefinger, showing the hand back and front, with the finger pointing upward. With a wavy motion, the number of thimbles is increased from one to four, which are counted by the left forefinger. Almost immediately, the left fingers swing behind the right hand and come out with their quota of four more.

Standard thimbles are used in this routine, but they must be the metal type. These are graduated in size, so it is quite easy to obtain three that fit neatly, but loosely, so they can be stacked to appear as a single thimble. This stack goes on the forefinger of the right hand. On the left hand, place four thimbles on the four fingertips and add a fifth thimble in thumb-palm position. You are then all set to go. However, a few suggestions can be made regarding this setup.

If seated at a table, you have a napkin or handkerchief spread in your lap beforehand. Have the three nested thimbles in the little change pocket inside your right coat pocket. The other five thimbles are in your left coat pocket. Secretly bring them from there and leave them on the napkin. From there, the left hand can work them into the required positions on the fingertips, with the fifth thumb-palmed. Or, if you have them in a stack, the right hand can go beneath the table and quickly set them on the left hand. This is done before people know that you intend to show some thimble magic.

When ready to perform, reach into your right coat pocket and bring out the three nested thimbles on the tip of your right forefinger, with the thumb and second fingers pressing from the sides to keep the thimbles together (Fig. 309). Turn your right side away from the table and point your forefinger straight upward. Spread the other fingers with your open palm toward the audience and keep the hand slightly in motion as you display what appears to be a lone thimble (Fig. 310).

The turn of the body gives sufficient distance for the hand to pause without dispelling this illusion, but now you resume the motion more rapidly, in larger circles. At the same time, grip the sides of the nested thim-

RAPID "ONE TO EIGHT"
Fig. 309. Three nested
thimbles on tip of right
forefinger held (as one) by
thumb and second finger.

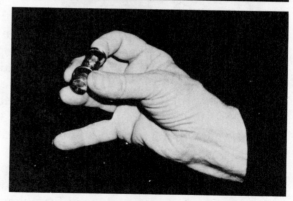

Fig. 310. Hand spread
with forefinger tilting upward, still showing thim-
bles as one.

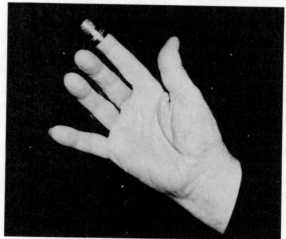

Fig. 311. Withdrawing in-
nermost thimble on fore-
finger. Thumb and second
finger grip outer thimbles.

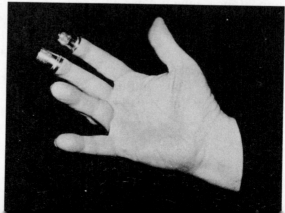

Fig. 312. Second finger inserted in remaining nested
pair of thimbles, showing
them as single thimble.

bles between the tips of your thumb and third finger, pointing the tips of the fingers toward the spectators. The forefinger is immediately withdrawn from the nest, bringing the innermost thimble with it, and the second finger is drawn back a trifle so that its tip can be inserted into the two remaining thimbles as soon as the forefinger comes clear (Fig. 311).

The tips of the fingers are then tilted upward so that the thumb and second finger can release their grip, enabling the right hand to show two thimbles, one on the forefinger, the other on the second finger (Fig. 312). The "thimble" on the second finger is actually a nested pair, so the hand repeats its circular motion and the fingertips are tilted forward, so that this time the thumb and fourth finger can grip the nested pair. The second finger is withdrawn, bringing out the inner thimble on its tip (Fig. 313).

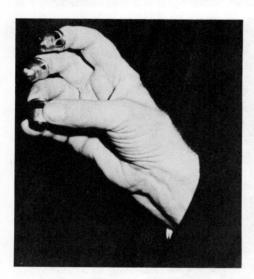

Fig. 313. Thumb and fourth finger have drawn outer thimble from second finger so third finger can be inserted in it.

The third finger is immediately inserted in the outer thimble, and the fingers are pointed upward. This enables the right hand to display three thimbles on the tips of its first three fingers; and the hand can be shown front and back, at any angle, as each is a single thimble. Meanwhile, the left hand, which all this time has been unnoticed, is brought from beneath the table, with all its fingers bent inward (Fig. 314). So all that the spectators see is the back of the left hand, fully fisted, as the right hand dips its fingers down toward the left.

Here the left forefinger makes a quick upward jab toward the tip of the right little finger. This gives the effect of a fourth thimble making an instant appearance, which can be helped by saying: "One, two, three thimbles—and one more!—makes four!" The move is easy, as you simply extend the left forefinger without disturbing the other fingers in the left hand. Also, if you place it squarely against the tip of the right little finger, it gives an effect of the right hand producing it (Fig. 315).

The right thumb and little finger immediately remove the thimble from the left forefinger. It can then be transferred to the left thumb and forefin-

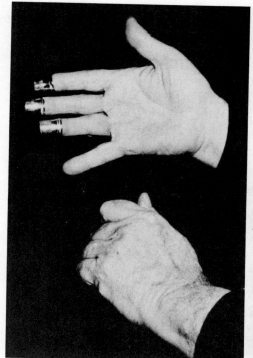 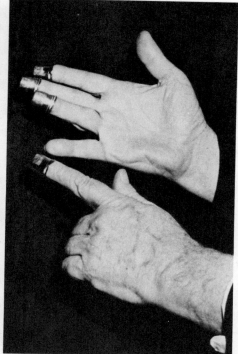

Fig. 314. Left hand coming up with hidden thimbles; one is hidden in readiness on left forefinger.

Fig. 315. Extending left forefinger with left quick upward jab to produce fourth thimble.

ger, which remain practically motionless. They placed it upon the tip of the right little finger, which comes up from beneath to receive it (Fig. 316). The right hand then shows all four thimbles on its fingertips and turns forward and downward, covering the left forefinger, which is still pointing upward.

This is the regular "four to eight" move (see Fig. 307) that enables the left forefinger to obtain the thumb-palmed thimble so the left hand can extend all its fingers, revealing the four additional thimbles when the right hand turns upward and backward.

When working in a standing position, especially before a larger audience, a good plan is to have the left-hand thimbles stacked in the right trouser pocket, from which the right hand secretly obtains them. Then, in the act of turning away, or laying some object aside, bring the right hand over to the left and successively place four thimbles on the left fingertips, with the fifth going into the thumb-palm position. Keep the left hand clenched close to the body, hiding its "load" of thimbles, while the right hand brings its three nested thimbles from the right coat pocket.

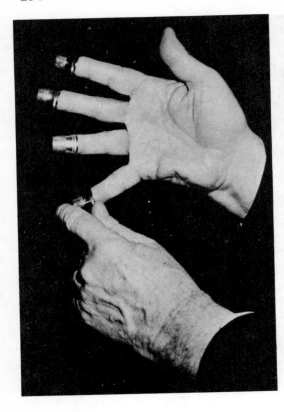

Fig. 316. Right thumb and little finger have removed thimble from left forefinger. Left thumb and forefinger now placing it on right little finger.

If you have to "set up" well beforehand, the best procedure is to put four of the left-hand thimbles in a holder and have the fifth in the left trouser pocket. While the right hand is bringing its "single" thimble from the coat pocket, turn to the left just long enough for the left hand to go to the trousers pocket and pick up its odd thimble, thumb-palming it on the way out. Then, turning to the right, three thimbles are produced on the tips of the right fingers while the left hand, at hip level, picks up the four thimbles from the holder or belt. With attention focused on the right hand, this can be done without haste or suspicion.

Some performers may prefer to delay the pickup from the holder until after the production of the fourth thimble. This enables the left forefinger to count the three thimbles on the right fingers, then make a stab in the air to produce a fourth thimble on its own. The left hand can place that thimble on the right little finger, at the same time showing itself quite empty. Then, while the right hand is showing itself back and front, the left hand goes to the holder and picks up the thimbles needed for the "four to eight."

The routine can be worked "full front" while either seated or standing, by keeping the back of the right hand toward the spectators while working up from one to three. This is good at very close range, as the fingers themselves hide the action of drawing off the outer thimbles from the nested group. With the production of the third thimble, the right hand should swing downward, so that the clenched left hand can come up behind it, between the right hand and the body, with its "load" fully concealed.

The left forefinger is extended and the hands are spread apart so that the tips of the left forefinger and the right little finger are side by side, bringing the fourth thimble into view. The usual transfer is made from left forefinger to right little finger. The left forefinger is then bent inward and under cover of the right hand; it picks up the thumb-palmed thimble so that both hands can be spread, with fingers wide apart, showing all eight thimbles.

With added practice and enough extra range, the "one to eight" can be performed still more rapidly with *four* nested thimbles instead of only three. Such thimbles are obtainable in standard sizes, but when stacked four high, the rims become too conspicuous unless the performer is standing at a safe distance from the spectators. With the right thumb or second finger pressing against the stack, it can be shown briefly as a "single" thimble *if* it is kept in motion. The production of a second and a third thimble follows the usual procedure.

This, however, leaves *two* thimbles still nested on the right third finger, though they appear only as one; and the hand, at this point, can be brought to a standstill. To bring the outer of those two thimbles to the tip of the right little finger, the performer faces forward, so the back of his right hand is toward the spectators, with fingers pointing upward. He doubles his fingers down into his fist, and in so doing grips the outer thimble in the center of his palm (Fig. 317). The third finger then moves upward, allowing the little finger to be inserted in the palmed thimble (Fig. 318).

All the fingers are then pointed upward, showing four thimbles on their

 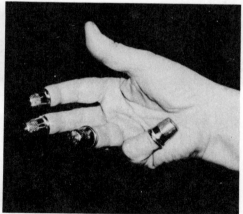

Fig. 317. Two nested thimbles already produced on first two fingers. Right palm gripping outer thimble so third finger can withdraw third thimble.

Fig. 318. Right little finger being inserted in palmed fourth thimble, ready to produce it (rear view).

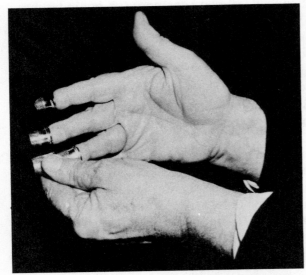

Fig. 319. Variation in production of third thimble. Left thumb and forefinger drawing outer thimble from pair on right third finger.

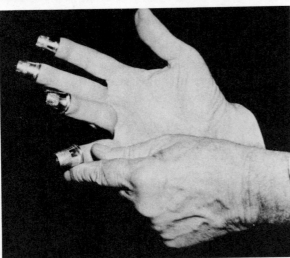

Fig. 320. Production of fourth thimble with left hand by simply placing it on tip of right little finger.

tips. Since the thimble on the little finger is the largest in size, some care is needed to keep in it place. The best way is to tilt the right hand forward, knuckles downward, so the right thumb can press against the thimble on the little finger, holding the thimble in place while the fingers are being pointed upward.

In this version, the left hand needs only four thimbles: one thumb-palmed, to be picked up by the left forefinger; the other three on the tips of the second, third, and fourth fingers, which are bent inward to hide them in the left fist. Since the production is being worked at longer range, the best plan is to set these beforehand while taking a new position in relation to the audience. The left forefinger is free to point to the right-hand thimbles as they appear on the right fingertips; and the four thimbles of the left hand are produced under cover of the right hand, in the conventional "four to eight" fashion.

A neat variation may be introduced after the production of the third thimble. The right hand is kept palm front, with fingers pointing upward, while the left forefinger counts the thimbles: "one—two—three." With the third tap, the left thumb and forefinger grip the outer thimble of the nested pair on the right third finger (Fig. 319). The right hand moves quickly downward, then upward, thrusting the tip of its little finger into the outer thimble and carrying it along, showing all four thimbles, well above the left hand. The performer comments: "And once more: one—two—three—four—" with the left forefinger counting them again (Fig. 320).

CHANGE-OVERS AND FLASHES

These moves are effective when introduced at intervals following the vanish of a thimble or prior to the production of one. They emphasize the fact that the hands are supposedly empty, although they actually contain a thimble.

DOUBLE CHANGE-OVER

With his right side toward the audience, the performer points with his right hand toward the empty left hand, showing it back front (Fig. 321). Slowly turning toward the right, he thrusts his right hand forward and draws his left hand inward until their fingers meet in V fashion (Fig. 322). Continuing his turn to the right, he brings the back of his left hand toward the audience and points to the right hand which is shown empty, back and front (Fig. 323). A reversal of the process brings the hands back to their original position, seemingly as empty as ever.

At the outset, the thimble is actually thumb palmed in the right hand (Fig. 324). As the hands are brought together laterally, the left thumb is bent downward and secretly inserted into the hidden thimble (Fig. 325), taking it from the right hand and immediately bending farther downward. By the time the body has completed its swing to the right (see Fig. 323), the thimble, firmly set on the tip of the left thumb, is safely hidden behind the palm of the left hand (Fig. 326).

The body is now turned to the left, with the hands naturally coming together as before (see Fig. 322), but this time the left thumb is not raised at all. Instead, it presses the thimble into the center of the right palm (Fig. 327), which immediately grips it and retains it with the center palm (see page 200). The beauty of this placement is that the right hand covers it so thoroughly that the hands continue their swing to the left without the slightest hesitation.

DOUBLE CHANGE-OVER

Fig. 321. Start of Doubl
Change-over. Audience
view of right hand point
ing to empty left hand.

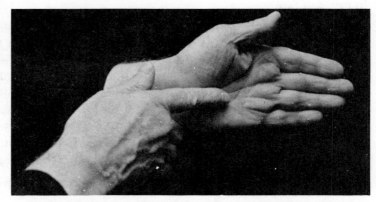

Fig. 322. Right hand mov-
ing forward so its fingertips meet those of left
hand. Move is followed
by swing of body to right.

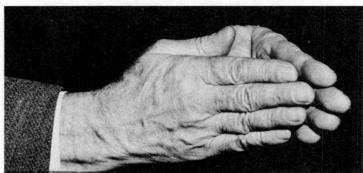

Fig. 323. Completion of
swing to right. Right hand
shown empty by thrusting
it beyond left hand (audience view).

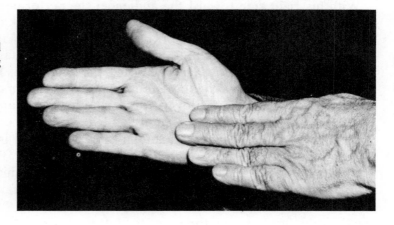

Fig. 324. Performer's view of original position. Thimble thumb-palmed in right hand as it points to empty left hand.

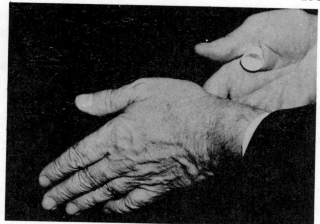

Fig. 325. Performer's view (from above). Left thumb taking thimble on its tip during swing of hands to right.

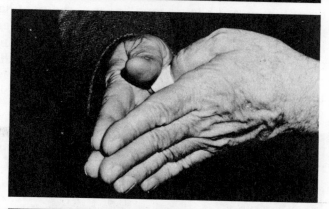

Fig. 326. Rear view of hands when right hand is shown empty. Tip of left thumb lowered to hide thimble.

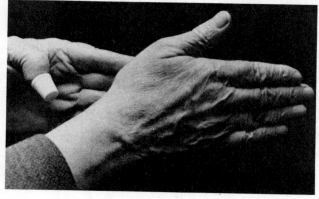

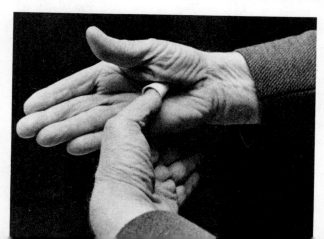

Fig. 327. Rear view of hands as they swing in reverse (from right to left), with left thumb secretly placing thimble in right palm.

This brings the hands back to their original position, with the right hand pointing to the "empty" left except that the thimble is now center-palmed instead of thumb-palmed, as at the start. This, of course, is both unnoticed and unsuspected by the observers. Ordinarily, it would mean that the right hand, in producing the thimble, would bring it to the tip of the third finger; but if the left thumb places the thimble in the right palm at just the proper angle it will be good position for production on the tip of the right second finger.

FINGERTIP FLASH

This is ideal for following a vanish in which a thimble is retained on the tip of the inward-bent second finger of the right hand (Fig. 301). With the right side toward the audience, the right forefinger points to the open left hand (from which the thimble presumably vanished) and then moves diagonally upward until it actually rests across the left palm. This brings the other fingers of the right hand below and in back of the left hand, so that the right second finger can bring its thimble-clad tip up behind the left wrist (Fig. 328).

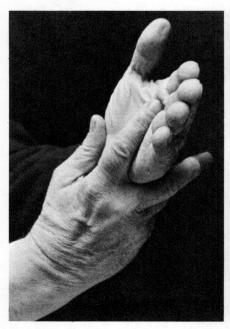
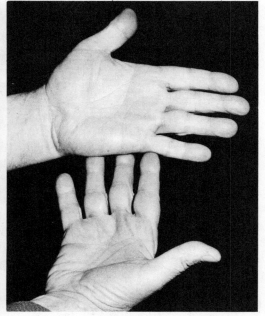

FINGERTIP FLASH
Fig. 328. Right forefinger moving upward across left palm, so right second finger (with thimble) can be extended behind left hand.

Fig. 329. Audience view after right has completed twist and is drawn downward, showing both hands empty with fingers fully extended.

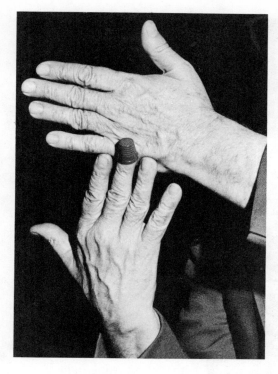

Fig. 330. Rear view. Tip
of right second finger conceals thimble behind left
hand.

This requires a slight outward twist of the right hand, which is continued
and accelerated to bring the right palm to the front, fingers extended
upward and hand drawn down until the tip of the right second finger — with
its thimble — is directly in back of the left hand, the tips of the other right
fingers being visible, or nearly so (Fig. 329), thus apparently showing the
hands completely empty. Note that the fingers of both hands, but most particularly the right, should be spread almost as widely as possible. This is
contrary to usual custom, and in this case it helps to bring the tips of the
right first and third fingers into full view, while the thimble remains concealed on the tip of the right second finger, which is behind the left hand, as
a rear view shows (Fig. 330).

The hands hold this "all clear" pose only momentarily; then they go into
an up-and-down motion in which the left hand is lowered until it conceals
the upper half of the right fingers, which allows the right hand to reverse its
twist (see Fig. 328), so the hands resume their original position. They are
then separated and the thimble can be produced as desired.

FULL-FRONT FLASH

With right side toward the audience, the right hand points to the left,
with a thimble concealed in the right hand, this time by the Finger-bend
Palm method. The body is then swung full front. During the swing, the left
hand is brought in front of the right, so that the backs of both hands are

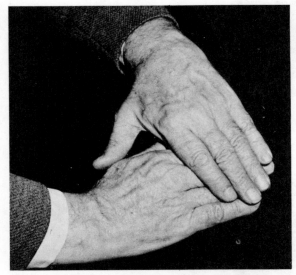

FULL-FRONT FLASH
Fig. 331. Backs of hands
turned toward audience,
left hand covering right,
so right thumb can gain
thimble from finger bend.

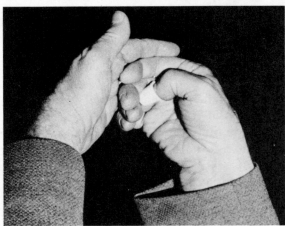

Fig. 332. Performer's
view of hands (from
above), showing right
thumb acquiring thimble
while left hand hides the
action.

toward the audience (Fig. 331). Under cover of the left hand, the right
thumb dips down into the bend of the right fingers and presses its tip into
the thimble (Fig. 332).

The left hand is then turned so its palm is toward the audience, with its
fingers pointing upward (Fig. 333). This enables the right thumb to extend
its tip in back of the left hand, keeping the thimble concealed during the action (Fig. 334). Using the right thumb as a pivot, the right hand is swung
upward to the right so that the palms of both hands are clearly shown
empty (Fig. 335), with the thimble safely hidden on the tip of the right
thumb, which is still out of sight behind the left hand, midway between the
left thumb and the left wrist (Fig. 336).

After a momentary pause, the moves are simply reversed, the body
being turned to the left during the process. This brings the hands back to
the original position, with the right fingers holding the thimble in their
bend. When showing the hands empty, the "flash" can be prolónged by

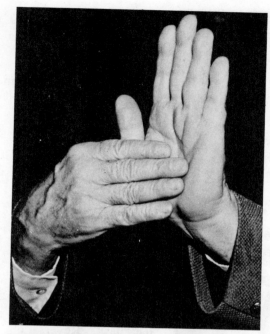

Fig. 333. Left fingers point upward and palm turns toward audience while right thumb (with thimble) is still bent forward.

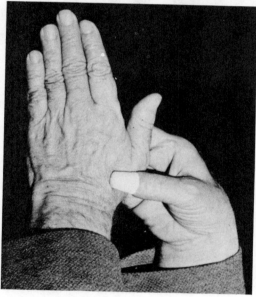

Fig. 334. Rear view showing how right thumb secretly extends its tip (with thimble) behind left hand.

keeping the hands in motion, back and forth from left to right, as if showing them to persons seated at the sides of the audience. Actually, they should be kept straight front, or nearly so, to prevent anyone from glimpsing the thimble from an angle.

However, the sidewise motion creates the illusion that the hands are turning, and it also helps to cover up the fact that tip of the right thumb is temporarily out of sight.

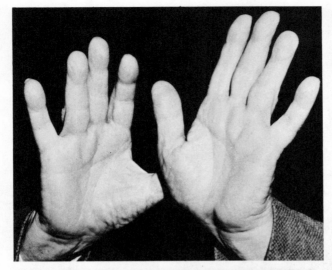

Fig. 335. Both hands spread wide to show them "completely" empty during a well-timed flash.

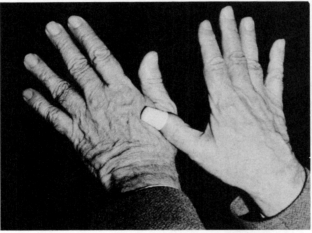

Fig. 336. Rear view during "flash". Reversal of moves as shown brings hands back to original position.

BACK-PALM FLASH

With a thimble "thumb-palmed" in the right hand, the performer stands with his right side toward the audience and displays his left hand wide open and palm frontward. To emphasize the left hand's emptiness, he brushes it up, then down with the tips of his right fingers (Fig. 337). When the right hand has gone beyond the left fingers the left hand is turned downward, so its back is toward the audience; and in the same action, the left hand covers the right thumb and fingers at a thirty-degree angle (see Fig. 331).

This enables the right fingers to bend inward unseen, and with the aid of the right thumb, transfer the thimble to the back-palm position (Fig. 338). By lowering the hands to waist level, then raising them to shoulder level,

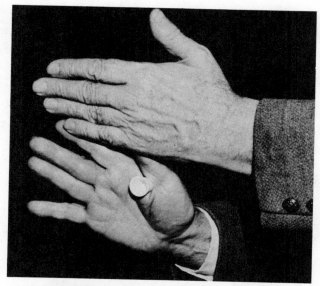

BACK-PALM FLASH
Fig. 337. Rear view of brushing action. Right hand has thumb-palmed thimble.

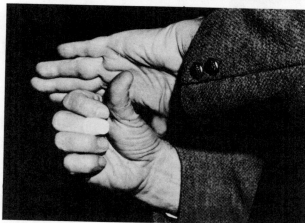

Fig. 338. Rear view of Back-palm Flash beginning. Right second finger using cover to bring thimble from Thumb-palm position.

the back-palming action is facilitated. On the upswing, the right hand is turned palm frontward (Fig. 339), with the right fingers still concealed by the left hand. The hands are now at a forty-five-degree angle, with the left fingers pointing outward, the right fingers pointing upward, and the thimble back-palmed (Fig. 340).

The left hand is then turned palm frontward in an upward action, revealing the right hand in full (Fig. 341). The back-palmed thimble is perfectly concealed behind the right second finger. However, it is best to treat this manipulation as a "flash" rather than hold the pose too long, because the right fingers cannot be spread—as with other change-overs—and to be consistent, the left fingers should also be kept close together. In fact, they must be kept closed when covering the right fingers in the early stages of the manipulation, so that pattern should be maintained throughout.

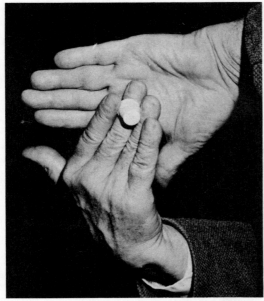

Fig. 339. Rear view. Right hand has manipulated thimble into Backpalm position and is already turned frontward.

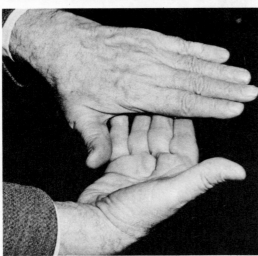

Fig. 340. Audience view of the same situation. Left hand is ready to be tilted upward and turned palm frontward.

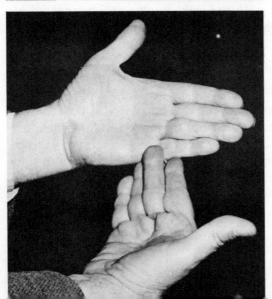

Fig. 341. Right hand drawn downward, showing hands "completely" empty with all fingers fully visible in this convincing audience view.

Following the "flash," the hands simply reverse the moves already described. The left hand is turned downward to hide the right fingers, which bring the thimble from the pack-palm position into the thumb-palm position. That done, the hands can be separated entirely to show their backs before turning the left hand palm frontward as in the starting position.

ONE-HAND FLASH

A neat move to precede the opening production of a thimble, this can also be used as a quick reproduction following a vanish. At the start, the performer is facing obliquely to the left, with a thimble "thumb-palmed" in his right hand. He drops his right hand to his side and swings his body to the right, pressing his hand against his right leg to hide the thimble while he turns.

Now, facing directly right, with his right hand completely out of sight, he brings the thimble to the tip of his right forefinger, bending it back behind the other fingers, which he keeps close together. Then, tilting his right hand at a backward angle, he brings it to shoulder level with a quick, upward sweep, with the arm well extended. Pausing momentarily, the right hand appears completely empty (Fig. 342), since the tip of the forefinger, with its thimble, is out of sight.

Actually, the other fingers hide the thimble, aided and abetted by the backward tilt of the hand (Fig. 343). After a brief "flash," the hand is

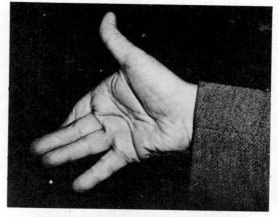

ONE-HAND FLASH
Fig. 342. Audience view of the One-hand Flash. Right hand being shown palm frontward with an upward sweep and backward tilt.

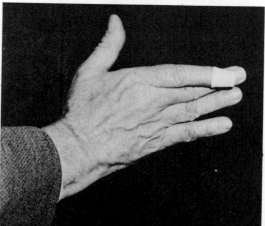

Fig. 343. Rear view of hand during flash, showing ingenious mode of concealing thimble behind extended fingers.

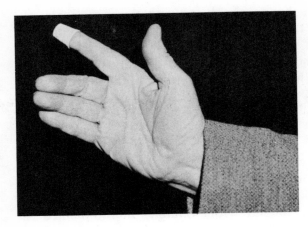

Fig. 344. Quick production of thimble on forefinger as follow-up to brief but deceptive One-hand Flash.

swung downward, with the fingers doubling inward behind the right leg. Then the hand sweeps upward, extending the forefinger only, so that the thimble appears on its tip when the hand stops at shoulder level (Fig. 344).

COLOR CHANGES

Causing a thimble to change color is a good effect, either in its own right or as part of a series of more extensive manipulations. Actually, two thimbles are used in such effects, so in impromptu work, a thimble can be casually brought from the pocket and replaced there after a few changes. The extra is simply picked up at the start and pocketed at the finish; meanwhile, the main aim is to convince the onlookers that only one thimble is being used. In routines where thimbles are produced and vanished, color changes are usually introduced while working with a single thimble, which is vanished and reproduced from the pocket or the coat collar, secretly obtaining the extra at that time. After the color changes, a thimble is vanished and reproduced from the pocket, with the extra being left there.

Since color changes depend on regular palming methods, along with moves used in productions, vanishes, change-overs, and flashes, those that follow will be described in such terms with references to the basic moves.

FINGER-SWITCH CHANGE

This is simply an adaptation of the Finger-switch Vanish (page 214). A red thimble is shown on the tip of the right second finger, while the other fingers are bent into a fist (Fig. 345). In this case, there is a white thimble already on the tip of the right forefinger, which is kept out of sight. The right side of the body is turned toward the audience; and the right hand,

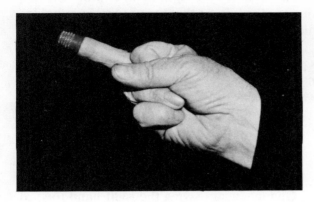

Fig. 345. Red thimble displayed. White thimble on right forefinger is hidden by right thumb.

with a sweep toward the left, bends its second finger inward, extending the forefinger instead.

This move enables the right forefinger to plant its thimble in the center of the open left hand, which is waiting to receive it (Fig. 346). The left fingers promptly close over the thimble, and when they are opened a few seconds later, the white thimble is seen instead of the red, giving the effect of an actual change of color.

Two pointers are helpful in this change:

First, if the right forefinger is pressed deep into the base of the thumb at the outset and the thumb is extended across the forefinger, covering the space between it and the third finger, the white thimble will be hidden, even if the right hand is shown from all angles. A brief flash is sufficient for this; and after the change, the second finger can be pressed beneath the base of the thumb in the same fashion, thus hiding the red thimble while turning the right hand so its thumb is toward the audience.

Second, for extremely close work, the right hand should be held at a higher level than the left, with the left hand tilted at a backward angle so

Fig. 346. Right hand planting white thimble in center of left hand. Left fingers then close immediately.

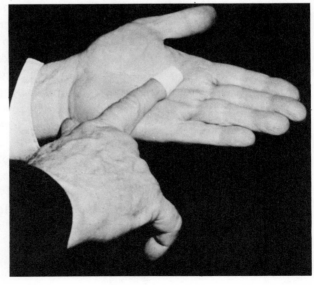

that it is almost palm upward. This enables the right hand to point its second finger downward as it swings to the left, so that the upturning knuckles of the right hand practically hide the fingertips while the "switch" is taking place.

Once the right forefinger is planted in the left hand, with the fingers closing over the fingertip, the hands should be raised to shoulder level, so that the left fingers are directly toward the spectators. The left hand can then be opened in the usual fashion.

REPEAT SWITCH

To repeat the Finger-switch Change, again swing the right hand toward the left, this time doubling the forefinger with the white thimble on its tip and planting the second finger with its red thimble in the left hand. Here, however, the right second finger should be immediately withdrawn, leaving the thimble in the left hand, which slowly opens and displays the red thimble between the tips of its thumb and first two fingers. This gives the right hand time to move downward and thumb-palm the white thimble from the tip of its forefinger, so the right hand can finish by pointing with its forefinger toward the red thimble. The left hand then places the red thimble on the right forefinger, as though it belonged there.

The right thumb and second finger can then loosen the thimble from the forefinger and drop it in the coat pocket, letting the palmed white thimble fall with it. Or, if you prefer to vanish the red thimble and reproduce it, proceed as follows:

Display the red thimble on the right forefinger, keeping the hand in motion while the right second finger regains the white thimble from the thumb-palm position. Keep the second finger bent inward so the thimble is hidden by the tip palm (page 203). With the right side toward the audience, the right hand plants the tip of its forefinger in the left hand, closing the left fingers over the red thimble. The right hand then executes the Take-away Vanish (page 208) so the left hand can be shown empty, and the right hand immediately goes into the coat or trouser pocket, where the right thumb and fingers loosen the white thimble, letting it stay in the pocket while the hand emerges, bringing out the red thimble on the tip of the forefinger.

Another type of vanish may be used if preferred—as an example, the Poke Vanish (page 210). Again, the second finger is bent inward to hide the white thimble, and the hands should be tilted well downward when the right forefinger pokes the red thimble into the left fist. There is no need to thumb-palm the red thimble following the poke. Simply retain it with the thumb and finger clip (page 203) and go directly to the pocket, where the red thimble is pressed back on the tip of the forefinger, while the white thimble is loosened and left in the pocket.

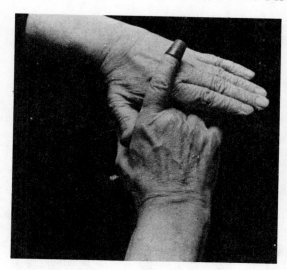

PUSH-THROUGH CHANGE
Fig. 347. Back of left
hand conceals white thim-
ble on second finger of
right hand while turning
downward and inward to-
ward knuckles of right
hand.

PUSH-THROUGH CHANGE

Start by showing a red thimble on the tip of the right forefinger. The thimble is poked into the left fist until it emerges above it, when to every-one's surprise it has become white, and the left hand is immediately turned frontward to show itself completely empty, apparently proving that only one thimble was used.

Have a white thimble on the tip of the right second finger, which is bent inward to hide it while the right forefinger displays its red thimble. Place the right forefinger against the open left palm. Then turn the left hand downward and inward, actually revolving it behind the upright forefinger of the right hand. This shows the back of the left hand (Fig. 347). It also brings the left hand close to the knuckles of the right hand, enabling the right second finger to swing upward and plant the white thimble in the bend of the left fingers (Fig. 348).

That simple move is perfectly concealed by the left hand, which forms itself into a loose fist and moves upward, secretly taking the white thimble with it. The right hand now executes the Poke Vanish by pushing the red thimble into the closed left fist and secretly bending the forefinger down so the red thimble can be clipped and stolen by the right thumb and second finger (Fig. 295). The right forefinger is immediately extended within the loose left fist, and a further thrust automatically forces the tip of the right forefinger into the white thimble, which is promptly pushed into view above the left hand (Fig. 349). To conclude the effect, the left hand is turned frontward to show itself entirely empty. This gives the right hand a chance to dip downward and grip the hidden red thimble between thumb and third finger so the right second finger is free to enter it and keep it con-cealed with the "tip palm."

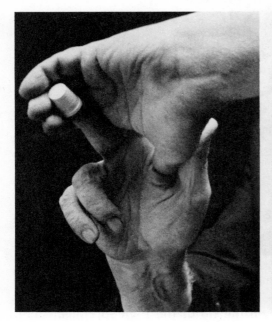 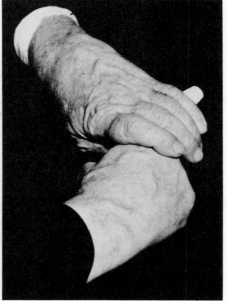

Fig. 348. Rear view of
right second finger planting white thimble in bend
of left fingers.

Fig. 349. Finish of push-
through with white thim-
ble emerging on tip of
right forefinger.

REPEAT PUSH-THROUGH

Since the positions of the two thimbles are now reversed, with the white
thimble on the right forefinger (Fig. 350) and the red thimble on the right
second finger, the color change be repeated exactly as done before. It
is simply a case of following the moves already given, except that the
change will be from white to red instead of from red to white.

A quicker "repeat" is possible, however, if the red thimble is retained in
the thumb and finger clip. The left hand is immediately turned downward
and forward behind the extended right forefinger, which displays the white
thimble. But in this case, the left thumb is bent inward and secretly inserted into the red thimble under cover of the left fingers (Fig. 351). From
there it is brought up into the bend of the left fingers as the hand is fisted,
and everything is set for the change of white to red.

THUMB THE THIMBLE

This is a neat, surprising manipulation originated by James Shannon,
who was one of the best thimble workers of his time. The performer starts

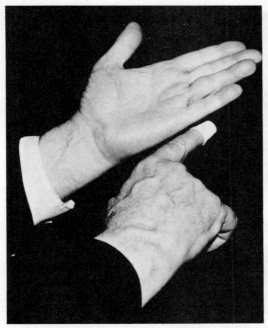

Fig. 350. White thimble
shown on right forefinger.
Red thimble hidden on tip
of right second finger,
ready to repeat change.

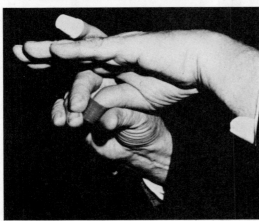

Fig. 351. Alternate form
of Repeat Change. Left
thumb "stealing" red
thimble from right thumb
and finger clip. Rear view.

with a thimble on his right forefinger, pokes it into his left fist (Fig. 352),
and without withdrawing his forefinger, he brings his right thumb upward,
showing the thimble on its very tip (Fig. 353)! This gives the magical effect
of an instant transposition of the thimble from forefinger to thumb, almost
as if it penetrated the back of the left hand.

Then, dipping his right thumb from sight below the left hand, the performer withdraws his right forefinger from his left fist, showing the thimble
back on the forefinger, exactly as it was to start. This baffling move bears
repetition; if performed rapidly and smoothly, it becomes even more
bewildering the more often it is shown. Yet, while practice is necessary to
gain the needed precision, the manipulation itself is of a basic type.

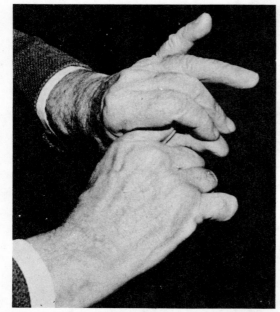

THUMB THE THIMBLE
Fig. 352. Right forefinger
completing poke of thim-
ble into left fist.

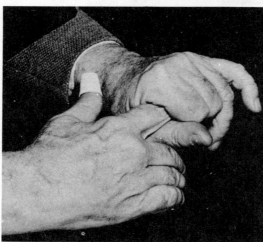

Fig. 353. Right thumb
swinging outward to show
thimble while forefinger is
still within left fist.

It is simply an extension of the Poke Vanish with a special follow-up.
The right forefinger is bent downward over the left thumb, so the thimble
can be clipped between the right thumb and second finger. But instead of
stopping there, it is pressed farther downward and outward by the right
thumb, so the third finger can come beneath it along with the second finger.
This not only frees the right thumb, but it also brings the mouth of the
thimble directly toward the tip of the thumb (Fig. 354), which is promptly
inserted in the thimble. All in the same move, the right thumb whips
upward and outward, bringing the thimble into view above the left hand.

To reverse the process, swing the right thumb down under the left hand,

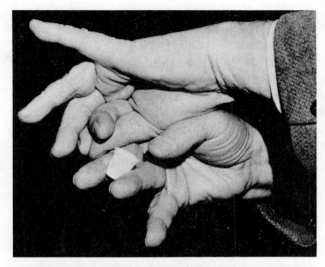

Fig. 354. Rear view showing intermediate position in rapid transfer of thimble from forefinger to thumb aided by right middle fingers. Right thumb is poised for insertion into clipped thimble.

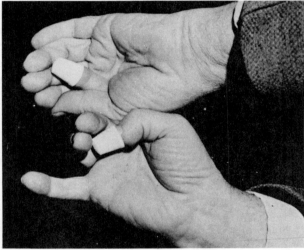

Fig. 355. Alternate method. Rear view shows right thumb gaining duplicate thimble from Finger-palm position.

clip it between the right second and third fingers, using the thumb to press it on the right forefinger, which promptly emerges from the left fist.

ALTERNATE THUMB THE THIMBLE

Here is another version of Thumb the Thimble that is exactly the same in effect, but is much faster, yet at the same time easier. The reason is that a neat bit of fakery is involved. You have a second thimble, unknown to the audience, concealed in the bend of your right fingers, with its mouth toward your right thumb. Show the original thimble on the right forefinger, poke it deep into the left fist, and simultaneously thrust the right thumb into the bend of the right fingers, picking up the duplicate thimble and swinging it into view (Fig. 355).

Reverse the move, putting the duplicate back in Finger-bend Palm position, and draw the right forefinger from the left fist, showing the original thimble on the fingertip. Worked alone, this might excite suspicion if repeated too often, but in conjunction with the regular method, it is great. You can start with the single thimble and after a few repeats vanish it, then reproduce it from your pocket, bringing along a duplicate that you have planted there, which you keep in Finger-bend position. Work the alternate version a few times, then vanish the original thimble and again reproduce it from your pocket, this time leaving the duplicate there.

MENTAL MAGIC

MESSAGE READING

Among mental effects, probably the most important is that of "reading" or "revealing" a question or a message that a person has in mind. The usual procedure in such cases is to have a person write a question, a name, or a number, on a sheet of paper that he keeps in his own possession for later verification, or that is folded and then burned so that no one but the writer can possibly know what it was. Hence when the performer gives the answer, the effect is more than magical; it is miraculous. That is why specialists in this type of work refer to themselves as mentalists rather than magicians, but actually they are one and the same.

Various gimmicks and devices have been invented and marketed to help the "mentalist" garner information in clandestine fashion. One time-honored item is a pad of paper that is quite ordinary except for the third sheet from the top. This has been waxed by rubbing paraffin evenly over its upper surface. The performer can casually thumb through the sheets, showing them to be quite plain, but when someone writes a question on the top sheet and tears it off, the third sheet picks up the impression. Later, in private, the performer rubs powdered graphite over the waxed sheet and literally "develops" the words written by the spectator.

The clipboard is a more modern device that serves a similar purpose. As its name implies, it is simply a smooth board with a heavy clamp at the top, and is normally used to hold sheets of paper such as bills, vouchers, and reminders. For mental effects, a single sheet with several perforated lines is attached to the board, enabling volunteers to write individual questions, tear them off one by one, and fold them so the performer cannot see what was written. The clipboard, however, is specially prepared with a thin paper surface that matches the wooden board. Beneath that is a sheet of carbon paper, with an ordinary white sheet under it.

Questions written on the perforated paper are therefore automatically reproduced in carbon copy, and once the performer is alone he can pull out the white sheet and learn all he needs to know. Like the waxed pad, the clipboard has not been well suited for close-up work, but in recent years, smaller boards have been devised, enabling the performer to pull out the carbon sheet and read the message practically under the eyes of the spectators, which makes it suitable for close-up work.

More adaptable to impromptu work is the "peek mirror," which is a polished metal disk the size of a large coin. The performer palms it in the bend of his right fingers (see page 3). He has a spectator write a name or number on a small blank card or sheet of paper and tells him to hold it a few feet in front of his eyes while he concentrates on what he has written and repeats it mentally, so the performer can "pick up the impression."

Since the back of the card is toward the performer, it is impossible for him to see the writing, and he keeps mentioning that fact, at the same time urging the spectator to hold the card higher and keep it vertical, even telling him to raise his chin, so he can keep the card exactly at eye level. The performer stresses the importance of this, saying that it prevents him from even glimpsing what was written; actually, it gives him the glimpse he wants, thanks to the palmed "peek mirror." While telling the spectator, "Keep the card straight up!" the performer moves his right hand *beyond* the card, bringing it *between* the card and the spectator's eyes. This enables him to see the writing reflected in the palmed mirror; and he gains a further glimpse when he moves his hand toward the spectator's chin, while suggesting that he raise his head higher.

This can be worked while seated opposite a person at a table, but care is needed to avoid bad angles if other observers are at the sides. Also, unless there is some leeway to allow for hand gestures, it is wise to specify that the person concentrate upon the date of a year or the initials of a friend, as these can be spotted fairly easily in a peek mirror, whereas full names or rows of figures can give trouble. One good test with a peek mirror is to have people hold up playing cards taken at random from their own pack. By aiming the "peek" for the index corner of the card, the performer can learn its name with a passing glance.

Many other devices used in mental effects are cataloged by magic dealers, and most will prove of value to anyone who wants to specialize in this branch of the mystic art. It must be remembered that nerve is the great asset when presenting mental effects; hence any suggestion of skill should be avoided. It is hard for some performers to realize that many spectators do not know that they were being tricked; instead, they are apt to take the result seriously and attribute it to ESP or some psychic ability on the performer's part.

This means that the performer will have to change the tempo of his work where misdirection is concerned, relying on casual comments and deliberate action rather than catch phrases and quick moves. Actually, the styles do not mix, but it is fairly easy to change from one mood to the other and stay with whichever seems best suited for the occasion or the audience.

Where both impromptu and close-up work are concerned, the best procedure is to practice and inject some manipulative skill into acquiring written questions without the spectator's knowledge. Sleights involving small objects, most notably coins or dollar bills, can readily be adapted to message reading. The basic method for these moves is termed:

BILLET SWITCHING

For this, you need slips of paper measuring approximately two by three inches, though the exact size may be varied according to individual choice. However, since one slip is to be "switched" for another, all should be identical when you have decided upon the size you prefer. You first fold the display slip or "billet" across, then down. You then open it and give it to a spectator, telling him to write a question, name, or number on the slip. After that, he is to fold it as it was and place it on the table.

Meanwhile, you have obtained a duplicate or "dummy" billet, which is blank and already folded. You clip this by the long edges between the first two fingers of your right hand, so it extends inward toward the palm. The dummy billet can be palmed before you hand the spectator his slip. It can be gotten from the right coat pocket or even from your lap while he is writing his question. Since you naturally turn away so as not to see what he is writing, acquiring the dummy is a very simple matter.

Once you have it, keep your fingers curled inward and your hand turned somewhat downward, with your thumb resting on your forefinger (Fig. 356). This is a natural position that hides the dummy from every angle. Tell the spectator to place his folded billet on the table—always referring to it as a "slip" or "question"—and if he sets it upright, all is ready. If he lays it flat, you set it up using your left thumb and forefinger to turn it toward you, resting it on its edges so that it resembles a tiny tent.

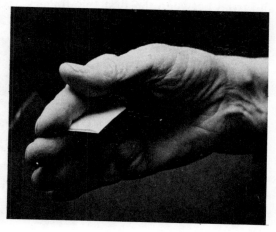

BILLET SWITCHING
Fig. 356. Dummy billet clipped at start between first two fingers of right hand and hidden by thumb.

Actually, you can arrange this placement beforehand by telling the spectator what you want him to do. Before handing him the blank paper, you say: "Write something on this paper, then fold it in half, like this—and again, like this. Then set it on the table like that, so that it will be impossible for anyone to see what you have written." With that, you open the paper and give it to him, while you specify that he can write a question, a name, a number, or whatever else he wants.

You can do all this while you have the dummy billet already clipped between the first two fingers of the right hand, but a better plan is to pick it up later, either when you are reaching in your pocket to find a pen or pencil for the spectator to use, or while he is writing his question. A very neat plan is to have the dummy attached to the clip of a pen or pencil, which is then placed deep in your shirt pocket, without using the clip to hold it there.

Reaching in your pocket, you take the upper end of the pencil between your right thumb and forefinger, so the slip is hidden within the bend of your right fingers. The right hand transfers the pencil to the left, which takes the upper end in the same manner, so that the first two fingers of the right hand can grip the dummy between them, with the right thumb aiding the process. The left hand simply draws away the pencil, leaving the dummy neatly clipped between the right fingers, in readiness for the billet switch. The left hand swings the lower end of the pencil outward while handing it to the spectator, thus carrying all attention in that direction.

Now for the billet switch itself:

After the original billet is placed tentwise on the table, you pick it up by cupping your right hand around it (Fig. 357). In this action, the right thumb presses the original into the bend of the second and third fingers, which grip it and retain it as the hand is raised. Note that the right hand is slanted inward during the pickup, but it immediately comes upright when it is raised, thereby concealing the spectator's slip perfectly in the finger bend. In that same action, the right thumb is thrust upward, forcing the dummy slip from between the first two fingers and pushing it into sight above the knuckle of the forefinger (Fig. 358).

Fig. 357. Right hand picking up original billet with thumb pushing it into bend of right fingers (rear view).

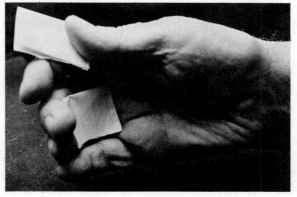

Fig. 358. Thumb thrusting dummy billet upward so it comes into view and is mistaken for original (rear view).

From the spectator's view, this is utterly deceptive, particularly so because no deception seems to be involved. The dummy comes in view so soon after the pickup of the original billet that most people will maintain that it never left their sight. In fact, with a little practice, the switch can be made almost instantly, with the lower fingers still palming the original slip away while the thumb is visibly pressing the dummy toward the tip of the forefinger.

Here the most direct procedure is to tell the spectator: "I want you to concentrate on what you have written on this slip while I press it against my forehead and try to obtain a mental impression." With that, you deliberately transfer the dummy billet to your left thumb and forefinger and turn your open left palm toward the spectator as you raise the slip to your forehead. This is a timely move, as anyone suspicious of a switch will be looking for it at this point, not realizing that it was done already.

One way to read the message is to keep your left hand pressed against your forehead and hold the dummy slip there. By then the hand should be turned inward to shield your eyes so that you can look downward without anyone noticing it. Your right hand goes to your lap with the spectator's slip and secretly opens it by pushing the tip of the thumb under a loose corner. If need be, you can turn your body somewhat to the right in order to see the writing more effectively.

With a question, you answer it as best you can, pretending that you are getting it mentally. The mere fact that you piece the question correctly is enough to nonplus most people, even though your answer may be hazy or even wrong. With names, it is a good policy to spell them out, letter by letter, as though you were groping for them. With numbers, you can go from figure to figure, getting them in the wrong order to start, then correcting yourself later. The whole idea is to avoid making things look too easy; otherwise people may suspect that you somehow gained access to the spectator's slip.

At intervals, you should lower your left hand from your forehead, as though to replace the dummy slip on the table; then raise it again and go back into your contemplative mood. At the conclusion, you actually leave it on the table, preferably on the left, and your right hand refolds the spectator's message while below the table edge and clips it between the first two fingers. You can then rest your right hand on the table as you look directly at the spectator and finalize your message. Folding your arms is also effective at this point, as it puts your right hand in perfect position to reach for the dummy slip and reverse the billet switch, giving the spectator's slip back to him, so he can open it and show people how right you were. Meanwhile, you have ample opportunity to pocket the dummy billet.

In the Crystal Perform the billet switch as described but instead of pressing the dummy billet against your forehead to "pick up telepathic impressions," you can gaze into a crystal ball and pretend to visualize the message in its depths. Such balls are available in various sizes from about two inches in diameter upward and add greatly to the effect. However, instead of a crystal ball, a large coin or medal can be used; in fact, almost any bright, shiny object will do.

A good procedure here is to start by putting the billet to your forehead, then remark that you can't seem to gain an impression, so you will try "scrying" — crystal gazing. You then set the dummy billet aside and bring out the crystal ball, or whatever object you are using. If you have already read the spectator's slip and have had time to refold it, you can switch it for the dummy then and there, and use the business of bringing out the crystal ball to furnish excellent misdirection.

For added effect you can still pretend to have trouble getting an impression, so you ask the spectator to open his slip and show it to someone else so that two people will be concentrating on the question. You then proceed with your revelation of the message, and since it all occurs after the spectator reopens his slip, he is apt to forget that it ever left his possession.

However, this method offers an alternative. If you have problems in reading the spectator's slip, or feel that you are taking too long about it, the alternative is to burn the dummy slip. For this you need a pack of matches and a receptacle such as an ashtray or a small plate or saucer. Lighting a match and setting fire to the dummy slip can be done quite easily while the spectator's slip is palmed in the bend of the right fingers, for the match pack helps to hide it.

This method makes it unnecessary to switch the spectator's slip for the dummy at the finish because you have already disposed of the dummy. Pocketing the spectator's slip after reading it in your lap is also easy. Merely pick up the match pack from the table and drop it into your pocket and let the spectator's slip go with it.

From the Ashes In this variation, you do not need the crystal ball or any other object used in scrying. Have a pack of matches and a receptacle handy and go through the usual routine of having the spectator write his question and fold it. Make the billet switch with your right hand and immediately transfer the dummy slip to your left hand, so your right hand can pick up the match pack — a very natural action.

Lay the dummy in the ashtray and open the pack of matches with your left hand. Take out a match and strike it with your right hand and lift up the dummy billet with your left thumb and fingers, just far enough to ignite it. The left hand drops the burning paper into the tray, while your right goes below the table and secretly opens the spectator's slip. Bring the ashtray close to the table edge with your left hand, which is then raised to your forehead, as though to shelter your downward gaze toward the burning billet.

Actually, you are reading the spectator's billet in the usual fashion and when the dummy burns out, you can stir the ashes with your left forefinger, as though that had something to do with divining the message. Since all emphasis is on the burning of the dummy billet, it becomes a very plausible procedure. At the finish, the right hand pockets the spectator's slip with the match pack.

Behind the Tablet This is a very impressive form of message reading, but if presented while seated at a table, care must be taken where side angles are concerned. Hence it is preferable to work it while standing or even walking about, keeping all observers well in front of you. You need a standard-size writing tablet, which you lay on the table at the start or hand to a spectator, whom you request to keep it until you need it.

From a small pad, you tear the usual billet, showing a spectator how to fold it after writing his question. Bring out a dummy billet clipped to a pencil, or get it from your pocket while you turn away so that you cannot see what the spectator writes. You do the billet switch and immediately burn the dummy, saying that you intend to write down impressions that come from the spectator's mind alone. For that you need the writing tablet, so you take it, along with a pencil, and begin drawing diagrams or listing random names. You can let people see these at first; then, as you concentrate more deeply, you keep them toward yourself. All this while, you have been concealing the spectator's slip in the bend of the right fingers. Now: Slide it under the thumb of the left hand, which is holding the tablet from its side.

In the course of further jottings, you bring the left forefinger to the near side of the tablet, so it can help the thumb open the spectator's slip under cover of the tablet. Your right hand can also help by pausing during its scrawls to spread the slip wider. Knowing the question, you naturally begin to formulate the answer; and here you can introduce a neat bit of byplay originated by U. F. Grant, popularly known as "Gen" Grant, who without doubt has the most inventive and ingenious mind of anyone in the creative field of magic.

After secretly reading the spectator's slip, you shake your head and begin to cross out your notations, saying that you just can't pick up impressions, so you will have to start all over. With that, you tear off the top sheet of the tablet, crumple it up, and throw it away or stuff it into your pocket. In doing this, you include the spectator's slip, getting rid of it entirely. You then begin making new notations on the next sheet of the pad, letting people see them as you do, and gradually you develop an answer to the spectator's question.

Pocketing the scrawled sheet is usually the best procedure; otherwise, some curious person might pick it up and open it to study your scrawls, only to find the telltale spectator's slip as well.

Find the Word Here you need a fair-sized dictionary to use with a highly convincing mental test dependent on the Billet Switch. You give the dictionary to a spectator, along with a pencil and a slip of paper of the customary size, and tell him to look through the dictionary and find a word he likes. He is to write that word on the slip, fold it, set it on the table, close the dictionary, and place it beside the slip, all while your back is turned.

You can emphasize that you have two good reasons for having the spectator go through the dictionary rather than simply pick a random word mentally. First, in looking through, he is sure to come across some unusual words that would not ordinarily occur to him; second, when he picks his word, you want him to read the definition as well, so that he can keep it in mind when writing it on his slip. With a word that has two or more meanings, he can concentrate on one while keeping the others in the back of his mind—in case you need them.

As with all effects of this type, the more you build up any such angles, the more impressive it becomes. Telling the spectator to concentrate on the word he has written and to repeat the definition mentally before folding the slip are good points to mention while your back is turned. Meanwhile, you have obtained your dummy billet, and when you turn around, you pick up the spectator's slip and make the customary switch. It is preferable to burn the dummy at this point, because otherwise you would have to leave it on the table, because you are now concerned chiefly with the dictionary.

This is where your procedure becomes neat indeed. Simply pick up the dictionary, saying that you will look through it and try to find the spectator's word while he concentrates on it. Bring your right hand beneath the book, pressing the spectator's slip up against it, and open it with your left hand, going down the columns with your left index finger. Pause, lowering the dictionary so that people can see its pages; then shift it to your left hand and tilt the book upward and bring your right hand above it, keeping the spectator's slip hidden in the finger bend. Note the page as you run your right hand up and down the page and slide the slip beneath your right thumb, closing the dictionary with your left hand.

Both hands are now clear, with the slip safely tucked away at a known page, while you ask the spectator a few pointed questions, such as: "Is your word a noun or a verb?" "Is it a long word or a short one?" "I get impressions of the letters 'R' and 'S.' Are either of those in the word you selected?" Regardless of the spectator's response, you open the book and go through its pages in batches, forward and backward, pausing at one spot or another. Finally, you tilt it your way again, open to the page where you left the spectator's slip, and unfold the slip while fingering the columns.

As soon as you have read the written word—for example, "panorama" —you simply leave the slip where it is and thumb through other pages openly, making suitable comments as, "Yes, I see the letter 'R'—I get an impression of 'R-A-M'—no, that isn't quite it. 'P-R-A-M'—but it has three syllables, maybe four." By then you have found the word "panorama" and are noting its definition, so you tell the spectator: "You are thinking of a picture—a large picture, like a view. Yes, here it is: panorama!"

With that you point out the word to people, close the dictionary, and put it away, leaving the spectator's slip lost among the pages, with your hands all clear. If you want to return the spectator's slip instead of burning it, you simply refold it after reading it and clip it between the first two fingers of one hand, which goes beneath the dictionary while the other hand turns to pages to find the chosen word. You are then ready to switch the spectator's slip for the dummy, which is still lying on the table. That done, you can carelessly flip through the pages saying, "Sixty-five thousand words to choose from and I picked the right one!" During that action, you leave the folded dummy anywhere convenient.

CENTER-TEAR METHOD

There is a development of the Billet Switch that is aptly termed the Center Tear and that is preferred by most close-up performers, for it does away with the switch entirely, though it still requires palming on a lesser scale. Actually, only one slip is used, but the "message" is generally limited to a name or a number; and in all cases, the slip must be torn into pieces that the performer either burns or openly puts in his pocket. This method has certain ramifications that make it specially deceptive, however.

You start with a sheet of paper about three inches square and fold it in half, then in quarters, as with the other billet tricks. Unfold it and draw a circle of one and one-half inches' diameter in the center. You tell a volunteer to write something within the circle, such as a name, a number, or date, or an address. He is then to refold the paper and place it on the table or give it to you directly. Either way, you take it between the tips of your thumbs and fingers so that you can tear it in half.

Keep the folded edges upright and to the left as you tear. Now put the right-hand pieces in front, away from your body, and tear from right to left. Again, put the right-hand pieces in front — that is, away from yourself. (Up to this point, keep your hands tilted upward and forward, and do the tearing openly so that people can see you have nothing but the spectator's slip.) Here lower your hands so that the backs of your fingers are toward the spectator, and as you do, your right thumb draws the nearest torn portion inward, so that it comes into the bend of the second finger. This enables you to raise your right forefinger a trifle and clip it between the first two fingers.

This happens to be the piece with the two doubled edges, which you continually kept at the rear of the batch. This piece is retained in the "finger clip" as your right thumb and fingers release the rest — the front pieces — and let them drop into a plate or ashtray. Or you can draw away those front pieces with your left thumb and fingers and either drop them into the ashtray or thrust them into your left coat pocket, showing them quite openly as you do. Either way, people take it for granted that they represent all the torn pieces; and after all, how could the retention of one tiny piece help you learn the circled message?

You will find this out when you open the palmed fragment with your right thumb, keeping it hidden in the bend of the right fingers. Though it represents only one fourth of the torn slip, it is the only part that counts. It forms the *exact center* of the original slip and it includes the *entire area* of the circle in which the name or number was written. Thus you have gained all you need to know, and after disposing of the other portions, you simply open the tiny slip secretly, read it, give the answer, and dispose of it later.

Various procedures for secretly viewing the "message" may be used during the burning stage. One is simply to keep the torn center clipped by the right fingers while both hands open the the match pack and while the right thumb and fingers tear out a match. The left hand closes the pack and holds it while the right strikes a match and does the burning, keeping the torn center hidden all the while. However:

For very close work, there is a type of "delayed action" that can be used very effectively once you have practiced it until it becomes entirely natural. This is to pick up the match pack with your left hand and open it by inserting your left forefinger beneath the flap, which enables you to bend the flap well back. Your right thumb and fingers come over to take a match, but in that action the right fingers tuck the clipped center down behind the matches and leave it there. The right hand removes a match and strikes it while the left hand closes the pack, but leaves the flap loose while laying it aside. When the odd pieces have been burned, the hands pick up the pack to close it, and either the left thumb or the right thumb goes behind the matches and draws out the torn center, sliding it into finger-bend position.

This allows the hands to be kept palms upward during the burning action, thus showing them entirely clear. The match pack, too, can be turned so people see the matches after the center slip has been neatly tucked away. You can even give the odd pieces another tear before burning them in the ashtray, which makes the batch look bulkier and makes it all the less likely that anyone will suspect that a portion of the original slip is missing.

In tearing the original slip, some performers prefer to draw away the center portion with the left thumb, so that it can be clipped between the left fingers instead of the right. The tearing process is exactly the same, with the right-hand pieces going to the front, so that the center still is toward you when the left thumb draws it away. But the handling of the match pack differs. The left fingers simply press the torn center beneath it, while the hands open the pack, take out a match, and close the pack in order to burn the odd slips. The pack hides the torn center all the while.

Reading the Message Practically all the methods used in reading a switched billet can be applied with the Center Tear. While dipping one hand below the table and secretly opening the torn center, you can pretend to concentrate by shading your eyes with your other hand and resting your elbow on the table. This enables you to look downward and read the circled message. Similarly, you can pretend to gain an impression from the ashes of the burned pieces.

By using a writing tablet to scribble impressions with a pencil, you can open the torn center while tilting the pad upward and holding it there with your left thumb. You then get rid of the torn center by crumpling it inside the scribbled sheet when you tear it from the tablet and thrust it in your

CENTER-TEAR METHOD

pocket. In this case you can use a smaller tablet than with the billet switch.

A smaller dictionary can also be used in the book test, where you have a person look up a word in a dictionary and write it within the circle. By slipping the torn center among the pages and opening it as you thumb through, your can learn the chosen word, turn to its page, and read it with its definition, showing the page as you do. The torn center can be left among the pages, or folded and removed with the finger clip. In all cases, it can be pocketed later with the match pack.

In addition, the Center Tear offers the following innovations, which are as baffling as they are unique:

Through the Crystal This is based on a neat method of using a crystal ball in reading a message that has been torn, then burned or pocketed. The old way is hold the ball above the table with one hand and open the message below the table with the other hand, so while pretending to gaze into the crystal, you can read the message. With the Center Tear such fakery is unnecessary. Since the slip is only about an inch and a half square, you can easily conceal it in the bend of the fingers and keep the written side toward you with the thumb holding it in place.

You do this without even glancing toward that hand, which can be beneath the table if you are seated, or at your side if you are standing. Pick up the crystal ball with your empty hand and transfer it to the hand that holds the torn center, keeping the back of that hand toward the spectators. Set the ball directly in the bend of the fingers, so that it covers the torn center and the thumb presses the opposite side of the ball to hold it there. You can now turn the ball at any angle, as long as you keep the palm of the hand upward or downward and the slip will not be seen, thanks to the curvature of the glass.

You can even turn it palm frontward, provided you keep it in motion and provided such action is brief. The final position should be palm upward, with the hand turned enough toward your eyes so you can gaze down into the ball as though expecting to read an answer in its depths. You will actually read it there if you keep your hand steady and toward the light, because the crystal will magnify the writing for your eyes alone.

From this method, Gen Grant has devised a still more ingenious system, ideally suited for impromptu work, namely:

From the Glass Instead of using a crystal ball, you use a glass or goblet partly filled with water, which makes it a very good effect for the dinner table, though it can be worked almost anywhere. Secretly open the torn center and work it into the finger bend, with the writing toward you, but in this case you pick up the glass of water, keeping the back of your hand toward the spectators and curving the torn center against the glass, a very natural position. State that you are using hydromancy, a form of divination by water, to learn the message.

As you tilt the glass one way and another and study the surface of the water, you turn it into the light so you can read the writing through the inside of the glass. A good plan here is to transfer the glass into the free hand before you give the answer. This enables you to keep tilting the glass and pretending to probe the water, while you lower the hand with the torn center to your lap or to your side. There you can fold it and get rid of it by pocketing it with the match pack that you have left on the table.

Name for Name This effect of Gen Grant's deserves top rating among Center Tears as it is foolproof from the performer's standpoint and an absolute convincer where spectators are concerned. You hand someone the usual square of paper with a circle in the center, stating that this represents his "circle of acquaintances," and in it he is to write the name of some person he has met but whom he is sure you would not know. For you to focus your mind on a single "thought target," you also specify that he is to write the person's *last name only,* then fold it along its cross creases.

You turn away while he writes the name; then pick up the paper, work the Center Tear, retain the vital piece, and burn or pocket the rest. So far it is standard procedure, but after a few moments of concentration and with no suspicious moves, you say that you are unable to gain an impression of the name because it is incomplete. Strangely enough, you need to know the person's first name in order to visualize the last name. This is not so strange, you say, because the spectator himself is thinking of *both* names, so it is not surprising that you should be confused.

To rectify this situation, you hand the spectator another paper square with a circle in the center and tell him to write the first name therein. Naturally, you turn away and read the name on the torn center already in your possession, which we will assume is "Larkin." As you turn back to the table, you can dispose of the torn center by picking up the match pack and pocketing both together, saying that you are not going to burn the new slip the spectator has just written.

Instead of tearing the new slip, you hold it to your forehead momentarily. State that it is just as difficult to get an impression of the first name as the last, so you will have to clarify the issue. With that, you deliberately unfold the slip and read the name, which we will assume to be "Roger." In a reflective mood, you then say: "Roger. I know a few Rogers. But none is the Roger you are thinking of, because I have never met him, nor even heard of him. But his name seems to be coming through, so keep concentrating on it. Roger—Roger—wait, I have it: Roger Larkin!"

You then show the slip to everybody so they can all see the name Roger. You tear it in half, then in quarters, *along the folds* while it is still open. This is a perfect "throw off" if anyone thinks back to the tearing of the previous slip. Here they actually see the circled name being torn into four separate segments that would be impossible to read, so they naturally assume that the first slip, with the name Larkin, was torn in the same fashion.

Instead of disposing of the torn center by pocketing it with the match pack, you can retain it in the bend of the fingers while you pick up the folded slip bearing the first name, in this case "Roger." In opening you automatically hide the torn center beneath it. When you tear the "Roger" slip across in two directions, tear the center of the "Larkin" slip with it and put them all in your pocket, thus making a very neat getaway.

Time out of Mind In this recent development in the Center-tear Method, the circle in the middle of the folded slip is marked with the numbers 1 to 12, to represent a clock dial. This gives the circle a special purpose, making the effect logical as well as deceptive. Since more than one dial will be used in the test, it is a good plan to mark them beforehand on the top pages of a square pad measuring three by three inches, so they can be torn off and used as required.

NOTE: A square pad can be cut two inches from the lower end of a standard three-by-five-inch pad. Or the bottom two inches can be turned up and torn off. The clock dial, of course, should be centered in the square portion above the fold.

You start by showing an ordinary watch, preferably one that is not running, and state that you will set it at some specific time, projecting a mental image of the time you have in mind. You give a spectator one of the paper squares and tell him to mark in hands, pointing to whatever time he thinks you have in mind. The hands should point directly to numbers, you say, so they will represent such times as 12:00, 12:05, 12:10, 12:15, and so on, all at intervals of five minutes. That makes 144 choices in all, but actually, that can be cut in half by using two hands of equal length, as it may be difficult for the spectator to differentiate between a long hand and a short hand while picking up a telepathically projected image.

You turn away and set the watch, telling the spectator to mark his dial while your back is turned, and then fold the paper in quarters, along the ready-made creases. When he has done that, you turn around and lay the watch face down beside his folded paper. You then say: "I will turn the watch face up; and if its hands point to the same numbers as yours, I want you to say, "Yes." If they are different, just say "No." Do not tell me what time you marked if I am wrong. Just say "No."

When you turn up the watch, its long hand is pointing to the 4 and its short hand to 8, signifying the time as 8:20. That would represent 3:40 if the hands were transposed. So you have two chances out of 144, or one in 72, that the spectator will say "Yes." If he does, you open his slip and lay it beside the watch so that everyone can see that the dials really match. Quite amazing, if it does happen, which it might, for this reason:

Many people automatically picture a watch or clock with its hands set as 8:20 because jewelers' signs often show imitation watches with their hands indicating that time. The hands also have a symmetrical or "balanced" appearance when pointing to the numerals 8 and 4, which may induce people to picture them that way. So you always have a chance for a lucky hit that will really flabbergast your audience. However, if you miss, don't worry. You are then ready for the sure-fire method that follows.

You pick up the spectator's folded slip, saying casually: "So we missed on that one. Let's try again." You tear the slip and retain the folded center as you reach for the watch. At the same time drop the remaining pieces in your pocket with your other hand. You pick up the watch as if to set it, but you remark, "Wait now! You already have your mind fixed on the time you marked on the paper dial. So I'm going to let *you* set the watch at that *exact time,* so that *you* can project *your* time thought, while I try to receive it and mark it down."

You give the watch to the spectator with your free hand, while you reach for the pad with the hand that secretly holds the torn center clipped between its fingers or in the finger bend. In picking up the pad, slide your fingers beneath and keep it hidden there as you take the pencil with your other hand. Turn your back saying, "Go right ahead and set the watch at the time you *already* have in mind. Then lay it on the table, face down, as I did."

With your back turned, you secretly open the palmed center, note its time, and slide the torn center deep among the pages of the pad. Then you use the pencil to mark that same time on the circular dial showing on the top sheet of the pad. Good byplay here is to hesitate until the spectator has laid the watch on the table. Then you turn around, make the final mark, pausing as though about to rub it out, but finally decide to leave it as it is. Tear the sheet from the pad, drop the pad and pencil in your pocket, and fold the sheet in four, laying it on the table beside the watch, just as the spectator did earlier.

This sets the climax. Tell the spectator to turn the watch face up, then unfold the paper and compare the dials. Or you can delegate both actions to other persons, since the result will always be the same. The fact that the dials match will seem a near miracle, and you will be completely free of the torn center from the spectator's slip. Some observers may even forget the original slip entirely, thinking that the spectator had free choice of setting the watch at any time he wanted.

Without the Watch The "time test" just described can be worked without a watch by having four sheets of dials on top of the pad. The routine is basically the same, but you must use a square of paper with its dial, instead of a watch. Start by tearing off two sheets—one for yourself, the other for the spectator. Turning away, you draw two hands on your sheet, one pointing to the number 8, the other to 4. State that you are projecting a "time thought" that the spectator is to copy if he can.

Both slips are folded and placed side by side, and you open yours first—just as you would turn up the watch. If the spectator says that its time—8:20 or 3:40—doesn't match his, you tear up your slip *openly*—that is, directly through the circle. You then tear up his slip, without bothering to unfold it, using the center tear. Practically in the same move, you pick up the pad, sliding the torn center beneath it, retaining it there while you tear off another sheet and hand it to the spectator, saying that you will "start all over." Then you add, "Since you already have a time in mind, mark it down again so as to avoid confusion in projection."

That leaves you with pad in hand, torn center beneath, ready to open it and copy it on the circular dial showing on the top sheet of the pad. Again, you tear it off, fold it, and lay it beside the spectator's folded slip while you pocket the pad, with the torn center snugly tucked away a few sheets down. The climax in this case comes when both new slips—yours and the spectator's—are unfolded and found to be identical.

TURN-OVER COINS

Three coins are laid on the table, and the performer turns his back, telling a spectator to start turning over the coins one by one. Each time the spectator turns a coin, he must say so, but he does not have to specify which coin, and he can turn them in any order that he wants, either repeatedly turning one while he ignores the others or anything else that occurs to him. He can stop when he wants, and having made his final turn-over, he is told to place his hand over one of the coins.

The performer turns about, studies the spectator's hand, or presses his pulse and states whether the coin lies "heads" or "tails." Whichever the case, when the spectator lifts his hand, the performer is correct. That could be luck, but when the test is repeated without a miss, it takes on the aspect of a real mystery. Yet the secret is actually quite simple.

The performer starts with all three coins heads up, thus showing an *odd number* of heads. When the spectator turns a coin, the performer mentally says "even"; when the spectator announces another turn, the performer mentally says "odd," and so on. When the spectator makes his final turn and says that he is stopping there, if the performer has reached "odd," he knows that an odd number of heads are upward, which means either three or one. If he has reached "even," it means an even number of heads are upward, either two or none. So after the spectator has placed his hand over the coin of his choice, the performer turns around and takes a passing glance at the two that are still uncovered.

If the performer has ended his count with odd:
Two heads showing will mean that the hidden coin is heads (three).
One head showing means that the hidden coin must be tails (one).
No heads showing proves that the hidden coin is heads (one).
If the performer has ended his count with even:
Two heads showing will mean that the hidden coin is tails (two).
One head showing means that the hidden coin must be heads (two).
No heads showing proves that the hidden coin is tails (zero).

In actual practice, this routine can be worked regardless of how many heads are showing at the start. With three heads, the performer begins counting from "odd," as described; with two heads, he starts from "even"; with one head, from "odd"; with none, from "even." Hence in repeating the effect, no new setup is needed; the performer can proceed with the coins exactly as they lie.

MULTIPLE TURNOVER

Basically, this is the Turn-over Coins using four, five, six, or more coins instead of only three. Actually, the extra coins make no difference. The performer simply notes whether the heads are "odd" or "even" at the start and switches as usual each time the spectator announces a turn-over. At the finish, the performer counts the heads, and if he needs another to make the total "odd" or "even," as the case may be, he knows that the hidden coin is a head. Conversely, if another head is not needed, the hidden coin will be a tail. Coins may be added or taken away, as though to complicate the test, but it makes no difference, as long as you note whether the heads are "odd" or "even" before the turning begins, and proceed accordingly.

The Multiple-turnover Method lends itself to another effect, however. Working with five or six coins, the performer tells the spectator to put each hand over a coin at the finish, instead of only one. Studying the spectator's hands, the performer says, "Both coins are alike. Look and see." This proves to be correct. Or he may decide, "One coin is a head; the other a tail," which turns out to be right.

The system is simply this:

> If the count ends on *odd* and heads are *odd* at the finish, both coins will be the same (two heads or two tails).
> If the count ends on *even* and heads are *even* at the finish, both coins will be the same (two heads or two tails).
> If the count ends on *odd* and heads are *even* at the finish, one hidden coin will be a head, the other a tail.
> If the count ends on *even* and heads are *odd* at the finish, one hidden coin will be a head, the other a tail.

FIND THE COIN

The performer tosses several nickels on the table, emphasizing that all are United States coins with one exception, a Canadian nickel, which is of the same size and weight as the others. When the performer turns his back, spectators drop the coins into his hand in any order they choose, yet the performer promptly picks out the Canadian nickel. After repeating the test a few times, the performer can vary it as follows:

The nickels are laid in the center of an ordinary handkerchief; a spectator gathers the corners of the cloth and shakes the coins about. The performer shows his right hand empty, dips it down into the handkerchief, and brings the Canadian nickel from the folds. Again, the test can be repeated with same result, leaving the spectators fully baffled.

Two different principles are involved in this effect, so that one version serves as prelude to the other. In the first test, you actually tell the Canadian nickel by the sense of touch. Test one with your thumbnail and you will find that the head side is so smooth that the nail slides over it. Turn the coin over and test the tail side to make sure. You will encounter a series of irregular obstructions.

Now try the same thing with a late-date United States nickel. The head will slow the thumbnail's progress somewhere along the line, while the tail will stop it abruptly. This must be tried from a few different angles to make sure, but once you have acquired the touch, the more certain it becomes. Since you can't be sure which side is "up" to start, a few turnovers may be needed for insurance. That makes it tougher for anyone who thinks that he has "caught on" to the trick.

If they really do catch on, they can be stopped cold by the second method, where the nickels are dumped into a handkerchief that is formed into an improvised bag. Here the performer steadies the bag with his left hand, while his right hand dips in and brings out the Canadian nickel so promptly that nobody else could hope to come up with it that fast, if at all. What's more, he can repeat it, so emphatically, that any would-be imitators will be left far behind.

In his left hand, the performer has a very small bar-shaped magnet. Canadian nickels are magnetic, whereas those of the United States are not. So by merely spreading the coins through the cloth with his left thumb and fingers, the performer actually finds the Canadian nickel, when the magnet becomes attached to it. He can even withdraw his left hand briefly, letting people see that it is empty, because the coin will hold magnet through the cloth. When the left hand finally steadies the handkerchief again, the right hand dips into the folds, goes directly to the magnetized nickel, plucks it free, and hands it to a spectator.

The magnet naturally drops into the left hand, which moves away, retaining it in the bend of the fingers, while the right hand dumps the U.S. nickels from the handkerchief, which is promptly transferred to the left hand. In pocketing the handkerchief, the left hand disposes of the magnet and can later bring out the handkerchief alone, if some spectator wants to try his luck at finding the Canadian coin.

CARDS AND DICE

This is a highly effective mental mystery, for it involves such common articles as three dice and a standard pack of playing cards. All these are so freely handled that subterfuge seems improbable, yet the working itself is practically automatic. The performer begins by thumbing through a pack of face-up cards, showing that they are well mixed and then mixing them further. He then lays the pack face down, brings out three dice, and gives them to a spectator, saying:

"Roll these three dice, add their total, and count off that many cards. Note the value of the card you come to, and count off that many more. My purpose is to predict your final card."

With that, the performer writes something on a slip of paper, folds it, and puts it in the card case from which he took the pack. If preferred, he can put the slip in a small envelope, or even leave it lying openly on the table.

The spectator rolls the dice, and we will assume that they show 6-3-4, for a total of 13. The performer takes the pack and deliberately deals cards face up from the top, laying each card on the one before, so that spectators can see them all, but again noting that they are in haphazard order. The thirteenth card proves to be the 6 of hearts, so the performer pauses and says: "A 6. We will deal six more cards." He does this, turning each card face up until he comes to the sixth, which he lays aside, face down, and tells the spectator to open the prediction. The spectator reads it—*jack of spades*—and the performer tells him to turn up the final card. It is the jack of spades!

A special setup is necessary for this trick, but if offers no apparent key to the mystery. You arrange a group of cards in the following order, from top to bottom: joker, S-5, C-9, D-A, D-Q, D-9, S-Q, S-10, C-K, C-6, H-9, H-8, D-3, H-6, S-2, C-4, D-K, H-2, H-A, S-J. Place this group at about the middle of the pack. When you show the pack face up, thumb through the cards in small clusters, sliding them from left to right with your right hand, transferring them from the bottom of the pack to the top—that is from front to back.

You can do this safely even with the setup, as this process does not disturb the order. You remark, "You can see that the cards are all well mixed," but after you have passed the joker and put the special group well to the top, you can do some actual mixing by pulling out half a dozen cards near the bottom and poking them in among others just above. Transfer these to the top and repeat the action with another half dozen; but as you approach the special group, stop mixing cards and just move clusters to the top until you have again passed the joker. Then you can resume your mixing with the bottom cards.

Finally, you remark: "We won't need the joker for this mystery, so let's get rid of it." You thumb through the face-up pack until you reach the joker. Thumb it forward so that it drops on the table and simply cut the pack at that point by moving all the front cards to the back of the pack. Turn the pack face down and your setup will then be on the top, beginning 5 of spades and running downward in the order already given.

When the dice are rolled, they will total from 3 to 18. A count of "3" will bring you to the ace of diamonds. You name it aloud, saying: "The ace of diamonds. We will spell it letter by letter, dealing a card for each letter: T-H-E A-C-E O-F D-I-A-M-O-N-D-S." Deal the cards as you spell and you will end on the jack of spades. If the dice show totals of 4 to 9, use the same process of naming the card and spelling it, but leave out the word T-H-E.

This rule applies to all suits *except* hearts. If the roll of the dice brings you to a heart, you simply announce the number of spots on the card as:

"A nine—very well, we will count off nine cards." In this case, you count an ace as one. If a roll brings you to a *low card*—less than a 5 in value—in any suit except hearts, you spell the *name of the suit*. Thus, with the 3 of diamonds, you would say, "A diamond! We'll spell it, a card for each letter: D-I-A-M-O-N-D." The same rules applies with the 2 of spades (S-P-A-D-E) and the 4 of clubs (C-L-U-B). The lone exception is the king of diamonds, which you term "a *red* card" and spell R-E-D from there down.

Always you will finish on the jack of spades, fulfilling your prediction, as shown in the following chart.

CHART FOR CARDS AND DICE

If dice roll "3," bringing count to D A:
Spell: T-H-E A-C-E O-F D-I-A-M-O-N-D-S

If dice roll "4," bringing count to D Q:
Spell: Q-U-E-E-N O-F D-I-A-M-O-N-D-S

If dice roll "5," bringing count to D 9:
Spell: N-I-N-E O-F D-I-A-M-O-N-D-S

If dice roll "6," bringing count to S Q:
Spell: Q-U-E-E-N O-F S-P-A-D-E-S

If dice roll "7," bringing count to S 10:
Spell: N-I-N-E O-F S-P-A-D-E-S

If dice roll "8," bringing count to C K:
Spell: K-I-N-G O-F C-L-U-B-S

If dice roll "9," bringing count C 6:
Spell: S-I-X O-F C-L-U-B-S

If dice roll "10," bringing count to H 9:
Count down 1-2-3-4-5-6-7-8-9

If dice roll "11," bringing count to H 8:
Count down: 1-2-3-4-5-6-7-8

If dice roll "12," bringing count to D 3:
Spell suit: D-I-A-M-O-N-D

If dice roll "13," bringing count to H 6:
Count down: 1-2-3-4-5-6

If dice roll "14," bringing count to S 2:
Spell suit: S-P-A-D-E

If dice roll "15," bringing count to C 4:
Spell suit: C-L-U-B

If dice roll "16," bringing count to D K:
Spell the color: R-E-D

If dice roll "17," bringing count to H 2:
Count down: 1-2

If dice roll "18," bringing count to H A:
Count down: 1 (for ace)

TRIPLE-COLOR TEST

Three colored marbles are used in this neat effect. All are of the same general size and appearance, except that their colors are different. For convenience, they will be termed red, white, and blue, although other colors may prove preferable, as will be discussed later. The performer gives the marbles to a spectator, then turns away, but extends his right hand behind him so that the spectator may drop one of the marbles therein. Facing about, the performer raises his right fist to his forehead and names the color of the marble. This may be repeated with continued success.

The secret is simple but subtle. Examine a batch of common marbles and you will find that they vary in size, though so slightly that the difference cannot be distinguished in ordinary handling. Select three of graduated sizes: small, red; medium, white; large, blue. Cut a square of fairly stiff cardboard, measuring an inch and a half to two inches in each direction; and in the center cut a circular hole, of sufficient size for the red marble to drop through freely. If the marbles are nicely graded, the white one will stick, but can be pushed through; while the blue will not go through at all.

After a little practice, the performer can proceed with the "color test." He holds the cardboard square unnoticed in the bend of his left fingers. He extends his right hand behind his back to receive a marble, reminding the chooser to keep the other two hidden. Facing about, with both hands behind him, the performer places the marble on the center of the cardboard and learns its color as described. He closes his right fist, raises it to his forehead, and names the color.

Opening his fist, the performer returns the marble to the spectator and offers to repeat the test, which he can do as often as desired. At any time, the cardboard gimmick can be slipped into the left hip pocket, while the right hand is being raised to the forehead. Always, too, it can be easily regained if the performer decides to accede to another request to "try it again."

Instead of the cardboard "fake," a small finger ring may be used, provided you can find one of the right size to go with the colored marbles. Actually, this is not too difficult, as cheap plastic rings are available at novelty counters, so by buying several, you will probably find one that will do.

Instead of marbles, the "color test" may be worked with small rubber balls, an inch or so in diameter. These come in various colors, and some are marked with numbers, like miniature pool balls. Some of these vary in size sufficiently to be identified with the aid of a special gimmick—in this case, a ring formed from a short piece of soft wire that can be shaped to just the required diameter, with its ends twisted firmly together. This is used to gauge the chosen ball in the usual manner.

MENTAL MOVES

This effect involves a coin and sixteen playing cards, which are laid face up in the form of a square. The performer turns his back and tells a spectator to place the coin on any card he chooses; then to move it about the square, as specified by the performer. The moves are sufficiently arbitrary to allow the spectator further choice or leeway. At the finish, however, the performer names the final card, as though he picks up the spectator's thoughts in progress.

First, arrange a layout as follows:

Club	K	Diamond	J	Diamond	Q	Diamond	6
Diamond	2	Spade	Q	Spade	3	Spade	5
Diamond	K	Club	J	Heart	4	Heart	Q
Diamond	7	Spade	K	Spade	9	Club	6

After the spectator has placed the coin on whatever card he wants, you state: "Now move the coin as I tell you, but if you are unable to move it, say nothing; just wait for the next move and go ahead with that. What I am trying to do is visualize the square and gain mental impressions of whatever happens there. Remember, you are to say nothing."

Pause dramatically, as if concentrating; then proceed:

"If you placed the coin on a *face card* (king, queen, or jack), move it to the *left* until you come to a *spot card* (ace to ten); then place it there" — pause briefly — "but if there is no spot card to the left, move the coin to the *right* until you come to a spot card and place it there."

Again pause briefly; then say:

"Of course, you may have put the coin on a *spot card* to start. In that case, move the coin straight *down* the line until you come to a *face card* and place it there; or, if there is no face card toward the bottom, move the coin *upward* to the first face card you see and place it there."

Another pause; then you proceed:

"Now note the *color* of the card on which you placed the coin. If it is *black,* move the coin either left or right to the first *red*. If it is *red,* move the coin either left or right to the first *black* card. In short, move either left or right to the first card of the *opposite color.*"

Following that, you continue:

"Note the *color* of the card where the coin is now; and this time move the coin up or down to the first card of the *opposite* color."

Pause again; then say:

"Now move the coin *diagonally* to the first card of the *opposite* color."

All is then ready for the final move, which is:

"This time, move the coin either to the right or straight downward to the first card of the *opposite* color. When you have done that, concentrate on the card itself."

After due deliberation, you announce that you have gained a mental impression of the "four of hearts," which proves to be the final card on which the spectator has concentrated.

Simply follow the procedure as described and the final move will end on the Heart 4 automatically, as a few trials will prove. Remember that with the first move, you must tell the person to move to the left (or down) *if he can;* otherwise, he may move to the right (or upward). With later moves, he can move either way you specify, though sometimes only one choice is possible. With all moves, be sure to specify that he must stop on the first or nearest card of the opposite type.

A dramatic way of naming the final card is to tell the spectator to remove all the rest and replace them on the pack, face down. He is then to lift the coin, and turn the chosen card face down, anywhere on the table, replacing the coin on it. That done, the performer turns around, touches the coin with his finger, then finally picks up the coin and presses it to his forehead, as though it could transmit the needed impression of the chosen card, which he names forthwith.

Any red spot card may be used instead of the Heart 4 for the final choice, provided that the performer takes care to remember it. Other cards in the layout may also be supplanted by any of their particular type.

DOUBLE-COIN SURPRISE

Here two coins are used, with a double prediction involving a square of sixteen face-up playing cards. A spectator is given a free choice of any card and told to place a coin on it while the performer's back is turned. The performer then adds further instructions regarding the placement of the second coin or another card. Following that, he asks a few casual questions and gains a correct mental impression of the card—or cards—that are in the spectator's mind.

A sample square of cards appears below, along with a four-word "key square," which the performer keeps in mind when laying out the square of sixteen cards:

D 6	H 3	S 5	D 2		B	A	L	E
D K	D Q	S 3	H J		S	T	A	R
H 5	S 8	D J	H A		L	O	R	D
C 9	C 2	S K	H 8		P	E	S	O

Note that the layout contains six pairs of cards of the same value at positions A-A (Heart 3 and Spade 3); L-L (Spade 5 and Heart 5); E-E (Diamond 2 and Club 2); S-S (Diamond K and Spade K); R-R (Heart J and Diamond J); O-O (Spade 8 and Heart 8). There are also four single cards represented by letters at positions B Diamond 6), T (Diamond Q), D (Heart A) and P (Club 9).

With his back turned, the performer tells the spectator to drop a coin on any card he wants; then, casually, the performer asks: "Do you see another card of the same value in the layout? That is, if your card happens to be a ten, is there another ten there?" Assuming that the answer is "Yes," the performer says, "Very well. Drop the other coin on that card."

The performer pauses as if to concentrate, then says:

"Look at the crossrow containing one of your cards. Tell me: Do you see another card of the *same color* as yours?" If the answer is "Yes," the performer asks, "And do you see a card of the *same suit* as yours?" If the answer to either question is "No," or if the answers to both questions are "Yes," the performer proceeds:

"Now look at the card that you covered with the other coin. Does its crossrow contain another card of the *same color?*" If the answer is "Yes," the performer asks, "Is there a card in that row of the *same suit* as yours?" Whatever the spectator answers, the performer promptly names both cards covered by the coins.

To accomplish this, the performer refers to a special chart of answers, as follows:

Chart of Answers

First Card: YES YES	*Second Card:* YES YES	Letters E-E	*Diamond* 2	*Club*	2
First Card: YES YES	*Second Card:* YES NO	Letters S-S	*Diamond* K	*Spade*	K
First Card: YES YES	*Second Card:* NO	Letters L-L	*Heart* 5	*Spade*	5
First Card: YES NO	*Second Card:* YES YES	Letters S-S	*Spade* K	*Diamond* K
First Card: YES NO	*Second Card:* YES NO	Letters R-R	*Heart* J	*Diamond* J
First Card: YES NO	*Second Card:* NO	Letters A-A	*Heart* 3	*Spade*	3
First Card: NO	*Second Card:* YES YES	Letters L-L	*Spade* 5	*Heart*	5
First Card: NO	*Second Card:* YES NO	Letters A-A	*Spade* 3	*Heart*	3
First Card: NO	*Second Card:* NO	Letters O-O	*Spade* 8	*Heart*	8

That takes care of all six "pairs" that may be picked; but in addition, there are four "singles" that may be chosen by the placement of the first coin, namely: Position B (*Diamond* 6); T (*Diamond* Q); D (*Heart* A); P (*Club* 9). The performer gains a clue to those from his preliminary question: "Do you see another card of the same value in the layout?" If the answer is "No," he knows that he is dealing with an "odd" card, and he promptly announces:

"Never mind the second coin. Just concentrate on the one card that you have covered. Then study the other three cards in the same column, or vertical row, running from top to bottom of the layout. Tell me: Do you see another card of the *same color* as yours?"

If the answer is "No," the card is at Position P—the *Club* 9.

If the answer is "Yes," the performer puts another query: "Do you see a card of the *same suit* as yours?"

If the answer is "No," the card is at Position T—the *Diamond* Q.

If the answer is "Yes," the performer proceeds with a third question: "Do you see a card of the *other color* in that column?"

If the answer is "No," the card is at Position D—the *Heart* A.

If "Yes," the card is at Position B—the *Diamond* 6.

This reduces to a simplified chart of answers covering "single" cards, as follows:

Chart of "Single" Answers

An answer of NO means P or *Club* 9   Answers YES NO is T or *Diamond* Q
Answers YES YES NO is D or *Heart* A   Answers YES YES YES, B or *Diamond* 6

Other "pairs" or "singles" may be substituted for those already given, provided they conform the four-word layout.

With <u>two cards</u>, ask about Horizontals.

Y-Y + Y-Y = E-E (♦2, ♣2)
Y-Y + Y-N = S-S (♦K, ♠K)
Y-Y + N = L-L (♥5, ♠5)

Y-N + Y-Y = S-S (♠K, ♦K)
Y-N + Y-N = R-R (♥J, ♦J)
Y-N + N = A-A (♥3, ♠3)

N + Y-Y = L-L (♠5, ♥5)
N + Y-N = A-A (♠3, ♥3)
N + N = 0-0 (♠8, ♥8)
*****
BALE ♦6 ♥3 ♠5 ♦2
STAR ♦K ♦Q ♠3 ♥J
LORD ♥5 ♠8 ♦J ♥A
PESO ♣9 ♣2 ♠K ♥8
(Over)

With a <u>single card</u> ask about Verticals.
<u>Card of same color?</u>
Answer NO = P or ♣9
If answer is YES, ask
<u>Card of same suit?</u>
Answer NO = T or ♦Q
If answer is YES, making it YES-YES, ask:
<u>Card of other color?</u>

Answer NO = D or ♥A
Answer YES = B or ♦6
****

B * * *   ♦6 * * *
* T * *   ♦Q * *
* * * D   * * ♥A
P * * *   ♣9 * * *

Fig. 359. These reference charts can be printed on opposite sides of a piece of cardboard the size of a playing card, which the performer holds beneath the pack while dealing the layout. After turning his back, he can easily and secretly refer to the proper chart while questioning and instructing the volunteer who places the coins.

SIX-SYMBOL TEST

This test is performed with three small disks, each bearing two symbols that are similar to those used in ESP experiments. Those recommended are: triangle, square, star, wavy lines, cross, pentagon. White poker chips are specially suited to this use, as they are about the right size, and the symbols can be drawn on them with pen or heavy pencil. However, if chips are not available, the designs can be traced on small cardboard squares.

While the performer's back is turned, a spectator turns over the disks, one by one, as often as he wants, and in any order, simply stating that he has turned one over, but without naming which one. It is up to the performer to "sense" which disks are being turned, and this is the finale:

When the spectator decides to stop turning the disks, he concentrates on one symbol that is upward and places his hand over it; for example, the star. The performer places his hand upon the spectator's, concentrates deeply, and names the symbol correctly. The test may be repeated, always with success.

Any similarity between this test and Turn-over Coins (described on page 267) is something more than accidental, for the two are actually the same from the performer's standpoint. The use of ESP symbols adds greatly to the effect, however, and lends a serious touch. At the same time it helps to disguise the subtle secret on which the test hinges. As with the coins, the key is to check heads and tails.

The performer classes three symbols as "heads," because they appear on what he regards as the "upper" sides of the disks. These are the *triangle, square,* and *star.* The corresponding "tails" or "lower" sides are the *wavy lines, cross,* and *pentagon.* As combinations, they are therefore:

| triangle | square | star |
| wavy lines | cross | pentagon |

These are easily remembered, because the *triangle* (upper) is composed of three lines like the *wavy lines* (lower); the *square* (upper) is composed of

277

four lines, as is the *cross* (lower); the *star* (upper) has five points, and the *pentagon* (lower) has five sides.

When the disks are laid on the table, you classify the total of visible "upper" symbols as *odd* (three or one), or as *even* (two or zero). Each time a person turns over a disk and announces it, you switch mentally from odd to even or vice versa. Example: The disks show (A) *wavy lines;* (B) *square;* (C) *star* representing an *even total; square + star = 2.*

A person turns over A, C, A, A, A, B, C, A; then places his hand over the middle disk (B), after announcing each turn with triangle, hand, star. The performer mentally tabs the turns as odd, even, odd, even, odd, even, odd, even, stopping there. He looks at the person's hand and notes the *triangle* (upper) and *star* (upper) showing at left and right. Since *two* upper symbols represent *even,* he knows that the *odd* disk must be a lower symbol, so he names the *cross;* and there it is.

As you try this for yourself, you will find that the simpler it becomes for you, the more puzzling it will be to those who witness it. That is the great aim in mental magic.

MATCHED THOUGHT

Three coins of different values — say a quarter, a dime, and a nickel — are laid on the table. The performer shows a loosely clenched right fist and states that he is projecting a thought that he expects someone to match and that the proof is in his fist. Gesturing to the three coins with his left hand, he tells a person to pick up whichever coin he wants. Assuming that the person takes the nickel, the performer says, "Hold your coin in your fist and keep it tightly closed, like mine. Concentrate on it and when we open our fists together, you will see that our thoughts are matched!"

The performer opens his fist as the other person does the same and shows that he, too, is holding a nickel, thus matching the person's thought.

The nickel is the best coin to use in this test, as there is a general tendency for a person to choose it as the middle-sized coin of the three. When he does, the result is automatic, as described. But if anyone makes another choice, the performer still can prove that the thoughts were matched by proceeding thus:

If the person picks up the dime, the performer says, "Good. Now pick up another coin with your other hand." Assuming that the person picks up the quarter, the performer says, "Fine. You have left me the nickel, exactly as I knew you would." With that, he picks up the nickel with his left hand, closes it, brings both fists together, and opens them, showing a nickel in each hand as he adds: "See how our thoughts match!"

This works just the same if the person picks up the quarter first and then the dime; it still leaves the nickel for the performer. But what if the person picks up the dime or quarter first and the nickel next, leaving the performer an odd coin that he doesn't want?

That, too, can be cleanly handled. The performer calmly ignores the coin that is still lying on the table and extends his open left hand, saying, "Now give me either coin you want." If the person hands him the nickel, the performer closes his fist over it and says, "So you want me to have the nickel. Let's see how well our thoughts match." He brings his fists together, opens them, and shows a nickel in each hand as he adds: "Perfectly!"

If the person keeps the nickel, he naturally hands the odd coin to the performer, who carelessly lays it aside and says, "So you are keeping the nickel. Hold it in your fist like this and concentrate." In short, the performer proceeds exactly as if the person had taken the nickel in the first place, and with the same result, as already described.

Obviously, this effect can not be repeated before the same group of people, but it can be worked in conjunction with similar tests described in this chapter.

NUMBER PREDICTION

Here is a subtle effect whereby the total of four seemingly random numbers can be accurately foretold. Four people are asked to call off numbers of four figures each, repeating any figures if they wish. The performer writes a total on a slip of paper, which he folds and seals in an envelope. Then, to prove that he has control over the result, he lets each person rearrange his figures to form an entirely new set of numbers. Yet, when added, the column of numbers produces the exact total that the performer put away.

As an example, suppose the numbers originally chosen are 7352, 5404, 3791, and 2866. The performer writes these in a column:

$$
\begin{array}{cccc}
7 & 3 & 5 & 2 \\
5 & 4 & 0 & 4 \\
3 & 7 & 9 & 1 \\
2 & 8 & 6 & 6 \\
\end{array}
$$

The performer then makes his prediction and tells the first person, "I'll now form a new number starting with any of your figures. Which do you want me to use?" Assume that the first person says "5," the performer asks the second person to name one of his figures, such as "4." The third person then chooses one of his, such as "3"; and the fourth names a "6" as his choice. The performer crosses off each figure as it is named and forms a new number from them:

$$
\begin{array}{cccc}
7 & 3 & 5 & 2 \\
5 & 4 & 0 & 4 \\
3 & 7 & 9 & 1 \\
2 & 8 & 6 & 6 \\
\end{array}
\qquad\qquad 5\ 4\ 3\ 6
$$

He calls for another figure from each person, such as "2," "4," "1," "2." He then crosses these out and writes the new number:

```
7  3 (5) 2              5  4  3  6
5  4  0 (4)             2  4  1  2
(3) 7  9  1
2  8 (6) 6
```

The performer calls for a further choice from each person, such as "7," "0," "9," "6." He crosses these out and writes the new number:

```
7   3 (5)(2)            5  4  3  6
5 (4) 0 (4)             2  4  1  2
(3) 7  9 (1)            7  0  9  6
(2) 8 (6) 6
```

Now the performer has each person call off his only remaining figure, and from this a final number is formed to complete the new column:

```
(7) 3 (5)(2)           5  4  3  6
5 (4)(0)(4)            2  4  1  2
(3) 7 (9)(1)           7  0  9  6
(2) 8 (6)(6)           3  5  7  8
                     1 8  5  2  2
```

Adding the four random numbers brings a total of 18522; and when the prediction is opened, it bears that very total: 18522.

Anyone will agree that a vast variety of combinations was possible; indeed, it can be proved mathematically, if you want to go to the trouble. But is is better to avoid all that. Otherwise, someone might gain an inkling to the simple but subtle system on which the trick depends, namely:

You begin by writing the four original numbers on the top half of a pad, showing them exactly as they were called off. Then, concentrating upon the numbers, you add the figures of the first number to form a "thousands" column; then the figures of the second number for "hundreds"; those of the third number for "tens," and those of the fourth number for "units." You write these quite small, toward the bottom of the page, forming a column, which you add:

```
First Number (7352)   7 + 3 + 5 + 2 = 1 7  *  *  *
Second Number (5404)  5 + 4 + 0 + 4 =    1 3  *  *
Third Number (3791)   3 + 7 + 9 + 1 =      2 0  *
Fourth Number (2866)  2 + 8 + 6 + 6 =        2 2
                                      1 8  5  2  2
```

Leave enough space near the bottom of the page to write the number 18522 in big, bold figures; then tear off that strip and fold it to serve as your prediction. Next, tear off your own calculation, crumple it, and put it in your pocket, leaving only the four original numbers (7352, 5404, 3791,

2866). Start forming the new numbers by having people choose their figures, as already described, and write them on the next sheet of the pad. Tear off the remainder of the top sheet with the original numbers and let anyone add the new numbers. The answer is sure to be 18522.

Why? Because you have simply transposed each horizontal row of figures into a vertical column. You added them across to make your prediction; the spectator adds the same figures down and gets the same total. The order of the figures will vary, according to the way they were called off, but that has no effect upon the total. Here are a few examples, using the same original numbers:

```
  2 5 1 8          3 4 9 8          7 0 7 2
  3 0 3 6          7 5 1 6          2 5 3 8
  5 4 9 6          2 4 7 2          5 4 1 6
  7 4 7 2          5 0 3 6          3 4 9 6
1 8 5 2 2        1 8 5 2 2        1 8 5 2 2
```

It is a good plan to ask the first person to "name a number with four different figures, anywhere from 1 to 9." This eliminates 0, so that when the first person starts new numbers with each of his or her four figures, an actual digit is involved. With the second person, you can say, "Use a 0 if you want; and it's all right to repeat a figure—anything from 0 up to 9."

With a reasonable amount of practice it is easy to form the magic-total mentally, starting with the thousands column and working to the right. In that case, all you have to do is write the magic total on the lower half of the sheet, tear it off, and fold it, as already described. This can be made still easier by limiting the number of people to three and by having each name a number of only three figures, which you add in terms of hundreds, tens, and units. For example:

```
    Original Numbers            Numbers from Chosen Figures
  5 2 7 = 1  4  *  *           2 0 3          7 8 1
  9 0 8 =    1  7  *           7 8 4   or     5 9 4
  3 1 4 =          8           5 9 1          2 0 3
        1  5  7  8           1 5 7 8        1 5 7 8
```

When working with an assistant, as some performers do, the mystery can be enhanced by stationing the assistant out of the audience's sight at the start. When people call off their original numbers, the performer repeats them loud enough for the assistant to hear. This enables the assistant to tabulate the total and write it on a slip that he seals in an envelope. Meanwhile, the performer is explaining that although all the figures have been selected at random, he intends to have the choosers themselves form them into new numbers that will produce a total that he has already predicted.

Here the assistant enters, bringing the sealed envelope on which people sign their names before the performer asks them to call off their figures in a new order. Or the assistant can "plant" the envelope in the performer's overcoat pocket, so that the performer can "remember" that he left it there. Naturally, he goes and gets it before proceeding with the test.

COLOR CARDS

This is a form of numerical prediction in which the result is fixed beforehand, so it is not only sure-fire, but also easy to do. By making up special cards, you force people to take the totals that you want, and therefore no mental calculation is needed on your part while you are performing the test.

Simply make up several sets of numbers on blank cards of different colors, such as red, white, yellow, green, and blue. The upper half of the accompanying list shows ten cards of each color, and each card bears a number that contains three digits. To present the effect in simple form, you use three sets of cards, thirty cards total — say, red, white, and blue — and mix them together. On a sheet of paper, you write the prediction "1459" and seal it in an envelope.

In performing, run through the cards, showing that no two are alike, and deal them in separate heaps according to colors. Give the red set to Person A, the white set to Person B, and the blue set to Person C. State that you will form three new numbers by letting each volunteer call off a figure in turn, with A giving you one of his figures to start the new number, B providing the second figure, and C the final figure.

Each takes a random card from his set: A's red card, for example, might be 256; B's white card, 932; C's blue card, 784. For the first number, A calls the figure 5, B calls the figure 2, and C decides on 4, so you write down the number 524. Since each must take another figure for the second number, A chooses 6, B takes 3, and C takes 7, so you write down 637. Since each has only one figure left, they fall in line: A = 2; 3 = 9; C = 8, which gives you the number 298, the last in the column. Added, your three numbers yield the total:

$$
\begin{array}{r}
5\ 2\ 4 \\
6\ 3\ 7 \\
2\ 9\ 8 \\
\hline
1\ 4\ 5\ 9
\end{array}
$$

This is your total, so you let the volunteers open the envelope. To their amazement, they find that your prediction is correct!

It is sure to be correct, because all the numbers on the red cards have figures totaling 13 when added across; whites total 14 across; blues, 19 across. Switched from horizontal to vertical, whatever numbers they choose will add up to 1459.

When you repeat the test, you can predict a different total by simply handing out the colors in a different order. If you give blue to A, white to B, and red to C, your total will be 2053. Or you can change the colors of some cards, giving a green card to A, a red card to B, and a yellow card to C. That would bring a predicted total of 1946.

Another method for this deception is to use four cards of different colors, with four volunteers: A, B, C, and D. If you should give them out in the order yellow, green, red, and blue to A, B, C, and D, respectively, your predictions would come to 17949. Other combinations will bring various totals; all you have to do is add up a sample set beforehand, and whatever numbers people take will give you the right total.

You can use more than ten cards to each set by simply forming other numbers that add the same across. For example, you could use numbers like 274, 346, 670, or 814 to make up extra red cards, as each adds to 13 across. The same applies to cards of other colors.

The lower half of the accompanying list is composed of sets of four figures, each to be worked with four people—A, B, C, and D—with each calling off figures in order. If you give out the cards in the order of red, yellow, green, and blue, forming four numbers of four figures each, your prediction would come to 20365. If the colors are given out in other orders, different predictions would result, as testing them will prove. Working a column of 4 × 4 takes longer than 3 × 3 but sometimes has a stronger effect.

Red	White	Blue	Yellow	Green
256	608	928	709	918
382	374	397	718	756
607	194	685	826	837
931	842	496	349	297
463	752	829	952	468
814	815	784	196	594
517	356	586	385	909
904	617	919	475	846
625	905	856	637	369
274	932	757	484	675
Total = 13	Total = 14	Total = 19	Total = 16	Total = 18

Red	Yellow	Green	Blue
6138	7428	9834	8935
7056	8193	6873	7864
1953	5097	5928	8296
4536	6870	9618	7198
1089	3486	8079	8395
2907	9273	3795	6973
3582	5169	2697	6892
9036	3738	8169	6937
8145	2874	3489	5983
7425	6195	6783	4786
Total = 18	Total = 21	Total = 24	Total = 25

SIXTH CARD—SIXTH SENSE

Six cards are taken at random from a pack of regular playing cards and placed face up on the table. A volunteer is asked to concentrate upon one and remove it from the rest. The proposition then is to tune his thought projection with that of another person, or recipient, who is in the next room or who may be reached by telephone.

Gathering the five odd cards, the magician holds them in a face-down pile and asks the chooser to call the names of those cards as he deals them, so the recipient may hear. All the while, however, the chooser should keep thinking of the sixth card, the one he chose but is not to name aloud.

So well do the thoughts attune that after the five odd cards have been called, the recipient is able to follow the projector's mind one step more and name the card that was mentally selected.

The secret depends upon a systematic but impromptu setup of the five odd cards. The person on the receiving end lists these cards as they are called and can promptly name the sixth of chosen cards. Here is the system:

First: Think of suits in the following order of value, high to low: diamonds, clubs, hearts, spades. If the volunteer chooses a diamond, pick up the *highest* of the five remaining cards; for clubs, *the second highest,* and so on. The lowest card in value does not figure. It is to be the "tab" card.

Having thus established the suit by the first card you pick up, think of that suit in three groups: high (A, K, Q, J); middle (10, 9, 8, 7); low (6, 5, 4, 3). You have four cards remaining to pick from. If the chosen card is *high,* take the card of highest value; if *middle,* take the second highest; if *low,* take the third highest. Don't worry about the deuce in this arrangement, nor the tab card mentioned previously.

You now have reduced matters to four choices, and on the table you have three cards. If the chosen card is in the high half of its group (A, K; 10-9; 6-5), use the highest card of the three that remain; if in the low half (Q-J; 8-7; 4-3), use the second highest to indicate. You still reserve the tab card.

Now your choice is one of two cards, such as an ace or a king, an 8 or a 7. All right; on the table are two cards (the tab card now figuring), so if you want to indicate the higher of a pair (as an ace), use the higher card; to show the lower (as a king), use the lower. This completes your setup.

Now for a simple example showing how easily this works. Suppose a spectator chooses the 9 of spades. The remaining cards on the table consist of the king of diamonds, jack of clubs, ten of clubs, 6 of hearts, and 4 of clubs, all by way of an example.

The *suit* is spades, the *fourth highest,* so you pick up the *fourth card* in value, the 6 of hearts, and hold it face up in your hand. That leaves: king of diamonds, jack of clubs, ten of clubs, and four of clubs.

The *group* is *middle,* the *second highest,* so you pick up the *second card* in value, the jack of clubs, and lay it face up on the first card you took. That leaves: king of diamonds, ten of clubs, four of clubs.

In the middle *group* the chosen card belongs to the *high* half (10-9), so you take the *highest* card on the table, the king of diamonds, and add it face up to those in your hand. That leaves: 10 of clubs, four of clubs.

In its *pair*, the chosen card is *low* (10-9), so you pick up the *low* card, the four of clubs, and add it to the group in your hand. Add the odd card, the ten of clubs, and turn the heap face down.

Here's the list the recipient gets when the cards are called one by one, and with it, the notations he makes when the list is complete:

6 of hearts—fourth highest—spades
jack of clubs—second highest—middle
king of diamonds—first highest—10-9
4 of clubs—lower of pair—9
10 of clubs

Note that each card, as listed, is eliminated in the later listings. You are through with the 6 of hearts after you learn the chosen suit; through with the jack of clubs after you get the chosen group, and so on.

If a deuce is chosen, give the *suit* with the first card you pick up. Then pick up the *tab card*—that is, the lowest card of those on the table. The next three won't matter. That low stranger that shouldn't belong stands for a 2 spot.

Should the joker be allowed as a choice, and should it be taken, simply start your setup with the lowest card on the table, the tab card. The rest follow in any order.

One final point: Should there be two cards in the group of the same value —as a 5 of diamonds and a 5 of spades—the one of higher suit takes precedence in your evaluation. That's not difficult to remember, as you are dealing with suit values anyway.

PAIRED CITIES

Ten small cards are used in this mental mystery. Each bears the names of two cities, as follows: LOS ANGELES—BOSTON; CHICAGO—LINCOLN; CAMBRIDGE—MEMPHIS; SALT LAKE CITY—MILWAUKEE; SEATTLE—MIAMI; SACRAMENTO—TACOMA; FORT WORTH—NORFOLK; HARTFORD—AKRON; SANTA FE—DENVER; WHEELING—TRENTON.

Cards are selected at random by different persons, up to as many as ten. These cards are kept from the performer's sight, and each person concentrates on the two cities named on his card, as FORT WORTH—NORFOLK. The performer then introduces a larger card, which lists the names of all twenty cities in four columns of five each, with a number at the head of each column:

1	2	3	4
LOS ANGELES	BOSTON	LINCOLN	DENVER
HARTFORD	CAMBRIDGE	WHEELING	CHICAGO
SEATTLE	FORT WORTH	MIAMI	MILWAUKEE
SANTA FE	MEMPHIS	NORFOLK	SALT LAKE CITY
AKRON	SACRAMENTO	TRENTON	TACOMA

Each person looks at each column and gives the number of the column or columns in which his two cities appear. The performer, concentrating on the list, picks up each pair of names mentally and calls off each correctly.

The method depends upon an ingenious system using a four-word formula, each word consisting of five letters. These words are TORSO, TIMID, PARMA, and SPEED, but you think of them in vertical columns, so they would appear like this:

T	T	P	S
O	I	A	P
R	M	R	E
S	I	M	E
O	D	A	D

Picture these letters as though they were superimposed on the corresponding cities in the four-column list, and spell the words mentally when you are told the columns in which a particular pair of cities appears. For instance: A person says he sees one of his cities in Column 2 and the other in Column 3. Spelling downward in Column 2, you come to "M" as the third letter. (T-I-M). When you spell down in Column 3, you reach "M" on the fourth letter. (P-A-R-M). That gives you FORT WORTH (in Column 2) and NORFOLK (in Column 3) as the M pair.

In some instances, a person will see both cities in the same column. You will then find two letters alike in the same word, and the cities will correspond accordingly. Example: If both are in the first column, you will find the letter "O" two down and another "O" five down. (T-O-R-S-O) That tabs the pair of cities as HARTFORD and AKRON.

The actual letter combinations are:

1-1, O-O. 1-2, T-T. 1-3, R-R. 1-4, S-S.
2-2, I-I.   2-3, M-M. 2-4, D-D. 3-3, A-A.
3-4, P-P. 4-4, E-E.

All these are different numerically, so the formula works automatically.

MATCHBOX MAGIC

Close-up tricks with match boxes and their contents are always effective, as they are especially suited to such work. Such common objects add an impromptu touch, and their apparent lack of preparation is also in their favor. Actually, preparation is an important adjunct to many matchbox tricks, and being unsuspected, it increases their effectiveness. Usually the preparation is both simple and inexpensive, making it all the more advantageous from the performer's standpoint.

For a starter, we have:

DROP THE BOX

The performer holds a match box in an upright position, some three or four inches above the table. He drops it straight down on its end and it remains standing upright. If other people try it, the box invariably bounces at an angle, landing on its side. Yet the performer can make it stand on nearly every try. Why?

Skill is not the answer, though some practice is necessary to make it work regularly. The real secret is a bit more subtle. The box is dropped from between the tips of the right thumb and fingers, which are pointed downward, thumb in back, fingers in front, which is natural enough. However, the box is first picked up by the left hand, thumb in back, fingers in front; and the left hand, holding the lower end of the box, transfers the upper end to the right hand, which takes it as described.

During that natural action, the left little finger is inserted in the cover of the box and pushes the drawer more than a half inch upward (Fig. 360, side view). The little finger is hidden by the other fingers of the left hand, and the right fingers, being in front of the box, completely conceal the upper end of the drawer as it emerges. When the box is dropped, the cover stops abruptly as it hits the table; but before it can bounce sidewise—as it ordinarily would—the descending drawer overtakes it, providing the stability that keeps the box upright (Fig. 361).

Make sure that the drawer fits rather loosely and is fairly well filled with matches, preferably with the heads upward. Too many matches may jam the drawer, preventing it from closing completely, which would give away the method. Though scarcely a trick in its own right, this is a good preliminary to other matchbox effects, particularly as it invites audience participation, which always rouses interest.

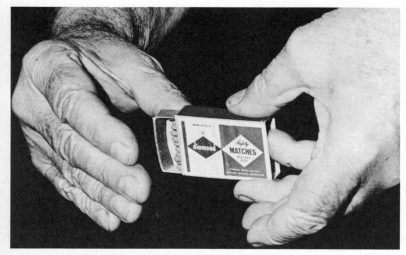

Fig. 360. Preliminary to Drop the Box. Left little finger secretly pushing drawer upward while box is taken between right thumb and fingers, which cover upper end.

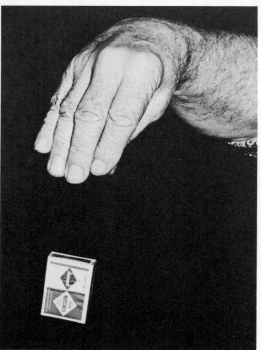

Fig. 361. Matchbox, released by right hand, automatically closes when it strikes table but remains upright.

MAGNETIZED MATCHES

Though old, this is still good, and affords a modern touch specially suited to present-day matchboxes, thus giving it a somewhat new effect. In its earlier form, which may still be used, the magician shows a well-filled box of matches with its drawer about half opened. Inverting the box, he pulls out the drawer completely, holding it between the thumb and fingers of his left hand, at opposite sides (Fig. 362). But the matches do not fall; instead, they remain in the inverted drawer as though held by some magnetic force, until the magician orders them to drop, which they do.

All that is required is a short match, broken off a trifle below the head. The box is about half filled with matches, and the short piece is wedged crosswise near the center of the drawer, to keep them in place (Fig. 363). The drawer is then pushed into the cover just far enough to hide the improvised crossbrace. Thus the matches can be shown in the partly opened box; and when the box is inverted, the drawer can be pulled out, yet the matches will stay. To make them fall, the performer loosens the wedge, which drops along with the regular matches and remains unnoticed among them.

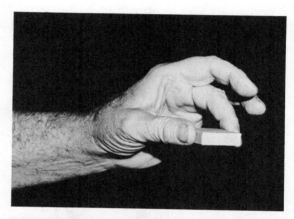

Fig. 362. Inverted match-box drawer mysteriously retains matches, which later fall to table.

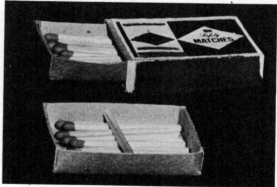

Fig. 363. Top: Preliminary view of partly opened box showing "loose" matches in drawer.

Bottom: Actual status of drawer before removal, with short match stick wedging matches in place.

Aside from the fact that the matches cannot be shown entirely loose to start, there is a slight problem in making them fall on call. One way is to shake them loose, but sometimes they are too tightly wedged to go. So the surer system is to slide the tip of the left little finger beneath the drawer and kick away the crossmatch. Even that takes a bit of maneuvering; hence some performers may prefer the modern version which follows:

MODERN MAGNETIC MATCHES

Here the matches are all shown loose at the start; in fact, the best procedure is to dump them all from the box and then replace them in the drawer, a few at a time, until it contains enough to "induce magnetism," as the performer terms it. He then inverts the drawer with his left hand, and the matches remain therein while he makes "magnetic passes" with his right hand. But the instant he snaps the fingers of his right hand the matches drop, without any noticeable action by the left hand, and everything may be examined.

This improvement depends on the fact that the drawer of a modern matchbox is made of flexible cardboard instead of thin, stiff wood. Hence, in dropping loose matches into the drawer, or while removing them, the performer can simply turn a full-sized match at an angle and wedge it diagonally across the drawer above the loose matches (Fig. 364). This causes two very noticeable bulges, but those are neatly covered by the thumb and finger of the left hand when the drawer is inverted (see Fig. 363). In fact, the more delicate the grasp, the better the concealment.

Fig. 364. View from below, showing slanted match holding the rest in place. Thumb and finger hiding bulges at sides of drawer before applying squeeze to release matches.

To release the matches, the left thumb and finger provide a slow but steady squeeze, and the diagonal match drops along with the rest, leaving no clue whatever. If there is any problem placing a diagonal match during the early stages, the performer can add or remove a few odd matches, making occasional tries, until he succeeds in secretly placing one. By having a short match lying on the table with some loose matches of regular length, he can always fall back on the old crosswedge method in a pinch.

LOOPING THE MATCHBOX

The cover of a matchbox is threaded on a piece of string about a foot and a half in length, and the string is tied in a loose loop (Fig. 365). A volunteer holds the ends of the string, and the performer covers the looped matchbox with a handkerchief. Then:

Reaching beneath the cloth, the performer tells his helpers to pull tightly on the ends of the string. They do, and when he whips away the handkerchief, the loop is no longer through the box cover. Instead, it is knotted around the outside of the cover (Fig. 366), which can be drawn from the knot and shown to be as intact as when it was first threaded on the string.

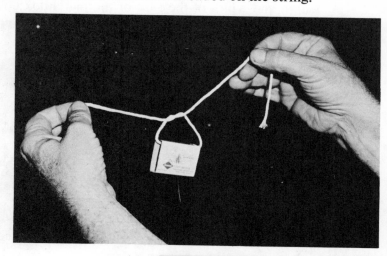

LOOPING THE MATCHBOX
Fig. 365. Matchbox cover, looped by knotted string, ready to be covered with handkerchief.

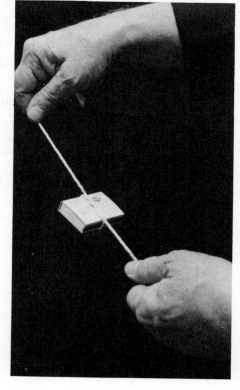

Fig. 366. After coverage: Removal of handkerchief shows knotted string tied around outside of box!

Simple but special preparation is needed for this marvel. The matchbox used must be the modern type that has a pasteboard cover. Inspection will show that such a cover has an overlap on one side, so it can be glued together. Beforehand, these overlapping segments are carefully worked apart so that the cover is open at that side (Fig. 367).

Now another innovation is brought into play; namely, "double stick" tape, a transparent mending tape that is gummed on both sides and is procurable in many stationery stores. Cut a strip of such tape to the exact length and width of the side of the matchbox cover. Use this to gum the separated portions lightly in place, and the cover will look perfectly normal.

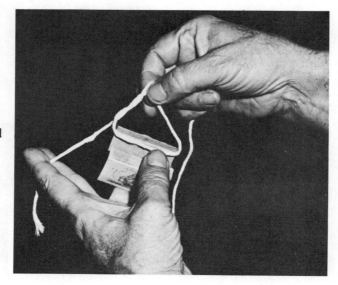

Fig. 367. The method (done beneath handkerchief): secretly opening double-taped side of box cover so string can be removed and looped around it.

Once the cover is threaded on the string, which is then knotted and the cloth draped over it, the performer secretly opens the side of the cover and removes it from the string. He then presses it back together, this time very firmly, even flattening the cover between his thumbs and fingers to make the sides adhere more solidly. He slips the reconstructed cover into the loop and tells people to pull the ends tightly, which makes the cover all the firmer. When the cover is lated pulled from the loop, it will actually stand close inspection; and when the performer slides the drawer into the cover to proceed with some other effect, the onlookers will be really baffled.

The result is further enhanced if Looping the Matchbox is worked in connection with the effect that follows:

MYSTIC KNOT VANISH

After removing the matchbox cover from the knot, the performer offers to work it in reverse without using the handkerchief, so that people can see for themselves how it is done. He slides the cover back into the knotted loop (as in Fig. 366) or simply reties it in that condition. Then, holding the cover upright, he runs the upper end of the string down through (Fig. 368), saying, "Let's put the string right through the cover—and then add the knot along with it."

In keeping with that statement, he draws the loop up from the cover, bunching the knot together, then stuffing it into the cover (Fig. 369). He lets two persons hold the ends and tells them to pull slowly and steadily. As they do, he adds, "Now that you have tightened the knot, I shall vanish it—like this!" He grips the matchbox cover, runs it back and forth along the string clear to one end, showing that the knot is gone (Fig. 370). The matchbox cover is then taken from the end of the string so that the string itself can be examined.

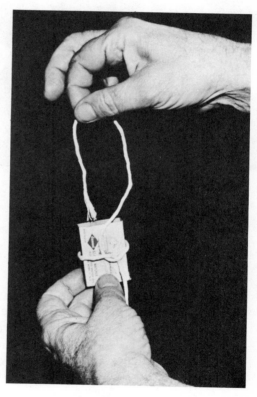

MYSTIC KNOT VANISH
Fig. 368. Matchbox cover tied with single-knotted loop. Loose end of string being dropped down through cover.

The nice part of this trick is that it practically works itself. In dropping one end of the string down through the tube the string goes through the knot and thereby unties it; but since the knot is still around the tube, it is temporarily kept intact. Bundling the knot into the tube surreptitiously disposes of the knot, and the mystery is complete.

SPECIAL NOTE: By working Looping the Matchbox and Mystic Knot Vanish in combination, they become the equivalent of a new effect and provide a perfect getaway for the faked matchbox used at the start. In his right coat pocket, the performer has a cover for a duplicate matchbox,

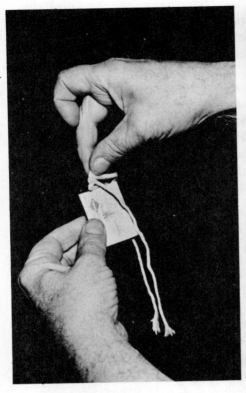

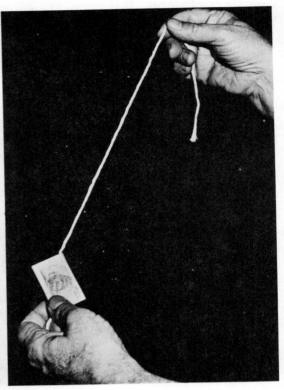

Fig. 369. Knot encircling
has been drawn clear of
box and is now being
pushed down into cover.

Fig. 370. Box cover
drawn along string, show-
ing that knot has magi-
cally vanished!

which is unprepared. After Looping the Matchbox, he starts to put the drawer back into the faked cover, then says, "Wait—I'll show you how it's done—but I won't need the handkerchief." Holding the cover in his right hand, he takes or picks up the handkerchief with that same hand and thrusts it into his pocket, where he drops the faked cover and brings out the unprepared one instead. Laying the drawer of the matchbox aside with his left hand, he transfers the cover from his right hand to his left and takes the looped string with his right hand, so that he can proceed with the Mystic Knot Vanish. Afterward the cover can be examined with the string, leaving no one any wiser.

HEADS AWAY

In simple form, this involves an ordinary matchbox, which is pushed halfway open in either direction, showing the heads of the matches pointing that way (Fig. 371). But when the performer pushes the drawer shut and out the other way, the heads have turned in that direction.

Some onlookers may suspect that the matches have heads on each end, but before anyone can become overly vocal on that score, the performer commands the heads to stay where they are. He can then show the bases of the matches at one end of the drawer and later cause them to appear at the other end. At the conclusion, the matches are dumped from the drawer and given for examination with the box.

The trick depends upon an easily made fake, consisting of a strip of cardboard cut from the bottom of another drawer. This is about half the length of the drawer and slightly narrower. To the strip is affixed a row of matches cut to about half their length (Fig. 372). A row of matches plus a

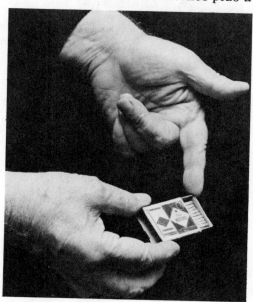

HEADS AWAY
Fig. 371. Drawer opened showing heads of matches at left. When drawer is pushed through cover, heads appear at right.

Fig. 372. Sliding fake previously inserted in drawer with heads to right. Real match heads are to left.

few extras are placed in the drawer, with their heads pointing toward the left. The fake is dropped upon them with its heads aimed the other way.

To show the real heads at the left, tilt the box downward to the right. This causes the fake to slide to the right of the box, so that the real heads are seen when the box is opened leftward (Fig. 373). By maintaining the tilt, the heads on the fake will show when the drawer is pushed out to the right (Fig. 374). To show the bases at either end, the box is simply closed and tilted to the left, so that the fake slides to that end. The drawer may then be opened as desired, from the left or the right.

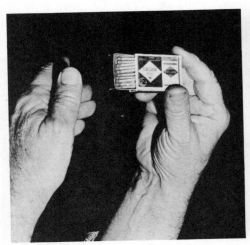 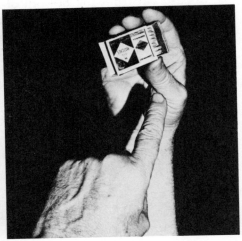

Fig. 373. When showing real heads at left, fake is concealed in drawer at right end, which is tilted downward.

Fig. 374. Box now closed and still tilted to the right, so heads of fake show at that end.

The drawer should never be pushed open as much as halfway, since beyond that, the fake might show. At the finish, however, the performer can turn the top of the box toward himself, tilt the box to the right, and pull out the drawer with his right hand while pressing his right thumb on the fake. He then dumps the contents into the bend of his left fingers, where the fake lies hidden under the loose matches, which can be shown freely but briefly. From there, the left hand, turning downward, spills the loose matches on the table, so that they can be examined along with the matchbox, while the left hand retains the fake in the bend of the fingers and pockets it at leisure.

NOTE: Since the loose matches slide downward when the box is tilted upward, too much space may show between the heads of the matches and the end of the box. This can be counteracted by cutting the ends from the drawer of another matchbox and inserting them at each end of the drawer used in Heads Away, gluing them in place. The interior of the drawer is thus reduced to the same length as the matches, which prevents them from sliding back and forth.

MATCHBOX VANISH

This is an effective item with any matchbox routine. One end of a matchbox is held between the base of the left thumb and fingers, so that it projects upward from the fist. The drawer is partly open, showing a full quota of matches (Fig. 375). The right fingers tap the drawer shut and give the box a harder tap, driving it down into the left fist. When the left hand is opened, the box has vanished!

It all depends on a neat, deceptive move, when the box is apparently tapped straight downward. Instead, the right hand presses at a forward angle, flattening the box across the knuckle of the left forefinger (Fig. 376, side view), clamping it in the bend of the middle fingers of the right hand, which press the other end of the box directly into the right palm. The per-

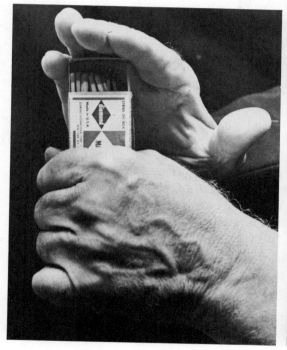

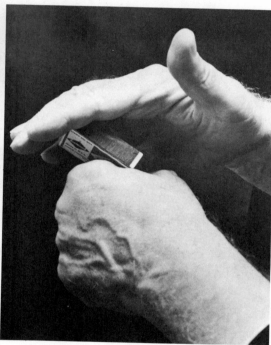

Fig. 375. Audience view at start of Matchbox Vanish, with right hand pushing box down into left.

Fig. 376. Side view of right fingers clipping matchbox with forward action after pushing drawer shut.

former immediately turns his body to the left, elevating his left fist and pointing to it with his right forefinger, and the left hand is opened with a rubbing motion to complete the vanish (Fig. 377).

The vanish can be worked with either a full box or an empty box, as desired. As a follow-up, the performer can reach into his right coat pocket and reproduce the missing matchbox from there.

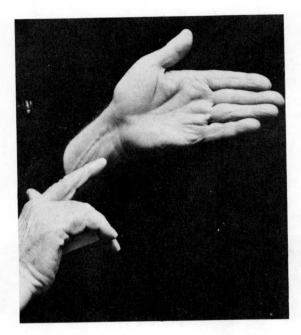

Fig. 377. Side view of right hand pointing to empty left after vanish. (Right hand purposely tilted upward to reveal box secretly retained in finger bend.)

Done smartly, this is a very surprising effect, and it serves an added function when worked with a faked matchbox—as with Looping the Matchbox or Heads Away. In such cases, the performer plants an ordinary matchbox in his pocket beforehand. After finishing the trick with the faked box, he vanishes it as just described; then, reaching in his pocket, he drops it there and brings out the ordinary box instead, tossing it on the table where it can be examined later or used in some other effect. Conversely, the vanish may be used to switch an ordinary matchbox for a faked one, which is equally useful.

ALTERNATE MATCHBOX VANISH

In this variation, the performer starts with his right side toward the audience and his left fist turned downward, so that the partially opened matchbox projects toward the onlookers. The right hand comes in front of the box, thumb upward (Fig. 378), and apparently presses the box into the left fist, from which it subsequently vanishes.

Actually, the right hand simply pushes the drawer shut and in the same action hooks the end of the matchbox in the bend of the third finger. The left fist is withdrawn just a trifle, enabling the right hand to swivel inward, bringing the matchbox with it (Fig. 379). The left hand is elevated back toward the audience, and the right forefinger points to it, exactly as with the standard vanish.

The matchbox may be reproduced from the pocket or switched for another box planted there, as in the regular method. In either version, if the

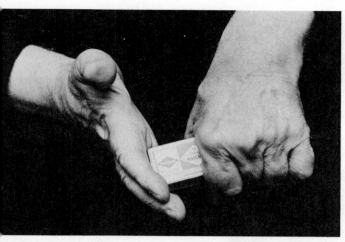

Fig. 378. Right hand pressing drawer shut as if to push box into left fist preparatory to "vanish."

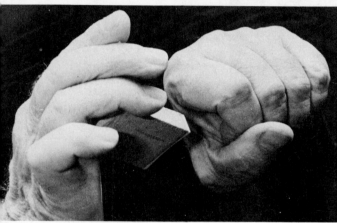

Fig. 379. Right third finger secretly retaining box as hands tilt upward (angle view from below).

performer is seated at a table he can dispose of the box entirely by letting the right hand drop it in his lap while the left hand is doing the vanishing act.

APPEARING MATCHES

The left hand shows an empty matchbox with the drawer well open. The right hand pushes the drawer shut and the left hand shakes the box, which rattles as though it contains matches. When a spectator opens the box, he actually finds it full of matches.

Two drawers are needed: one full, the other empty. Beforehand, insert the full drawer at the left of the cover, almost fully in; and insert the empty drawer at the right, just enough to hold it there (Fig. 380). In displaying the box, hold it so that it extends from the left fist, as with the Alternate Matchbox Vanish (see Fig. 378). The left fist hides the projecting full drawer, so that only the empty drawer is seen.

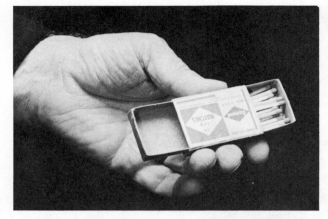

APPEARING MATCHES
Fig. 380. Original setup for matchbox, with empty drawer projecting from left and full drawer from right, to be concealed by fist.

Fig. 381. View of action from below. Right hand secretly removing empty drawer while left little finger bends inward to halt full drawer.

The right hand openly and deliberately pushes the empty drawer about half shut, while the left little finger is bent inward, acting as a barrier to stop the hidden full drawer as it emerges from the other end of the cover. Up to this point, the hands can be pointed frontward and downward; but now they swing leftward, so that the right hand hides the matchbox, as in the Alternate Vanish.

Here the right hand moves forward, bringing the empty drawer with it in the crook of the third finger, while the left little finger moves in beneath the others, pushing the full drawer forward into the cover (Fig. 381, angle view). Thus the right hand takes away the empty drawer and points its forefinger toward the left hand, which swings upward while shaking the matchbox to prove that matches have mysteriously arrived therein. While a spectator is opening the box and finding it full, the performer secretly drops the empty drawer into the right coat pocket.

VANISHING MATCHES

In effect, this is just the opposite of the Appearing Matches. The performer shows a partly opened matchbox, which is well filled with matches. He pushes the drawer shut with the fingers of the right hand and gives the box to a spectator, who opens it only to find that the matches are gone.

This can be worked by simply reversing the drawers at the start, so that a full drawer extends from the right end of the matchbox while the empty drawer is concealed by the left hand, rather than the other way about. The right hand then steals and pockets the full drawer, while the left secretly pushes the empty drawer into the cover. However, this move requires special handling of the full drawer because of the loose matches.

This is obviated in the method that follows:

INSTANT VANISHING MATCHES

Here the left hand displays the matchbox at the tip of the thumb and fingers, with the drawer projecting at the right end of the box, chock full of matches. The right hand closes the box in the usual manner and points to the left hand, which immediately opens the box and completes a seemingly instantaneous vanish.

This is done with the aid of an easily constructed and totally unsuspected fake that can even be introduced into a borrowed box of matches. Cut the drawer of a matchbox in half, crosswise. Take one half and trim the upper edge of its sides and end, making it about an eighth of an inch shallower than the other half. Turn the shallow half upside down and place it upside down in the normal half, using glue to keep it in place. Cut a row of matches in half and glue them to the inverted insert, with their heads toward the end of the half-drawer (Fig. 382).

Push this slightly into the cover of a matchbox, so that it looks like a half-opened matchbox with its drawer full of matches. Then push an empty drawer well into the left end of the cover and hold the matchbox in the left hand, with the thumb across the left end to hide the protruding end of the empty drawer.

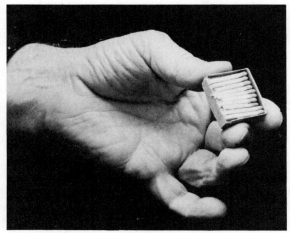

Fig. 382. Fake used for Instant Vanishing Matches and subsequent tricks, with row of half matches glued in place.

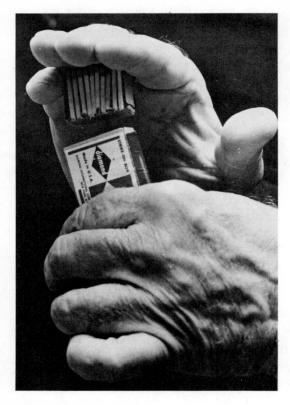

Fig. 383. Instant Vanishing Matches, rear view. Performer apparently presses drawer down into cover of matchbox, but actually removes fake in finger bends. Note how little finger acts as anchor.

The right hand approaches the box, thumb upward, and apparently pushes the drawer shut, but actually removes the fake in the bend of the third finger (Fig. 383). By simply toying with the box the left hand can close it completely, while handing it to someone to prove that the matches have vanished; this, while the right hand disposes of the fake. However, since the fake is easily and naturally concealed, the right hand can simply turn palm downward and use its forefinger to push open the empty drawer, and the left hand retains the matchbox until the vanish is complete.

TURNABOUT HEADS

In this quick effect, the left hand shows a half-opened matchbox with the match heads aimed toward the right. The right hand closes the drawer, then pushes it clear through, showing that the heads have turned completely about. Box and matches are given for immediate examination.

This utilizes the same fake as Instant Vanishing Matches, but in this case the drawer of the matchbox is filled with matches. Their heads, however, are pointed toward the left, while those of the fake are toward the right. The fake is stolen by the third finger of the right hand, which turns downward so that the forefinger can push the drawer completely through the box, to show that the heads have turned about.

THROUGH THE TABLE

This is a neat variant of Instant Vanishing Matches suited for the table worker. The performer sets a matchbox upright, with the drawer half open at the top, showing a full quota of matches. The right hand taps the drawer downward from above, and the left hand goes beneath the table, bringing up a handful of matches. When the box is opened, it is empty, proving that the matches were driven through the table.

The fake half drawer is used again as with Instant Vanishing Matches, but the take-away is different. While the left hand steadies the box with the fake protruding upward, the right fingers come down over the fake and lift it away while pretending to drive the drawer down into the cover. The real drawer is empty and the loose matches are planted in the performer's lap beforehand. The fake can be dropped in the lap while the left hand is tossing its matches on the table, so that both hands will be free to gather the matches and replace them in the box.

MATCHBOX DO AS I DO

Presented as a impromptu effect, this will prove to be a real baffler, and it becomes even more perplexing when repeated. The performer brings two matchboxes from one pocket, shows that each is filled with matches, and gives one to a spectator, keeping the other for himself. Each lays his matchbox on the table, with the drawer partly open to show the matches, and the performer tells his victim, "Now do exactly as I do and see what happens!"

The performer closes his box, raises it up on its side, then on end, down flat again, and so on, giving the victim just enough time to copy each move or to correct him if he goes wrong. Finally the performer states, "That's enough; now let's see how we stand." He pushes his drawer open. The victim does the same, but curiously, the performer's drawer is upside down, while the other drawer is right side up.

Chidingly, the performer decides that the spectator must have made a wrong turn, so he suggests that they start all over. But again, the victim misses somewhere, for one drawer finishes upside down and the other is right side up. No matter how often it is tried, the results go awry; and for a finish, both boxes are opened completely to show that there was no fakery whatever.

Actually, though, some preparation is needed. First, the cover of each box must be identical on top and bottom, so that no one can be sure just how often each has been turned over. This is easily fixed by using boxes with distinctive labels. Soak two extra covers in a bowl of water, peel off the labels, then paste one to the underside of each box used in the trick.

Next, take one of the extra drawers and cut off about a half inch from one end. This large section forms a simple fake, which is placed over the

Fig. 384. Preparing for Matchbox Do as I Do. Drawer with cut-off end is inverted and fitted over regular drawer of match-box.

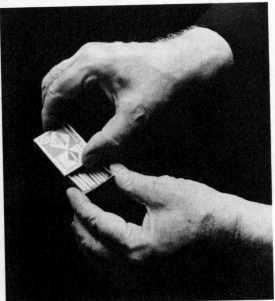

Fig. 385. Drawing real drawer through to left. Tip of right thumb is low-ered to retard inverted "fake" drawer.

right end of the drawer of the performer's matchbox (Fig. 384); and the two are pushed into the cover together. In opening the drawer, use the right forefinger to push it very slightly to the left; then extend the right thumb over the left end of the cover to grasp it, and pull the drawer well out with the left thumb and forefinger (Fig. 385).

Here the tip of the right thumb keeps the fake from coming along, so the matches can be displayed quite fully. To show the drawer apparently up-side down, keep the right forefinger against the right end of the box and push the drawer inward with the left forefinger until it is completely within the cover. The right forefinger is then lifted, so that the left forefinger can

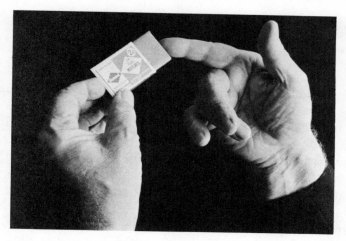

Fig. 386. Left finger pushing drawer through cover, with right forefinger ready to push "inverted drawer" back again after it emerges.

push the drawer through, fake and all, with the right thumb and forefinger pulling it about halfway out. The fake fits so neatly and is so unsuspected that people never think it is the bottom of an inverted drawer (Fig. 386).

Naturally, the performer cannot present the trick this abruptly, because if he turned over the box to show the matches, people would see the real bottom of the box instead. So he utilizes the moves just described as part of a well-calculated routine, which throws observers completely off the track.

It proceeds as follows:

The performer brings out the two "double sided" matchboxes, shows that each contains matches, and gives the ordinary box to a spectator, keeping the one with the fake for himself. Each box should be partly opened toward the left, showing its matches. The performer closes his box; the spectator does the same, and each sets his box on the table. Then the performer announces and makes this series of moves, which the spectator copies:

> Turn the matchbox upward toward yourself, resting it on its long side.
> Tilt the box upward to the left, standing it on end.
> Bring the box straight downward toward yourself, so that it lies flat.
> Tilt it upward to the right, so it stands on its side.
> Tilt it up on its end toward you.
> Flatten it down to the right, topside up.
> Tell the spectator—now your victim!—to push the drawer open to the left, just as you do.

The victim does and finds, to his surprise, that his matches are showing, while the performer's drawer is upside down. To rectify this, the performer has the spectator turn his box over, so that both drawers are upside down. The boxes are again set on the table, and he then calls for these moves:

> Turn the box upward and away, resting it on its side.
> Tilt the box upward to the left, standing it on end.
> Bring the box straight downward toward yourself, so that it lies flat.

Tilt it upward to the right, so that it stands on its side.

Tilt it up on its end with the top side away from you.

Flatten it down to the left, bottom up.

Tell the victim to push the drawer open to the left, just as you do.

This time the victim's drawer is upside down, while the performer's is right side up, showing its matches. The performer tells the victim to turn over his box, so that they can start all over again, both with matches up and "Try to do it right."

All is then in readiness to repeat the double routine, with exactly the same results. One repetition should be enough, unless the performer introduces some innovations of his own to throw the victim farther off the track.

To dispose of the fake, the performer pushes the drawer shut with his left forefinger and then on through, so it can be pulled out by the right thumb and the third finger. (The inverted fake is hidden by the fingers of the right hand, which are turned downward for that purpose.) The left thumb is extended clear to the right of the box, so it can stop the inner end of the drawer before it is completely pulled out (similar to Fig. 385, reversed). The right hand simply keeps on going, taking along the hidden fake, which it drops in the coat pocket while the left hand is placing the opened matchbox on the table.

Another way of disposing the fake is for the left hand to pull the drawer entirely clear and exhibit it freely, while casually turning over the cover, so the fake remaining within is no longer inverted. The left hand then pushes the drawer into the cover so that it slides into the fake while the right forefinger blocks the right end of the cover. Now the drawer is pushed clear through and shown by the right hand as though the fake were part of it. The left hand exhibits the empty cover, and the drawer and fake are pushed back into it.

TURNABOUT MATCH

The closer this trick is shown, the better, as it involves a comparatively small objects, a wooden match. The performer shows a match, holding one end between the tips of his right thumb and forefinger, then pushes it head first into his loosely closed left fist until it is completely gone from sight. (His fist is turned downward during the procedure.) Then:

Deliberately turning his left fist upward, the performer inserts his right thumb and forefinger beneath his left little finger and draws the match into sight again. To everyone's surprise, the head emerges last, and when the left hand is opened it proves to be entirely empty. This final action can be delayed long enough to frustrate suspicious observers who think that a duplicate match is involved. Afterward, the one and only match is given for examination.

The mystery depends upon a tiny but simply made fake in the form of an extra match head, which is cut from another match and carefully glued to the base of the match used in the trick (Fig. 387). When actually showing the match, the real head (seen here on tip of right forefinger) is concealed between the tips of the right thumb and fingers, which hold it in a pincer grip. The match goes into the left fist with the fake head first.

Care is taken not to reveal the real head at the final moment; and after the left fist is turned upward, the right thumb and forefinger gain a pincer grip on the fake head before drawing out the match and showing it. The left thumb and forefinger then take the match and give it for inspection, with the right thumb and forefinger gripping the fake head so tightly that it comes free and remains hidden between them. By lowering the right hand and releasing pressure, the tiny match head will drop to the floor, unnoticed.

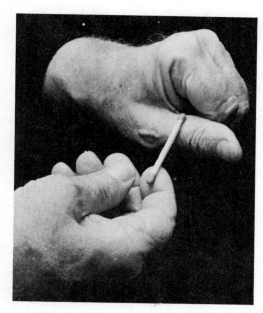

Fig. 387. Start of Turn-about Match. Right hand pushing match into left fist, glued head first. Right thumb would cover real head (purposely shown here in full view).

Instead of removing the fake head and giving the match for immediate inspection, the trick can be repeated a few times. Simply turn the left fist downward and push the match through again. It makes no difference which head is on view at the start, but the performer should always finish with the fake head clipped between the right thumb and forefinger, ready for detachment.

ALTERNATE TURNABOUT

This makes an excellent repeat for the Turnabout Match, as it can be worked with an unprepared match. Hence it can be shown after the origi-

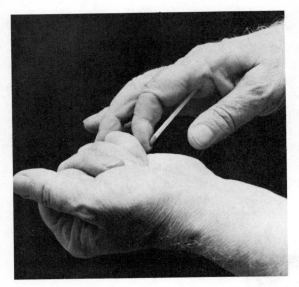

Fig. 388. Turnabout with ordinary match. Performer's view of right hand apparently pushing match head first into left fist, but actually sliding thumb and forefinger forward.

nal match has been examined, but it is equally good in its own right. The effect is exactly the same: The right thumb and forefinger insert a match head-first into the bottom of the left fist. When the fist is turned upward, the match is drawn out, and the head emerges last.

The method is neat indeed. The right hand does not push the match into the left fist at all. Instead, the right thumb and forefinger simply slide along the match, with the right forefinger covering it as they progress. This gives a perfect optical illusion of the match being pushed into the fist (Fig. 388).

The main point is to make sure that the head of the match is actually hidden in the fist before the "push" is started. From then on the deception is perfect, even when done deliberately. Once the match appears to be fully in the left fist, the right forefinger is thrust deep enough to go just beyond the head of the match, and the tip of the right thumb presses the match against the tip of the right finger. Thus the right hand can be withdrawn, bringing the match along.

This move is natural and the match is completely hidden by the right forefinger, which should be bent slightly inward. When the left fist is turned upward, the tips of the right thumb and forefinger are thrust beneath the left little finger, pushing the head of the match deep enough for the left little finger to grip it. Then, deliberately, the right thumb and forefinger pretend to draw the match into view, by sliding back along it. This is a reversal of the forward slide whereby the match was apparently pushed into the fist. When the right thumb and forefinger reach the outer end, they simply bring the match along, so its head comes into view and the left hand may then be shown empty.

A good preliminary to this method is to push the match into the left fist, with the head pointing to the left; then turn the fist upward and open it, showing the match lying in the left hand, with its head pointing to the right. This can be repeated a few times; then the performer goes into the moves just described, apparently pushing the match head first into the fist and drawing it out with the head still pointing to the left, making a real surprise.

PENETRATING MATCHES

Here is a close-up match trick that increases in effect the more you practice it. In fact, it can become quite bewildering if you give it enough attention, for any twist or turn of your hands aids in the deception. Yet the effect is simplicity itself—as is true with so many close-up effects. Two wooden matches, one in each hand, are held lengthwise between the tips of the respective thumbs and forefingers. You bring your hands together, as though trying to make the matches penetrate each other, and suddenly they do. Now you show them mysteriously linked, making it apparently impossible to draw them apart.

Yet after a few tries, they come apart; and to prove that it really happened, you continue to link and unlink them in the same baffling fashion, finally drawing them completely apart and allowing them to be examined. The trick can be repeated, as many times as you wish.

The easiest and surest method of accomplishing this neat deception is as follows:

In pressing the ends of the right-hand match between the tips of the thumb and forefinger, work the match from the tip of the forefinger to the side nearest the second finger. This enables you to clip it secretly between the tips of the first and second fingers (Fig. 389). Now, as you keep bringing the matches together, as if trying to find a proper angle, raise the right

Fig. 389. Start of "penetration" showing matches between thumb and finger of each hand, ready to be linked.

Fig. 390. Base of match, clipped between right fingers, being lifted for swift passage. Base is later shifted to forefinger.

Fig. 391. Completion of thrusting move. Apparently the solid matches have penetrated each other, while retained by thumb and forefinger.

fingers, bringing the match up with them. That gives you enough space to slide the left-hand match through the opening (Fig. 390), and the penetration is completed.

Don't stop there, however. Immediately shift the end of the match onto the very tip of the right forefinger as you raise or turn your hands so that the spectators can get a closer view (Fig. 391). Once your hands are again in motion, shift the end of the match back between your first two fingers and you can slide the matches apart as surprisingly as you interlocked them. At times you can put them together and take them apart immediately, without making the shift in between. You may also switch to slow-motion tactics by trying from one angle, then another, or by turning your hands this way and that until, suddenly, you've done it. All these maneuvers add to the overall effect.

ALTERNATE PENETRATION

The effect here is almost identical with the one just described, except that it is a little more difficult to accomplish. Counteracting that is the fact that Alternate Penetration gives you better coverage and therefore enables you to work more slowly. Unlike the original method, where it is best to press the head end of the match against the tip of your thumb, here the head must be pressed against the tip of your forefinger.

The reason is this: The lower end of the match is secretly wedged beneath your right thumbnail. This enables the right thumb to retain the match in an upright position when you raise your right forefinger. The left-hand match goes through the gap *above* the match (Fig. 392), instead of below, as in the original version. While you must be careful not to lose the match in transit, it is easy to tilt the hands so your left fingers hide the action, which can be slowed accordingly. Also, if the right-hand match tilts too much, it can be brought upright by pressing it against the inner bend of the left fingers.

Worked alternately, these two methods are very effective, since spectators who think they are catching on to one will be more easily baffled by the other.

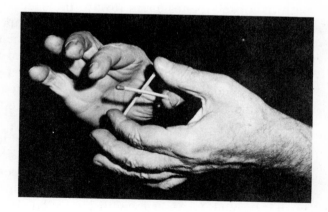

Fig. 392. Alternate Penetration. Base of right-hand match secretly wedged beneath thumbnail, allowing space between match head and forefinger.

HALF-MATCH PENETRATION

This clever variation of Penetrating Matches is worked with a large kitchen match, the "nonsafety" type that can be struck anywhere. Since the match is large, you break it in half, pressing the upper half between the tip of your right forefinger and thumb, the lower half between your left thumb and forefinger. You then proceed with the usual penetration, apparently pushing each half back and forth through the other.

The method here is quite ingenious. Beforehand, moisten the tip of your right forefinger. When you press it against the head of the match, you will find that the match will stick (due to the sulphur content). As a result, you can thrust the half matches back and forth as if they actually penetrated each other. The fact that they are shorter than full-sized matches makes it all the more difficult for observers to detect the lift, which in this case can be slight indeed.

Breaking a single match in half is necessary in this version in order to reduce the weight of the portion that you lift with your right forefinger, for if it is too heavy, it is apt to fall free. It is always worthwhile to carry a few kitchen matches, just to have one handy for this trick.

MATCH THROUGH HAND

Originally presented as a bit of byplay, this penetration effect is actually a gem of close-up deception, well worth the trifling amount of practice needed to acquire it. Attention to detail is the important requisite, as a few tests will prove.

A large match is shown at the tips of the left thumb and second finger. The head of the match is pointed straight upward and the palm of the hand is turned toward the audience, showing the hand otherwise empty. The right hand, also shown empty, takes the match by the head and presses the other end against the back of the left hand, which is turned palm downward, with its loosely bent fingers toward the spectators.

With a sudden thrust, the right hand apparently pushes the match straight through the left hand, which simultaneously extends its fingers to show that the match has "actually" pierced the hand and is literally dangling from it. A twist of the right fingers, a grimace on the part of the performer, and the match drops to the table, so that the right hand, moving clear of the left, can point to the match while the left hand is shown unscathed.

The right hand then picks up the match by its lower end and shows it, head upward, between the tips of thumb and second finger, exactly as the left hand showed it at the start. Having thus convinced the onlookers that only one match is involved in the mystery, the performer can proceed to push it through his right hand, using his left hand to make the thrust, with the same phenomenal result.

Now to explain the mystery:

Two matches are used in the trick. One is concealed beforehand in the bend of the left second finger. The fingertip presses the blank end of the match so that the head is pressed against the base of the finger. This area of the palm should be moistened slightly jut before starting the trick. With the hidden match thus placed (Fig. 393), the right hand displays a match between its thumb and forefinger and sets it upright between the tips of the

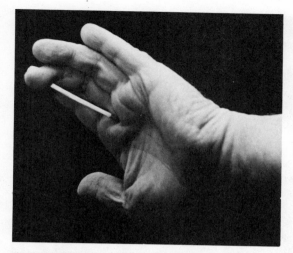

Fig. 393. View from below showing duplicate match with moistened tip in readiness to appear when left fingers are stretched.

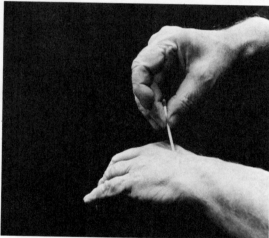

Fig. 394. Side view of right hand pushing match down on back of left hand. Note how sliding action gives effect of penetration.

left thumb and second finger, so it can be shown with the left hand palm front, without revealing the hidden match.

Now the bent left fingers are turned toward the spectators so the right hand can take the visible match and thrust it downward upon the left hand (Fig. 394). During the thrust, the right thumb presses the original match into the bend of the right second finger, which clamps it so the head is firmly against the finger base (similar to Fig. 393 position). At the same time, the left fingers are stretched to full length and the hidden match is seen dangling from the moistened base of the left second finger, to which the match head naturally adheres (Fig. 395).

This gives the effect of an actual penetration. As a natural follow-up, the right hand picks up the match once it is dropped from the left, taking it between the tips of the thumb and the second finger, thus keeping its own match concealed behind the thumb.

Fig. 395. Audience view of right hand completing push through with left hand stretching to show match completing penetration.

By moistening the base of the right second finger beforehand, the penetration can be repeated by having the left hand apparently thrust its match through the right hand. It can even be continued a few more times—left, right—if desired, once the performer has acquired sufficient precision.

TABLE MAGIC

For many years, after-dinner tricks gave impromptu magicians a chance to display their budding talents with whatever objects were handy, and the practice eventually developed enough to arouse the interest of advanced performers as well. Meanwhile, close-up magic was coming to the fore and injecting skill into impromptu work. It was inevitable that the two types of presentation should merge to a marked degree, and the result, table magic, is now regarded as a special magic form of its own.

From one viewpoint, table magic should involve articles commonly found at the dinner table, such as glasses, sugar lumps, and napkins, but this could limit it too strictly. Coins, matches, and other items the performer might have with him can logically be pressed into service while working at a table. Conversely, objects can be taken from the table and used to present tricks elsewhere, so there is no hard-and-fast rule for table-magic props. The tricks allotted to this section have been chosen primarily because they seemed appropriate for the setting and the occasion.

Some specialists in table magic have developed extensive programs devoted entirely to this type of work involving vanishes that are quite baffling when skillfully presented. These depend upon special moves and well-timed misdirection that carries attention elsewhere while articles are dropped secretly into the performer's lap. This technique is termed "lapping," and like "sleeving," it should not be overdone, particularly by beginners, as spectators are apt to suspect where the "vanished" articles went, even though they did not see them go.

FOUR-COIN BAFFLER

For a truly open-handed deception under the most exacting conditions, this is a standout. You begin with four coins, all identical in appearance, such as four half dollars, and put them on the table, two toward the left, two toward the right. Extending your hands palm upward, you ask someone to place a coin in each hand (Fig. 396). That done, you close your left fist and have the person place a coin on your left knuckles.

Now you do the same with your right hand, having the second coin placed upon your right knuckles (Fig. 397). You then remark, "If I turn my hands over, the outer coins will naturally fall off." Suiting your words with action, you turn your knuckles downward, and the coins drop as you said they would (Fig. 398).

315

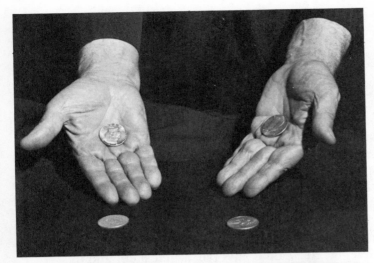

FOUR-COIN BAFFLER
Fig. 396. Start of Four-coin Baffler. A coin shown in each hand; two others ready for placement on knuckles.

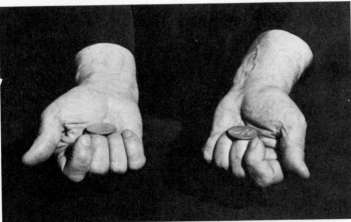

Fig. 397. Hands after spectator places "outside" coins on knuckles. Each still has a coin inside.

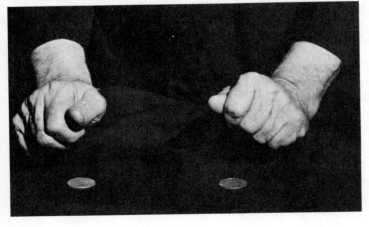

Fig. 398. Simple turnover move in which "outside" coins are apparently dropped from knuckles onto table.

Again turning your fists knuckles upward, you ask your helpers to replace the coins, one on the outside of each hand, which they do. You then say that you once met a gambler who claimed that he could make the inner coins magnetize the outer coins so they would not fall. He used to win bets on it, but of course there was a catch to it, and here was how he did it.

With that, you slide the outer coins down over your knuckles, so you can press each coin between the base of the thumb and the fingernails (Fig. 399). That way, you turn your hands downward without losing the coins. After bringing your knuckles upward, you continue:

"But that gave me an idea for a better trick. I have two coins in each hand, one inside, the other outside. Suppose I should pass one coin invisibly from my right hand to my left. That would be more than magnetism; it would be magic. Watch!"

You make a throwing motion with your right hand and then open the fingers of both hands upward, letting the outer coins slide inside as you spread your hands wide. To everyone's surprise, the left hand contains three coins, while the right hand holds only one!

While the spectators are still blinking in surprise, you close your fists again and extend your right hand, saying, "And to prove it really happened, suppose I make the fourth coin pass invisibly, too!" With that, your right hand makes a throwing motion and you open it, showing it empty. When you open your left hand, all four coins are there!

Fig. 399. Demonstrating the gambler's squeeze whereby the "outside" coins are retained after being replaced on knuckles (the "inside" coins are both in left hand).

Now for the explanation, which depends upon a few simple but subtle moves. The coins are placed fairly as described—one inside each hand and one outside. But as you turn your hands downward, open the right hand far enough to let the inner coin fall along with the outer; and at the same time press the fingers of the left hand against its outer coin, drawing it into the hand with the coin already there (Fig. 400). One coin tends to fall farther than the other.

With a little practice, this knack is easily acquired, and since the onlookers see two coins fall to the table, they naturally suppose that both were outside coins. The hands are turned downward and inward, thumbs swinging toward each other, a few inches above the table, so the move is well covered, adding to the illusion. Furthermore, it is all done before anyone has reason to suspect it.

The business of having people replace the coins on the upturned knuckles (so you can show how the gambler hoaxed his victims) is simply an excuse for having dropped the coins earlier. Now, since you already have three coins in the left hand and only one in the right, passing one "magically" from right to left is simply a matter of showmanship. When you open your hands, there they are.

Now for the fourth coin. Keeping your palms upward, spread your hands well apart, showing the coins plainly, but gradually sliding the three left-hand coins well back into the left palm, while the right hand keeps its coin closer to the fingers. Casually, as though you were finished, you bring the hands close together and look up at the spectators, making some remark such as, "Amazing, wasn't it?"

The instant that you see that their attention is diverted from the coins, bring the outside edge of the right hand against the tips of the left fingers and turn the right hand downward (Fig. 401), letting its coin drop on the left fingers and avoiding any telltale click. The right hand partly covers this, if anyone glances that way. All in the same action, both hands are fisted, turned downward, and moved well apart, finally turning upward as they were originally.

All is then ready for the "magical" passage of the fourth coin. You go through the mystic motions as described and show the right hand empty with all four coins in the left hand.

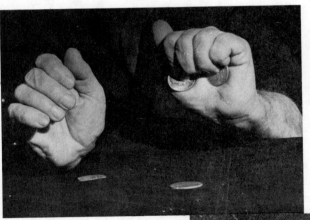

Fig. 400. View of turn-over from below, showing how left fingers gather in their knuckled coin with the coin already retained while right hand lets both its coins fall.

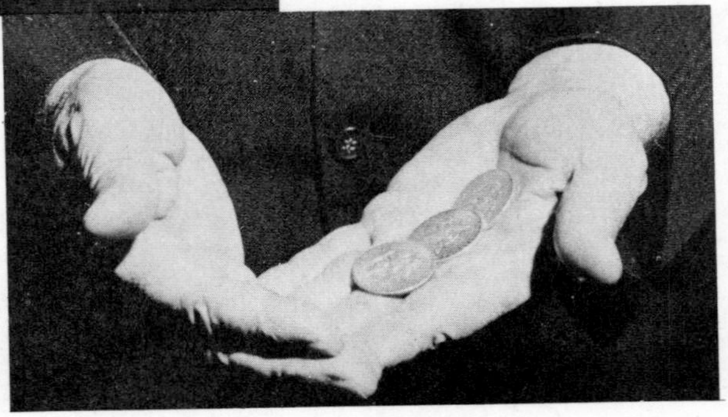

Fig. 401. Right hand dropping fourth coin onto left fingers. By swinging hands leftward, back of right hand hides this action.

MAGIC SUGAR LUMPS

Here we have three separate table tricks involving lumps of sugar, each a good close-up mystery in its own right, and all suitable for combination in a triple routine where one surprise follows another in bewildering succession. Each will be described and explained individually, then linked to the next in order:

FOUR-LUMP ASSEMBLY

You take four lumps from a sugar bowl, or simply bring them from your pocket and set them on the table so they form the corners of a square, six inches or more apart. You cover two diagonal lumps, one with each hand, wiggle your fingers, and command, "Go!" When you lift your hands, one lump has traveled from the left corner to the right.

Covering the two lumps with one hand, an odd lump with the other, you cause the odd lump to "go" in the same fashion. You then cover the three lumps with one hand, the fourth with the other, and when the hands are lifted, all four lumps are seen congregated at the right corner.

The swift assemblage depends upon an extra lump of sugar that is palmed in the right hand, either in taking the lumps from the bowl or beforehand. The right hand sets the four visible lumps at the corners of the imaginary square (Fig. 402), which for convenience can be regarded in the following order from the performer's viewpoint:

$$4 \qquad 1$$
$$2 \qquad 3$$

Cover Lump 4 with the left hand, Lump 3 with the right, remarking, "Suppose I cover two sugar lumps like this—" With that, lift your hands and bring the left toward you to cover Lump 2, while the right again covers Lump 3, as you say, "Or this pair." Then lift your hands again, and turn the

MAGIC SUGAR LUMPS
Fig. 402. Original arrangement of four sugar lumps. Extra lump is palmed in right hand.

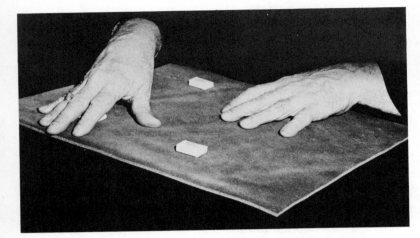

Fig. 403. Right hand covering Lump 1, about to drop extra while left palm picks up Lump 2.

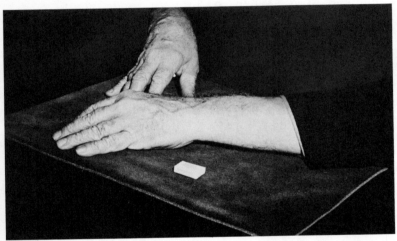

Fig. 404. Left hand covering two lumps while right palm picks up Lump 3.

left palm upward so it can make a circling gesture toward the group as you add, "It really doesn't matter which pair I cover."

With the right forefinger, point to Lump 2, then to Lump 1, saying, "So suppose we take this pair." With that, you place the right hand over Lump 1 and turn the left hand downward over Lump 2 (Fig. 403). Follow this preliminary procedure carefully and people will gain the impression that you showed the palms of both hands, though the right is back upward all the time.

Now comes the smooth, well-timed sequence. As you wiggle your left fingers, press the hand downward and palm Lump 2. This is a simple pickup, since the oblong lump can be gripped by the ends rather than the sides. Lift both hands and at the same time release the extra lump from the right palm so it joins Lump 1. This is timed to the word "Go!"

Immediately the right forefinger points to the two lumps at Corner 1 as you say, "And here we have two." Draw the right hand inward, turning it downward over Lump 3, while the left hand moves over to Corner 1 and covers the two lumps there (Fig. 404). Wiggle the right fingers while palm-

Fig. 405. Right forefinger pointing to three lumps now at Corner 1. Note extra lump picked up by right palm. Left forefinger indicating final lump at Corner 4.

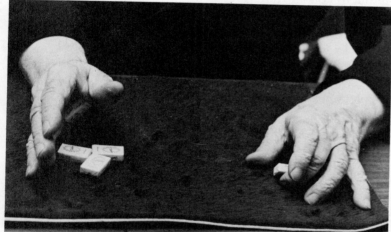

Fig. 406. Right hand covers three lumps and releases extra while left palm picks up lump at Corner 4.

ing Lump 3 and say, "Go!" Lift the left hand and turn its palm upward and raise the right hand, back upward, to show that its lump is gone.

Point to Corner 1 with the right forefinger, saying, "Here we have three." Be sure to keep the palmed lump concealed (Fig. 405). Then point to Lump 4 with the left hand. Plant the left hand downward on Lump 4, cover the three lumps at Corner 1 with the right hand (Fig. 406), and announce, "Now for the fourth and last!" Palm Lump 4 with the left hand, which is lifted to show that the lump is gone, and raise the right hand to let everybody see the four lumps assembled at Corner 1 (Fig. 407).

With one surprise topping another, the effect of this is cumulative, leaving observers all the more baffled. Hence it is unwise to linger following the climax. You should either dispose of the sugar lumps immediately or proceed with the next effect of the sequence. The simplest disposal is to gather up the four visible lumps with the right hand and toss them into the left, which turns upward to receive them. This adds the four to the extra, but before anyone has a chance to note that there are five, you drop them all back in the bowl or pocket them.

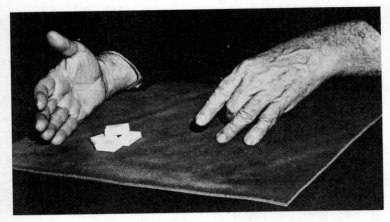

Fig. 407. All four lumps
assembled at Corner 1,
with left hand moving
away with palmed extra.

However, as a special touch, you can add a very convincing move called
the Palm Toss. After lifting the right hand to show the four lumps at
Corner 1, you pick up the lumps with the left hand, dropping them in the
open right hand, one by one. In so doing, the first lump should be placed in
the very center of the right palm, the rest being loosely arranged toward
the fingers.

Count them as you place them: "One—two—three—four—" and with
the final count, turn the right hand downward and the left hand upward,
giving the lumps a very slight toss from right to left. The toss is actually
covered by the right hand, and with it you retain the first lump in the right
palm, letting the three loose lumps fall into the left hand, which immediately spreads wide to show what appears to be the same four lumps, but
one, of course, is the extra that was already palmed in the left hand (Fig.
408).

After thus "proving" that only four lumps were involved, the left hand
dumps its four lumps back into the right, which puts them away with the
fifth lump, which it now has palmed.

The alternative is to follow with the second effect in the sequence,
namely:

Fig. 408. Right hand
throws "four" lumps into
left, but retains palmed
lump (performer's view).

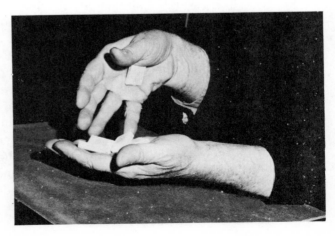

THROUGH THE TABLE

Four lumps of sugar are stacked in a pile, which for convenience will be numbered 1, 2, 3, and 4 from top down to bottom. One hand covers the stack while the other hand goes beneath the table. When the upper hand is lifted, one lump has apparently been pushed through the table, because only three are seen. The lower hand promptly brings the missing lump from beneath the table.

The stack of three is covered with one hand and another lump is driven through the table, the lower hand bringing it from beneath. The two lumps are covered and another is sent through; finally, the fourth and last lump penetrates the table in the same surprising fashion.

As with the Four-lump Assembly an extra lump is needed, and again, it should be palmed in the right hand to start. If worked in sequence you begin Through the Table with the "palm toss" from right to left, thus showing four lumps in the left hand and secretly retaining the fifth in the right. Drop the four lumps on the table and stack them alternately with each hand (Fig. 409).

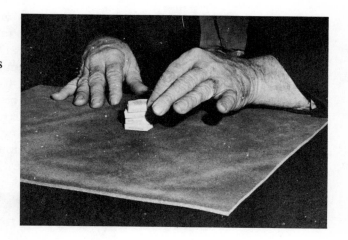

Fig. 409. Left hand stacks fourth lump while right hand carries its palmed lump beneath table.

Now thrust the right hand beneath the table and press down on the stack with the left hand. Palm Lump 1 and lift the left hand and announce, "There goes one lump—through the table!" Bring up the right hand and toss its lump on the table just beside the stack. Pick up that same lump with the left hand, thrust the left hand under the table, and press down on the stack with the right hand.

Palm Lump 2 from the stack with the right hand, saying, "There goes another through the table—" bringing up the left hand and tossing its two lumps to the right of the stack. Gather those with the right hand so the left hand can press the stack and send a third lump through. Toss the three lumps on the table with the right hand, gather them with the left hand, and use the right hand to press the fourth lump through.

Having the lumps stacked helps in palming, so this effect can be worked rapidly until the last lump. Then, by drawing the lump along the table or by tilting the lump on edge if it's oblong, you can often gain a quick grip. You can end the trick after throwing the four lumps from the left hand, by simply gathering up the lumps with the right hand so that the palmed extra joins the visible four, then dropping the lot in the sugar bowl or your coat pocket.

Or you can proceed with the third effect of the sequence:

COME-BACK LUMP

Three lumps of sugar are lying on the table. You pick up two with the right hand and drop them in your left, putting the third in your pocket. When you open your left hand, out fall all three lumps. The third lump has come back! Not only that, it also keeps coming back as fast as you repeat the trick. By way of variation, you thrust your right hand beneath the table and send the third lump up through to the left fist. You can repeat that along with the pocketing process as often as you wish.

As a surprise climax, you make a magic pass with your right hand, and when you open your left hand, no sugar lumps fall out, because all three have completely vanished! That, indeed, is a baffling finale.

Again, you start with a sugar lump secretly palmed in your right hand and three lumps on the table. If this trick is a follow-up to Through the Table, put the fourth lump back in the bowl or lay it completely aside before proceeding with the Come-back Lump routine.

With the right hand, drop a visible lump in the open left hand. Do the same with a second lump, letting the palmed lump fall with it (Fig. 410) and then close the left hand into a loose fist. Take the remaining lump with

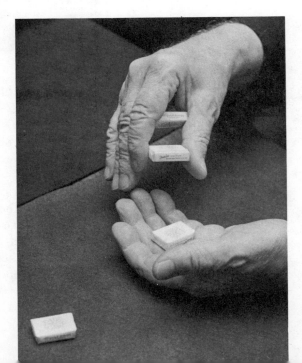

Fig. 410. Right hand secretly drops its palmed lump along with other two (performer's view).

your right hand and palm it as you put it in your right pocket. As you bring your right hand from your pocket, open the fist and let the three lumps fall to the table.

Before people recover from their surprise, repeat the process, saying, "one—two—" dropping two lumps in the left hand and the palmed lump with them; then add, "—and the third in the pocket." Put it there, palming it as before, and you will be all set to continue. In pretending to drive the third lump up through the table, palm it in the same way, simply changing your comment to suit the action. This variation naturally enhances the effect; but there is another procedure that adds still more misdirection.

That is to drop the palmed lump along with first lump that you place in the left hand, immediately closing the left fist so that no one can see that it holds two lumps instead of only one. As you do this, you count, "one—" and tilt the left fist to the right, so that the thumb comes directly upward. Pick up the second lump with your right hand, counting "two—" and move the left thumb aside so that the right fingers can tap the "second" lump down into the loose left fist, with the left thumb promptly closing the gap. Put the remaining lump in your right pocket, remarking "three," and toss the three lumps from the left hand.

Since you are a "move ahead" of any suspicious spectators, this will invariably catch them off guard. In repeating this maneuver, you can tilt the left fist still farther to the right, so that its knuckles are well upward. This gives you an excuse to turn the right hand palm upward as its fingers push the "second" lump into the left fist. This adds another puzzling touch for the benefit of skeptical onlookers.

You can also speed the action by picking up the first and second lumps together, counting, "One—two" and dropping the palmed lump with them in the left hand. The "third" lump is either pocketed or sent up through the table, being palmed as usual, to be ready for the next "repeat."

Here a note should be injected regarding the term "as usual" where palming is concerned. Up to this point, the "usual" palm is preferably the Standard Palm where most performers are concerned. But some may find the Finger Bend more natural, particularly with the Come-back Lump. Also, the Front-finger Grip can be used effectively at various stages of the full routine.

This applies directly to the finale that features both the Come-back Lump and the entire routine of the Magic Sugar Lumps, namely, the complete evanishment of the "three" lumps.

You lead up to it as follows: With the right hand, drop Lumps 1 and 2 into the left hand, letting the palmed lump go with them. As before, put the third lump in the right coat pocket, but this time simply leave it there. Slide the three lumps from the left hand and apparently you are ready for another "repeat." But now you have no "extra" palmed in the right hand.

There are just three sugar lumps on the table. Take up the first, saying, "One" and hold it between the tips of the right thumb and fingers as you apparently place it in the left hand. Instead, you draw it back with the right thumb and palm it with the Finger Bend; or simply retain it with the Front-finger Grip. Close the left hand immediately, as if the lump were really there.

With the right thumb and fingers, pick up the second lump, saying, "two," and carry it directly above the closed left hand, which is kept knuckles upward, opening as if to receive it. Repeat the placement move, retaining the second lump as you did the first, by using either the Finger Bend or the Front-finger Grip. Again, close the left hand as if it held two sugar lumps.

Pick up the third lump with the right thumb and forefinger and show it triumphantly as you announce, "three!" while keeping the other two lumps in the bend of the right fingers. Deliberately put the third lump in your right coat pocket and drop all three. Bring the right hand from the pocket as usual, make a mystic pass over the left hand, and ask, "How many?"

When they all say, "three," you calmly respond, "none." Open your left hand to justify it, brush it with your open right hand to prove it, and turn your right hand palm upward, brushing it with the left hand to confirm it. Thus you complete one of the greatest deceptions in all close-up magic.

Why is it so great? You have conditioned your audience to the point where the keener observers think that you are trying to outwit them with the "one—two—three" caper. They think they have it solved, while every-one else is going along happily with you, and discover much to their dismay that they're all wrong.

So even if you are a bit slow on the final take, you can't lose. The smart set is looking for a "load" instead of a "steal," which leaves them flab-bergasted. The regular customers are going along with you, trustingly as ever, and they too are properly mystified.

COINS THROUGH TABLE

Connoisseurs of close-up conjuring regard this as among the best of table tricks and frequently refer to it as the "Han Pin Chien Coins" in honor of a Chinese magician who first introduced it in America. Some skill is required, but careful timing is the most important item, and the trick should be practiced with that in mind. The original version is described herewith, followed by the latest variant.

The magician, seated at a table, takes several small coins in each hand, then adds a larger coin to the right-hand group. Actually, one set should duplicate the other, though that is generally not mentioned. Thus the left hand might hold, say, a dime, two nickels, and two pennies; the right hand, a dime, two nickels, and two pennies, plus a quarter dollar. Or each hand could hold a quarter instead of the dime; in that case, the right hand would require a half dollar as its largest coin. The usual procedure is to borrow some small change and simply pick out coins that will equalize the groups.

With the coins in their respective hands, the performer closes his fists and places his right hand beneath the table. He raises his left fist and gives it a downward swing, knuckles first, opening his hand just before it reaches the tables so as to trap its coins and prevent them from scattering. He raises his hand and points to the coins with his left forefinger, remarking, "All small coins here in the left hand."

Gathering the coins with his left hand, he brings up his right hand from beneath the table and swings it down in the same manner, trapping its coins, then showing them, as he comments, "And all small coins in this hand—except for the one large coin. Remember that!" He gathers the coins with his right hand and thrusts it beneath the table, at the same time raising his left fist and saying, "Now watch what happens this time!"

With that, he smacks his left hand flat on the table and then lifts it, all in the same action. All the coins are gone from his left hand, apparently driven through the table top! Nonchalantly, the magician brings his right hand from beneath the table, opens it deliberately, and pours out the full quota of coins, showing that those from the left hand have joined those in the right. Yet the table is intact.

Check the routine as given and the method will be easy to follow, as it depends upon two secret moves, which the uninitiated observers do not suspect. When the right hand goes beneath the table for the first time, it leaves all its small coins on the right knee, stacking them there loosely and retaining only the extra coins (Fig. 411). Meanwhile, or shortly thereafter, the left hand smacks its coins down upon the table, counts them, and gathers them up.

COINS THROUGH TABLE
Fig. 411. While left hand retains its small coins above table, right hand, below table, has stacked its small coins on right knee, retaining large coin.

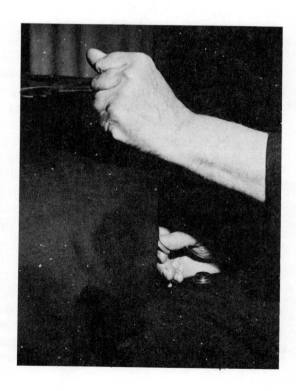

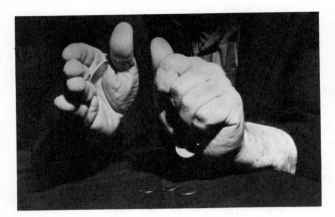

Fig. 412. Right hand slapping downward with large coin and trapping small coins that left hand secretly releases.

The right hand comes up from beneath the table, closed in a fist as though it still held its group of coins, though actually it has only the large one, which can have its edge protruding slightly between thumb and forefinger. The left forearm is resting on the table, extending toward the right at a forty-five-degree angle. The right hand is raised above the left (Fig. 412) and is then swung straight down toward the table, spreading wide as it nears the knuckles of the left hand, which are extended upward. At the same instant, the left fingers open slightly, letting the coins drop from the left hand. The open right hand, carrying its long large coin, overtakes the falling coins with its swift downstroke and traps them on the table, while the left fist tightens and moves toward the left.

To all appearances, the right hand has simply slammed its coins on the table the way the left hand did earlier, as each move is an exact simulation of the other. Everyone supposes that the left hand still has its group of coins; hence they take it that the small coins now on display belong in the right hand, along with the large coin that was originally there. So the right hand gathers up all the loose coins and goes beneath the table, where it secretly picks up the stack of coins that it placed on the right knee. All that remains is to slam the left hand flat on the table, raise it to show that its coins are gone, and bring out the entire lot with the right hand, which drops them openly upon the table, concluding a most startling mystery.

The downswing of the right hand and the opening of the left fingers should be practiced until they are timed to exact precision. If the dropping coins have a tendency to scatter, tilt the left hand lower and more to the right, so it is almost directly beneath the right hand when the latter begins its swing. Hence the left hand makes a quick, short motion, slightly upward and toward the left, slowing as it continues in that direction.

This is natural enough, as the left hand merely seems to be avoiding the descending right hand. But the motion hides the opening of the left fingers, which can therefore be opened wider, so that the left hand practically pulls away from the dropping coins, letting them drop vertically. This makes it all the easier for the right hand to clamp them as it flattens, and the left fist has ample time to tighten as it completes its sideward swing.

If all the spectators are seated at the performer's left, the secret transfer of the coins is completely covered by the back of the left hand. The move is partly covered by the right hand where persons on the performer's right are concerned, but the "drop" may be detected if the left hand releases its coins too soon. A good way to avoid this is to work the coins to a position between the left fingertips and the heel of the left hand. A quick opening of the left fingers will then provide an instant drop.

Latest Variant: To present Coins Through Table in a bolder, faster, but somewhat easier style, the following course is recommended:

Set up two equal groups of coins, one for each hand, as in the original method. Take a larger coin and instead of adding it to the right-hand group, place it forward, by itself, saying, "I may not need this coin, so I'll try the trick without it. But if I do need it, I'll have it handy."

Gather the equal groups in left and right hands respectively; thrust the right hand beneath the table and secretly stack its coins on the right knee, meanwhile jingling the left-hand coins openly as you announce:

"The purpose is to drive these coins squarely through the table — like this!"

With that, you close the left fist, raise it, and give it a downward slam-bang, opening it as it reaches the table, as if you expected to do exactly what you said. Instead, when you raise the left hand, the coins are still there, so you gather them up, jingling them as you continue:

"It didn't work, so we'll have to start all over. Here's one batch of coins in my left hand" — close your left fist and turn it downward and at the same time bring the right fist up from beneath the table — "and another batch in my right hand."

With that, you execute the original "drop" from the left hand as you bring the empty right hand slam-bang downward, trapping the dropped coins beneath, saying: "Just the way we started." You raise the right hand, point to the coins, and then pick up the large extra coin, placing it with the group as you declare:

"But this time we'll add the big coin, as I should have done before. You ask why? Because I need it as a magnet." As you talk, you gather the coins in the right hand, the large coin among them. "Yes, I said a magnet. When I put my right hand under the table" — close your right fist and thrust it there — "the magnetic coin will pull these left-hand coins down through."

At that you raise your left fist as if it still held its coins, while your right hand simultaneously gathers its original batch from your right knee, and you end with the triumphant note:

"Just like this!"

Slam-bang the left hand flat on the table, show its coins gone, and at the same time bring out the right to dump the entire quota into view. Pick the large coin from the double group and pocket it, commenting, "You see what I mean by a magnetic coin?"

The first advantage of this variation is in the secret placement of the right-hand coins on the right knee, which is easier than the original method because the right hand is unencumbered with the large "magnet" coin. Again, when the right hand traps the dropped coins from the left hand, the right hand is still unencumbered with the extra, making that move easier. Next, adding the extra coin to those in the right hand provides good misdirection, as the trick really seems to be just beginning when actually it is as good as over. The added slam-bang of the left hand is like another honest try, stepping up the climax.

Some performers are sure to prefer the old original "Han Pin Chien" rather than the variant; but many will find it good policy to practice both methods and alternate them with doing the trick for persons who have seen it before, since the different approach provides misdirection in itself.

STRAIGHT THROUGH

This alternate for Coins Through Table is a master effect in its own right and can be presented under the most exacting conditions. Instead of showing several small coins in each hand, two large coins of half-dollar size are used in each hand, making four in all. A fifth coin is also needed, such as a large foreign coin of copper, or a souvenir medal. (A quarter can be used, even though it is smaller in size.) Whatever the fifth coin, it will be referred to as the "extra."

Lay two halves at the left of the table; two halves at the right, with the extra just beyond. Pick up the two half dollars with the right hand and then the extra. With your left hand, pick up the half dollars at the left. Then:

Slap the left-hand coins on the table, gather them up, and slap the right-hand coins in the same way: two from the left, three from the right (Fig. 413). Gather up the right-hand coins and dip the hand beneath the table. The left hand strikes the table hard and flat. Its coins are gone, and up from beneath the table comes the right hand to drop all five coins on top!

Here is the procedure: In picking up the two half dollars at the right, rest them loosely near the base of the right fingers, one slightly overlapping the other (Fig. 414). Close the right hand into a fist, turning it downward; as you do, press the coins into the Thumb-fork Palm (Figs. 17 and 18). Keep the thumb close to the hand to hide the edges of the two half dollars and extend the forefinger just enough to pick up the extra coin between the first joint of the forefinger and the tip of the thumb (Fig. 415).

Keep the extra coin in sight, but with the right hand well fisted as you turn it thumb upward, so no one will suspect that the half dollars are gripped in the thumb fork. The left hand then picks up its two half dollars and lets them rest on the bend of the fingers, just as the right hand did with its pair (see Fig. 414).

Partly close the left hand, then turn it downward with a swing, trapping its coins beneath it. Keep the left hand slightly cupped, thumb pressed close against it as you raise the hand and point to its half dollars, saying, "Two coins in the left hand." Pick up the two coins with the left hand and

STRAIGHT THROUGH
Fig. 413. Preliminary move, showing right hand about to pick up its coins after actually slapping them on table. Cupped left hand holds two coins.

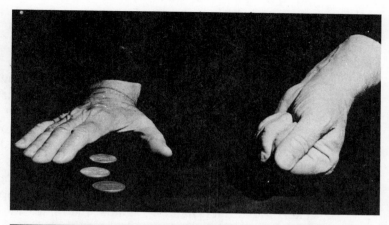

Fig. 414. Each hand showing two coins of half-dollar size. Right hand about to pick up fifth coin of larger size. Preliminary action.

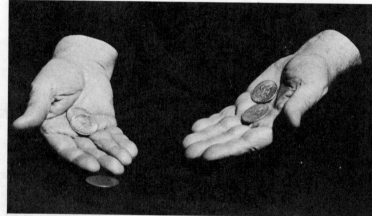

Fig. 415. Left hand has slapped its two coins on table and is about to pick them up. Right hand still holding larger coin in view. Preliminary action.

fist them loosely, keeping them on the tips of the downturned fingers and remark: "And three coins in the right hand" (see Fig. 416).

With that, swing your hand hand downward and leftward at a slant, opening it, but keeping it a trifle cupped. People actually see the extra coin fall, and simultaneously, the left hand releases its two half dollars, so that the right hand traps them with the extra coin—the left hand moving away just rapidly enough to get clear, tightening its fist as though it still held its coins (Fig. 417).

In lifting the right hand, keep it cupped just as you did with the left, but keep it toward you, so that no one sees the two half dollars gripped in the thumb fork (Fig. 418). Turn the right hand down, gather up the visible half dollars and the extra coin, and close the right fist. You are then ready for the climax.

So far, neither hand has been out of sight. Now the right hand dips beneath the table, the left hand whams downward on the top and turns up empty, while the right hand comes up and flings all five coins on the table. Assuming the audience has seen that before, you can spring a surprise by dipping the left hand beneath the table and keeping the right hand above. Then slap the left hand up against the underside of the tabletop and dump the coins from the right hand, promptly bringing the left hand into sight to show it empty.

Fig. 416. Right hand preparing to repeat preliminary slap, secretly thumb-palming two half dollars while keeping larger coin in sight.

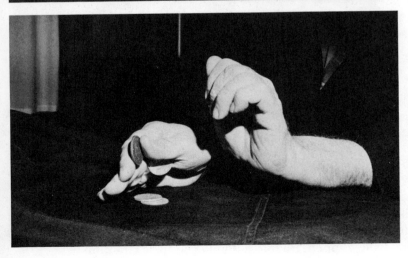

Fig. 417. Right hand completing slap, trapping two coins secretly dropped by left hand. Right hand is letting larger coin fall while retaining its thumb-palmed half dollars.

Fig. 418. Right hand picking up large coin and two
half dollars from left hand.
Note right hand's own
half dollars still secretly
thumb-palmed.

Either way, you do not have to be seated at a table to present this effect.
You can stoop forward while standing and "drive" the coins through either
a table or a shelf. Or, seated in one chair, you can work the trick on another chair instead of a table. Finally, instead of a penetration, the effect
can be shown as a transposition entitled:

HAND-TO-HAND

This is identical with Straight Through up to the point where one hand is
ready to go beneath the table. There, instead, both hands are kept in sight
and turned knuckles upward. The left hand makes a throwing motion
toward the right and is spread to show itself empty. The right hand
promptly opens and lets all five coins—four half dollars and the extra—
trickle triumphantly onto the table.

The method, of course, is exactly the same as with Straight Through,
though dependent on a variation of the famous Han Pin Chien "move."
The effect, when done as a pure transposition, closely resembles the Four-
coin Baffler (see page 315). Simply by dispensing with the extra coin and
starting with two half dollars in the left hand and two in the right, you can
make that resemblance closer still. The only difference is that with the
Baffler, the coins pass one at a time, while with Hand to Hand both go together.

When persons who like the Four-coin Baffler ask to see it again, you can
show them Hand to Hand with only four coins and leave them more flab-
bergasted than ever.

THROW-OVER

Though simply an incidental move, this is well worth the practice, as it
can be used as a follow-up to various table tricks in which coins are involved. The move itself has three variations:

SIMPLE PASSAGE

Both hands are extended palms upward, with a coin lying at the base of the right middle fingers. Simultaneously the hands are turned inward and downward, flattening against the table-top, several inches apart. They are lifted and the right hand picks up the coin, to display it as before and with the left hand also extended palm up, as it was originally. Again, both hands turn downward; this time the right hand begins a rubbing motion, finishing with the fingertips, and when they are raised, the coin has vanished. The left hand is then lifted, showing that the coin has mysteriously arrived there.

It's all done on the second turn-down. The right hand ordinarily starts slightly to the right, in order to make a circular motion to the left and trap the coin beneath. But in this case it swings directly toward the left, literally throwing the coin beneath the left hand as the latter makes its turn-down. While a bold, long throw usually eludes detection, it is better to swing the right hand close to the left, if several persons are watching from various angles. In that case, the right hand should start a sweeping motion toward the right the moment it slaps the table, working well away from the left hand. Thus the hands are well apart when they are lifted to show that the coin has passed from right to left.

MUTUAL ATTRACTION

In this case two coins are used, preferably two of the same type, though that is not absolutely necesssary. One is shown in each hand; the hands are slapped palms down and later lifted to show that the coin from the right hand has joined the coin on the left.

Again, the throw-over move is utilized, but while the right hand is making its accustomed throw, the left hand does a shorter revolution, simply flipping downward to trap its coin beneath, while the other is arriving from the right. But just before the turn-down, the left fingers are tilted upward far enough for the coin to slide down toward the left palm, where it is later trapped.

As a result there is no clash of coins, as the coin from the right is trapped beneath the left fingers. This can be accentuated by thrusting the right hand a trifle forward just before the throw-over. In lifting the left hand, the fingers should draw their coin toward the palm, so both coins will be together.

TRANSPOSITION

Here the coins must differ in appearance, as a penny and a nickel; or two larger coins, say a quarter and a half dollar, or foreign coins of contrasting metals. One is shown in the right hand, the other in the left; when the hands are slapped on the table, then raised, the coins have changed places.

This requires a double throw-over, executed simultaneously by each hand. Again, the right-hand coin should be at the base of the fingers; the left-hand coin should be well toward the palm. With large coins, the right thumb can thrust its coin outward, while the left hand draws its coin inward, just before the vital move, so there is no chance of the coins clicking each other in transit.

Once practiced sufficiently to gain the needed precision, this double throw-over becomes almost automatic; and since the action of the hands is identical, they can be brought fairly close together, then drawn apart, in a continuous move.

JUMP-OVER DICE

This neat table trick with a pair of dice—one red, the other green—is well worth the practice needed to master it. The performer places the red die in his left hand, closes his left fist, and says, "Red on the left." He then picks up the green die with his right hand, closes his fist, and adds, "Green on the right." To emphasize the situation, he slaps each hand flat on the table and raises both hands to show the location of the dice.

This whole procedure is repeated with the statements, "Red . . . left, green . . . right," but this time, the performer remarks, "Now, watch!" Keeping his hands well apart, he lifts them and shows the green die on the left and the red die on the right. Mysteriously, the dice have jumped from one hand to the other.

In the preliminary showing of the dice, the right hand picks up the red and places it in the left hand, which closes over it. This leaves the right hand free to pick up the green die, forming a fist over it too. This procedure is important, as it sets the pattern for the deception that follows. When the hands are slapped flat on the table—left first, then right—the red is naturally seen on the left, the green on the right.

So far, all fair and square. But in repeating the process, trickery enters the start. The right hand, in apparently placing the red die in the left fist, actually retains it in the bend of the right fingers. Turning downward, the right hand picks up the green die and apparently fists it as before. Only the tips of the fingers are brought over it, however, as it is held for the next and all-important move.

At this point, the left hand is empty, while the right holds both dice—the red in the finger bend, the green almost at the fingertips. Putting both elbows on the table, the performer brings his fists close together, gesturing the left above the right as he repeats, "Red on the left" and brings the left hand straight downward, spreading it flat while simultaneously the right fingertips release the green die, which falls ahead of the left hand and is thereby trapped beneath it.

Sliding the left hand well to the left and taking the green die along, the performer nonchalantly adds, "And green on the right." He slaps his right hand flat, well to the right, trapping the red die beneath it. This is a perfectly normal move that seems executed exactly as before. Hence, when the hands are lifted, the surprise is complete.

NOTE: The drop just described is an adaptation of the move used in Coins Through Table (page 328); hence it can be used for a coin transposition as well. Dice are preferable because of the color contrast available; but the routine is also effective with coins of different sizes, such as a half dollar and a quarter, or with a copper coin and a silver coin both the same size. In either case, the procedure is the same. One coin is retained in the bend of the right fingers and the right hand then picks up the other and puts it in position for the drop, which follows.

STRING A RING

The magical placement of a solid finger ring on a length of string while both ends are being held has long been regarded as an ideal close-up mystery. Various ways have been devised to accomplish this result; and the best of these, performed at a table with the ring, a string, and handkerchief, is described herewith, in its simplest and perhaps move effective form.

A two-foot length of string is stretched along the table and the ring is laid upon it, near the center. A handkerchief is spread over the string, leaving the ends in full view. The performer then slides his hands beneath the cloth and manipulates the ring briefly, with the ends of the string continually in sight. That done, he raises the string from the table, drawing its ends taut, with the handkerchief draped over the string. When he gives the ends to a spectator and whisks away the cloth, there is the ring on the very center of the string, proof that the impossible has again been accomplished.

It all depends, of course, on what is done beneath the handkerchief, but the effect is so phenomenal that it is almost impossible for anyone to fathom what goes on there. Yet the procedure is so simple that you can soon learn to work it sight unseen. Just practice it a while without the handkerchief as cover and you will soon find yourself presenting this near miracle.

First, make sure that the ring is laid *over* the string to stress that you propose to string the ring magically. Now, under cover of the handkerchief, you hold the ring steady with your left hand while your right thumb and fingers draw a loop up through the ring and carry it off toward the right (Fig. 419).

Take that loop and tie it around the main portion of the rope, to the right of the ring (Fig. 420). (All you need is a simple, single knot, the easiest of all knots.) This done, go back to the ring and draw another loop up through with your left thumb and forefinger and insert your thumb in the loop as you complete the action (Fig. 421).

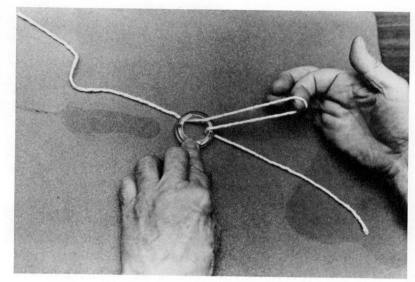

Fig. 419. Right forefingers drawing loop up through right, which is steadied by left hand (under cover of handkerchief).

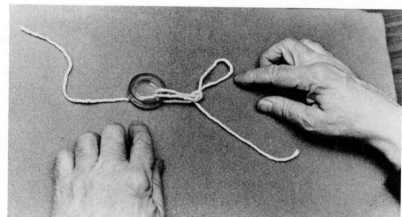

Fig. 420. Hands have tied loop to right of string (still under cover; ends of string should show).

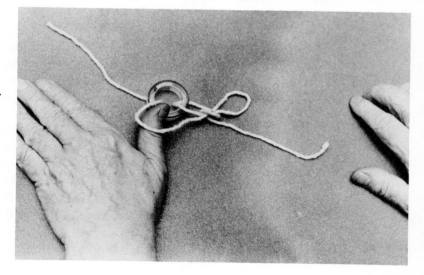

Fig. 421. Left thumb has drawn another loop up through ring and is engaging it under cover (ends of string remain in view).

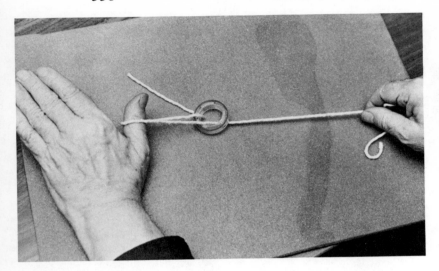

Fig. 422. Right hand visibly drawing its end of string while left hand (beneath handkerchief) rapidly pulls loop toward left.

Now you say to a spectator: "Just take the ends of the string and draw them apart." You lift the string, with your right hand close to its end, your left thumb in the loop, drawing your own hands apart in order to give the ends to the spectator. This action automatically draws the left end through the ring (Fig. 422) and brings the end into the left hand as the hand emerges from beneath the cloth. This is never noticed, because the left hand, moving outward, hides the string as it moves inward.

A final tug of the ends, as you give them to the spectator, will untie the knot, so when you take away the handkerchief the ring is neatly threaded on the string. Often, you can let the spectator supply the last pull, even after you have drawn away the handkerchief. The sight of the knot will puzzle him; and when his pull dissolves the knot, leaving the ring on the string in its place, he will be utterly mystified.

MAGNETIC PENCILS

A neat twist on an old trick where a pencil is placed against the palm of the right hand and is apparently magnetized there by gripping the right wrist with the left hand to "create the necessary power." The primary difference in this case is that seven pencils are used instead of only one. But there is a further difference, as will be shown.

The pencils are laid across the right hand, which is held palm upward to receive them. The right thumb is then extended across the pencils to keep them in place. The right hand is then tilted upward so that its back is toward the onlookers; simultaneously, the left hand grips the right wrist, fingers below, thumb above. The right thumb is then raised and brought into view. Amazingly, the pencils ahere to the right hand as though mysteriously magnetized.

The secret is this: The left hand, in gripping the right wrist, extends its forefinger inward behind the right palm (Fig. 423), pressing the pencils in place and relieving the right thumb of its burden. Thus the right thumb swings to the front, and the miracle is complete. And a miracle it is— unless observers note that those clutching left fingers are one too few (Fig. 424).

By keeping the right hand slightly in motion, the missing finger is apt to be overlooked, and the trick can be brought to a quick termination, either by swinging the right thumb inward to grip the pencils as they were originally, or by simply withdrawing the left forefinger and letting the pencils drop to the table as the left hand relaxes its supposedly "magnetic" grip.

MAGNETIC PENCILS
Fig. 423. Performer's view of "magnetic" pencils, showing left forefinger secretly extended to retain the pencils.

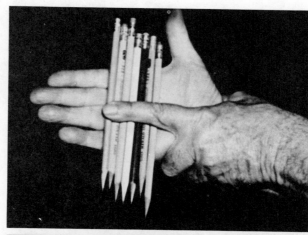

Fig. 424. Spectator's view of pencils being "magnetized" by gripping right wrist. Note absence of left forefinger.

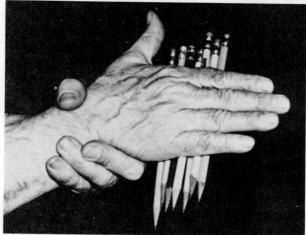

IMPROVED METHOD

If asked to repeat Magnetic Pencils, the performer runs the risk of a smart guesser being ready to count his fingers, particularly as someone may be familiar with the old trick in which only a single pencil was used. Imagine the surprise when the performer repeats the trick, showing all four fingers of the left hand as they grip the right wrist, even wiggling them to show that they are real. Yet the pencils stay "magnetized" as usual (Fig. 425).

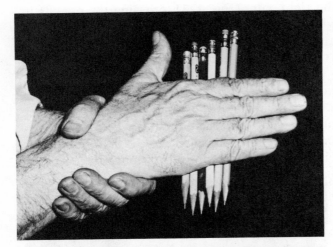

Fig. 425. Improved version of Magnetic Pencils. Spectators see all four fingers of left hand, yet pencils do not fall.

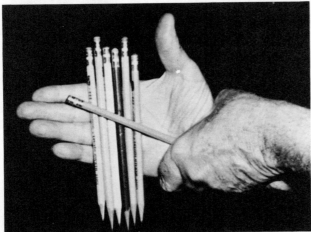

Fig. 426. Withdrawn pencil gripped in place by left hand so that right thumb can be fully extended.

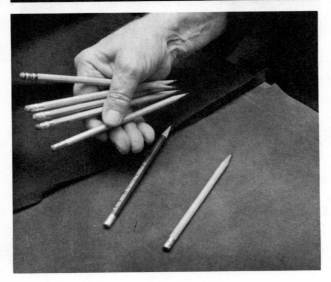

Fig. 427. Right hand dropping "demagnetized" pencils on table. Note how right thumb grips the extra, letting it go with the clump.

The difference here is in the pencils. A count shows only six instead of seven. (Compare Figs. 424 and 425.) In starting from the original position, the left thumb and forefinger grip the lower end of the outermost pencil — the one nearest the right fingers — and swivel it directly toward the right wrist, while the back of the right hand is tilted upward, bringing its back toward the onlookers, with the right thumb still retaining the pencils.

This enables the left hand to include the extra pencil in its grip when it encircles the right wrist. Pointed straight from right wrist to right fingers, the extra pencil clamps the rest in place, unseen by the audience (Fig. 426). The left hand, while applying the clamp, can thus show all its fingers. For a finish, the right thumb can come inward and grip the extra pencil along with the others, to display them in a clump; or they can all be dropped to the table, the extra along with the rest (Fig. 427).

PERFECT MAGNETIC PENCIL

Ideal for close-up work, this version of the Magnetic Pencils is simplicity itself. With your left hand, you place a pencil against the upturned fingers of your right hand, where it remains as though magnetized, and is shown at all angles. While the pencil remains upright, the left hand is placed palm to palm with the right, and whenever the hands are separated, the pencil clings to the left fingers instead of the right.

This surprising transfer can be repeated time after time, always with the same result, and with each separation of the hands, the free hand can be rubbed against the coat sleeve and shown with fingers wide apart to prove that no adhesive substance is used. At the finish, the pencil is rolled freely between the hands and given to a spectator for inspection, while both hands are shown at the closest range.

The secret depends upon an ordinary straight pin, which is pushed into a side of a hexagonal pencil, about an inch below the upper end. The pin should be inserted at a forty-five-degree angle, so that when the left hand places the pencil against the spread right fingers, the pencil can actually be hung from the right second finger. When the left hand first displays the pencil, its fingers cover the pin, and once the pencil is in position the right fingers are brought together to that the pin is hidden between the first two fingers of the right hand.

Standing with his left side toward the audience, the performer can tilt his right hand forward and backward and even point his fingers downward, provided he does not go far enough to show the pinhead projecting behind his first two fingers. Then comes the convincing move: The left hand is brought palm to palm with the right, and the magician swings to the left, bringing his right side toward the audience. Timed to this action, he spreads his fingers slightly and moves his right hand forward. This gives the pencil a half turn and swivels the pin from the first two fingers of the right hand to a corresponding position between the left fingers (a rolling motion), which are then immediately closed.

When the right hand is withdrawn, the pencil is "magnetized" by the left, and the right hand can be shown freely. Then, by again pressing the right hand palm to palm with the left, a reversal of the preceding move swivels the pin back to the right hand, which again imparts its "magnetic power" to the pencil. This sequence can be repeated as often as desired with the same baffling effect.

At the finish, the hand nearest the audience simply draws the pencil upward and forward, while the fingers of the other hand maintain their grip up on the pin so that it remains there, allowing the front hand to pass the pencil for examination. During this procedure, the rear hand is lowered and the fingers are spread sufficiently to let the pin drop to the floor unnoticed.

This effect can be worked at very close range with the performer seated at a table by simply shifting his arms from left to right and vice versa. For the finale, the hands should be clear of the table edge, so that one hand can carry the pencil forward and drop it on the table, while the other is lowered just past the table edge, letting the pin fall when the fingers momentarily dip from sight.

MAGNETIZED KNIFE

For a quick, effective close-up baffler, this is just about tops. The performer lays a table knife across the outspread fingers of his left hand and brings his right hand toward the left in order to interlace the fingers of both hands. This is done automatically and immediately, and the hands are raised with their backs toward the audience. To everybody's consternation, the knife adheres to the palms of the hands as though magnetized.

When the hands are drawn apart, the knife drops to the table, as though suddenly demagnetized. The knife can be examined, then replaced exactly as before, again regaining its magnetic quality, as often as required.

The secret is both subtle and simple. In bringing the hands together the right second finger is bent inward (Fig. 428) so that it comes above the knife instead of below. Thus three fingers of the right hand come between four of the left hand. When the hands are raised to the vertical (Fig. 429) nobody notices that there are only seven fingers instead of eight.

The missing finger does the trick, for it provides the needed clamp to keep the knife in place. The simple act of drawing the hands apart releases the knife and disposes of the lone clue to the mystery.

SUPERMAGNETISM

While this effect is limited to certain types of table knives, it is so

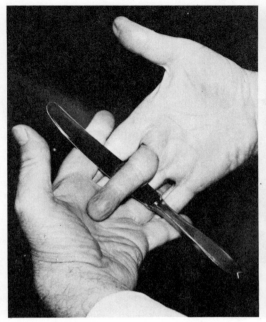

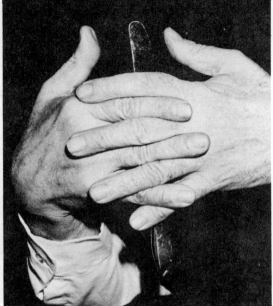

MAGNETIZED KNIFE
Fig. 428. Performer's
view showing right second
finger sliding below knife
as fingers are interlaced.

Fig. 429. Audience view
of "magnetized" knife.
Pressure of missing right-
hand finger keeps knife in
place.

surprising that it is well worth the necessary practice just to be ready with
it when the opportunity arises. Picking up a table knife with his left hand,
the performer lays the blade across his right second finger and presses the
very tip of his right forefinger against the edge, near the end of the blade.
He points his fingers straight down toward the table, yet the knife refuses
to fall from its precarious position. Finally, the left hand removes the knife
and offers it for examination.

A knife with a heavy handle is required, and some experimentation is
necessary to gain the proper knack. If you hold such a knife with its blade
pointing upward and press the tip of your forefinger against the edge near
the end, you will find that by tilting your hand backward, the weight of the
handle will act like a counterbalance and keep the knife in position. However, as you tilt your hand forward, the weight of the handle becomes too
great if kept in the vertical position.

However, by pointing the fingers downward (Fig. 430), the knife assumes a horizontal position and thus equalizes the balance. The force
applied by the downward pressure of the forefinger is counteracted by the
weight of the handle, and by spreading the fingers, or bending the second
finger slightly inward, the knife can easily be retained in what is seemingly
an impossible position.

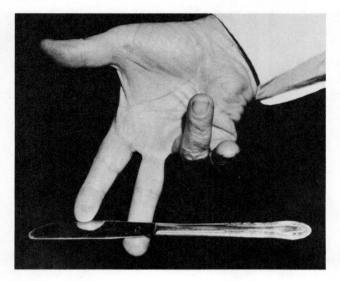

SUPERMAGNETISM
Fig. 430. Final position
with fingers pointing down
so pressure of forefinger
counteracts weight of
knife handle.

SALT VANISH

From an ordinary glass salt shaker, the performer pours a quantity of
salt into his left fist, brushes away a few loose grains with his right fingers,
and spreads his left hand wide open with a sudden, upward toss. Instantly
and mysteriously, the salt has vanished completely from the left hand!

The trick can be ended then and there, particularly when working at a
table, where it can be introduced as an impromptu effect. As an added
climax the performer can show both hands empty, raise his right hand high
in the air, and from it pour the missing salt into his outstretched left palm,
which lets it trickle back into the salt shaker.

A special gimmick is needed for this trick but it is one that is literally invisible before and after the vanish and the reproduction. Moreover, it is a
very common article—a small plastic pill bottle, one-half inch or slightly
more in diameter, and about two inches in depth. This size container will
fit neatly into the average salt shaker.

In preparation, the fake is imbedded deeply in the shaker, which is about
two thirds filled with salt. By shaking it while the fake is being pushed
downward, the salt is forced upward around it so that the shaker appears
to be almost filled with salt. The shaker cap is then screwed in place and all
is ready for the following procedure:

The performer picks up the shaker between the tip of his left thumb and
the bend of the left fingers. Turning the back of his left hand toward the
spectators, he unscrews the cap with the thumb and fingers of his right
hand and lays it near the edge of the table. At the same time, the left thumb
draws the shaker slightly downward, so it can be retained in the finger
bend while the thumb is raised sufficiently to press the lip of the projecting
fake against the forefinger. The right hand then comes from below, grips

the shaker between thumb and finger bend to draw it straight downward, and leaves the fake secretly gripped between the thumb and forefinger while fully hidden in the bend of the left fingers.

The left hand is then cupped in a loose fist, with the thumb across the top of the fake to keep it hidden until the hand is raised above the eye level of the spectators. The left thumb next moves aside, allowing the right hand to pour salt from the shaker into the cupped left fist. This should be done openly and deliberately so people can see that the salt is really being poured. When the fake is about half filled, the performer places the shaker beside the cap and swings to the left so the fingers of his left hand are directly toward the spectators, with the thumb raised slightly to make sure the lip of the fake is hidden.

Here comes the subtle touch: The right hand approaches the left fist and pretends to brush away a few grains of loose salt. In that process, the right hand pauses long enough to dip the tip of its second finger into the concealed fake and presses it firmly home. The right hand is then drawn upward, bringing the fake with it.

Once clear, the right hand is brought toward the body, so that the left hand can be swung upward and above it. The right hand lowers gradually, keeping its fingers bent inward, with the exception of the forefinger. The forefinger points upward toward the left hand, directing attention there, while the left hand spreads open with the toss that "vanishes" the salt. The fake, meanwhile, remains concealed on the tip of the right second finger, which presses it closely against the heel of the right hand.

While attention is still focused on the left hand, the right hand reaches for the salt shaker. By raising the second finger, the tube is easily gripped between the thumb and the last two fingers, so the tip of the second finger can be drawn clear. By lowering the right hand loosely around the shaker, the fake is replaced therein during the natural action of picking up the shaker. The left hand, after swinging frontward to emphasize its emptiness, picks up the cap and replaces it on the shaker. To aid this, the right hand tilts the shaker to the left, until it is nearly horizontal. Thus in screwing on the cap, the fake is pushed deep into the salt, so when the shaker is raised upright, its salt will be at the same approximate level as the salt in the fake.

ALTERNATE ROUTINE WITH REPRODUCTION OF SALT

Instead of replacing the fake in the shaker, the right hand retains the fake on its second finger and moves upward, placing its forefinger slantwise across the left palm to prove that the salt isn't there. The right hand extends its fingers behind the left hand; at the same time, the right hand pivots so it comes palm frontward and moves gradually downward until even its extended fingers are almost totally visible.

The term "almost" applies particularly to the right second finger, which is neatly hiding the fake behind the left hand. This is an extension of a thimble move (page 213), which is even more effective in this case, considering that nobody knows that a fake is involved. So instead of a momentary "flash," a sizable pause is allowable here. A reversal of the move brings the fake back into the right fist, which closes around it and then:

The first hand reaches higher than the left, closes in a fist while drawing the fake from the tip of the second finger, and then majestically pours the vanished salt into the outstretched left palm. From then on, it is easy. The right hand picks up the salt shaker, calmly "loading in" the fake, which is now empty and therefore invisible inside the shaker. The left hand tosses away the loose salt, picks up the cap, and screws it on the shaker, forcing down the fake lower into the bed of salt than it was originally placed.

Instead of slipping the fake into the shaker, it can be retained in the bend of the right fingers while the right hand picks up the shaker between tips of thumb and fingers. The right hand is then turned palm toward the audience. The fake remains invisible behind the glass shaker while the left hand deliberately pours its salt into the shaker and adds the cap. The right hand turns its back toward the audience, lays aside the shaker, and later pockets the empty fake. A good excuse is to bring out a handkerchief to wipe a few stray grains of salt from your left hand.

If observers are at side angles, the simultaneous showing of both palms can be omitted. In that case, the performer simply reproduces the salt by reaching upward with his supposedly empty right hand. Due to the easy concealment of the fake in the bend of the fingers, this abbreviated version is highly angleproof.

FIST TO FIST

This is perhaps the most popular version of the Salt Vanish treated as a transposition rather than as a vanish and a reproduction. The performer "steals" the fake from his left hand as already described; then swings face front, spreading his arms wide, so that the fingers of both fists are directly toward the spectators. The left hand, supposedly containing the salt, goes through the "vanishing" motions, and as it is shown empty, the right begins a squeezing action, turns thumb down, and lets the salt pour into sight as though it had traveled up one arm, across the performer's back, and down the other arm, thus passing from fist to fist.

No need to show both hands empty between times, as the action seems continuous. Instead of letting the salt trickle to the floor, the performer can turn his left side to the audience, recapturing the falling salt in the outstretched left hand. Disposal of the fake is handled by one of the methods already described.

VANISHING SALT SHAKER

Even the title of this excellent table trick should be kept a secret until the climax, when it then becomes self-evident. Up to that point, attention is focused upon a borrowed coin—any denomination from a penny to a half dollar—which the performer intends to vanish.

While seated at a table, the performer borrows a coin and places it in front of him. Next, he sets a salt shaker on the coin, gives it a slight twist, and lifts it as though expecting the coin to disappear, but it is still there. Another try results in another failure, and noting that the shaker is slightly tilted by the coin, the performer decides that more covering is needed. So he folds a napkin into quarters and drapes it over the shaker, pressing it firmly to show the shape.

Another lift and the coin is still there. So the performer moistens his fingertip, reaches up under the cloth, and dabs the bottom of the shaker, but it still fails to pick up the coin. He even turns the coin over and sets the napkin-covered shaker upon it, but again the coin fails to go. So, with a resigned gesture, the performer says, "Since I can't vanish the coin, I'll vanish the shaker—like this!"

In emphasis, he spreads his right hand and drives it downward with full force on the humped-up napkin, which flattens under the blow. While spectators still stare goggle-eyed, the performer picks up the napkin with his right hand and flings it aside, showing that the salt shaker is really gone, leaving only the coin. Then, casually dipping his left hand deep in his inside coat pocket, he brings out the missing shaker, replaces it on the table, and returns the borrowed coin to its owner.

Misdirection is the keynote of this grand effect. The performer proceeds as described, until he raises the napkin and the shaker as though expecting the coin to come with them. As he leans forward, glancing at the coin in dismay, he turns it over with his left hand while his right hand naturally withdraws toward his body and releases the shaker from within the napkin folds so that it drops past the edge of the table into his lap. The right hand should dip to table level, so that no one sees the shaker drop; but it promptly moves upward and forward to set the napkin—and presumably the shaker—squarely upon the turned-over coin.

Since the folds of the napkin retain the shape of the shaker, all is ready for the right hand to deliver its convincing smash. But as the right hand poises, drawing attention upward, the left hand slides naturally to the performer's lap and grips the shaker lengthwise, pressing its fingers at the cap and the heel of the hand at the base. The right hand flattens the napkin, plucks it up, and tosses it aside. As the onlookers glance in that direction, the left hand comes up with the palmed shaker and dips inside the coat as though going to the inside pocket. The vanished shaker is then produced and shown at the tips of the thumb and fingers.

Timing is important here. Actually, the misdirection is so good that the moves are almost automatic; but that is no reason to be lax. Instead, a very special technique is essential: While the right hand is flamboyant, the left hand should be deliberate. In short, the quick, surprising vanish should be counterbalanced by the cook, calculated reappearance of the elusive salt shaker. Just concentrate on presentation; the deception will take care of itself. Experience will show how the routine can be varied to suit your own style, or the inclinations of the spectators.

If you wear a vest, a neat way to produce the shaker is to lower your left hand earlier and secretly slide the shaker up beneath your vest. You can work it farther up while the right hand is busy vanishing the imaginary shaker. Then, leaning back, you can unbutton your vest and bring out the shaker at the level of your chest, leaving everyone wondering how it ever got there. That is the way it was done originally, and with vests coming back in style, the old way may very well prove to be best.

SUPERSALT

Passing salt magically from hand to hand is naturally a good table trick, but it is often more effective when performed while standing, though still at fairly close range. The added distance, however, enables the performer to utilize a newer device than the customary "inner tube," and this in turn increases the amount of salt used in the trick, which greatly enhances the effect.

The new device consists of an *outer* tube, which fits closely around the salt shaker. Such a tube can easily be fashioned from a plastic tube used by coin collectors, or a tube containing tacks, which may be purchased at a hardware store. Cut down this tube to about half the height of the salt shaker so it fits over the lower half of the salt shaker; and since the tube is transparent, it will not be noticed. By having such a shaker handy, you can proceed with the following routine:

Pick up the shaker with your left hand and hold it cupped in a loose fist as you face the audience and unscrew the top with your right hand. Lay the top on the table and with your right hand, draw the shaker upward from the left and at the same time tighten the left fist, so that it retains the outer tube. The right hand then pours salt into the left fist, where it actually fills into the hidden tube, which holds a sizable amount.

Now you turn your right side toward the onlookers, so your right hand can brush loose salt from the left fist while dipping both middle fingers down into it. (This move is covered by the right hand, whose back is toward the spectators with its knuckles upward.) Both fingers are needed in order to press their tips down into the tube and spread them there, so they can lift it when the right hand is brought upward. [An alternative move here is to clip the left rim of the tube between the tips of the right forefinger and second finger. The exact procedure depends partly on the size of the tube in relation to the fingers, or according to which way seems easiest to manage it.]

In any case, the right fingers "steal" the salt-laden tube. With the back of the right hand hiding the action and with the aid of the right thumb, the tube can be easily brought into the curl of the right fingers as they form a fist, which assumes an upright position with the thumb on top. While this can be done under the very nose of a keen spectator, distance must be taken into consideration when performing before a group in order to avoid bad angles due to the size of the tube.

With the left hand extended to the left and the right hand to the right, all that remains is simply vanishing the salt from the left fist and then pouring it from the right. The Left-hand Vanish may be any that works well. The salt can be poured into the empty left hand, which promptly dumps it on a plate; or the right hand can pour it directly on the plate itself. Either way, the left hand is then free to pick up the salt shaker and place it in the right fist, pushing it down into the transparent tube. The left hand then screws the cap on the shaker, which is laid aside by the right hand, thus concluding the deception.

With a straight-walled glass salt shaker, particularly one with an ornamental design, and a snugly fitting outer tube, this device can defy detection at the closest ranges.

ROLL THE BILLS

One of the most deceptive of close-up table tricks. Two bills of different value are used — say a ten-dollar bill, which is shown in the right hand, and a five-dollar bill, shown in the left. These are placed on the table so that they form a V, with the ten overlapping the five.

Now the hands begin to tightly roll the bills outward from the point of the V. When they are almost completely rolled, the performer places his right forefinger on the corner of the ten-dollar bill, reminding the spectators that it is uppermost.

Slowly, methodically, he unrolls the bills, simply reversing the original action. But when the bills are fully unrolled, they have magically changed places, for the five, the left-hand bill, is now overlapping the ten, the right-hand bill.

You will have to try this one to see how baffling it can be, for the secret, though simple, is subtle; and the action is almost automatic. Have the ten-dollar bill slightly advanced when you start (Fig. 431) so that the five-dollar bill will be rolled a little faster (Fig. 432). This means that the five-dollar bill will be fully rolled when you place your right forefinger on the corner of the ten-dollar bill. At that moment, the corner of the five-dollar bill will be coming up beneath the third finger of your left hand, so instead

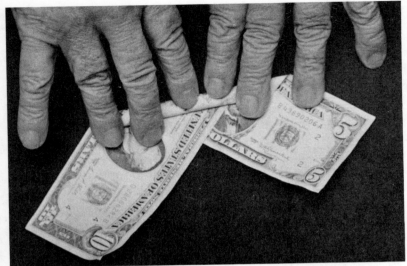

ROLL THE BILLS
Fig. 431. Start of roll. Ten-dollar bill laid above five-dollar bill and extended to performer's right.

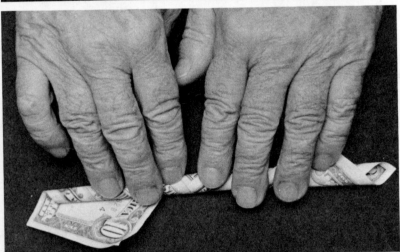

Fig. 432. Roll nearing completion. Upper (ten-dollar) bill is well advanced as left third finger presses corner of lower (five-dollar) bill.

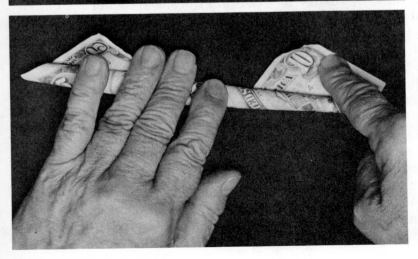

Fig. 433. Right forefinger pressing corner of upper bill while left third finger secretly releases corner of lower bill, transposing their positions.

of pegging it, like the ten, you just raise your left third finger and let the corner of the five do a flipover (Fig. 433).

That's all! When you unroll the bills, the five will be on top. As an added touch, you can have a spectator put his finger on the ten-dollar bill and keep it there, but when the bills are unrolled, the five-dollar bill will still come out on top.

TURN-UP GLASSES

Although fairly well known, this trick is still effective and forms a good prelude to others that are somewhat more complex. In effect, three drinking glasses are placed in a row, with the center glass turned up and the end glasses mouth down. Pointing his thumbs downward, the performer picks up a glass with each hand and turns them over simultaneously, replacing them exactly where they were. He repeats this action twice, making three times in all; and at the finish, all three glasses are turned up.

The moves are quite simple, but if executed rapidly, they are difficult to follow. Counting the glasses as "1, 2, 3" from left to right, turn over 1 and 2 on the first move; 1 and 3 on the second move; and 1 and 2 on the third move. If asked to "do it again," the routine can be varied by turning over 2 and 3 on the first move; 1 and 3 on the second move; and 2 and 3 on the third move. This works out just the same.

Now, however, comes the "catch" that can turn this into a real baffler. Having brought all three glasses mouth up, the performer suggests that somebody else try it. To give the volunteer a good start, the performer takes the middle glass and turns it mouth down, so the glasses are arranged "up," "down," and "up." From this position it is impossible to bring all the glasses mouth up in the three turnovers. People will try it repeatedly and fail, never guessing that the glasses have been placed differently at the start.

FIVE-GLASS FOOLER

Here is an excellent elaboration of the three-glass "turnup" that often baffles persons who have seen the older effect. Five glasses or paper cups are used instead of only three, and at the outset they are arranged alternately up, down, up, down, and up. Again, the performer turns over two glasses at a time, one with each hand, and in three such moves, he brings all five glasses mouth upward.

Counting the glasses as 1, 2, 3, 4, 5, the following sequence does it: Turn over 1 and 4; then 2 and 5; then 1 and 5. A good variant is: 2 and 5; 3 and 4; 3 and 5. Still another: 1 and 5; 2 and 5; 1 and 4. By simply turning down the glasses at positions 2 and 4, the performer can immediately repeat the turnover process, again bringing the glasses all mouth up.

The "catch" in this case is to turn down glasses 1, 3, and 5 whenever a victim wants to try it. From that position it is impossible to bring all five glasses mouth up in three turnovers. The fact that they are down, up, down, up, and down instead of up, down, up, down, and up is seldom noted even by astute observers.

FULL AND EMPTY

This is an early version of the six-glass Two at a Time stunt, with an ultramodern twist. Instead of using "up" and "down" glasses, all six are up, but they are alternately full and empty. The idea is to move them by pairs, and in three moves to bring them into separate groups of three fulls and three empties.

This is beautiful, because you can't do the turnover caper used in One Less Move. So it has to be done legitimately Two at a Time, as described under that head. For once, the performer, and not the victim, is nonplused. Or is he?

Perhaps not. After performing the trick as required, the performer throws this sockdolager at the spectators:

By moving *just one glass,* and *without touching* any other, the performer guarantees to bring the full glasses on one side and the empties on the other. Impossible? After everyone has agreed that it is, the performer shows how simple it really is.

He picks up glass 5, which is full, and pours it into glass 2, which is empty. He then puts glass 5 back where it belongs. He has moved just one glass without touching any other, and the feat has been accomplished.

SPECIAL EFFECTS

DIME TO DOLLAR

This qualifies as an absolute close-up effect, for the closer to the audience you perform it, the better, provided you limit it to just a few observers.

You display a dime at the very tip of your right thumb and second finger, which hold it edgewise, with the full surface of the coin directly toward the spectators. Everyone can see that your hand is otherwise empty (Fig. 434), for your palm is frontward and your fingers are widespread. Your left hand is also shown empty.

However, when you bring your hands together and perform a simple twisting action, the dime is gone and instead you are holding a full-sized silver dollar, which you toss on the table with a convincing clank.

The method requires a special placement prior to the trick. The dollar is set edgewise directly behind the dime and held horizontally between the right thumb and finger. Small though the dime is, it conceals the dollar perfectly from the front, while the thumb and finger hide the big coin from the side angles. The only way a spectator can glimpse the hidden coin is from above or below, so the proper procedure is to work the trick close to the eye level of the spectators.

When bringing the hands together, point them toward each other. The right thumb and fingers swing into a vertical position—fingers above,

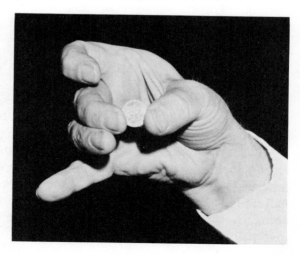

Fig. 434. Start of sequence (spectator's view). Dime shown openly between tips of right thumb and second finger.

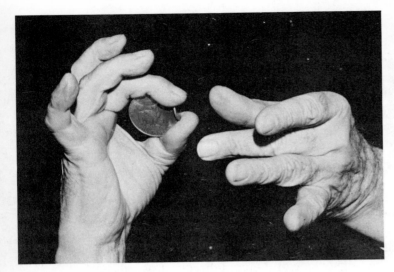

Fig. 435. Side view of Dime to Dollar showing dollar concealed edgewise behind dime with left hand poised to take coins from right.

thumb below — but the left thumb and fingers are kept horizontal and wide apart (Fig. 435). This enables the left hand to take the coins from the right as the hands tilt downward and forward. The thumbs push the dollar into sight, and the right hand lets it drop on the table while the dime is retained in the bend of the left fingers. You can then pick up the dollar with your left hand and drop it into your pocket, letting the dime go along with it.

Instead of using a silver dollar, you can use two half dollars by placing one upon the other and setting the two edgewise directly behind the dime, which will hide them as effectively as it will a silver dollar. In this case, each hand lets a half dollar clank on the table. Both coins and the dime can then be pocketed unless you prefer to add this touch:

Pick up the dollar (or half dollars) with your right hand, and move your left hand to your right elbow saying, "Look!" Then draw the dime from behind your elbow with the tips of your left fingers and remark, "Here we have the 10 per cent interest on the dollar."

QUICK DIME VANISH

This is a neat trick in its own right, but it is particularly good as a follow-up to Dime to Dollar after the reproduction of the dime from the elbow, as it requires two half dollars and a dime.

Hold a half dollar horizontally between the tips of the right thumb and forefinger. With your left hand, place a dime on the half dollar; then lay another half dollar over that, so the dime will be sandwiched between the two half dollars. To convince people that the dime is really between the larger coins, show the left hand entirely empty, then snap your left fingers, saying that you will cause the dime to vanish.

COIN THROUGH THE HAND

This is an excellent effect at very close range. The left hand is held palm upward, with the thumb pointing forward, while the right fingers and thumb press a coin held edgewise against the left palm. The performer states that he is trying to push the coin through the hand. After a few unsuccessful attempts, he turns the left hand back up and says, "Let's try it on the back of the hand." He gives a hard push, bringing his right fingers flush with the back of the left hand, which is held in a loose fist; then he draws his right hand slightly away and turns his left hand palm upward, saying, "Not through yet!"

Turning his left hand back upward again, he immediately repeats the pressing action with the right thumb and fingers. He finishes with a rubbing motion of the right fingers, which are turned sideways to show that the coin is gone as he adds, "That push did it!" The left hand is again turned palm upward and opened, showing that the coin has actually arrived there.

Good timing and one neat move are the only elements needed. Pressing the coin edgewise against the left palm is simply a preliminary move to throw observers off guard. With each thrust, the coin is only partly covered by the right fingers, so it is shown openly when the performer turns the hank back upward and starts to push it down from there (Fig. 436). This time he covers the coin completely with his right fingers (Fig. 437), retaining it in position with his right thumb as he turns the left hand palm upward (Fig. 438).

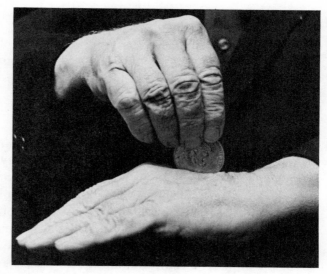

COIN THROUGH THE HAND
Fig. 436. Start of push with right hand pressing coin edgewise against back of left. Spectator's view.

With the remark, "Not through yet," the performer turns the left hand palm down, barely grazing the tips of the right finger as it passes. During that momentary concealment, the right thumb releases the coin, letting it drop into the left hand (Fig. 439), which is already closing to receive it. As soon as the back of the left hand is upward, the right fingers and thumb

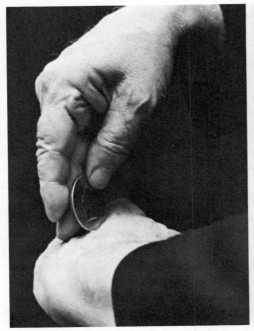 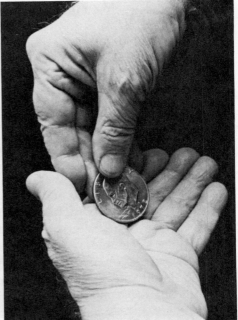

Fig. 437. Side view of
right fingers covering coin
with downward pressing
action.

Fig. 438. Rear view of
right hand about to re-
lease hidden coin after left
hand has been turned
palm upward.

revert to their pushing action, as if they still held the coin. Rubbing the
coin away and showing it in the left hand completes the penetration effect.

SLOW-MOTION PENETRATION

As a follow-up or alternate for Coin Through the Hand, this is an ideal
effect. The performer holds a coin edgewise between his right fingers and
thumb and presses it down against the back of his closed left hand as
though seeking a soft spot between the left knuckles. After a few deliberate attempts, he raises his right fingers with a rubbing motion and opens his
left-hand palm upward to show that the coin has really gone through.

Here deception takes place the moment the right fingers completely
cover the coin. The right thumb relaxes pressure so that the coin falls flat
(Fig. 440), thus letting the tip of the right thumb press its outer edge and
draw it lightly backward. Continuing that secret action, the right thumb
slides the coin down and around the inner edge of the left hand, between
the left thumb and the knuckle of the left forefinger (Fig. 441), finally
pressing it into the left palm. Still unseen, the right thumb returns to join

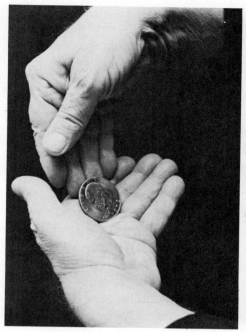

Fig. 439. Rear view show-
ing coin released. Left
hand about to close and
turn back upward so right
can resume its push.

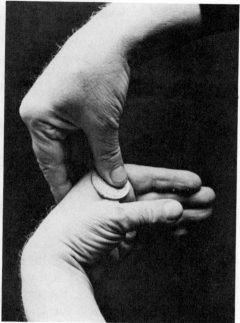

SLOW-MOTION
PENETRATION
Fig. 440. Side view of
right fingers secretly flattening hidden coin so
thumb can press down on
outer edge.

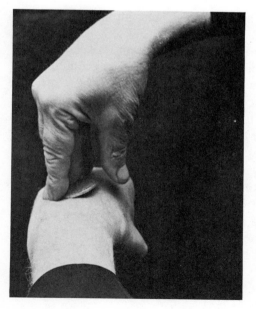

Fig. 441. Rear view of
right thumb secretly sliding coin around inner edge
of left hand into palm.

the right fingers in their slow rubbing action, and the penetration is
complete.

COIN THROUGH HANDKERCHIEF

Here is an excellent close-up effect in which an ordinary coin penetrates an unprepared handkerchief in a manner both deliberate and deceptive. A large coin and a large handkerchief, particularly one with an ornamental border, add to the effectiveness of the routine.

To start, the coin is held at the tips of the right thumb and first two fingers in display position. The left hand drapes the cloth over the coin so that its shape shows at about the center. To prove that the coin is really there, the left hand moves forward and downward, grips the front corner of the handkerchief, and raises it up over the coin and far enough back so that the coin can be fully seen.

That done, the left hand carries the front corner forward and downward, covering the coin as before; then the left hand comes up and grips the coin through the center of the cloth so that the right hand can be drawn from beneath. The right hand then helps the left hand twist the center of the cloth, and the coin can be struck against a table to prove its presence there. But when the hands squeeze the center folds, the coin emerges through the cloth in an uncanny fashion. Later the handkerchief is spread completely to show that it is free from holes and that no duplicate coin was involved.

Now for the explanation: In placing the handkerchief over the coin, the left thumb pushes the cloth down between the coin and the right thumb, forming a small tuck or pleat that the right thumb retains by pressing through the cloth (Fig. 442). Thus, when the front corner of the handkerchief is folded back by the left hand to show the coin, the pleat is still behind it (Fig. 443).

This trifling detail passes notice, but serves a very important purpose because:

It enables the left thumb and fingers to grip the front and rear corners of the cloth (Fig. 444) and carry them both forward as one, over the coin and downward. From the front—as viewed by the spectators—the cloth appears to be draped exactly as it was before the front corner was lifted to show the coin, but now the coin is actually behind the center pleat. The left hand promptly comes up to grip the center (Fig. 445), and during the action the left thumb presses the coin against the back of the pleat, keeping it in place. The right hand, now released, is brought downward as though coming out from beneath the handkerchief.

The rest is pure showmanship. The left hand gathers some loose cloth near the coin and folds it behind the coin toward the right (Fig. 446), and the right hand makes a similar fold across to the left, so the coin is tightly imbedded in a double fold and the handkerchief can be shown from all angles. Working together, the hands then loosen the cloth sufficiently to squeeze the coin upward from the folds, as though actually penetrating the center of the handkerchief (see Fig. 448).

NOTE: In originally draping the handkerchief over the coin, it is a good plan to place the coin well forward, so the rear corner will hang lower than

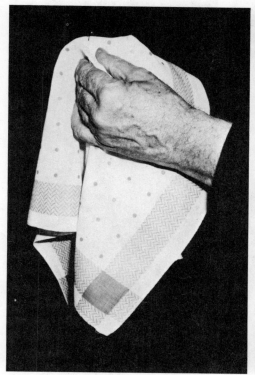

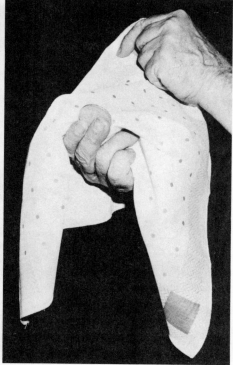

COIN THROUGH
HANDKERCHIEF
Fig. 442. Left hand has
covered displayed coin
with handkerchief, and
left thumb is secretly
forming a pleat between
coin and right thumb.

Fig. 443. Left hand lifting
front corner of cloth to
show coin still beneath.
Right thumb presses se-
cret pleat against rear of
coin.

Fig. 444. Left hand about
to bring front and back
corners of handkerchief
forward as one. Side view
shows how right thumb
still holds pleat.

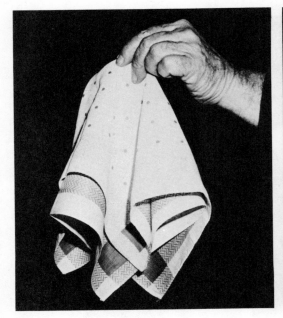
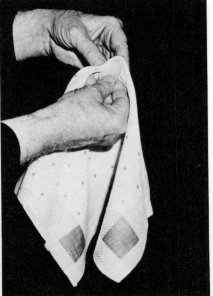

Fig. 445. Rear view of left
hand taking handkerchief
from right, with left thumb
pressing cloth downward
to hide coin under pleat.

Fig. 446. Audience view
of hands twisting center of
cloth around coin.

the front. Thus when the rear corner is secretly carried forward it will be
mistaken for the original front corner, which it hides completely.

ALTERNATE PENETRATION

Here, the effect is almost identical to the Coin Through Handkerchief
sequence, but the essential moves are quite different. It is an excellent
variant, as the performer can switch from one version to the other when
working the trick for persons who have already seen it.

Starting with the coin in display position in the right hand, the left hand
covers it with the handkerchief and lifts the front corner of the cloth to
show the coin again. (In this case, the front corner of the handkerchief
should hang considerably lower than the rear corner, so that after the coin
is shown, the front corner is brought down legitimately and alone.)

The left hand releases the corner, then goes up and apparently grips the
coin through the cloth and lifts it along with the handkerchief; but actually
the right hand retains the coin as it emerges from beneath (Fig. 447). This
move, though bold, is very natural, as the right hand is brought down in the
usual manner but without showing itself, for the front corner of the
handkerchief hangs low enough to hide the coin.

Without hesitation, the right hand moves upward behind the handker-chief and calmly slides the coin beneath the left thumb, which is still help-ing the left fingers to retain the shape of the coin within the center of the cloth. Once the coin is safely planted in back, the hands are able to apply the double fold, setting the scene for the upward squeeze (Fig. 448), which forces the coin "through" the handkerchief.

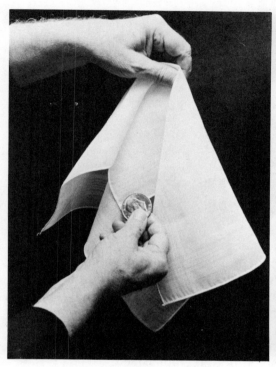

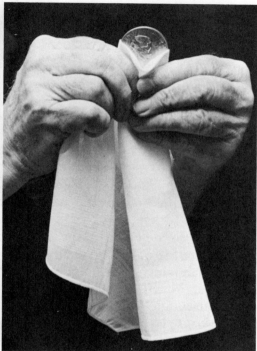

Fig. 447. Alternate Pene-tration. Rear view of left hand apparently lifting coin in handkerchief while right hand secretly retains it.

Fig. 448. Audience view of climax. Hands squeez-ing coin upward through double folds of cloth to simulate an actual pene-tration.

ADVANCED PENETRATION

This can be classed as an expert form of the Alternate Penetration of the Coin Through Handkerchief sequences, for it involves back-palming the coin. Actually, skill plays only a minor part, because the necessary moves are made under cover of the handkerchief and there is no need for speed. The procedure is the same as with the Alternate Penetration up to the point where the left thumb and fingers pretend to grip the coin through the

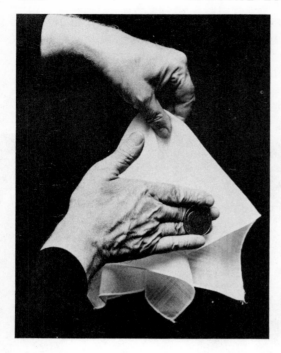

ADVANCED PENETRATION
Fig. 449. Rear view of left
hand supposedly holding
coin beneath center of
handkerchief. Right hand
has back-palmed coin
while beneath the cloth
and is now coming clear.

center of the cloth, so the right hand can move downward with the coin.

Here the right hand pauses long enough to back-palm the coin beneath the handkerchief and point its fingers at a downward angle (Fig. 449). That done, the left side of the body is turned toward the audience, and in the same action the left hand raises the handkerchief, with the coin apparently in the center, while the right hand is lowered and extended so that its open palm comes in full view. Since the coin is back-palmed, the right hand appears to be quite empty, but this should not be emphasized.

Instead, the right hand is raised casually to shoulder level while the left hand is turned around so its thumb is toward the audience, thus showing both sides of the handkerchief and increasing the impression that it is gripping the coin within the center of the cloth. All in the same action, the left hand is brought up to the supposedly empty right hand as the performer comments that he will twist the coin tightly in the handkerchief.

The right thumb is brought downward in front of the handkerchief to join the left, while the right fingers dip behind the center of the cloth. Once there, the right fingers simply swivel the coin from the back of the hand to the front, so the fingertips can press the coin into the cloth. From there, the cloth can be twisted or folded around the coin in the usual fashion, putting it in position to be squeezed up.

In this version of the penetration effect, the performer must use a coin he can properly back-palm. This eliminates all coins smaller than the half-dollar size, which is usually the best for most performers. Even if the fingers must be slightly cramped to conceal a half dollar behind them, the fact that the hand is in constant motion during the procedure will prevent anyone from noticing it. With a broader hand, a dollar coin may prove preferable, and the larger size should add to the effect.

LOOPER DOOPER

Though more a puzzle than a trick, Looper Dooper makes a nice interlude between more impressive effects. It is particularly good when other people try it and find themselves unable to duplicate the performer's wizardry.

The performer shows two loops of cotton: a dark-colored loop, which is doubled around his left thumb, and a light-colored single loop, which dangles from the dark one, enabling him to draw the single loop downward with his right thumb and first two fingers. The tips of the left thumb and forefinger are held firmly pressed together, while the right hand brings the lower end of the single loop upward and downward—and then!

To everyone's amazement, the loops have transposed themselves. The doubled upper loop is now the light-colored one; the single lower loop is the dark one. The change is so quick it actually looks magical; and it can be repeated instantly, bringing the loops back to their original position, with the doubled dark loop above and the single light loop below. This effect can be repeated as often as desired.

To set up the trick, push the dark loop horizontally through the light loop, holding the ends of the dark loop in each hand so the light loop hangs between (Fig. 450). Bring the ends of the dark loop together and push the left forefinger through them while pressing its tip against the tip of the left thumb. From there it is a simple matter to slide the doubled dark loop over the left thumb, so the single light loop can be drawn downward (Fig. 451).

LOOPER DOOPER
Fig. 450. Dark loop being drawn through light loop as preliminary to actual effect.

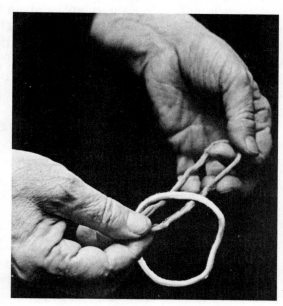

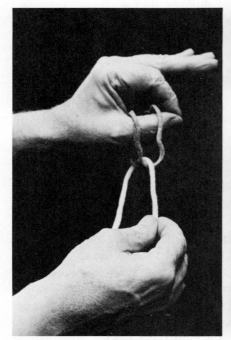

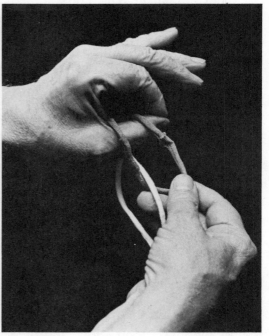

Fig. 451. Ready for action. Dark loop doubled around left thumb, with light loop drawn downward.

Fig. 452. Right thumb and forefinger gripping upper loop while second finger releases lower loop.

From there, the "switch" is worked as follows: In gripping the bottom of the lower loop between the right thumb and the first two fingers, keep the right forefinger somewhat extended so that the lower loop is really gripped between the thumb and second finger, and the forefinger is free to act on its own. Bring the right hand upward and grip *any portion* of the upper loop between the tips of the right thumb and forefinger, and at the same time release the lower loop by letting it slide from the right second finger (Fig. 452).

Draw the right hand downward, keeping the left thumb and forefinger tip to tip. so the upper loop is pulled around them and becomes a single lower loop while the original lower loop is whisked upward to replace it as a doubled loop (Fig. 453). This may be repeated indefinitely, and once the knack is acquired, the action becomes too fast for the average eye to follow.

LINK THE CLIPS

Here is another puzzling effect of a highly ingenious nature. The props are simply a dollar bill and a pair of paper clips, preferably of the "jumbo"

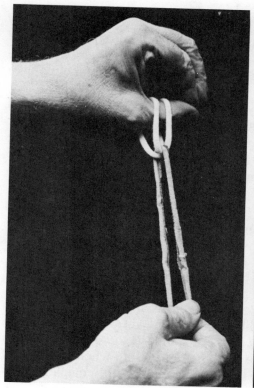

Fig. 453. Right hand completing quick downward pull, instantly transposing loops.

Fig. 454. Link the Clips setup. Bill has been folded in thirds and clips attached: Right clip grips bottommost portion and inner fold; left clip is attached to outer fold and top of bill.

two-inch size. The bill is folded crosswise in thirds; one third being folded under from the left, and another third folded over from the right. The paper clips are then slipped onto the upper edges, and all is set for a real surprise.

The bill is held horizontally, with the clips at the outer edge. The ends of the bill are drawn apart, and quite amazingly, the clips are projected from the edge of the bill, and land on the table linked together!

It all depends on the placement of the clips at the start of the trick. Fix the clip at the left so it holds the two upper folds together, while the clip at the right holds the two lower folds (Fig. 454). Draw the ends of the bill slowly apart and you can watch the clips join themselves, slow-motion style. In actual performance, this should be done a little faster, finishing with a short tug just as the clips merge, which shoots them across the table and insures a perfect link.

TRIPLE LINKS

In this new form of the linking clips, three are fastened to the edge of the bill and they all link together when the ends of the bill are drawn apart. Clips of standard size should be used in this case, as the jumbo clips take up too much space.

Fix the first two clips as already described, but keep the lower and center folds shorter than usual so that the upper fold will overlap well over to the right. Now fold the overlap under the bill and turn the underside upward. The bill will then have four folds, and you simply fix the third clip to the two folds that are now uppermost, placing it between the other two clips.

The bill is then ready for action, and when you pull the ends, the clips will skim free to form a triple link when they land.

TRIPLE-KNOT TRICK

This classic among "dissolving knot" effects is highly effective when presented in a smooth yet fairly deliberate manner, yet with no hesitation during the process. To all appearances it is a standard square knot with an intricate third knot that should make it all the tighter; but when the ends of the string or rope are pulled, all the knots dissolve in a truly magical manner.

The simplest way of tying the self-untying knot is as follows: Bring the right end of the cord across in front of the left and tie a single knot (Fig. 455). Bring the left end across in front of the right and tie another single knot (Fig. 456), making a "square knot." Push the right end through the

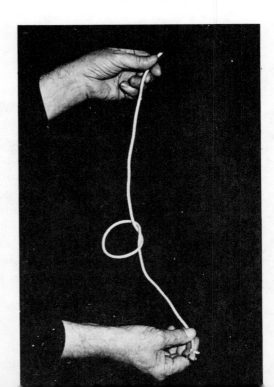

TRIPLE-KNOT TRICK
Fig. 455.

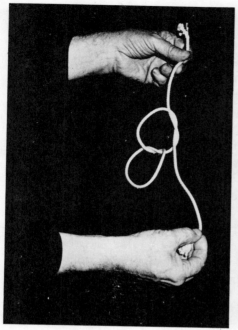

Fig. 456.

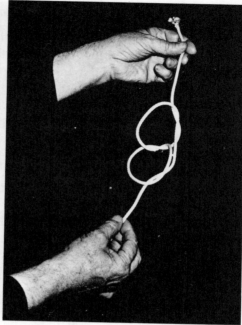

Fig. 457.

lower loop from the front (Fig. 457) and bring it up so it can be pushed through the upper loop from the front (Fig. 458). Pull the ends steadily apart and the "knots" will tighten, then seemingly dissolve.

With some groups, this can be shown as a "do as I do" effect, in which the performer passes out short lengths of string to various spectators and tells them to tie a triple knot exactly as he does. As they draw the knots tight, they blow on them, but only the performer blows hard enough, or magically enough, for his knots dissolve while the others remain snarled.

The reason is that simple though the moves appear, they are actually difficult to follow, as one false step can ruin the entire process. When people unloose their knots and copy the performer's moves once more, they are just as apt to fail again; and anyone lucky enough to succeed on the first try generally misses on the second. The same applies to succeeding tries as well, especially if the performer reverses his moves, working from left to right instead of from right to left, thus confusing the spectators still more.

Fig. 458.

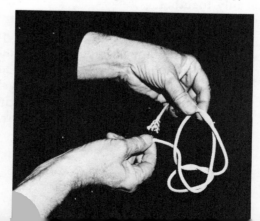

MULTIPLE-KNOT TRICK

An effective elaboration of the Triple-knot Trick in which up to a dozen knots are tied in all, bunching the center into an almost solid mass. Yet by drawing on the ends and manipulating the center coils, the performer gradually disposes of all the knots, drawing the cord straight and clear.

The method, though apparently complex, is quite simple. Start with a Triple Knot, and before drawing it too tight, go right ahead with another. After finishing that, add another—and still another, if desired. Even persons familiar with the simpler version seldom realize what is going on, as it is hard for them to keep track of the loops through which the end of the rope is thrust. But regardless of the total, all the "knots" can be worked free.

A good procedure here is for the performer to hand the ends of the rope to two different spectators, telling them to pull or relax the ropes as he specifies. That enables him to work on the center coils, pushing them through one another until they all come completely loose.

QUICK-KNOT VANISH

Showing a three-foot length of soft rope stretched between his hands, the performer proceeds to tie a single knot in the center, then dangles the rope by one end and shakes it to prove that the knot is genuine. But when he grips the rope by the other end and gives it a slight tug, the knot vanishes instantly!

Some special but unsuspected preparation is required for this effect. Beforehand, take a two-inch strip of transparent mending tape and roll it around the rope with the sticky side out, so that the tape adheres to itself and forms a ring. Slide this loop to one end of the rope, then form a similar ring and slide it to the other end. By holding the ends of the rope, you hide the tape and can show the rope under the very eyes of the spectators.

Stepping back to a longer range, you slide one hand, then the other, along the rope as though measuring it to find the center. Each hand brings along its ring hidden between thumb and fingers. When both rings are near the center, you go through the motions of tying a knot. What you actually do is bring the right-hand portion of the rope across the left-hand portion from above, so the left thumb and fingers can press the two gummed rings firmly together.

While the left hand holds the loop thus formed, the right hand thrusts its end of the rope down through. The rope can then be dangled by the right end, giving the appearance of an actual knot; but when the left hand tugs the lower end, the adhesive gives way and the "knot" instantly vanishes.

To conclude this surprising trick, grip the center of the rope with both hands and draw the hands apart, taking along the gummed rings as you draw the rope to its full length and show it to be quite ordinary. If a spectator wants to examine the rope, offer him the center, and when he takes it, simply draw the gummed rings off the ends.

KNOT AND RING

A string or thin rope is threaded through a ring, which can vary in size from a finger ring to a bracelet, though a wooden curtain ring is perhaps the most effective. A knot is tied in the string and the threading process is continued, apparently knotting the ring more firmly on the string. Yet while the ends of the string are held by spectators, the performer mysteriously removes the ring from the cord, which is simultaneously unknotted.

Start by threading the ring on the string; then tie a single knot by placing the left end of the string across the right (Fig. 459). Then push the right end of the string through the ring from the left (Fig. 460). After that, bring the free right end of the string around to the left of the ring and push it through the loop from front to back (Fig. 461). Bring the ends of the string together and draw them upward with the right hand while the left hand takes the ring and pulls it downward. The result is that the ring is apparently tied, but is actually only looped to the center of the cord.

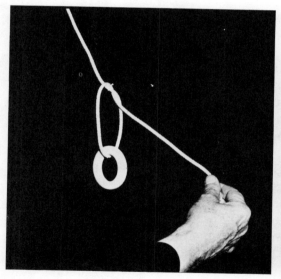

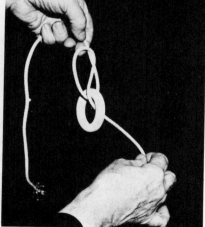

KNOT AND RING
Fig. 459.

Fig. 460.

Give the ends of the cord to the spectators, while you take the ring and slide the sides of the loop downward, releasing the ring from the center of the cord, magically and completely, with no trace of a knot. With a small ring, this can be done under cover of the hands, as they release the ring.

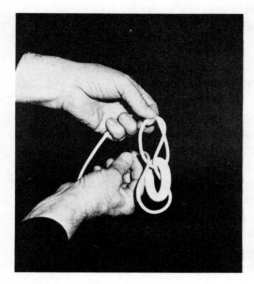

Fig. 461.

With a large ring, it is better to spread a handkerchief over it, then reach beneath and slide the loop apart, bringing the ring into sight beneath the cloth and thus adding a touch of mystery as a climax.

RING AND TRIPLE KNOT

In this combination of close-up effects with ring and string, the ring is triply tied to the center of the cord, yet comes free, knots and all, almost as readily as with the simpler versions. It takes longer and therefore requires more practice, but its very intricacy enables it to baffle the keenest observers. In a sense, it is an elaboration of the Knot and Ring, as it starts with the same moves, namely:

Thread ring on string; tie single knot, left end in front of right (see Fig. 455), and push right end through ring from left (see Fig. 460). Here you switch to the Triple-knot routine, bringing the right end across in front of the left and tying another knot to form an upper loop as well as a lower. Push the left end through the lower loop from front to back (Fig. 462), then bring it forward and upward and thrust it through the upper loop from front to back.

Draw the ends tight, and the result will be a beautiful snarl with all the look of a double knot from which the ring can not possibly be extricated (Fig. 463). Here it is simply a case of spreading the sides of one "knot" down around the ring (Fig. 464), then repeating the process with the other to free the ring.

The original "knotting" will be facilitated if the hands retain a hold on the ring during the process, or let the ring rest flat on the table, so the ends of the string can be guided more effectively. With a large ring this too can be done under a cover.

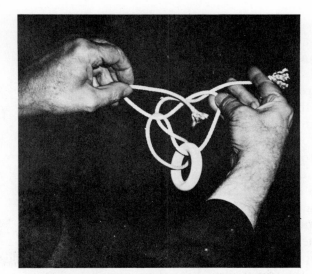

RING AND TRIPLE KNOT
Fig. 462. Final tie of effect. Left end of cord pushed through lower loop, from front to back.

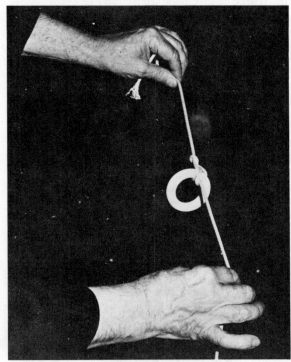

Fig. 463. "Double knot" created by tying procedure when drawn tight.

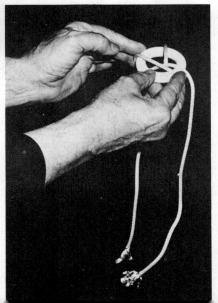

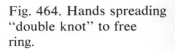
Fig. 464. Hands spreading "double knot" to free ring.

TUBE AND KNOTS

Here is an old effect with a novel touch that gives it a forceful impact. The simple requirements are a transparent plastic tube, open at both ends, and a two-foot length of cord. The tube, which should be about two inches in length, can be easily prepared by cutting the bottom from a pill bottle.

Standing the tube upright, the performer circles it with the cord and ties a simple knot near the bottom, keeping the long end uppermost. He ties a second simple knot with the long end, and he ties another simple knot (also with the long end) near the top of the tube. He then takes the free upper end of the cord and drops it down through the tube (Fig. 465).

Now the left hand lifts the tube so that the right thumb and fingers can draw all the knots upward and stuff them down into the tube (Fig. 466). This obviously snarls the knots so thoroughly that only a magic touch could rectify it. The performer provides that touch by taking the ends of the cord and drawing them apart horizontally as the spectators watch the knots dissolve visibly within the transparent tube (Fig. 467).

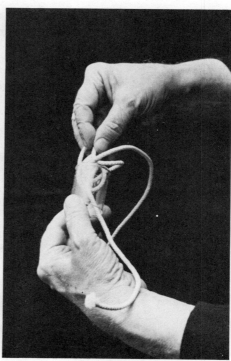

TUBE AND KNOTS
Fig. 465. This shows two simple, single knots already tied around tube, with right hand dropping free end of string down into tube.

Fig. 466. Right hand is now drawing off knots encircling tube and is pushing them into tube itself.

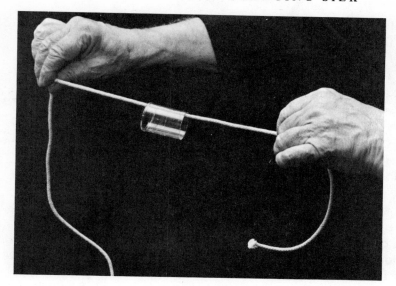

Fig. 467. By simply drawing on ends of string, knots have visibly untied themselves within tube!

It's all automatic. Tieing the knots as shown and dropping the end of the cord down through the tube will untie them, but no one will realize this until the ends of the cord are drawn apart with the tube dangling between. Even then they won't understand it, which makes it truly magical. Originally this sequence was worked with a single knot and a metal tube. With a triple knot and a transparent tube, the effect is proportionately greater.

COLOR-CHANGING SILK

Facing toward the left, the performer dangles a red silk handerchief from the tips of his right thumb and forefinger, while he shows his left hand empty, full front. He lowers his left hand, lays the red silk across it, forms the left hand into a loose fist, and draws the red silk slowly through.

After repeating this a few times, he draws the red silk through more slowly while turning his body so that he faces to the right, and he finishes the process with the palm of the right hand openly toward the audience. *One* corner of the red silk is gripped between the first two fingers of the right hand. The far corner is held between the first two fingers of the left hand, which forms a loose fist, thumb upward with its back toward the spectators.

The performer again faces to the left, releasing the left end of the silk while the left fist is raised to shoulder level and turns its thumb downward. The right hand then pokes the silk down into the left fist, and as the silk emerges below the fist, its color has amazingly changed from red to green. After poking in the last red corner, the performer brings his right hand down to the dangling green corner and draws it taut. He then pulls the green silk entirely clear and lets it dangle from the right hand while the left fist is turned thumb upward and deliberately opened, palm front, showing itself entirely empty.

Still facing to the left, the right hand draws the green silk through the loose left fist, exactly as it did with the red, once again turning the right hand palm frontward to show it empty. He crumples the green silk and pockets it or lays it aside and proceeds with some other effect. Onlookers are left quite mystified by the clean-cut transformation. The most convincing part of the sleight is that the silk — first red, then green — can be shown so deliberately and at such close range that any preparation would *seem* impossible.

Actually, two silks are used — one red, the other green — with each made of thin material and measuring about 12 inches square. Also required is a fake in the form of a stiff tube, measuring $2\frac{1}{4}$ inches in length and $\frac{7}{8}$ inch in diameter, although these specifications can be modified to suit individual performers. The tube is open at both ends, and the standard form is usually of metal, with its exterior painted a flesh color. A tube can also be rolled from thin cardboard and its overlapping edges affixed with gummed tape. The exterior is covered with strips of thin, flesh-tinted surgical tape. Or a length of plastic tubing can also be covered with surgical tape to produce the same result.

To prepare, the green silk is pushed or "loaded" into the tube, corner first. The tube is then wrapped loosely in the red silk and placed in the performer's pocket or laid casually on a table, and all is ready for presentation.

The performer picks up the red silk with his right hand and faces toward his left, drawing the silk clear with his left hand. This lets the tube settle in his right hand, which has its back toward the audience. The right thumb and forefinger still hold a corner of the red silk, while the right second finger presses the upper end of the tube to wedge the lower end against the heel of the hand. This lets the right hand draw the red silk through the left fist easily and naturally (Fig. 468) while keeping the tube from view.

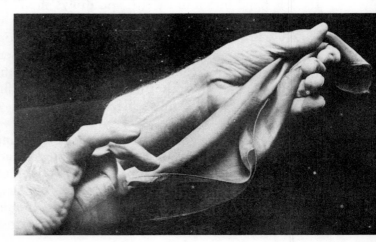

COLOR-CHANGING SILK
Fig. 468. Right hand openly drawing red silk through cupped left hand. Right hand should be turned forward and downward to hide fake extending from second finger, which is bent inward.

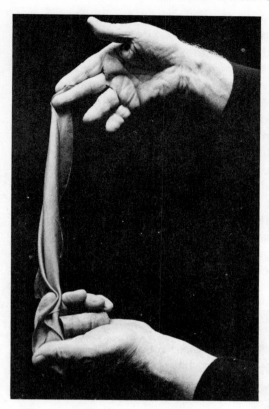

Fig. 469. Finish of final "draw through." Performer has secretly dropped fake in cupped left hand, so right hand can be shown empty while drawing red silk taut. Left fingers hide fake from spectator's view (performer's view looking downward).

Before the final draw, the right hand comes above the extended fingers of the left hand, which are cupped upward against the outer edge of the right hand. The body is turned frontward and the right hand drops the tube in the bend of the left fingers, which receive it crosswise (Fig. 469). That is when the right hand begins drawing the red silk through the loose left fist, while the body turns completely to the right. The right hand carries attention by drawing the red silk upward to the right, while the left hand is raised thumb upward, bringing the back of its loose fist toward the spectators.

The right hand is now turned palm front, while the tube is safely nestled in the bend of the left fingers. As a change-over in which an object is secretly transferred from one palm to the other, this is excellent in its own right, but drawing the silk through the left fist makes it just about perfect. The silk covers the tube during the entire action and provides misdirection, but the tube, being flesh-colored, is scarcely visible anyway. Keeping the left thumb over the upper end of the tube prevents any premature glimpse of the green silk, and all is ready for the color change.

This is accomplished by turning the body to the left and turning the left fist thumb downward but keeping its back somewhat toward the audience while the right fingers push the red silk down into the left fist. This forces the green silk from the bottom of the tube; and between pokes, the right hand comes down in front of the left in order to draw the green silk downward, so that it emerges neatly, as if the red silk were actually turning green (Fig. 470). This natural action provides a subtle sequel; namely:

When the upper corner of the red silk is almost entirely gone from view, the right second finger delivers a final poke, and in the same action the upper edge of the tube is clipped between the tips of the second and third fingers. The right hand is immediately raised, bringing the tube with it (Fig. 471), and in the same natural fashion it comes down in front of the left fist to take a last tug at the lower corner of the green silk. All eyes naturally follow the downward sweep of the right hand, never suspecting that it brought along the red silk in a hidden tube no one knows about (Fig. 472).

Everyone looks to the left hand as the right hand tugs the green silk clear, and to their surprise, the left hand is opened and shown empty. The right hand draws the green silk through the left fist a few times, then follows with the change-over that shows the right hand empty like the left. All that remains is to bundle the green silk around the unsuspected tube and lay them both aside or put them away.

Fig. 470. Front view of color change in progress. Right second finger secretly pushing red silk into fisted tube, so green silk can emerge below.

NOTE: The tube used in this change can be improved by cutting two crosswise slits in the opposite walls at the very center. A strip of cloth, two inches long and one-half inch wide, is run through the slits and its ends are taped firmly in place. The loose strip then forms a divider or "two-way bag" that prevents a silk from emerging at the wrong end. The green silk is first loaded from the bottom; when the red silk is poked down from the top, it stays put while only the green emerges.

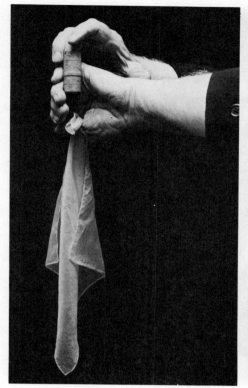 

Fig. 471. Rear view at finish of "push through." Silk has apparently changed from red to green, and right hand is stealing tube (with red silk) by clipping it between fingers.

Fig. 472. Rear view of color change near completion. Right hand has descended with stolen tube and is giving green silk final downward tug so that left hand can be turned toward spectators and shown empty.

SPECIAL COLOR CHANGE

Here is an extension of Color-changing Silk involving other features and finishing with a repeat change that tops off a most effective routine. The performer starts with the color change as already described, emphasizing that the silk is slowly changing from red to green and that many people think that it is real magic. But after turning to the right and completing the change-over with the green silk he pauses and closes the right hand in a loose fist, like the left hand. Then:

Raising both fists with their knuckles toward the audience, he faces directly frontward. He grips the opposite corners of the green silk between

SPECIAL COLOR CHANGE
Fig. 473. Spectator's view of performer "materializing" red silk from supposedly empty left hand. Green silk is draped over left wrist.

Fig. 474. Rear view immediately following steal of tube. Right hand, with clipped tube, is drawing green silk from left wrist in order to brush left fist with it.

the thumb and forefinger of each hand and stretches the silk on a level between them as he says, "Actually, it isn't magic. It's simple psychology. Any psychologist will tell you that if you stare steadily at a green object— like this handkerchief—the retina of the eye will form an after-image of a red handkerchief. This is because red is the opposite color of green—the complementary color, as psychologists term it. Let me show you!"

With that, the performer faces to the left and extends his left hand at shoulder level while his right hand drapes the green silk over the left forearm. Pointing to the green silk with his right forefinger, the performer continues, "While you concentrate on that green silk handkerchief, a red silk handkerchief automatically materializes in my left fist, proving the theory of complementary colors and reflex images. Look! Here it is already—"

With his right thumb and forefinger, the performer reaches up past his left thumb and slowly plucks the red silk into sight, drawing it downward, saying, "You see how the green image induces the red reflex. You must take it slowly, that's all, to make sure that the red silk is fully materialized." He continues the process (Fig. 473) until the red silk comes entirely clear. Dangling it from his right hand and holding it briefly beside the green silk, he says:

"Now when I push the red silk slowly down into my left fist, it dematerializes." Suiting word to action, his right fingers start poking the red silk down into his left fist as he reminds his audience: "That's what I did originally—remember? Only then, the red came out green, because a green handkerchief had naturally materialized in my left fist. But now it can't materialize because it is already here. See?"

The right hand pauses to point to the green silk, then resumes its pokes as the performer adds: "Once the red silk is in the left hand, it will dematerialize." Finishing the downward pokes, the right fingers steal the tube as they did before. The difference is that *then* the green silk had fully emerged from the left fist; *now* nothing is coming out. Now the right hand reaches for the dangling green silk, carrying the hidden tube along (Fig. 474), and whips the green silk against the left hand, saying, " . . . if we provide a touch of green to help."

The left hand turns thumb upward, opening to show that the red silk has vanished, while the right hand lets the green silk dangle (Fig. 475). "And so," says the performer, "that leaves us with a green silk handkerchief." He draws the green silk through his left fist and executes the change-over, leaving the tube in his left hand as he faces to the right. Then, swinging

Fig. 475. Spectator's view of vanish. Right hand has flicked left fist with green silk, and left hand is now being shown empty. All is now ready for color change from green to red.

fully to his left, he raises his left hand, back to the audience, and reverts to the original color change, thus:

He pushes the green silk down into the left fist, letting the red silk emerge. The only difference is that instead of red becoming green, green is changing into red. That's where the performer delivers his pay line: "If you don't believe that if you keep looking at green steadily, it will turn to red—just go out to your car and drive down the street to the first traffic light." He pushes the green silk down to the last tip. "It will be green until you get there"—here the right hand steals the tube, goes down to the bottom tip of the dangling red, and grips it as the performer adds—"and then it will be red!"

With that he whips the red silk free, opens the left hand, and shows it empty. He draws the red silk through the left hand a few times, turns to the right, and executes the change-over once more, dropping the tube from the right hand to the left finger bend, exactly as before. This leads to the usual finish of stretching the silk between the apparently empty hands, the only difference being that in this routine the silk is red instead of green. The performer then wraps the silk loosely about the tube and casually puts them away together.

SILK TO EGG

Once known as the "Egg Kling Klang," or simply the "Kling Klang," this provides a maximum effect with a minimum of skill. A few props are required, but they are easy to obtain or simple to prepare, so the routine is well worth the trouble. Props needed are a small silk handkerchief—8″ × 8″ or so—a ladies' stocking (dyed red), and a hollow egg with a hole (obtainable from any magic dealer).

The magician shows a red silk handkerchief dangling from the thumb and fingers of his right hand. Turning his right side toward the audience, he brings his hands together, extends them in cupped fashion, and uses his thumbs to work the silk down into his hands. This done, he turns the back of his left fist to the audience as though it retained the silk, while his right hand goes to its coat pocket. Naturally, onlookers suspect that the wizard is brazenly trying to get away with the silk, but he blandly opens his left fist and shows the silk still there.

Then, bringing his right hand from his pocket, he repeats the maneuver—two or three times, if he so desires, depending on the attitude or patience of the audience. Each time, he asserts, "I want you to be *sure* that the silk is really in the left hand—" and invariably some skeptical spectators demand to see it there. Finally, after fumbling in his pocket, the magician brings out his right hand so impatiently that a corner of a red silk comes along with it, but he simply points his right forefinger at his closed left fist and insists, "Now you *know* the handkerchief is in my left hand."

Hearing guffaws from the skeptics, the wizard looks down, sees the red corner projecting from his pocket, and says, "No, no—that's not the handkerchief." He draws it out with his right hand and it proves to be a silk stocking, which he dangles in tantalizing fashion as he adds: "This is a red silk stocking I use as a magic wand. The handkerchief is still here in my left hand, but when I wave the stocking over it"—he does this slowly and deliberately—"the handkerchief is transformed into an egg!" With that he turns his left fist forward, opens it, and displays an egg at the tips of his left thumb and fingers.

Before the observers snap from their surprise, the performer indulgently offers to reveal the mystery. He either lays the stocking on the table, or drapes it over his left forearm. He then raises his left thumb, and discloses a hole in the egg, from which he draws out the missing handkerchief, and remarks: "It's done with a hollow egg, made of plastic. All I had to do was push the handkerchief into the fake egg and it looked like magic." He starts to push the silk back into the egg, then remarks "But if I had done it that boldly, you might have suspected something. So I ran in the business of the silk stocking to throw you off the track."

Pulling the handkerchief from the egg, he continues, "Let me explain the whole thing from start to finish. Beforehand, I put the hollow egg and the stocking in my coat pocket." He places them there, as stated. "So I began by showing you the silk handkerchief, which I really took in my left hand." He does this openly, showing his right hand empty, then adds: "But I kidded you by sneaking my right hand to my coat pocket, like this,"—he thrusts his right hand into his coat pocket—"and then showed you that the handkerchief was in my left hand all the while."

He adds: "While I was showing the handkerchief, I brought out the hollow egg in my right hand and put it in my left." He goes through this action, this time letting people glimpse the egg. "Then I worked the silk into the egg and kept it in my left hand, while I slid my right hand to my pocket and drew out the silk stocking." Again, he matches the words with actions. "So all I had to do was wave the stocking and show the phony egg, taking care to keep my thumb over the hole. That's how simple it is."

Now comes the real surprise. Still showing the egg, the performer states, "Of course, sometimes somebody asks, 'Is that a real egg?' and when I say, 'Yes' they say, 'Then let's see you break it!' So in a case like that"—the performer reaches for a glass that is resting on the table—"I always do." With his other hand he cracks the egg on the edge of the glass, and to the audience's amazement, it proves to be a real egg, just as he said.

Despite the fact that the performer actually explains aspects of the trick as he proceeds, he continually keeps a jump or more ahead of the spectators, so that the routine has a cumulative effect. One surprise tops another until the climax, which leaves people wondering how any of it was done. Originally, the "Kling Klang" was a favorite with stage magicians, but the modern version can be done at very close range and is practically angle-proof.

The performer starts with the stocking and hollow egg in his right coat pocket, but he has a real egg there as well. He proceeds exactly as described, first fooling the spectators, then explaining how he brought out the hollow egg and worked the handkerchief into it, which he really did, the first time. But in demonstrating the process, he brings the real egg from his pocket, letting people glimpse it as he places it in his left hand. He refers to it as the "hollow egg," which is the only one the audience knows about, and so closely resembles a real egg that no one will suspect the difference.

When he says, "Then I worked the silk into the egg and kept it in my left hand . . ." he really works the silk into his right hand, closing his fingers over it, with the exception of the right forefinger, which points to the left fist, even letting people glimpse the real egg, since they will suppose that it is the hollow egg with the silk inside it. Thus he actually gets rid of the silk by secretly placing it in his pocket with his supposedly "empty" right hand—a very neat touch, indeed. He brings out the silk stocking, waves it magically, and shows the supposedly hollow egg, classing it as such until he finally breaks it.

Summarized, the whole routine is replete with misdirection, with the performer explaining just enough to cover up the rest all the more effectively. At the finish, he breaks a real egg, a truly magical transformation, with no trace whatsoever of an ordinary silk handkerchief or a hollow plastic egg that became a real one. That's magic. Or should we say Magic, with a capital "M."

OKITO COIN BOX

This classic of close-up magic is unusually intriguing because it requires a special pillbox that is entirely free of trickery and can be examined by the most skeptical onlookers. Curiously, when the effect was first devised, an ordinary pillbox was used, but its effect was so puzzling that special boxes were introduced to facilitate handling and increase the mystery. There is nothing more baffling to the average spectator than to view a trick involving some device that he feels sure must be mechanical yet proves to be entirely innocent.

The basic effect is as follows: The performer shows a small round box just large enough to receive a half dollar, which is dropped into the bottom portion of the box. A loose-fitting lid is placed on the box, which is shaken by the left hand so that everyone hears the coin rattle inside. The right hand then takes the box, while the left hand is formed into a fist and turned thumb downward, so that the box can be rested on the back of the left hand.

With his right forefinger, the magician gives the box a slight tap, and as he opens his left fist, the coin apparently drops through his left hand and lands with a plunk on the table. There is no question about it being the same coin, for the magician immediately opens the box and offers it for inspection. At the same time, he shows both his hands to be entirely empty.

The method is simple but subtle. Rest the box on the middle fingers of the left hand fairly close to the tips, and drop the coin openly in the box. Pick up the lid between the tips of right thumb and forefinger and bring it over the box in order to close it (Fig. 476). As you do, spread the middle fingers of the left hand slightly, so that the very tip of the right second finger can come up between them and turn over the box in the direction of the left palm (Fig. 477). As the box falls on the base of the left fingers, the right hand places the lid upon the undersection. The left thumb then pushes the box forward toward the fingertips so that it can be shaken, and the coin rattles inside.

The rattle occurs, however, each time the box is shaken upward, giving the impression that the box is properly closed with the coin duly inside. The right thumb and fingers then slide the box to the center of the left palm, where it is openly displayed (Fig. 478). The coin is presumably

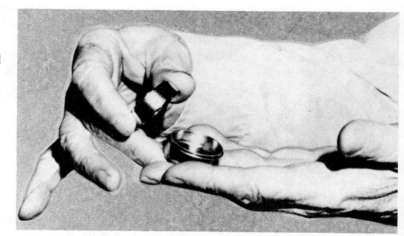

OKITO COIN BOX
Fig. 476. Right thumb and forefinger placing lid on box containing coin. Right second finger is about to tilt box upward (side view).

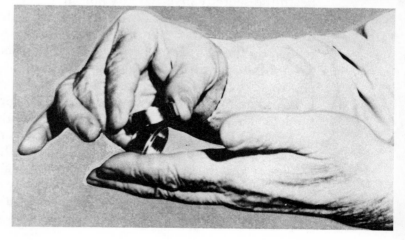

Fig. 477. Right second finger secretly completes turn-over of box while placing lid upon it (side view).

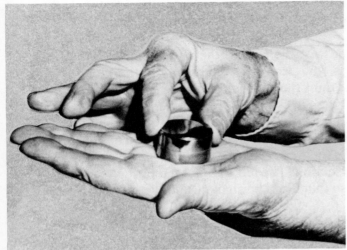

Fig. 478. Right hand slides closed box from left fingers to center of left palm.

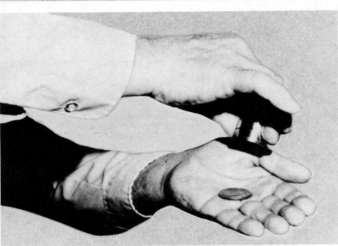

Fig. 479. Right thumb and fingers lift box from left hand, secretly leaving coin in left palm (performer's view).

within the closed box, although it is actually resting on the left palm beneath the secretly inverted box bottom.

When closing the box, the back of the right hand should be turned toward the spectators, thus hiding the secret turnover. Now that the box is resting on the left palm, the performer turns his left hand so its thumb is toward the spectators, and at the same time brings his left thumb inward and slightly cups his left fingers to block off a view from that angle. This enables him to lift the box between his right thumb and fingers as he turns the left hand inward (Fig. 479) while leaving the coin unseen in the left palm. The left hand is immediately fisted and its back turned up, so the box can be placed thereon (Fig. 480). As the right hand taps the box, the left fist opens and the coin apparently drops through the left hand (Fig. 481). All that remains is to show the box empty.

This, too, can be done quite simply. To open the box normally, the left thumb and fingers would grip the bottom half of the box, while pointing

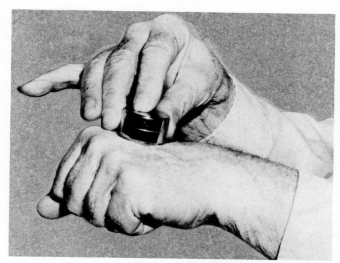

Fig. 480. Right hand places box on left hand. Coin is secretly retained in closed left fist.

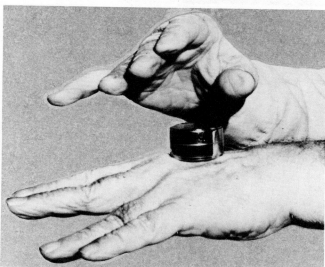

Fig. 481. Right hand completing tap of box. Left fingers have opened, letting coin drop—as if knocked through hand.

upward, with the right thumb and forefinger approaching horizontally to remove the lid, by gripping it from opposite sides. In this case, however, the left thumb and fingers approach in the same horizontal fashion from their side, gripping the box accordingly (Fig. 482). Now both hands are turned with thumb and fingers upward are swung well apart with a slight flourish, showing the box and lid both empty, as they are extended for examination (Fig. 483).

The routine just described was used with the early forms of the Okito Coin Box and was named after its inventor, Theo Bamberg, a master of close-up magic, who presented an oriental act under the stage name of Okito. The boxes ranged from simple ones made of tin and used for holding tacks, to those specially made of brass, and others neatly turned from mahogany and other woods. Any and all of these boxes are still usable in the manner just described, but many magicians prefer to use the—

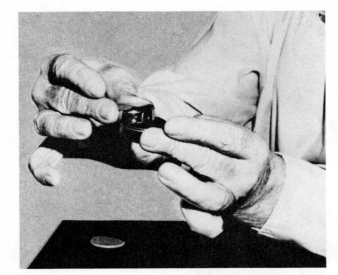

Fig. 482. Thumb and fingers of each hand open box and separate pieces in sideways motion. Coin now lying on table.

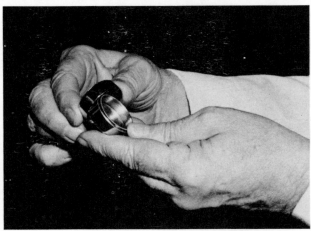

Fig. 483. Palms turned upward by simply twisting them in opposite directions to show inside of lid and empty box.

IMPROVED OKITO COIN BOX

This refined box design was developed by Carl Brema, a master technician in the manufacture of magical appliances, as well as a skilled performer. Years ago, this author described Brema's devices as "mechanical appliances that truly belong to the future art of conjuring," and that prophecy has held true with many items, among them the Improved Okito Coin Box. It is still the box style most used today, some sixty years since its conception.

The improved coin box has a recessed flange around its upper edge so that the lid, instead of coming down over the box, fits neatly on the flange, just as many lids fit neatly on cooking pots. The bottom of the box, which is rather thick, has a similar flange, so that the "turnover" can be handled in the usual fashion. There is also a flange around the top of the lid, giving the box a symmetrical appearance. Due to its balanced construction, this box can be closed by means of a very deceptive move.

Poise the box on the tip of the left second finger, with the first and third fingers pressing against the sides. Drop the half dollar in the box and take the lid between the right thumb and fingers, which are pointed downward as though to plant the lid on the box from above. Instead, the lid is tilted to a nearly vertical position, in order to provide coverage for the simultaneous action: The very tip of the left thumb presses the edge of the box undersection, so the outer edge tilts upward, and the lid can be pressed beneath it (Fig. 484). By simply continuing pressure with the right hand, the box automatically swings up to vertical position and the flange will lock in place even before the turnover is completed (Fig. 485).

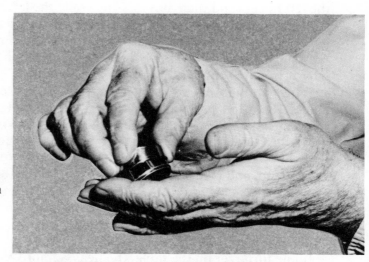

IMPROVED OKITO BOX
Fig. 484. Edging lid beneath undersection of box under cover of right fingers. (Coin is in undersection.) Note thumb position (side view).

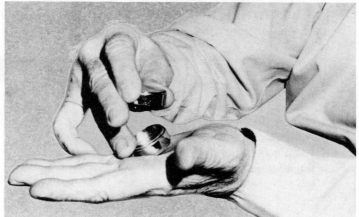

Fig. 485. Side viewing showing right third finger secretly tilting box forward as thumb and forefinger put lid in place.

This move is so good that you can first close the box legitimately, open it to show the coin, then repeat the action using the turnover without fear of detection. The move can be done with other types of boxes too, but more coverage is necessary, as this is specially suited to the Brema box because of its weight. However, from this move developed an alternate or reverse procedure that is excellent with the Brema box but is almost as good with others and provides natural coverage under the very eyes of the onlookers.

Start by placing the box underside flat on the outstretched left palm and drop the coin in it. Point the left fingers toward the spectators and take the cover between the tips of the right thumb and forefinger. Keep the lid level as you bring it forward from the heel of your left hand to place it on the box. The right middle fingers are extended, and this enables the tip of the right third finger to tilt the box forward. As the right hand continues its forward motion, the box underside automatically inverts itself beneath the lid, and the extended right fingers conceal the action (Fig. 486).

As the cover is clamped home, the right hand slides the box to the tips of the left fingers and then moves away while the left thumb presses down on the top of the lid so that the box can be shaken up and down, and the coin will rattle in the customary fashion. Due to the complete coverage by the right fingers, the entire move can be executed quite deliberately, which is why it is suited to almost any box.

When working at a table, the turnover can be executed by the right hand alone. Have the box underside lying on the table with the lid beside it. Drop the coin in the box, pick up the lid with the right hand, and cover the box with a forward slide, while the middle fingers cover the turnover. If the table has a cloth, it is an easy matter to tilt the box toward you with your right thumb and place the tip of the second finger beneath the box in order to pick up the coin with it. Otherwise, the right fingers must draw the box off the edge of the table, where the right thumb comes up from beneath to trap the coin within the inverted box. Either way, the right hand promptly plants the box upon the outstretched left hand.

In the turnover on the table, the heavy, improved type of box facilitates the one-hand action. It is also advantageous in another highly convincing maneuver generally known as the "hand-to-hand toss." It is always good

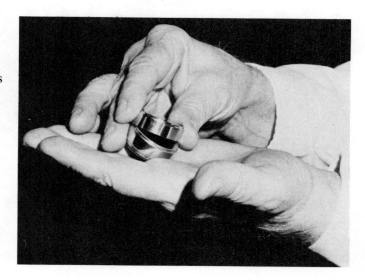

Fig. 486. Closing the inverted box. Right fingers hide entire action from front. Coin is in bend of left fingers (side view).

policy to transfer the box from one hand to the other while shaking it. With a heavy box, however, the performer can actually toss it back and forth with no chance of losing the coin as the box drops just as rapidly. With a light box, a short toss is generally safe if done at a downward angle, so that the box is dropped from hand to hand, rather than being tossed. This should not be overdone, for a light box is apt to bounce off at an angle if dropped too hard.

This routine may be concluded with the coin passing from the box through the left hand, as in the original version, or it can be supplanted by the following variation.

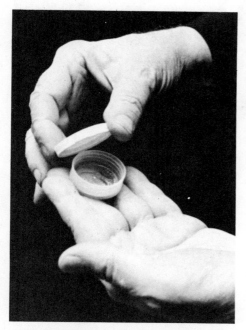

NOTE: The following photo sequence shows the original Okito routine performed with an improvised coin box consisting of an opaque screw cap from a plastic bottle and a cover from the lid of a simple pillbox or cylinder for collecting coins of half-dollar size.

Fig. 487. Right hand placing lid of box containing half dollar. Middle fingers of left hand are slightly spread.

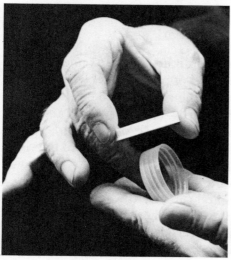

Fig. 488. The turnover. Second finger of right hand comes up between left fingers to tip box inward.

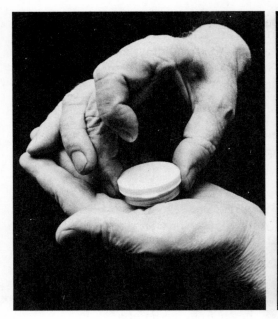 

Fig. 489. Completion of
turnover. Right hand
places lid on inverted box.

Fig. 490. Right hand lifts
box to place it on back of
left hand, leaving coin in
left palm.

All these pictures are
shown looking downward
from performer's view-
point, with back of right
hand hiding turnover from
spectator's view.

COIN THROUGH CARD

This variation came in with the Improved Okito Coin Box and is generally regarded as a Brema innovation. Instead of placing the box on the left
palm, it is retained on the right fingers with the right thumb pressing down
on the lid. The left hand takes a playing card — or any card of about the
same size — with thumb and fingers at the left side of the card, thumb
above, fingers below. The card is tilted slightly downward toward the right,
and the right hand approaches from that direction with the box, while you
state that you will place the box upon the card.

In so doing, the right fingers are pointed directly toward the card, and
the right thumb is drawn back to press the inner edge of the box downward
with its tip. This forms a gap between the inverted box and the coin, which
is resting on the left fingers, allowing you to insert the card edgeways in be-

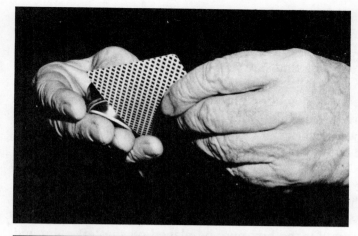

Fig. 491. Sliding playing card between coin and inverted box. Space between elements purposely exaggerated here (performer's view).

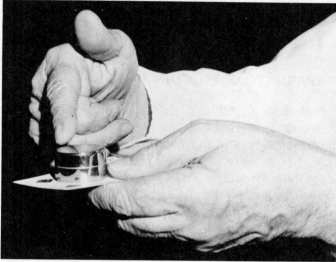

Fig. 492. Right forefinger taps cover of inverted box. Left finger ready to release coin from beneath so it will apparently "pass through" card.

tween them (Fig. 491). This is done in a continuous motion while the body is turned slightly to the left. As the right thumb openly thrusts the box on top of the card, the right fingers slide the coin beneath, where it is pressed up against the card by the second finger of the left hand and retained there, while the left thumb presses the card from above.

The card is then held level by the left hand, and gripped between the left thumb and forefinger, which keep a firm hold while the right forefinger taps the top of the box (Fig. 492). Simultaneously, the left second finger releases the coin, which drops to the table as though magically penetrating both the bottom of the box and the card. The right thumb and forefinger immediately lift the box with a pincer grip so that the left hand can show both sides of the card and toss it on the table. All is then ready for a final and most convincing move.

The right hand holds the box above the outstretched left hand, and the right thumb and forefinger grip sections of the box at the join. The grip is eased, allowing the box to drop to the left hand, several inches below. But just before the release, the tip of the right second finger is moved beneath the edge of the box, retarding that side as it drops. As a result, the inverted box does a turnover as it falls, and lands right side up in the left hand, which extends the box to a spectator, showing it empty and giving the impression that it was right side up all the time.

This drop works with lightweight boxes, but is most effective with a Brema-type box, due to its weighted bottom.

However, with the heavy box, still another move is possible. Instead of dropping the box, the right hand simply places it on the left fingers, so that the right thumb and fingers can lift the lid a trifle while the left thumb and fingers do the turnover with the inverted section of the box, bringing it back to starting position. Or the box may be placed on the left palm and slid forward with the right hand, making the turnover in progress.

TRANSPARENT OKITO COIN BOX

After many years of evolution, the Okito Coin Box took on a new look as a transparent plastic box. Onlookers think they see all that is going on in the box, yet actually find themselves more mystified than ever. This innovation was the brainchild of modern magic's most inventive genius, U. F. Grant, of Columbus, Ohio. Popularly known as Gen Grant, he has supplied the magic world with some of its most artful devices, especially in the realm of close-up wizardry.

Grant's plastic box has a depth of one-half inch, with a quarter-inch lid, and is wide enough to accommodate a coin of the highly effective silver-dollar size, although the smaller half-dollar and quarter coins can be used quite as readily. Many magicians prefer the half-dollar size, as such coins are more apt to be available. A standard poker chip may also be used to add a colorful effect to the routine, which begins in the usual fashion with the performer dropping the coin in the box and covering the coin with the lid. Any of the standard turnovers may be used, but Grant, a past master at misdirection, has devised a "pickup" turnover that is ideally suited to the transparent box but may be used with opaque boxes as well, especially when working at a table.

Show the box closed to start and remove the lid with your left hand. Place the lid slightly toward your left on the table while your right hand sets the box underside on the right side of the table. Drop the coin in the box with your right hand (Fig. 493) and then pick it up with your left hand, thumb and fingers pointing downward. At that moment, you pause and reach for the cover with your right hand. The thumb and fingers also point downward, and the right wrist naturally crosses the left (Fig. 494).

Now, as you draw your hands together to place the lid on the box, the

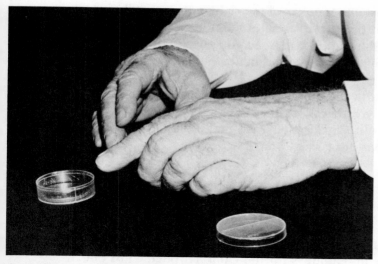

TRANSPARENT OKITO BOX
Fig. 493. Start of Transparent Box routine. Left hand points to coin placed in box by right hand. Note position of lid toward left.

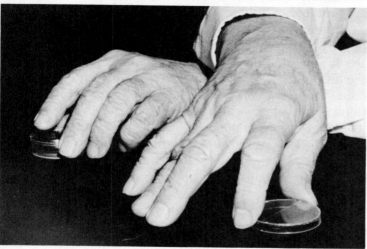

Fig. 494. Left hand picking up box containing coin while right hand reaches over to pick up lid.

Fig. 495. Left hand turning palm upward under cover of right hand, which promptly places lid on inverted box. Coin rests on fingers.

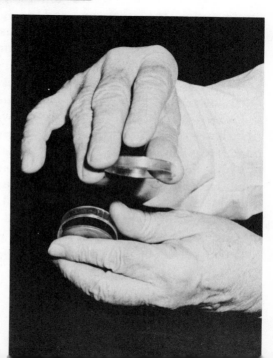

left hand turns palm upward under cover of the right, automatically inverting it (Fig. 495). Not only is this turnover natural but it's also undetectable. With the transparent box, the audience can see you putting the lid on while it is resting flat on the left fingers. The coin is beneath the mouth of the box, and appears to be within it.

The coin may be shaken in the box, which in turn may be passed from hand to hand and even given a few short tosses. Tosses are particularly effective with a dollar-size coin, because its width and weight help to keep it trapped within the open-bottom box.

COIN THROUGH CARD (WITH TRANSPARENT BOX)

With the box and coin finally resting on the left fingers and the left thumb pressing from above, all is in readiness for the Coin Through Card effect. Here, however, you have the problem of hiding the coin when the card is slid beneath the box. Again, Grant has provided an ingenious answer: Simply use two cards instead of only one.

The right hand picks up the first card, thumb above, fingers below (Fig. 496), and slides it beneath the left thumb, which is raised a trifle, then lowered to keep the card in place. The right hand then picks up the second card and holds it at a slight downward angle while the left hand slides the box above the card and the coin beneath, as in the usual method (Fig. 497). Here it may prove easier to slide the lower card between the box and coin, rather than having the left hand provide the main action, but either way, the move can be done deliberately, because the upper card provides complete coverage.

Cards, box, and coin are now transferred to the right hand, which, with thumb above and fingers below, literally clamps them with the box neatly sandwiched between the cards and the coin in readiness beneath. The left forefinger taps the upper card, and the right second finger releases the coin, which drops to the table with its accustomed plunk. The upper card is lifted by the left hand and an added feature is introduced. Instead of having to open the box immediately to show it empty, the performer lets people look right through it and see for themselves that the coin is really gone – a most convincing sequel to the penetration.

The left hand then lifts the box between thumb and fingers, while the right hand gives the bottom card for examination. This leaves the right hand free to return to the box and grip it with thumb and fingers pointing upward. The hands are now in position to reverse Grant's pickup turnover. The left thumb and fingers lift the lid and place it on the left side of the table and pass above the right hand, which uses the coverage to turn the box over and set it on the right side of the table. Its opening is now upward, so that anyone can pick it up and inspect it. Other forms of the turnover can be used if preferred.

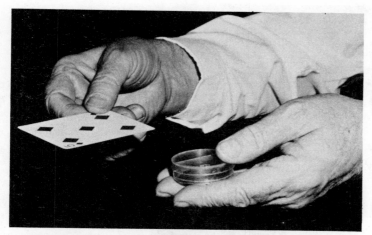

Fig. 496. Left hand about to raise thumb so right hand can cover box and coin with card. This done, right hand slides another card beneath box as left hand leaves space between box and coin.

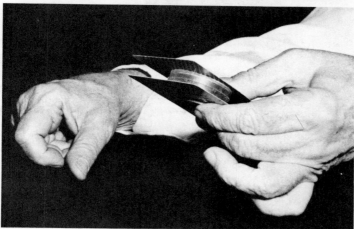

Fig. 497. Final position. Top card hides box supposedly containing coin, which is now below bottom card and secretly retained by left fingers in readiness for drop-through (view from below).

NOTE ON PLASTIC BOXES FOR OKITO ROUTINES: It is not difficult to make up a suitable box for the Transparent Okito Box routine, though the Grant box is preferable when obtainable through magic dealers. Many modern pillboxes are made of transparent plastic and can be cut down to the half-inch height. Some of these come with opaque caps that are usable, but that modify the working style. There are also half-inch screw-top caps that are entirely opaque and can be used as an old-style Okito Coin Box. A cap from a regular pillbox can serve as its lid. Some pillboxes are the right size for a half dollar, but better still are plastic containers used by coin collectors, since they come in the required sizes.

SUPER COIN BOX

Early in the development of the Okito Coin Box, a special type of box was produced with a recessed bottom of the proper size to contain a single coin. This can be used exactly like the Okito Coin Box, but can also serve

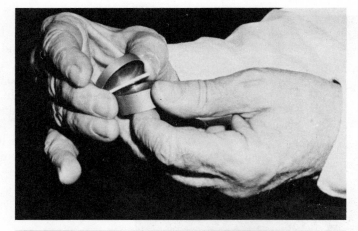

Fig. 498. Right hand placing lid on inverted box, letting coin drop into recessed bottom.

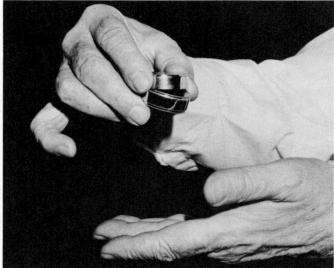

Fig. 499. Right forefinger retards inverted box so it will turn over as it drops to left hand and retain coin in recess.

to vanish a coin completely—or apparently so—in connection with other coin tricks. Here is the procedure:

The right hand drops the coin in the box, which is held in the left hand. The right hand then picks up the lid and holds it inverted so that the left hand can dump the coin from the box into the lid. The right hand then dumps it back from lid to box and this is repeated, back and forth, apparently to emphasize the solidity of the box, but actually for another purpose.

Sometime during the tossing, the performer closes the box as he dumps the coin in it, then he repeats the back-and-forth procedure. When he finally closes the box, he does the turnover using the simple method with the right middle finger (page 383), but since the coin is in the lid, the box must be turned over before the lid is tilted downward. This action is covered by the right hand as the body is turned to the left, with the result that the coin is trapped between the inverted box and the lid (Fig. 498).

The box can now be shaken freely and the coin rattles inside. For the vanish the right hand holds the box between the tips of thumb and forefinger, above the outstretched left hand. It then drops the lower section of the box into the left palm, using the tip of the right second finger to make the box turn over as it drops (Fig. 499). The left hand is extended to show that the box is clearly empty, and the right hand casually places the lid mouth downward on the table. This move directs suspicion to the lid, but before anyone has time to pick it up and look at it, the right hand lifts the box from the left hand and, at the same time, turns the left hand downward to retain the coin in the left palm. The performer then lays the box beside the lid, or even sets it on the lid. Someone is almost sure to pick up box and lid, only to examine both and find the coin is really gone.

If preferred, the box can be dropped on the left fingers, using the same turnover. In this instance, the coin is retained in the bend of the left fingers when the right hand takes the box away. In either case, a very short drop is all that is needed. A slight sweeping action of the right hand will help cover the turnover, while at the same time drawing more attention to the right hand and the suspicious lid.

For the Penetrating Coin effect, close the box as just described and trap the coin between box and lid. Then grasp the box with both hands, left below and right above, and lift the lid slightly with the right hand and flip the box mouth upward beneath the lid, trapping the coin beneath it. With the box lying on the left fingers, they press the coin into the recess beneath it, and any suspicion is immediately allayed because the box can be shown freely and even passed from hand to hand or set on the table, so long as it is not turned bottom up (although this can be done casually, if you keep your fingers beneath to hide the coin).

The box is finally slid to the left palm. Then the box is lifted by the right thumb and fingers and set on the back of the left hand, which has been turned downward and fisted to retain the coin. The right fingers tap the box, and the left hand opens and releases the coin. The closed box is then handed to a spectator so that he can open it and find that the coin is gone.

The card penetration follows a pattern similar to that of the usual penetration. With the left hand holding a playing card tilted slightly downward, the right hand approaches and slides the box above the card while the right fingers are lowered sufficiently to slip the coin beneath, where the left second finger retains it. At the tap, the coin drops through the card, and in this case, too, the box is handed to someone so that he can open it and find it empty.

MULTIPLE-COIN PENETRATION

Here, the Super Coin Box produces the effect of four or more coins penetrating the hand simultaneously, although they are shown in the box after it has been placed upon the back of the left fist. The box is closed and

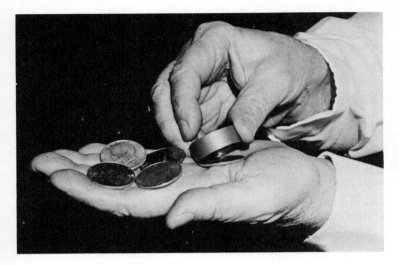

MULTIPLE-COIN
PENETRATION
Fig. 500. Right hand se-
cretly covering up coin
with recessed bottom of
box while sliding box
along left hand so four remaining coins can be
stacked inside.

tapped, and instantly the coins drop. The box may then be shown empty and examined.

For this neat effect, you need an extra coin. Assume that you are using a box just large enough to contain four coins of half-dollar size. In your left hand, you hold five such coins, jingling them so that no one can tell exactly how many coins you have. You place the box alongside the coins, spreading them somewhat, so that you casually slide the box across them with your right hand. This enables you to press the box firmly and to secretly carry along one of the coins in the recessed bottom (Fig. 500) as you slide the box to the tip of your left fingers. You then pick up the loose coins with your right hand and openly feed them into the empty box, counting "one—two—three—four—" as you let them fall there.

Now, instead of picking up the cover from the table and placing it on the box, you can let it wait until later by simply taking the box with your right hand and placing it in the center of your left hand. Actually, you turn the box over, by tipping it upward with the right second finger, using the original Okito move (page 384). The cover is not needed at this point, since the coin in the bottom recess will pass for the top coin of the stack after the box is turned over.*

The left hand is cupped loosely around the box, leaving just enough space for the right thumb and fingers to lift the box straight upward. The stack of coins stays in the left hand, which tightens into a fist to hide the coins completely once the box is removed and turns back upward, retaining the four coins while the right hand places the box on the back of the left hand. This again follows the old Okito move, but since the recessed coin is

---

* If preferred, the lid can be picked up and put on the box during the turnover, as with the original Okito Coin Box. After sliding the box to the center of the left hand, the lid can then be lifted to show that all the coins are in the box, as they appear to be due to the recessed coin. The lid is replaced on the box, which is then set on the back of the left hand, ready for the climax.

still showing, the onlookers suppose it to be the top coin of the stack and suspect nothing.

That is, they will suspect nothing if you don't let them get a flash of the coins in the left hand when the right hand is making its lift. This is why the left hand must be almost fisted, rather than merely cupped. It is also a good plan to tilt the left hand a trifle toward your body, with the left thumb hiding the view from the front. Once the box is resting on the back of your left hand, you can be quite deliberate telling onlookers to watch the coins closely while you put the lid on the box. Stress the word "coins" as you say this.

Tap the covered box, and simultaneously open your left fist to let the coins clatter to the table. Immediately take the box and lid by the sides with your right hand, extend your left hand palm upward, and let the box drop from the lid into your left hand. Here you keep your right second finger extended, causing the box to turn over as it falls. The result is that the spectators will be looking at an empty box. But the extra coin is hidden in the recess beneath it. Don't make the drop a long one. You can almost lay it in your left hand by raising your right hand as you release the box, but don't stop after showing the box empty.

With your right hand, lay the top aside and pick up the loose coins, jingling them as you spread them in your hand. The left hand comes over holding the "empty" box with thumb above and the fingers below. With a sliding motion, the left hand lays the box on the coins, releasing the extra coin from the recess so that it secretly rejoins those in the right hand. Leaving the box in the right hand, the left hand is free to pick up the top and show it; then the left hand takes the box from the right and gives both the box and the top for examination, while the right hand displays the coins.

ALTERNATE PROCEDURE

A simpler but bolder procedure is this:

After letting the coins drop from the left hand, take the box and lid by the sides with the right thumb and forefinger, extend the second finger beneath, and let the box drop squarely on the coins, turning over as it does. In this case, a drop of several inches is advisable, and if done accurately, the box will bounce away from the coins and leave its extra coin with them. Pick up the box with the left hand and pass it for examination while the right hand does the same with the lid. Gather up the coins with your right hand and the trick is done.

Don't try this on a table with a hard top unless you are very sure of yourself, as the top is apt to bounce too far. A table with a cloth covering lessens the bounce, and if you are working with a close-up pad the result will be still better, as you can practice it with the pad until you have it down to perfection.

NOTE ON PLASTIC BOXES FOR MULTIPLE-COIN PENETRATION ROUTINES: Some plastic boxes containing thumbtacks and similar items have recessed bottoms. Cut the box down to the right size for the number of coins you intend to use. Six to ten coins would be a good choice; in fact, the more coins the better, for it gives people less chance of noticing that there is one more coin at the finish than at the start.

Since most of these plastic boxes are transparent, you are confronted with a slight problem that can be easily overcome. Simply apply a strip of colored masking tape around the box edge. If it is not wide enough, overlap it with another strip. Cut out a circular piece of tape or colored paper and fix it to the bottom of the box. For the lid, use the cover of a pillbox; these are usually white and therefore not transparent. Being flimsier than a metal box, the plastic type may have to be handled more carefully when performing the coin penetration, but the overall procedure is essentially the same.

REPEAT-CIGAR PRODUCTION

This is one of the most deceptive of close-up effects, yet the necessary moves are quite easy. However, it depends on perfect timing; hence it must be practiced until the action is practically automatic. In effect, you reach straight upward with the right hand and produce a small cigar at the tips of your thumb and fingers. You transfer the cigar to your left hand, which openly places it in the left coat pocket. Then:

A mere moment later, you produce another cigar with the right hand and you immediately transfer it to the left, which pockets it as before; then you produce a third cigar, a fourth, and so on, pocketing each in the same fashion, until the supply seems inexhaustible. Generally, it is best to wind up the production with a dozen or so; otherwise people will begin to wonder how your pocket can hold them all.

Actually, only two cigars are used, with one in each hand. Each is clipped between the tips of the first and third fingers, with the cigar extending down into the palm, so it remains unseen when the back of the hand is toward the audience. The right hand moves forward and upward, and during that action the right thumb comes beneath the cigar and pivots it upward (Fig. 501) so that it appears at the fingertips (Fig. 502).

During the production, you should be faced almost directly toward the audience. This allows the left hand to come up beside the right and keep its duplicate cigar concealed. The right hand tilts downward, to the left, as though to transfer the cigar to the left hand, but instead the right fingers bend inward, so that the right thumb can swivel the right-hand cigar back to its original position. This action starts just as the tips of the right fingers meet the fingertips of the left hand (Fig. 503).

Next you turn gradually to the left, and as the right thumb draws its cigar into the clip-palm position, the left thumb pivots its cigar to the tips of the

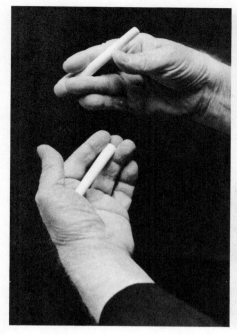

**REPEAT-CIGAR
PRODUCTION**
Fig. 501. (Chalk sticks
shown here for clarity.)
Right hand producing
cigar at tips of thumb and
forefinger; left hand ap-
proaching from below.

Fig. 502. Rear view of
production showing how
right thumb pivots cigar
upward, with left hand
holding duplicate clipped
in readiness.

Fig. 503. Rear view of
pretended transfer. Right
hand swiveling its cigar
down into finger clip as
left thumb starts to pivot
duplicate upward.

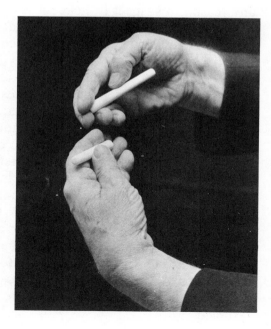

Fig. 504. Rear view of completed "transfer." Right-hand cigar is clipped from sight just before left hand shows duplicate.

left fingers to produce it (Fig. 504). The action of each hand is timed to the other but in reverse, so that when the left hand tilts its fingers upward to reveal the duplicate cigar at their tips, it looks exactly as though the original cigar had been transferred from the right hand to the left, which moves away with the visible duplicate while the right hand retains the unseen original. This key move is done on the off-beat at a time when no one has any reason to suspect it; hence it is utterly deceptive.

When you deliberately place the left-hand cigar in the coat pocket, the left fingers bend inward so the thumb can swivel the duplicate cigar back to the clip-palm position. As you turn your body straight toward the audience, extend your right hand forward and again produce the original cigar. Simultaneously, the left hand emerges from the pocket, approaches the right hand, and the transfer is repeated. This goes on and on and on—and on, leaving the onlookers more and more bewildered until you finally drop the duplicate cigar in your pocket. You then produce the original cigar once more, and this time actually transfer it from the right hand to the left, which pockets it legitimately to conclude the routine.

SPECIAL NOTES: As part of the deceptive timing, the right hand should produce its cigar with a rather quick thrust, whereas the left hand may bring its cigar into sight quite casually, as if there were no relation between the two moves. Occasionally the left hand can leave the duplicate cigar between the tips of the right thumb and forefinger, as though the productions were ended. Then the right hand makes an actual transfer to the left, which makes ensuing transfers all the more natural when the productions are resumed.

Instead of cigars, king-sized cigarettes, or larger, may be used in this routine. Short, stubby pencils are equally adaptable, as they can he sharpened down to the most desirable size. Two identical penknives of proper proportions will also prove quite effective, while other suitable objects may occasionally suggest themselves.

With cigarettes or pencils, a neat sequel is to have a dozen or more already in the left coat pocket. After finishing the production, these can be brought out and handed around as souvenirs, as though they had really materialized from nowhere to be put away one by one.

Another follow-up, especially with cigars, is to end the routine by having the right hand take the duplicate cigar and put it in the right coat pocket, secretly dropping the palmed original with it. The left hand then goes to its coat pocket and turns it inside out to show it empty, thus "proving" that the cigars have vanished as surprisingly as they appeared.

RESTORED PAPER NAPKIN

This was originally a prolonged effect in which the performer tore and restored a paper napkin and then repeated the trick with the aid of an extra napkin to "show how it's done," only to have the extra napkin restore itself as well. Keeping with modern tempos, a simpler procedure is followed today. The audience is shown how the trick is done at the very start. The original napkin and the extra are openly exhibited so that the spectators are baffled before they even expect it. In this form the Restored Paper Napkin makes an excellent opening for both large and small audiences. (See accompanying photo sequence for detailed descriptions.)

Three identical napkins are used, and small sizes are preferable. Beforehand, crumple one into a tight ball and roll the other two loosely around it, letting their edges overlap. This bundle can be carried in the right coat pocket, or simply laid on a table or some other handy place where it will be ready when needed. You begin by showing the rolled-up napkins while you tell your audience:

"You know, magic is much easier to perform than most people suppose. All this talk of digital dexterity—how 'the quickness of the hand deceives the eye'—has been concocted to throw people off the trail. What you really use is 'misdirection' which means that you draw attention one way when everybody should be looking in the other direction. The best way to illustrate this is to show you a simple trick that you can do for yourselves, once you see how easy it really is. All you need is two ordinary paper napkins, rolled up like this. Before doing the trick, you unroll them."

Here you show the rolled napkins with your right hand while turning your right side toward the audience. Your left hand approaches and the left thumb and fingers draw away the two ordinary napkins and unroll them simultaneously. The right fingers press the extra napkin into the right palm, and the left hand then draws the outer napkin completely clear. The right

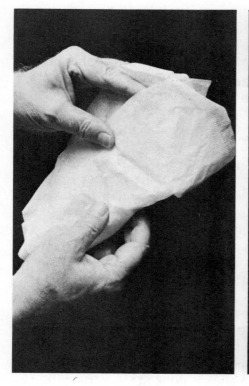

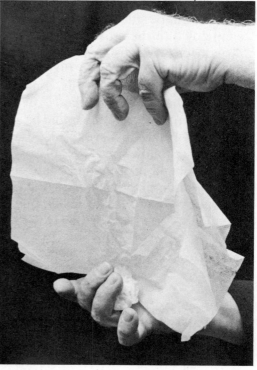

The following illustrations show step-by-step procedure with Restored Paper Napkin routine.

Fig. 505. Right hand showing two loosely rolled napkins, with left hand starting to unroll them. Note how left thumb and forefinger separate napkins to show them singly (audience view).

Fig. 506. Rear view of left hand continuing to unroll napkins, with right fingers automatically retaining tightly wadded extra napkin (X) originally hidden within loose napkins.

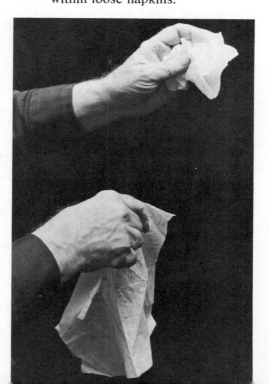

Fig. 507. Audience view of hands showing visible napkins separately, with left hand rolling its napkin (A) into a ball, which goes beneath left fingers.

thumb and fingers retain the inner napkin of the rolled pair, so that each hand displays a visible napkin.

Now you continue: "And now you roll one napkin into a tight ball, which you hide beneath the fingers of your left hand." You do this openly, crumpling the left-hand napkin (Napkin A) with your left thumb and fingers, but not as tightly as you want people to believe. After pressing Napkin A beneath the fingers with the left thumb, you bring your left hand inward and turn its back toward the spectators as you add: "But before you begin the trick, be sure to turn the back of your left hand toward the audience, like this. This is very important."

Meanwhile, you are casually displaying the right-hand napkin (Napkin B), keeping the extra (Napkin X) palmed in the right hand, which still has its back toward the audience. Bringing your hands together, you announce: "Now you show people a napkin in your right hand, the only napkin that they know anything about. You proceed to tear it in half, then in quarters." Actually, you tear Napkin B exactly as described, then you add, ". . . and you roll it into a tight ball so it looks exactly like the napkin hidden under your left fingers."

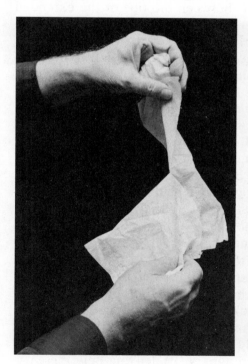

Fig. 508. Left hand openly showing its rolled napkin (A) while hands tear the single napkin (B). Right hand still secretly retains extra napkin (X) in finger bend.

Fig. 509. Rear view of tearing process. Right hand keeping extra napkin (X) hidden beneath visible napkin (B) so hands can be shown from any angle.

You naturally tear Napkin B with both hands, using the very tips of your thumbs and fingers, and people may glimpse Napkin A beneath your left fingers. Keep Napkin X (the extra) palmed deep in the right hand. Squeeze the torn napkin (B) very tightly so that it will be smaller than Napkin A. There are two reasons for this: First, the torn pieces will be well crumpled together, and second, you can secretly add the palmed extra (Napkin X) to Napkin B without having anyone suspect it.

This is accomplished both naturally and neatly by the following procedure. Grip the crumpled pieces of Napkin B with your left thumb beneath and your left fingers above. Slide them down into the right palm and press them against the palmed extra (X). The left thumb is moved below the extra (X) and presses it upward against the torn napkin (B) while squeezing both tightly together. In the same continuous move, the left hand is turned thumb upward and raised clear of the right hand. It now holds Napkins B and X. The combined napkins are brought into sight, but with the extra (X) now above, and the torn napkin (B) below.

Now face forward and casually turn the right palm toward the spectators so they can see it is empty, while you raise the left hand, holding what appears to be simply the torn napkin (B) between the tips of the extended thumb and first two fingers. The other fingers of the left hand retain the napkin (A) that you planted there originally. As if to recapitulate, you state, "So here you have the torn pieces at the tip of the left thumb and fingers"—with the right forefinger, point to the combined Napkins X and B "while under the other fingers, you have the good napkin that nobody knows about." Point to Napkin A while keeping the right-hand palm front so that everyone can see it is empty, but do not mention this fact. Then turn the left hand inward as you add, "Of course, as I told you before, always keep the back of your left hand toward the audience, so that nobody can see the good napkin you're hiding there."

At this point you pause, raise your right-hand palm frontward, and state: "Now comes the misdirection, so watch closely while I show you how easy it is." Turn your body to the left so that your right side is again toward the audience. This brings your left hand palm front and leaves the good napkin (A) under the left fingers and the torn napkin (B) at the tip of the left thumb and forefinger. The extra napkin (X) is capped above, unknown to the spectators. Bringing your right hand over to your left you say, "All you do is squeeze the torn pieces, tuck in the loose corners . . ."

Working on the torn napkin with the thumb and the first two fingers of both hands, you pretend to do exactly that, but in the process your right thumb and fingers steal away the torn napkin (B), leaving only the extra napkin (X) in sight. The right fingers secretly press the torn napkin (B) into the right palm, and you announce dramatically, . . . and suddenly you thrust your right hand into your trouser pocket!" Do this, taking along the torn napkin (B), and with your right thumb you push it into a corner of the pocket. Then, with a laugh, you continue, "And immediately you bring your hand out and turn your pocket inside out, showing it empty."

Fig. 510. Audience view of thumbs and fingers of both hands squeezing torn napkin (B) into a ball. Left hand openly shows its napkin (A) while right hand continues to keep extra napkin (X) hidden in finger bend.

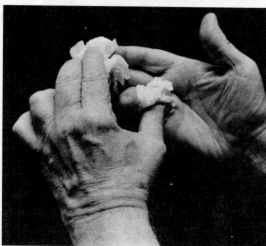

Fig. 511. Rear view of left thumb drawing extra napkin (X) from bend of right fingers to press it against torn napkin (B) in order to show both as one.

Turn your pocket inside out and show the right hand empty, as stated; then ask, "Why do you do this? Simply because nobody can watch your right hand, down here, and keep an eye on your left hand, over there, both at the same time." Pause with the right hand, keeping it palm front, and gesture with the left hand, also keeping it palm front. Then add, "This is where the misdirection enters. While your right hand is pushing the pocket back in place, your left hand neatly switches the torn napkin for the good one."

Your right hand finishes pushing in the pocket and points to the left hand, which openly exchanges one good napkin (A) for the other (X). This is easily done with a rotary action with the thumb drawing the supposedly torn napkin (X) downward into the bend of the fingers and then working Napkin A up to the fingertips. As you complete this action, turn the back

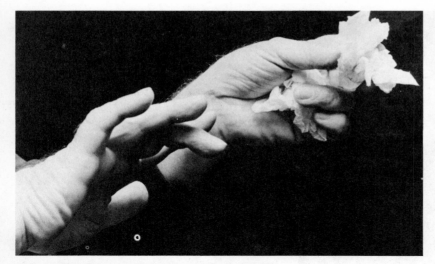

Fig. 512. Left hand displays torn napkin at fingertips and original napkin (A) in finger bend. Actually, torn napkin (B) includes extra napkin (X) so right hand can be shown empty.

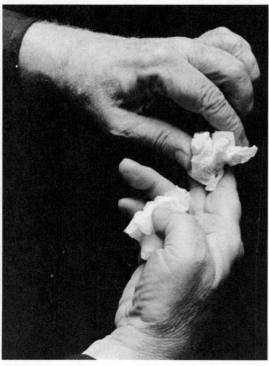

Fig. 513. In squeezing torn napking (B) at fingertips, right thumb secretly draws it away, leaving extra napkin (X) between left thumb and finger (rear view).

of the left hand toward the spectators and remark, "Of course, you should always keep the inside of your hand toward yourself, so that nobody ever sees the good napkin that you put there to start; and naturally, they won't see you make the switch."

At this point you should be facing directly toward the audience so that you can bring your hands together and open out the napkin showing at your fingertips, saying, "Then all you have to do is open the only paper napkin the people know about. To their amazement, instead of being torn

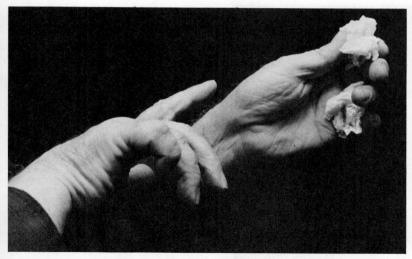

Fig. 514. Performer's view. Right hand pointing to extra napkin (X) at left fingertips and original napkin (A) in bend of left fingers. Right hand is going to pocket with torn napkin (B) hidden in bend of fingers.

Fig. 515. Right hand has come from pocket after leaving torn napkin (B). Right hand is pointing to left hand, which is openly switching one napkin (X) for the other (A).

in small pieces, it is fully restored and as good as ever!"

You now lay the "restored" napkin (A) on the table, or let it flutter to the floor. Turn your left side toward the audience so that you can wave your right hand, back and front, showing it empty. At the same time keep the back of your left hand toward the spectators. You can emphasize this action with the comment: "The trouble is, you have to do the rest of your tricks with one hand, because only your right hand is empty and you are stuck with the torn napkin here in your left hand." You pause, face front again, and show the inside of your left hand with the lone napkin (X) tucked beneath the left fingers and ruefully add, "That's why you seldom see magicians do this trick. They have no way of getting rid of the torn pieces." Then, brightening a bit, you continue.

"Of course, if they tried some real magic, like blowing on the torn

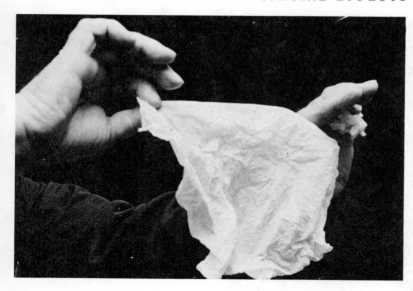

Fig. 516, Right hand showing itself empty while left hand helps it unroll original napkin (A). Left hand keeps showing supposedly torn napkin (X) beneath its fingers, later opening it to show that it, too, is restored.

napkin"—here you push the napkin up to your fingertips—"and repeating a magic word like 'abracadabra' and really meaning it, they might get results like this!"

Slowly, carefully, you open out the supposedly torn napkin to show it completely restored. Let everyone see that your hands are completely empty as you remark, "There, you see the torn napkin is completely restored, and my hands are just as empty as when I started!"

With that you drop this napkin along with the first and proceed with your next trick, adding the casual comment, "So now you know exactly how it's done."

NOTE: Many modern trouser pockets are fashioned with a cross-cut, horizontal opening instead of the vertical type, so that they lack an upper inside corner where the torn napkin can be thrust in order to turn the pocket inside out and show it apparently empty. However, some of these modern-style pockets are fitted with a smaller inside pocket for carrying keys or loose change. By using a small napkin, the torn pieces can be pushed down into the change pocket. When the entire pocket is turned inside out, the torn napkin will be snugly concealed in the change pocket, which will be at the back.

If an inner pocket is lacking, it is an easy matter to sew one in place, but even without an inner pocket the regular routine can be followed closely by simply keeping the torn napkin palmed in the right hand while turning the pocket inside out and pushing it back in again, all in one action.

It requires practice to blend smooth action with patter. Instead of saying, "And immediately you bring your hand out . . ." you cut your statement to, "And immediately you turn your pocket inside out and push it in again." Then bring your right hand out and add, "And show your right hand empty, like your pocket!"

To key the words to the action, leave the torn napkin in the pocket when you bring your hand out. Done neatly, this is as convincing as showing both the pocket and the hand empty simultaneously, but it must be done briskly instead of deliberately. After you have shown your right hand empty, you can, of course, go into a slow-motion style when pointing to the left hand to show how it takes advantage of the misdirection.

ALTERNATE ROUTINE

Although the described routine is quite effective when the performer is standing at close range, it may present a problem when the performer is seated at a table. Often he can ease back in his chair and rise sufficiently to thrust his right hand in his trouser pocket, but this can prove awkward. It is preferable to go to the right coat pocket if it has an inner change pocket. You simply tuck the torn napkin into the inner pocket and turn the entire pocket inside out, keeping it close to the body, so that the inner pocket will stay completely out of sight.

To hide the inner pocket successfully, the right thumb and fingers should draw the larger pocket straight upward and keep it that way before thrusting it back in place. Meanwhile the pocket can be clipped between the first two fingers so that the back of the hand can be tilted toward the body, giving the spectators a view of the empty palm. This applies to both the trouser pocket and coat pocket, whichever you happen to be using. Of course, if the coat pocket lacks an inner pocket, keep the torn napkin palmed during the drawing-out action and finally leave it in the pocket after pushing the latter back in place.

GLOSSARY-INDEX

This lists the principal terms used in this book, with reference to the pages on which they are first explained. It also includes descriptions of special effects and devices used in close-up and manipulative magic, which are not covered in the text and therefore have no page references. These require specially manufactured appliances obtainable through magic dealers. They have been mentioned as adjuncts specially suited to the needs of close-up workers.

Advanced Penetration (Coin Through Handkerchief), 361-63

Alternate Ball on Fist Production, 94-95

Alternate Coins Through Body, 75-76

Alternate Fingertip Production, 92-93

Alternate Matchbox Vanish, 298-99

Alternate Penetration (Coin Through Handkerchief), 360-61

Alternate Penetration Matches, 311

Alternate Restored Paper Napkin Routine, 411

Alternate Roll-over Color Change, 154-55

Alternate Salt Vanish, 345-46

Alternate Super Coin Box Procedure, 399

Alternate Thumb-fork Palm, 13-14

Alternate Thumb-palm, 36-38

Alternate Thumb the Thimble, 251-52

Alternate Turnabout Match, 307-9

Anti-gravico: A clever effect in which water remains in an ordinary "pop" bottle when it is inverted. Performed with the aid of a special gimmick supplied by magic dealers.

Appearing Matches, 299-300

Back and Front Clip, 25-26
  for a vanish, 26

Back and Front Palm coin, 17-22
  for a production, 22
  for a vanish, 22
  thimble, 204-7

Back-finger Clip, 23-25
  for a vanish, 24, 25

Back-finger Grip, 18, 19

Back Palm
  billiard ball, 90
  coin, 18, 19

Back-palm Flash, 240-43

Back Palm Off, 40-41

Back-palm Transfer, 135-36

Back Thumb Clip, 26, 27-28

Ball and Shell, 168-69

Ball and Silk Vanish, 122

Ball and Tube: A close-fitting double tube of metal that supports a small ball, which mysteriously moves downward and upward when the inner tube is secretly released or pushed up by the fingers.

Ball Clip: Device of pliable wire that is pinned beneath hem of coat to hold a small billiard ball or golf ball, so the performer can obtain it as needed.

Ball from Wand Production, 103-4

Ball Glass: A specially made glass with a hole in back, so a ball can

Ball Glass: *cont.*
    be rolled out and palmed when
    the glass is covered with a cloth.
Ball Holder: A Ball Clip or Ball
    Tube.
Ball of Wool: A trick depending on
    a flat, hollow slide that is open
    at both ends, and large enough to
    accommodate a half-dollar. A ball
    of wool (yarn) is wound around
    one end and the ball is put in the
    coat pocket, with the other end
    of the slide held upward. During
    the course of the trick, the
    performer drops the borrowed
    coin into the slide, inverts the
    ball of wool, and draws it from
    his pocket, leaving the slide there.
    The ball of wool is then given to a
    spectator, so when he or she
    unrolls it, the coin is found
    inside.
Ball on Fist Production, 93-94
    Alternate, 94-95
Balls, 85-86
    See also Billiard balls
Ball Tube: A cloth tube containing
    several balls which can be released
    singly by squeezing a flexible ring
    at the lower end. Various types
    are obtainable from magic dealers.
Bamberg, Theo, 385. *See also* Okito
Basic Change-over, 127-28, 129-30
Behind the Hand Production, 217
Behind the Tablet, 259
Billet Switching, 254-61
Billiard-ball change-overs, 126-30
    Basic, 127-28, 129-30
    combination Flash and, 141
    Delayed, 129, 130
    general description of, 126-27
    Improved, 128, 130
    notes on, 129-30
Billiard-ball color changes, 149-58
    Fist, 149-53
    Full-front, 155-56
    Roll-over, 153-54
        Alternate, 154-55
    sample routines, 157-58
    Special, 193-95
    Throw, 156-57

Billiard-ball flashes, 140-49
    combination Change-over and, 141
    Crisscross, 141-43
    Finger, 147-49
    Forearm, 140
    general description of, 126-27
    Sleeve, 140-41
    Thumb, 143-45
    Thumb-front, 145
    Turnabout, 145-47
Billiard-ball productions, 91-104
    Ball from Wand, 103-4
    Ball on Fist, 93-94
        Alternate, 94-95
    Draw-Apart, 99-100
    Elbow, 102, 103
    Fingertip, 91-92
        Alternate, 92-93
        Reverse, 95-96
    "Four to Eight," 179-81
    general data on, 91
    Knee, 102
    Slow-Motion, 101-2
    Through the Hand, 100-1
    Thumb Squeeze, 97-98
Billiard balls, 85-195
    Back Palm, 90
    basic manipulations, 86-90
    Display Position, 87
    Double Palm, 89,90
    Finger-bend Palm, 87
    palming, 86
    size of, 85
    Standard Palm, 88
    Thumb Palm, 88-89
    Triple Palm, 89
Billiard balls, Multiplying, 158-95
    Ball and Shell, 168-69
    Fifth-ball Routine, 192-93
    Final-ball Vanish, 178-79
    Four-ball Twirl, 184-86
    "Four to Eight" Production, 179-81
    "Four to One" Routine, 187-92
    "One to Four" Routine
        Rapid (with solid balls), 163-68
        with shell, 171-78
        Standard, 158-63
    Special Color Change, 193-95
    Two-way Twirl, 170-71
    White and Red Transposition, 181-
        84

Billiard-ball transfers, 131-40
  Back-palm, 135-36
  general description of, 126
  Reverse, 132-33
  Simple, 131-32
  Slow-motion Steal, 134-35
  Thumb and Finger Steal, 133-34
  Turn-around, 137-38
    Double, 138-40
    Reverse, 138
Billiard-ball vanishes, 104-25
  Ball and Silk, 122
  Final-ball, 178-79
  Fingertip, 118-19
  Fist
    Improved, 120-21
    Simple, 119-20
  French Drop, 106-8
  Hand-to-Hand, 105
  Hit-down, 121
  Lay-over, 125
  Palm, Simple, 105
  Pincer, 108-9
  Pour, 104, 105-6
  Push, 109-11
  Roll
    Fingertip, 112-14
    Simple, 111-12
    Thumb, 114-16
  Slow-motion, 124-25
  Snatch, 122-23
  Swallow, 108
  Throw, 105
  Toss, 116
    Swing-about, 118
    Two-hand, 116-17
Brema, Carl, 386, 390
Brema Coin Box, 386-89
Brush-over Change, 64

Cards and Dice, 269-72
  chart for, 272
Center Palm, 200-1
Center-Tear Message Reading, 261-
  67
Change-overs
  billiard ball, 126-30
    Basic, 127-28, 129-30
    combination Flash and, 141
    Delayed, 129, 130
    general description of, 126

Improved, 128, 130
    notes on, 129-30
  coin, 63-65
    Brush-over, 64
    Multiple-coin Transfer, 64-65
    Placement, 64, 65
    Simple, 63
    Sleeve Action, 63-64
  thimble, 233-36
    Double, 233-36
Chop Cup: A special mechanical cup
  used in modernized version of
  Cups and Balls.
Clipboards, 253
Coin Box
  Brema, 386-89
  Okito, 382-95, 398
    Improved, 386-89
    Transparent, 392-94, 395
  Super, 395-97
    Alternate Procedure, 399
    Multiple-coin Penetration, 397-
      400
Coin Catcher: Any of various
  mechanical devices used for
  bringing coins to fingertips instead
  of using sleights.
Coin change-overs, 63-65
  Brush-over, 64
  Multiple-coin Transfer, 64-65
  Placement, 64, 65
  Simple, 63
  Sleeve Action, 63-64
Coin changes, 53-55
  French Drop, 54-55
  Palm Drop, 54
  Palm Drop 2, 54
  Palm-to-palm, 54
  Pickup, 55
Coin Dropper: A mechanical device
  inserted inside a hat brim, where it
  drops coins singly into the hat.
Coin flashes, 5
Coin Holder: A device for holding a
  load of coins under the vest,
  where they can be obtained by the
  left hand, prior to performing the
  Miser's Dream.
Coin productions
  Back and Front Palm, 22
  Coin-star, 66-68

Coin productions, *cont.*
  Downs Palm, 15, 17
  Edge Palm, 9-11
  Elbow, 62
  Finger-bend Palm, 4-5
  Fingertip, 62
  Five-coin Routine, 71-72
  Four-coin Vanish and Recovery,
    69-71
  Knee, 62
  Miser's Dream, 14, 76-83
    Full-front, 80-83
    recommended palming methods,
      79-80
  Multiple-edge Palm, 60, 61
  Multiple Finger Bend, 55-56
  Multiple Standard Palm, 59
  Simple, 62-63
  Spread-away, 62
  Standard Palm, 9
  Sweep, 62-63
  Thumb-fork Palm, 12, 14
Coin Roll, 50-51
  One-hand, 53
  Two-hand, 53
Coin-roll Vanish, 50, 51-53
Coins, 1-83
  Back and Front Clip, 25-26
  Back and Front Palm, 17-22
  Back-finger Clip, 23-25
  Back-finger Grip, 18, 19
  Back Palm, 18, 19
  Back Thumb Clip, 26, 27-28
  basic manipulations, 1-28
  comedy routines, 76, 79
  Dime to Dollar, 353-54
  Display Position, 2
  Double-coin Surprise, 275-76
  Downs Pakm, 14-17, 69, 70
  Edge Palm, 8, 9-11
  Find the Coin, 268-69
  Finger-bend Palm, 3-5
  Fingertip Display, 3
  Four-coin Baffler, 315-18
  Front-finger Clip, 22-23
  "Han Pin Chien," 326, 330, 333
  for manipulations, special, 1
  Matched Thought, 278-79
  Multiple Downs Palm, 61-62
  Multiple-edge Palm, 60-61

Multiple Finger Bend, 55-58
multiple manipulations, 55-58
Multiple Penetration, 397-400
Multiple Standard Palm, 58-60
Single-coin Palms, 1-2
size of, 1
Standard Palm, 6-9, 21-22
Thumb-crook Palm, 11
Thumb-fork Palm, 12-13
  Alternate, 13-14
Turn-over, 267-68
  Multiple, 268
See also Palming Coins
Coins and Glass, 68-69
Coin-star Production, 66-68
Coins Through Body, 72-75
  Alternate, 75-76
Coins Through Table, 326-35
  Hand-to-Hand, 333
  latest variant on, 329-30
  Mutual Attraction, 334
  Simple Passage, 334
  Straight Through, 330-33
  Throw-over, 333-35
  Transposition, 334-35
Coin Through Card, 390-92
  with Transparent Box, 394-95
Coin Through Handkerchief, 358-61
  Advanced Penetration, 361-63
  Alternate Penetration, 360-61
Coin Through the Hand, 355-57
  Slow-motion Penetration, 356-57
Coin vanishes, 28-53
  Back and Front Clip, 26
  Back and Front Palm, 22
  Back-finger Clip, 24, 25
  Back Palm Off, 40-41
  Coin-roll, 50, 51-53
  Downs Palm, 15, 16-17
  Edge Palm, 9
  False Drop, 41-44
  Finger-bend Palm, 3-4
  Fist, 44-46
  Four-coin Vanish and Recovery,
    69-71
  French Drop, 39-40
  Multiple-edge Palm, 61
  Multiple Finger Bend
    Side-drop, 57, 59
    Slide, 57

Multiple Standard Palm, 59-60
  Pickup, 60
  Throw, 60
One-by-One, 65-66
Palm Off, 40
Pull-away, 29-30
Quick Dime, 354
Reverse, 30-33
Slow-motion, 46-48
Squeeze, 49, 50
Standard Palm, 9
Take-away, 38
Thumb-fork Palm, 12, 13
Thumb-palm, 33-36
  Alternate, 36-38
Coin Wand: A mechanical wand that produces a coin at its tip, used as an adjunct for the Miser's Dream.
Color Cards, 282-83
Color changes
  billiard ball, 149-58
    Fist, 149-53
    Full-front, 155-56
    Roll-over, 153-54
    Roll-over Alternate, 154-55
    sample routines, 157-58
    Special, 193-95
    Throw, 156-57
  thimble, 244-48
    Finger-switch, 244-46
    Push-through, 247-48
    Repeat Finger-swtich, 246
    Repeat Push-through, 248
Color-changing Silk, 373-77
  Special, 377-80
Come-back Lump, 324-26
Comedy coin routines, 76, 79
Crisscross Flash, 141-43
Crystal balls
  In the Crystal, 257-58
  Through the Crystal, 263
Cups and Balls: A classic effect performed with three specially shaped metal cups and several small balls which vanish, appear, and multiply beneath the cups. Various long-tested routines based on simple moves are supplied with the equipment by most magic dealers.

Decorative balls, 85
Delayed Change-over, 129, 130
Dice
  Cards and Dice, 269-72
    chart for, 272
  Jump-over, 335-36
Dime to Dollar, 353-54
Diminishing Ball: A hollow ball containing a half-size ball which is released with a throwing move from the right hand to the left, while the right hand palms the large ball. Further changes can be made with smaller balls to continue the routine. Sold by magic dealers, 85, 86
Display Position
  billiard ball, 87
  coin, 2
  thimble, 197-98
Double Change-over, 233-36
Double-coin Surprise, 275-76
Double Palm, 89, 90
Double Turn-around Transfer, 138-40
Downs, T. Nelson, 14, 17, 25, 57, 69, 72, 75, 76
Downs Palm, 14-17, 69, 70
  Multiple, 61-62
  for a production, 15, 17
  for a vanish, 15, 16-17
Draw-apart Production, 99-100
Draw-off Vanish, 212
Drop the Box, 287-88

Edge Palm, 8, 9-11
  for a production, 9-11
  for a vanish, 9
Egg Bag: A cloth bag measuring about 8 by 8 inches, open wide at the top, and with a double side open at the bottom that forms a hidden pocket. An egg placed in the bag drops into the pocket when the bag is inverted, so the bag can be turned inside out, proving that the egg is gone, only to be recovered when the maneuver is reversed. Modern forms of this century-old standby are sold by

Egg Bag: *cont.*
  magic dealers, with special routine
  instructions included.
Egg Kling Klang, 380, 381
Elbow Production
  billiard ball, 102, 103
  coin, 62
  thimble, 217
Excelsior Clip: A metal hook
  combined with a spring clamp that
  can be attached to the edge of a
  half-dollar to make it serve as a
  Hooked Coin. Sold by stationers
  as Spring Hooks. Highly useful in
  closeup work.
Extrasensory perception (ESP), 254,
  277

Fake: A trick device that imitates a
  genuine object, such as a Shell
  Coin or a Half Thimble; also, a
  device that is completely unnoticed,
  such as a Glass Disk or a Thumb
  Tip.
False Drop, 41-44
Feke: A term sometimes used to
  describe a fake of the second type.
Fifth-ball Routine, 192-93
Final-ball Vanish, 178-79
Find the Coin, 268-69
Find the Word, 259-61
Finger Bend, Multiple, 55-58
  for a production, 55-56
  Side-drop Vanish, 57,59
  Slide Vanish, 57
Finger-bend Palm
  billiard ball, 87
  coin, 3-5
    for a production, 4-5
    for a vanish, 3-4
  thimble, 201
    for a production, 201
    for a vanish, 201
Finger Clip
  Simple, 204
  Thumb and, 203-4
Finger Flash, 147-49
Finger-switch Change, 244-46
  Repeat, 246
Finger-switch Vanish, 214-15

Fingertip Display, 3
Fingertip Flash, 236-37
Fingertip Production
  billiard ball, 91-92
    Alternate, 92-93
    Reverse, 95-96
  coin, 62
  thimble, 216
Fingertip Roll Vanish, 112-14
Fingertip Vanish, 118-19
Fist Color Change, 149-53
Fist to Fist, 346
Fist Vanish, 44-46
  Improved, 120-21
  Simple, 119-20
Five-coin Routine, 71-72
Five-glass Fooler, 351-52
Flash Paper: Chemically treated
  paper that ignites instantly when
  touched with a match.
Folding Coin: A specially constructed
  coin that can be folded in three
  sections, which spring open when
  released. Such a coin can be
  thrust down through the neck of a
  bottle, then shown inside. Shaken
  out through the neck, it is caught
  by the waiting hand and changed
  for a solid coin that can be given
  for examination.
Forearm Flash, 140
Four-ball Twirl, 184-86
Four-coin Baffler, 315-18
Four-coin Vanish and Recovery,
  69-71
Four-lump Assembly, 319-22
"Four to Eight" Production
  billiard ball, 179-81
  thimble, 220-25
"Four to One" Routine, 187-92
French Drop Change, 54-55
French Drop Vanish
  billiard ball, 106-8
  coin, 39-40
From the Ashes, 258-59
From the Glass, 263-64
Front-finger Clip, 22-23
Front-finger Grip, 18
Full and Empty, 352
Full-front Color Change, 155-56

Full-front Flash, 237-40
Full-front Miser's Dream, 80-83
"Full Front" Routine, 225-26

Gimmick (Gaff): A special or secret device used in mechanical effects. Akin to Fake.
Glass Disk: Cut to the size of a half-dollar or a dollar, a plain glass disk can be changed for a borrowed coin under cover of a handkerchief. Held through the cloth, it is then dropped into a tumbler partly filled with water, where it "vanishes" by remaining unseen when the handkerchief is removed.
Golf balls, 85
Grant, U. F. (Gen), 189, 190, 191, 259, 263, 264, 392, 394, 395

Half-match Penetration, 311-12
Half Thimble: A thimble cut in half from top to bottom. One half is placed on the tip of the middle finger with back of the hand toward spectators. The hand is doubled, turned palm frontward, and opened to show thimble gone. A reversal of the action results in its reappearance.
Handkerchief Ball: A hollow ball of plastic or thin metal, containing one or more silk handkerchiefs. The performer manipulates it exactly like a miniature billiard ball to show hands empty, then works the silks into sight between his hands as though producing them magically. The silks can be vanished by reversing the process to show the hands empty by means change-overs and other ball moves.
Hand-to-Hand (Coins Through Table), 333
Hand-to-Hand Vanish, 105
"Han Pin Chien Coins," 326, 330, 333
Heads Away, 294-96
Hit-down Vanish, 121
Hollow balls, 85

Hook Coin: A large coin with a hook soldered to it. With his or her left side toward spectators, the performer shows the coin in his right hand, lowers it, and hooks it to his coat or trouser leg as he begins a quick upward toss, showing his hand empty. Later, he can secretly reclaim the "vanished" coin and reproduce it. *See* Excelsior Clip.

Improved Change-over, 128, 130
Improved Fist Vanish, 120-21
Improved Magnetic Pencils, 339-41
Improved Okito Coin Box, 386-89
Instant Vanishing Matches, 301-2
In the Crystal, 257-58
Inward Take-away Vanish, 209-10

Jump-over Dice, 335-36

Kling Klang, 380, 381
Knee Production
    billiard ball, 102
    coin, 62
    thimble, 217
Knife, magnetized, 342, 343
Knot and Ring, 369-70

Lay-over Vanish, 125
Link the Clips, 364-65
    Triple Links, 366
Looper Dooper, 363-64
Looping the Matchbox, 290-92

Magician's Wax: A special type of wax that can be quickly attached to coins, cards, or other items, yet is just as easily detached. A high-grade beeswax often serves the same purpose.
Magic Sugar Lumps, 319-26
    Come-back Lump, 324-26
    Four-lump Assembly, 319-22
    Through the Table, 323-24
Magnetic Pencils, 338-39
    Improved, 339-41
    Perfect, 341-42
Magnetized Knife, 342, 343

Magnetized Matches, 288-89
  Modern, 290
Matchbox Do as I Do, 303-6
Matchboxes (matches), 287-314
  Appearing Matches, 299-300
  Drop the Box, 287-88
  Heads Away, 294-96
  Looping the Matchbox, 290-92
  Magnetized Matches, 288-89
    Modern, 290
  Matchbox Do as I Do, 303-6
  Matchbox Vanish, 297-309
    Alternate, 298-99
  Mystic Knot Vanish, 292-94
  special note, 293-94
  Penetrating Matches, 309-14
    Alternate Penetration, 311
    Half-match Penetration, 311-12
    Match Through Hand, 312-14
  Through the Table, 303
  Turnabout Heads, 302
  Turnabout Match, 306-7
    Alternate, 307-9
  Vanishing Matches, 300-1
    Instant, 301-2
Matched Thought, 278-79
Match Through Hand, 312-14
Match to Flower: A quick opener in
  which a match is lighted and
  instantly changes into a flower at
  very close range. An automatic
  device supplied by magic dealers.
Match to Silk: Another instantaneous
  close-up effect serving as a
  prelude to a handkerchief routine.
Mentalists, 253
Mengal magic, 253-86
  Cards and Dice, 269-72
    chart for, 272
  Find the Coin, 268-69
  Matched Thought, 278-79
  Mental Moves, 274-77
    Double-coin Surprise, 275-76
  Message Reading, 253-66
    Behind the Tablet, 259
    Billet Switching, 254-61
    Center Tear, 261-67
    Find the Word, 259-61
    From the Ashes, 258-59

    From the Glass, 263-64
    In the Crystal, 257-58
    Name for Name, 264-65
    Reading the Message, 262-63
    Through the Crystal, 263
    Time out of Mind, 265-66
    Without the Watch, 266-67
  Number Prediction, 279-83
    Color Cards, 282-83
  Paired Cities, 285-86
  Six-symbol Test, 277-78
  Sixth Card — Sixth Sense, 284-85
  Triple-color Test, 273
  Turn-over Coins, 267-68
    Multiple, 268
Mental Moves, 274-77
  Double-coin Surprise, 275-76
Message Reading, 253-66
  Behind the Tablet, 259
  Billet Switching, 254-61
  Center Tear, 261-67
  Find the Word, 259-61
  From the Ashes, 258-59
  From the Glass, 263-64
  In the Crystal, 257-58
  Name for Name, 264-65
  Reading the Message, 262-63
  Through the Crystal, 263
  Time out of Mind, 265-66
  Without the Watch, 266-67
Miller, Welsh, 69
Miser's Dream, 14, 76-83
  Full-front, 80-83
  recommended palming methods,
    79-80
Multiple-coin Penetration, 397-400
Multiple-coin Transfer, 64-65
Multiple Downs Palm, 61-62
Multiple-edge Palm, 60-61
  for a production, 60, 61
  for a vanish, 61
Multiple Finger Bend, 55-58
  for a production, 55-56
  Side-drop Vanish, 57, 59
  Slide Vanish, 57
Multiple-knot Trick, 368
Multiple Standard Palm, 58-60
  Pickup Vanish, 60
  for a production, 59

Throw Vanish, 60
for a vanish, 59-60
Multiple Turn-over Coins, 268
Multiplying Billiard Balls, 158-95
Ball and Shell, 168-69
Fifth-ball Routine, 192-93
Final-ball Vanish, 178-79
Four-ball Twirl, 184-86
"Four to Eight" Production, 179-81
"Four to One" Routine, 187-92
"One to Four" Routine
Rapid (with solid balls), 163-68
with shell, 171-78
Standard, 158-63
Special Color Change, 193-95
Two-way Twirl, 170-71
White and Red Transposition,
181-84
Multiplying Thimbles, 218-33
"Four to Eight" Production, 220-
25
"Full Front" Routine, 225-26
"One to Four" Production, 218-20
Rapid "One to Eight" System,
226-33
Mutual Attraction, 334
Mystic Knot Vanish, 292-94
special note, 293-94

Name for Name, 264-65
Nickels and Dimes: An automatic
close-up effect in which a stack of
nickels is covered with a metal
cap and transformed into a stack
of dimes. A precision-made
appliance. No skill needed.
Number Prediction, 279-83
Color Cards, 282-83

Okito (Theo Bamberg), 143, 385
Okito Coin Box, 382-95, 398
Improved, 386-89
Transparent, 392-94, 395
One-by-One Vanish, 65-66
One-hand Coin Roll, 53
One-hand Flash, 243-44
"One to Eight" System, Rapid, 226-
33
"One to Four" Production, 218-20

"One to Four" Routine
Rapid (with solid balls), 163-68
with shell, 171-78
Standard, 158-63

Paired Cities, 285-86
Palm (billiard ball)
Back, 90
Back-palm Transfer, 135-36
Double, 89, 90
Finger-bend, 87
Simple Vanish, 105
Standard, 88
Thumb, 88-89
Triple, 89
Palm (coin)
Back, 18, 19
Back and Front, 17-22
for a production, 22
for a vanish, 22
Downs, 14-17, 69, 70
for a production, 15, 17
for a vanish, 15, 16-17
Edge, 8, 9-11
for a production, 9-11
for a vanish, 9
Finger-bend, 3-5
for a production, 4-5
for a vanish, 3-4
Multiple Downs, 61-62
Multiple-edge, 60-61
for a production, 60, 61
for a vanish, 61
Multiple Standard, 58-60
Pickup Vanish, 60
for a production, 59
Throw Vanish, 60
for a vanish, 59-60
recommended method for Miser's
Dream, 79-80
Single-coin, 1-2
Standard, 6-9, 21-22
for a production, 9
for a vanish, 9
Thumb, 33-36
Alternate, 36-38
Thumb-crook, 11
Thumb-fork, 12-13
Alternate, 13-14

Palm (coin), *cont.*
 for a production, 12, 14
 for a vanish, 12, 13
Palm (thimble)
 Back and Front, 204-7
 Back-palm Flash, 240-43
 Center, 200-1
 Finger-bend, 201
  for a production, 201
  for a vanish, 201
 Thumb, 198-99
  for a production, 199
  for a vanish, 198-99
 Thumb-bend, 199-200
 Tip, 203
Palm Drop Change, 54
Palm Drop Change 2, 54
Palming Coins: Special coins or
 tokens of half-dollar and dollar
 size often used in the Miser's
 Dream. Their chief advantages are
 sharply milled edges and thinner
 bulk than regular coins that enable
 the performer to handle a greater
 number simultaneously. Most
 palming coins have become
 collectors' items and are now
 worth far more than the genuine
 currency that they represent, 1
Palm Off, 40
 Back, 40-41
Palm-to-palm Change, 54
Palm Toss, 322
Paper Napkin, Restored, 403-11
 Alternate Routine, 411
Peek mirrors, 253-54
Pencils, magnetic, 338-39
 Improved, 339-41
 Perfect, 341-42
Penetrating Matches, 309-14
 Alternate Penetration, 311
 Half-match Penetration, 311-12
 Match Through Hand, 312-14
Penny and Dime: A shell penny, with
 dime that fits inside it. Supplied by
 dealers along with instructions for
 various tricks in which it is used.
Perfect Magnetic Pencil, 341-42
Pickup Change, 55
Pickup Vanish, 60

Pincer Vanish, 108-9
Ping-Pong balls, 86
Placement Change-over, 64, 65
Pocket Production, 217
Poke Vanish, 210-11
Pop Production, 216
Pour Vanish, 104, 105-6
Pull: A cup or tube attached to a
 length of cord elastic that runs up
 the performer's sleeve or under his
 coat and extends through the belt
 loops of his trousers. Small objects
 pushed into the fist are secretly
 inserted in the pull, which is then
 released so the hand can be shown
 empty. Commonest is the
 Handkerchief Pull for vanishing
 silks, while a Clutch Pull is made
 to grip a billiard ball and carry it
 beneath the coat. Smaller devices
 are the Cigarette Pull, Coin Pull,
 Match Pull, which all go up the
 sleeve.
Pull-away Vanish, 29-30
Push-through Change, 247-48
 Repeat, 248
Push Vanish, 109-11

Quick Dime Vanish, 354
Quick-knot Vanish, 368-69

Ramsay, John, 216
Rapid "One to Eight" System, 226-
 33
Rapid "One to Four" Routine (with
 solid balls, 163-68
Reading the Message, 262-63
Repeat-cigar Production, 400-3
Repeat Finger-switch Change, 246
Repeat Push-through Change, 248
Restored Paper Napkin, 403-11
 Alternate Routine, 411
Reverse Fingertip Production, 95-96
Reverse Transfer, 132-33
Reverse Turn-around Transfer, 138
Reverse Vanish, 30-33
Ring and Triple Knot, 370-71
Roll-over Color Change, 153-54
 Alternate, 154-55

Roll the Bills, 349-51
Roll Vanish
  Fingertip, 112-14
  Simple, 111-12
  Thumb, 114-16
Rubber balls, 85, 86

Salt Shaker, Vanishing, 347-48
Salt Vanish, 344-49
  Alternate, 345-46
  Fist to Fist, 346
  Supersalt, 348-49
  Vanishing Salt Shaker, 347-48
Shannon, James, 248
Shell balls, 85, 86
  making, 86
Shell Coin: A coin so completely
  hollow that it can fit over a solid
  coin of the same type that has
  been reduced in diameter to
  accommodate the shell. Used for
  "multiplying" one coin to two or
  "reducing" two to one.
Shirt Collar Production, 217
Side-drop Vanish, 57, 59
Silk, Color-changing, 373-77
  Special, 377-80
Silks: A popular term for silk
  handkerchiefs (12-inches square or
  larger), used in manipulative magic.
  Most silk tricks depend to a great
  degree on special appliances sold
  by magic dealers.
Silk to Egg, 380-82
Simple Change-over, 63
Simple Coin Production, 62-63
Simple Finger Clip, 204
Simple Fist Vanish, 119-20
Simple Palm Vanish, 105
Simple Passage, 334
Simple Roll Vanish, 111-12
Simple Transfer, 131-32
Single-coin Palms, 1-2
Six-symbol Test, 277-78
Sixth Card—Sixth Sense, 284-85
Sleeve Action Change-over, 63-64
Sleeve Flash, 140-41
Slide Vanish, 57
Slit Glass: A drinking glass with a
  horizontal slit cut in the side on a
  level with the bottom. Coins
  dropped in the glass slide out
  unnoticed into the performer's
  hand, enabling him to produce
  them over and over, or vanish
  them entirely by covering the glass
  with a cloth. Obtainable from
  magic dealers.
Slow-motion Penetration, 356-57
Slow-motion Production, 101-2
Slow-motion Steal, 134-35
Slow-motion Vanish
  billiard ball, 124-25
  coin, 46-48
  thimble, 215-16
Snatch Vanish, 122-23
Special Color Change, 193-95
Special Color-changing Silk, 377-80
Special effects, 353-411
  Brema Coin Box, 386-89
  Coin Through Card, 390-92
    with Transparent Box, 394-95
  Coin Through Handkerchief, 358-
    61
    Advanced Penetration, 361-63
    Alternate Penetration, 360-61
  Coin Through the Hand, 355-57
    Slow-motion Penetration, 356-57
  Color-changing Silk, 373-77
    Special, 377-80
  Dime to Dollar, 353-54
  Knot and Ring, 369-70
  Link the Clips, 364-65
    Triple Links, 366
  Looper Dooper, 363-64
  Multiple-knot Trick, 368
  Okito Coin Box, 382-95, 398
    Improved, 386-89
    Transparent, 392-94, 395
  Quick Dime Vanish, 354
  Quick-knot Vanish, 368-69
  Repeat-cigar Production, 400-3
  Restored Paper Napkin, 403-11
    Alternate Routine, 411
  Ring and Triple Knot, 370-71
  Silk to Egg, 380-82
  Super Coin Box, 395-97
    Alternate Procedure, 399
    Multiple-coin Penetration, 397-
      400

Special effects, *cont.*
   Triple-knot Trick, 366-67
   Tube and Knots, 372-73
  Sponge Balls: Small balls made of
   sponge rubber, which enable the
   performer to press two balls tightly
   together and show them as one.
   He places this "ball" in a
   spectator's hand, telling him to
   hold it tightly; then, taking a single
   ball, the performer vanishes it (as
   described under Billiard Balls) and
   the spectator, opening his fist, is
   amazed to find it with the ball
   already there. From this, more
   elaborate routines have been
   developed, which are supplied by
   dealers along with extra sponge
   balls of whatever sizes, shapes, or
   color are required.
Spread-away Production, 62
Squeeze Vanish, 49, 50
Standard Fingertip Production, 216
Standard "One to Four" Routine,
   158-63
Standard Palm
  billiard ball, 88
  coin, 6-9, 21-22
    for a production, 9
    for a vanish, 9
Straight Through, 330-33
Stretched Shell: A shell coin that has
  been increased in diameter during
  manufacture so that it will fit over
  a regulation coin of standard size.
String a Ring, 336-38
Sucker Trick: Any trick in which
  the performer pretends to "give
  away" the secret, only to baffle
  the spectators later.
Sugar Lumps, Magic, 319-26
  Come-back Lump, 324-26
  Four-lump Assembly, 319-22
  Through the Table, 323-24
Super Coin Box, 395-97
  Alternate Procedure, 399
  Multiple-coin Penetration, 397-400
Supermagnetism, 342-44
Supersalt, 348-49
Swallow Vanish

  billiard ball, 108
  thimble, 215
Sweep Production, 62-63
Swing-about Toss Vanish, 118
Switch: A secret "change" of an
  item (as a coin) for a duplicate.
  See Change-over

Table magic, 315-52
  Coins Through Table, 326-35
    Hand-to-Hand, 333
    latest variant on, 329-30
    Mutual Attraction, 334
    Simple Passage, 334
    Straight Through, 330-33
    Throw-over, 333-35
    Transposition, 334-35
  Five-glass Fooler, 351-52
  Four-coin Baffler, 315-18
  Full and Empty, 352
  Jump-over Dice, 335-36
  Magic Sugar Lumps, 319-26
    Come-back Lump, 324-26
    Four-lump Assembly, 319-22
    Through the Table, 323-24
  Magnetic Pencils, 338-39
    Improved, 339-41
    Perfect, 341-42
  Magnetized Knife, 342, 343
  Roll the Bills, 349-51
  Salt Vanish, 344-49
    Alternate, 345-46
    Fist to Fist, 346
    Supersalt, 348-49
    Vanishing Salt Shaker, 347-48
  String a Ring, 336-38
  Supermagnetism, 342-44
  Turn-up Glasses, 351
Take-away Vanish
  coin, 38
  thimble, 208-9
    Inward, 209-10
Thimble change-overs, 233-36
  Double, 233-36
Thimble color changes, 244-48
  Finger-switch, 244-46
    Repeat, 246
  Push-through, 247-48
    Repeat, 248
Thimble flashes, 236-44

Back-palm, 240-43
  Fingertip, 236-37
  Full-front, 237-40
  One-hand, 243-44
Thimble Holders, 224-25
Thimble productions, 216-18
  Behind the Hand, 217
  Elbow, 217
  Finger-bend, 201
  "Four to Eight," 220-25
  Knee, 217
  "One to Four," 218-20
  Pocket, 217
  Pop, 216
  Shirt Collar, 217
  Standard Fingertip, 216
  Thumb Palm, 199
  Thumb to Finger Bend, 203
  Trouser Cuff, 217
  Vest Pocket, 217-18
Thimbles, 197-252
  Back and Front Palm, 204-7
  basic manipulations, 197-207
  Center Palm, 200-1
  Display Position, 197-98
  Finger-bend Palm, 201
  Simple Finger Clip, 204
  Thumb and Finger Clip, 203-4
  Thumb-bend Palm, 199-200
  Thumb Palm, 198-99
  Thumb the Thimble, 248-51
    Alternate, 251-52
  Thumb to Finger Bend, 202-3
  Tip Palm, 203
Thimbles, Multiplying, 218-33
  "Four to Eight" Production, 220-25
  "Full Front" Routine, 225-26
  "One to Four" Production, 218-20
  Rapid "One to Eight" System, 226-33
Thimble vanishes, 208-16
  Draw-off, 212
  Finger-bend, 201
  Finger-switch, 214-15
  Poke, 210-11
  Slow-motion, 215-16
  Swallow, 215
  Take-away, 208-9

  Inward, 209-10
  Thumb Palm, 198-99
  Thumb to Finger Bend, 202
  Twist-away, 213-14
Through the Crystal, 263
Through the Hand Production, 100-1
Through the Table
  Magic Sugar Lumps, 323-24
  matches, 303
Throw Color Change, 156-57
Throw-over, 333-35
Throw Vanish, 105
  Multiple Standard Palm, 60
Thumb and Finger Clip, 203-4
Thumb and Finger Steal, 133-34
Thumb-bend Palm, 199-200
Thumb Clip, Back, 26, 27-28
Thumb-crook Palm, 11
Thumb Flash, 143-45
Thumb-fork Palm, 12-13
  Alternate, 13-14
  for a production, 12, 14
  for a vanish, 12, 13
Thumb-front Flash, 145
Thumb Palm
  billiard ball, 88-89
  coin, 33-36
    Alternate, 36-38
  thimble, 198-99
    for a production, 199
    for a vanish, 198-99
Thumb-roll Vanish, 114-16
Thumb Squeeze Production, 97-98
Thumb the Thimble, 248-51
  Alternate, 251-52

Thumb Tip: A flesh-colored metal tip that fits over the thumb up to the first joint. Originally used for switching a torn strip of paper for a duplicate of the original. The Thumb Tip has been expanded to include vanishes or productions of small items and a variety of other effects. Oversized Thumb Tips can accommodate fair-sized silks and may even be used for the Salt Vanish instead of the usual fake. Thumb Tips are obtainable from magic dealers along with general instructions for their use.

Thumb to Finger Bend, 202-3
  for a production, 203
  for a vanish, 202
Time out of Mind, 265-66
Tip Palm, 203
Toss Vanish, 116
  Swing-about, 118
  Two-hand, 116-17
Tourniquet, 40
Transfers, 131-40
  Back-palm, 135-36
  general description of, 126
  Multiple-coin, 64-65
  Reverse, 132-33
  Simple, 131-32
  Slow-motion Steal, 134-35
  Thumb and Finger Steal, 133-34
  Turn-around, 137-38
    Double, 138-40
    Reverse, 138
Transparent Okito Coin Box, 392-94,
    395
Transposition, 334-35
  White and Red, 181-84
Triple-color Test, 273
Triple-knot Trick, 366-67
Triple Links, 366

Triple Palm, 89
Trouser Cuff Production, 217
Tube and Knots, 372-73
Turnabout Flash, 145-47
Turnabout Heads, 302
Turnabout Match, 306-7
  Alternate, 307-9
Turn-around Transfer, 137-38
  Double, 138-40
  Reverse, 138
Turn-over Coins, 267-68
  Multiple, 268
Turn-up Glasses, 351
Twist-away Vanish, 213-14
Two-hand Coin Roll, 53
Two-hand Toss Vanish, 116-17
Two-way Twirl, 170-71

Vanishing Matches, 300-1
  Instant, 301-2
Vanishing Salt Shaker, 347-48
Vest Pocket Production, 217-18

Waxed pads, 253
White and Red Transposition, 181-84
Without the Watch, 266-67
Wooden balls, 85